# WHEN GOD OPENS A DOOR...

## *Run Through It*

===========================

*or you will miss the miracles God has for you*

*by*

*Tommy Watson*

Order this book online at www.trafford.com
or email orders@trafford.com

Most Trafford titles are also available at major online book retailers.

Note for Librarians: A cataloguing record for this book is available from Library
and Archives Canada at www.collectionscanada.ca/amicus/index-e.html

Printed in Victoria, BC, Canada.

ISBN: 978-1-4269-1607-6

Library of Congress Control Number: 2009934086

*Our mission is to efficiently provide the world's finest, most comprehensive book publishing
service, enabling every author to experience success. To find out how to publish your book, your
way, and have it available worldwide, visit us online at www.trafford.com*

*Trafford rev. 9/18/2009*

All scripture quotations, unless otherwise indicated, are taken from the Holy Bible, New
International Version®, NIV®.
Copyright © 1973, 1978, 1984 by Biblica, Inc.™
Used by permission of Zondervan. All rights reserved worldwide.

 www.trafford.com

**North America & international**
toll-free: 1 888 232 4444 (USA & Canada)
phone: 250 383 6864 ♦ fax: 812 355 4082

# Contents

# Acknowledgements

FROM TIME TO TIME, I have read in other books the acknowledgements by the author. I wondered if those names were listed just out of friendship, or did the people really help. <u>Now I know</u>! This book would never have been finished if we had not received help from those more knowledgeable in book writing and with more computer expertise.

There was Mary Ruth Howes who critiqued the manuscript, using her years of publishing experience to get our stories in order and onto CD. I will be forever grateful for her help, as well as for her encouragement, knowing that if she said a story was okay, it was okay.

When we needed computer help, which was quite often, Johnny Reeves was "Johnny-on-the-spot," regardless of his schedule. Charles Koch threw in his valuable "two cents"— and we didn't even have to pay him the two cents.

For months, as we neared the completion, we became more concerned about a cover for the book. Along came Ken Reeves with his excellent photography. Thank you, Ken, for the <u>visual</u> encouragement to <u>run through that open door</u> and experience God's miracles.

Our daughter Tracie performed the final editing of this project and discovered that the rules of grammar are *very* confusing. She will happily continue her career as a nurse!

To get my experiences on paper and into book form would have been impossible without the excitement, skill, and persistence of my wife Mollie. Many of the stories we both experienced, and through many of the doors we walked together.

This book is dedicated to our four children, their spouses, and our nine grandchildren: Lorna, Alea, Brandon, Brittany, Courtney, Kayla, Devery, Kiley, and Brady, who have patiently waited for its completion. Their encouragement and prayers have been priceless. We trust that they, and all others who read it, will know that our God is a great God.

# Preface

IT WAS A NEW and thrilling experience moving to south Florida from our church in a small Texas town. We were young and needed all the help we could get. Mr. James was a grand old man, a retired railroad worker, and a deacon in our new church in the suburbs of Miami. He and Mrs. James were very caring of their young pastor's family, even to the point of baby-sitting with the four young children. They were loving and kind servants of God.

Knowing the love Mollie had for flowers, Mr. James brought over one day a lovely big bronze-toned alamanda plant in a bucket. After digging a deep hole next to the mailbox in our front yard, he took the plant out of the bucket and placed it gently in the hole, watered it well and packed down the dirt. He got into his car to leave, backed up, and backed right into the alamanda. He patiently did the work again: dug the soft dirt out of the hole, put the alamanda into the soil, added more dirt and packed it down. We all laughed and thanked him graciously. Getting into his car again, he backed up—and, yes, again he backed into Mollie's lovely alamanda bush.

I am reminded that we are all so much like Mr. James. We dig, we plant, we water. But then in a thoughtless moment, we err. We move too quickly without thinking—or praying—and we must go back to repair the damage. But—we must keep on planting and watering and God will give the increase.

WE HAD TAKEN OUR first group of 49 bicyclists to Europe. I was to drive ahead in the van to find a campsite and purchase the supper food. I had more difficulty than I had expected so it was getting late in the afternoon. When I turned back to meet the cyclists and lead them to our campsite, they could not be found. I searched all the country roads, but I came up empty. I questioned everyone I saw.

"Have you seen 49 cyclists all wearing orange t-shirts?"

"No" was the only reply I got.

Only one man evaluated my predicament: "You—have lost 49 cyclists—all wearing orange shirts?"

"Yes sir, I have!"

The man looked puzzled, then gave a most accurate evaluation: "You are stupid!"

Looking back, I am not happy about some "stupid" things I have done, but I am very grateful that when I ignorantly put myself out on a limb, God didn't saw off the branch. He gently lifted me down and redirected my efforts in serving Him. He saw my heart and continually opened unbelievable doors for service. My prayer is always:

*"Show me your ways, O Lord, teach me your paths; guide me in your truth and teach me, for you are God my Savior, and my hope is in you all day long." (Psalm 25:4-5)*

## Who is Tommy Watson?

Tommy Watson is a "nobody." This is not a statement of false humility. I assure you he knows very little about humility, false or true.

## Why should a "nobody" write a book?

This book is written to remind us there are a lot of "nobodies" in the Christian faith—young people and older people—through whom God would like to work some modern day miracles for His glory. We want to challenge them to look for "open doors" through which God wants them to run.

Some of our stories are miracles that we experienced in Russia, China, Romania, Cuba, Honduras, East Germany, and South Africa. However, God is not limited to working miracles in other countries only. He can "open doors" for you right where you live.

## Who is going to believe these miracles happened in the life of one person?

This question has been asked of me. Here are my answers:

<u>My wife</u>: She experienced some of these miracles with me and felt the Lord would have us share them. She did the work, drawing the stories out of me and putting them down in a readable form.

<u>My children and my grandchildren</u>: They know me well, and this book is written for them.

<u>My church family</u>: For thirty-five years it encouraged me to "color outside the lines" and to "think outside the box." The members of First Baptist Church of Perrine worked, watched, and prayed while becoming one of the largest congregations in Miami, Florida.

## My prayer:

*"Let them know that it is Your hand, that You, O Lord, have done it."* (Psalm 109:27)

**My promise to you:**

After you have read this book, if you do not feel it is worth four times the amount you paid for it, I will personally sit down, take out a pen, and write you the most sympathetic letter you have ever read.

**Don't wait around! Run through that open door and experience the miracles God has for you.**

# I. IT ALL BEGAN

# 1
## Growing Up

*"Grandma had seventeen children and raised five of us."*

THE DEPRESSION YEARS WERE tough years! I have often heard people say that they grew up during those years, but they didn't know they were poor, because everyone was poor. Well, I <u>knew</u> we were poor! We were poor—but proud. It was 1935 and Miss Cuthrel was my teacher in the second grade. I remember it well. As she often did, she checked our fingernails and teeth, and when she came to my desk she paused and said, "Tommy, I bet I know what you had for breakfast this morning. You had eggs, because some of it is still on your mouth." We did have eggs, but since we were poor, my little mind thought that only poor people had eggs, so I said, "No, Ma'am. That's not eggs. That's mustard. We had hot dogs for breakfast."

One day, also when I was in the second grade, I came home from school and saw a sign in our front yard, which I thought was a quarantine notice for scarlet fever, as I had seen them on other houses and been told what they meant. It wasn't a quarantine sign, but as I got closer, I saw it said "for sale." An enforcement officer "suggested" we put our furniture out in the yard to sell because, my mother told me, we couldn't pay our rent. I knew that Miss Cuthrel lived somewhere near our house because I often saw her drive past in her shiny gray

1934 Plymouth. On this day I surely hoped that Miss Cuthrel didn't see the sign—I didn't want her to know we were poor.

Eleven years later, when I was working for A&P stores, I bought a 1934 Plymouth—but it didn't look like Miss Cuthrel's. It had no headlights so I attached some to the fenders where they were supposed to be on those cars, and since it had no headliner, I bought some red material to brighten the interior. A Nabisco salesman, to whom I gave a good display area in the A&P, offered to paint my car if I bought the paint. He painted it gray—just like Miss Cuthrel's—but I added red wheels. This was the first car owned in my family. Neither my parents nor my older brother and sisters had a car. I sold it to "Slick" Johnson for $250, but I had a hard time getting the money until his mother put pressure on him.

My mother, Virgie, was the oldest child in the family of 17 children born to Kennie and Annie Vick who lived their entire married lives in one small two-story house, 509 Florida Ave. in Portsmouth, Va. (This was quite unlike me! I once counted 16 houses I lived in by the time I was 16 years old.) My grandfather, Kennie Vick, was a full-blooded Cherokee Indian, having been adopted into the Vick family. My parents owned the house next door to them but lost it during the Depression through gambling, and it was there where I was born, to join my brother Buddy, and my two sisters, Laurie Lee and Mary Ellen. Three years later Rosie was born.

My father, Oscar Watson, at various times worked for the Seaboard Railroad, ran a tavern, and worked away from home as a cook in a CCC camp. He was basically a kind man—but—he was an alcoholic. The last thing I remember him asking me to do was to get him his whiskey ration book.

My mother was sickly during my early school years, so I lived at Grandma's house with aunts and uncles only a few years older than I. Mother died of hemochromatosis. I remember well when I was in the fifth grade, standing out in the hall for punishment, when the principal came and told me my mother had died. I didn't cry. I was hardened to "hurts" but was a continual behavior problem to my teachers. I was sent home from school so often that I became quite an expert in knife throwing in Grandma's backyard. I slumped through grade school, never learning, really, how to read, write, or spell. My high school years were different because athletics became my life, and I would do anything to play sports. I graduated from high school, certainly not with the highest academic record, but with three letters in football, two in basketball, and two in baseball, where I led my team in hitting. I thank God for coaches who encouraged me to succeed in something that interested me.

Because I was an extrovert, and because of athletics, I was elected president of both my sophomore and junior classes, and president of the Student Council, and most popular student in my senior year. Also I was elected as president of the Student Council of the seven high schools in the county. Although I certainly didn't know it then, God was preparing me for a life of leadership and service in His Kingdom work.

The war was on, and for two summers during high school years, I worked for the Seaboard Railroad standing on a scaffold, catching hot rivets in a can as they were thrown to me, and putting them in a hole on the coach. At Christmas I worked for the post office, walking house to house with a mailbag. My friend, Ed Austin, who later became the mayor of Jacksonville, Florida, got me that job.

When my older sister, Laurie, graduated from high school, she got a job at the A&P grocery store, rented a little apartment, and brought Mary Ellen, Rosie and me to live there. My father, who was living above the bar where he worked, also stayed with us after he lost both his legs and could no longer work.

BRIEFLY, THAT IS MY early life story. I must not forget where I came from or I may forget who I am. But then one day, I read more about my life:

*"Brothers, think of what you were when you were called. Not many of you were wise by human standards; not many were influential; not many were of noble birth. But God chose the foolish of the world to shame the wise; God chose the weak things of the world to shame the strong. He chose the lowly things of this world and the despised things—and the*

*things that are not—to nullify the things that are, so that no one may boast before Him. It is because of Him that you are in Christ Jesus, who has become for us wisdom from God—that is, our righteousness, holiness, and redemption."*
*(I Corinthians 1:26-30)*

# 2

# Miss Minnie

*"I was rich because Miss Minnie was rich!"*

Miss Minnie lived right around the corner from Grandma's house and just three houses down. Every Christmas, I gave her a twenty-five cent pound box of chocolate-covered cherries. It was not because I thought it was more blessed to give than to receive, but because I knew that Miss Minnie thought it was more blessed to give than to receive. I knew that my twenty-five cent box of candy would assure me of a $20 bill from her. (That was half the salary my father earned <u>a month</u> for working as a cook at the CCC camp.) Miss Minnie also gave me $2 each Sunday for walking her blind sister, Miss Maude, to Broad Street Baptist Church, just two blocks away from their house.

Miss Minnie trusted me and knew that I would always carry out her instructions. One instruction was, "Never mail anything that Miss Maude gives you to mail." That intrigued me because Miss Maude, though slightly older, was a very independent lady even though she was blind. Miss Maude would not ride to church in the same car with her sister, and that too, puzzled me, to the point that one day I asked her the reason why. "Tommy," she said, "Miss Minnie is on the wrong team and I am on the right team." Little did I know how true that was!

It was dark one night when Grandma answered the knock at the door. It was Miss Minnie. She told Grandma she needed me to go with her to the church and help her find a way to get in, in order to retrieve her purse she had left. Strange, I thought. Pastor Archer, living next door, would have been happy to unlock the door for her. He knew her well, as she was a regular attendee and certainly among the top givers in the church. I found an unlocked window, and with some effort we were able to push it up enough for me to climb through. I made my way through the dark building until I found the seat where Miss Minnie had left her purse. It was a fat purse. Out of respect for Miss Minnie, and knowing that I would be rewarded, I didn't once think of opening it. I climbed back through the window, pushed it down, and—true to fashion, Miss Minnie placed a $20 bill in my hand. I was rich because Miss Minnie was rich!

Broad Street Baptist Church had a thriving Girls' Auxiliary with over 100 girls attending every week, studying missions and memorizing Bible verses. Miss Minnie was the leader and she knew that in these depression years, candy and ice cream would bring the crowd. A few of us 11- and 12-year-old boys hung around outside the church, knowing that when the girls left, Miss Minnie would have the same treats for us. Frankie Carmichael was the ringleader of these boys. He was the toughest of us all and had the well-deserved reputation for breaking out the most streetlights with his left-handed accuracy. He was our hero. (Six years later I played first base on a team when Frankie pitched a no-hitter in one of our games.)

Miss Minnie's best friends in the church were the Murphy's. Although I was only 13, Miss Minnie asked me to go out to dinner with her and the Murphy's, including their daughter, Patsy, to the fanciest restaurant in Norfolk. Having never eaten in a restaurant, I wasn't sure what I should order. My older sister, Mary Ellen, having taken Home Economics in school, told me that if I ordered steak I should cut and eat only one piece at a time, as that was the proper thing to do. So with that bit of knowledge, I felt comfortable and ordered steak. Having finished eating, and while the adults were visiting, Miss Minnie handed me ten dollars worth of quarters to play the slot machine. So Patsy and I spent them all and learned this very valuable lesson—the odds are against you in gambling. Six years later I was working in a pool hall at night. Following the war, because of the demand, it was almost impossible to buy new cars, but one night Patsy picked me up at the pool hall in her new 1946 Plymouth coupe, given to her for her high school graduation by Miss Minnie.

It wasn't until I had finished college and was in seminary that the news spread across the nation that for *twenty-five years*, Miss Minnie Mangum had been embezzling money from the Norfolk Commonwealth Building and Loan Association, where she worked. It was the largest embezzlement by a woman in banking history! Although Miss Maude was totally blind, she could see clearly the difference between wrong and right in morality. My grandma, however, until her dying day, believed that Miss Minnie was framed. "She was too good to do anything like that." Why, she had given Grandma and Granddad a beautiful set of hand-painted, gold-trimmed dishes for their 50th wedding anniversary! One of those dishes, a gift from Grandma, is on display in Mollie's antique china closet, collecting dust, and reminding us of Miss Minnie's generosity and her fateful end.

While I was still in seminary, I went back to my native Portsmouth, Va. with a desire to see Miss Minnie. She was out on bond, but she had no desire to see me. Her sentence was nine years, and for nine years she taught the women's Bible study in prison. I hope and pray that Miss Minnie got on the "right team."

# 3

# Mitsuo Fuchida—God's Grace and Forgiveness

*"I'm going back to ask for forgiveness."*

I WAS 13 YEARS old—I remember it well. Together with my two uncles, who were only a few years older, I stepped out of the movie theater into the crisp December air in Portsmouth, Virginia. Jumping into the car, Ralph turned on the radio and we heard the news blaring across the airwaves: Pearl Harbor had been bombed by the Japanese, and much of the Pacific fleet was destroyed. Over 2,000 American men were killed. It was Dec. 7, 1941. Fear overwhelmed my young mind; anger gripped my heart as it did all Americans, young or old. Truly, this was a "day of infamy" as our President Roosevelt stated. How could this have happened? Who could have planned and carried out such a treacherous and secret attack on an unsuspecting people? It was many years before I found the answer.

His infamous words "Tora, Tora" (Attack, Attack), which sparked the beginning of America's participation in WWII, came easily, as he had been personally and meticulously chosen by General Tojo to select and train the 360 pilots who would fly this mission of attack. His name was Mitsuo Fuchida, a Japanese Air Force Commander and flying ace, loyal to the core, dedicated to the task, faithful to his country and his emperor, and to Gen. Tojo, the power behind the throne. His nation had not been invaded in more than a thousand years.

Japan continued on the offensive, capturing territory throughout Asia and the Pacific. Its plans were now to attack the island of Midway to use as an advance base, as well as to entrap and destroy the U.S. Pacific Fleet. Because of communication intelligence success, the U.S. Pacific Fleet surprised the Japanese forces, sinking the four Japanese carriers that had attacked Pearl Harbor only six months before. The Battle of Midway (June 4-7, 1942) is considered the decisive battle of the war in the Pacific. Now the Americans and their Allies took the offensive in this part of the world. And where was Mitsuo Fuchida during this critical period following the Battle of Midway? He was on an aircraft carrier with a broken leg, writing the story of the naval battle of Midway, which became required reading at the U.S. Naval Academy.

Although he was the lead pilot at Pearl Harbor, beginning the Pacific war in December, 1941, few people know he risked his life to help end the war. When General Douglas MacArthur called for the surrender of Japan and the signing of the surrender to be on the deck of the USS Missouri, the kamikaze pilots vowed to shoot down any plane that made an attempt to fly the Japanese officials out to surrender. It was a white plane with a green cross—and Mitsuo Fuchida was the pilot. He stood on the deck of the USS Missouri at the surrender ceremonies.

But that is not the end of the story, as he explained to me during the days he was in our home in Miami. Following the war, he said, he was a broken and disillusioned man. He was wrestling with flashbacks, probing the meaning of his life. While boarding a train in Tokyo, a man put into his hand a leaflet with the striking title "I Was a Prisoner of Japan." It was written by Jacob DeShazer, a U.S. Army Air Corps corporal who was a bombardier when Gen. Jimmy Doolittle's Raiders razed Tokyo, reversing the tide of the Pacific war. DeShazer and his crew ran out of fuel, bailed out over China and were taken to a Japanese prison camp where they survived three years of cruel torture and starvation. But there, also, DeShazer found Jesus as his Savior, later becoming a missionary to Japan, having learned from Jesus: *"Father, forgive them, for they do not know what they are doing." (Luke 23:34)*

It was DeShazer's pamphlet that was handed to Mitsuo Fuchida. Also, he had learned of many Japanese prisoners who had been ministered to by a woman whose parents had been missionaries to Japan, but had been beheaded by his countrymen. Such love and forgiveness he could not comprehend. Obtaining a Bible, Fuchida soon became a Christian and later an evangelist, sharing his testimony of God's forgiveness through Jesus, the Prince of Peace, throughout Japan and America.

As he preached from my pulpit, and stayed in our home doing some writing, I saw one of the most beautiful miracles of God's grace and forgiveness. Sitting at our small dining table, eating some Japanese food, Captain Mitsuo Fuchida asked for our prayers as he was going back to Pearl Harbor. It was for the December 7, 1961, twentieth anniversary of the bombing of Pearl Harbor. "I am going back," he said, "to ask forgiveness in Christian love. It is something I <u>must</u> do."

Much has changed in my life since that day, December 7, 1941, when I was just thirteen. I, like Mitsuo Fuchida, also needed to find forgiveness. I was nineteen when I gave my life to Jesus Christ, and my whole life changed. Just as surely as Fuchida chose to fly the plane with the green cross of surrender, I chose to take up the cross of Jesus and surrender to Him.

# 4

# May 4<sup>th</sup>

*"I saw a pamphlet behind a can of peas."*

I LOVE TO PREACH! I think all preachers who are called of God love to preach. When I was saved at nineteen, God gave me a testimony and a message, and I promised Him then that I would always be faithful to share that message with others.

On May 4th, 1947, two of my friends and I drove up to a little Baptist church, Highland Park, in Portsmouth, Virginia, because we knew there were some pretty girls there. It was my car—a 1934 gray Plymouth with red wheels. We entered the church and sat down close to the back. The song leader impressed me since he was smiling. Because the pastor of the church was in the hospital, the sermon was preached by a layman, Sandy Nesbit, who spoke about the woman with an issue of blood who came behind Jesus and quietly reached out and touched the border of His garment. (Luke 8:44) She was miraculously and completely healed. The story was new to me and fascinating. I heard the speaker say, "Jesus is walking by tonight and it may be the last opportunity to reach out and touch Him." God spoke to me, and I knew that I wanted, and needed, to be healed from my sin. I got up out of my seat and walked to the front and I, too, touched the border of Jesus' garment and was made whole. Mr. Nesbit opened his Bible and read and explained to me Romans 10:9 and 10, and verse 13. This too, was new to me.

*"That if you confess with your mouth, 'Jesus is Lord,' and believe in your heart that God raised Him from the dead, you will be saved. For it is with your heart that you believe and are justified, and it is with your mouth that you confess and are saved…For everyone who calls on the name of the Lord will be saved."*

I left the guys and the girls, got into my car, drove a few blocks, and parked—"and this poor man cried." I looked up into the sky and the stars were brighter. My load of sin was gone. I was forgiven. I was a new person. Psalms 34:6 became a favorite verse of mine. *"This poor man cried, and the Lord heard him, and saved him out of all his troubles."* (KJV)

At this time at 19 years of age, I was doing much of the ordering for the largest A&P grocery store in the Philadelphia unit, which reached from Philadelphia to Florida. I also stocked the store on Friday nights and ran the night crew. Because of a special need in another A&P store, I was asked to temporarily fill in the gap. It was there one day that I saw on a shelf a pamphlet called "Four Things God Wants You To Know." Earlier that morning a lady (or man) was pushing her grocery cart down the canned vegetables aisle when God reminded her to stick that pamphlet behind a can of peas because "someone" needed it. No, I don't know who the lady or man was, but I do know who the "someone" was. I picked it up and every day during my lunchtime, I climbed up into the loft of the store and memorized all of the Bible verses until they were my own. What a wonderful way for a new Christian to grow in the Lord and learn to share his faith! I wonder who that person was who put that pamphlet there. Some day I will meet her in Heaven and thank her for the treasure she gave me early in my spiritual growth.

Soon after my salvation, I went to talk to a pastor whom I knew because he was always at our football games and was very popular in our town. I wanted to tell him what happened to me—that I had been saved. He looked at me, smiled, and said, "Tommy, you've always been all right." I am so glad that he was *not* preaching the night that God spoke to me. The pastor might have told me I was all right, and I would have gone out into the night as dirty as I came in. No, I hadn't been all right. I was a sinner needing God's grace and forgiveness.

I don't remember a definite "call" to preach, but I soon knew that was what God had for me to do. After taking my first steps in spiritual growth, I was baptized at Highland Park Baptist Church and the same night preached my first sermon. It was from Romans the 10th chapter, and although I am sure it was not profound, it was definitely from experience. Since some of the youth in our town were attending Columbia Bible College, and since I knew I needed some Bible training, I decided that I would enroll there although I had very little money for college. I sold my birthstone diamond ring to the butcher at the A&P store for $70, and I sold my 1934 Plymouth car for $250. My sister Laurie gave me $100.

I was definitely not college material since I had stumbled through grade school and bluffed and cheated my way through high school. The only reason I stayed in school was because of sports. Now, however, I had a goal and that was to learn the Bible in preparation to preach the Word, but that meant I would have to learn how to study, how to read and write. My roommate who worked in the registrar's office told me that I had the lowest score on the entrance exam of anyone in the school. Yes, I had a long way to go, but I am thankful that God uses the "weak" things of this world to accomplish His purposes.

My Biblical studies at Columbia Bible College under godly professors *grounded* me in the Word, and the weekly Saturday night street meetings in downtown Columbia, South Carolina gave me the opportunity to *preach* that Word. Every Saturday night the streets were alive with soldiers from Fort Jackson, eager for any kind of entertainment. After some good trumpet and vocal music by some of our students, I often preached my "Devil's Toolbox" sermon. I had painted a bright yellow toolbox with red-lettered words naming various sins. Inside the box I had placed some of the "tools" of the Devil, which he uses to attract and destroy young people and old alike, and one at a time, I pulled these tools out. At one point of the sermon I took a chain from the box, had one of the men wrap it several times around my wrists and lock it with a padlock. As long as I was chained, the crowd listened, and I used this opportunity to tell how Satan has us bound in his power, how we are all sinners unable to free ourselves, and that "the wages of sin is death." Christ came to set us free from the bondage of sin. At that point in the sermon, I escaped from the chains. On many occasions we had as many as 10 to 15 soldiers step forward to give their lives to Christ and they were immediately counseled by the eager, dedicated college boys. Their faces flash before me now: Joel, Bruce, brothers Burt and Bill, Cecil, Gus, and others. This was our training field for personal evangelism and I will ever be grateful for it.

However, I had much to learn in personal evangelism. Since I needed summer work, my friend Joel Ortendahl invited me to go home with him to Pleasantville, N.J. just outside Atlantic City, stay with him and his mother, and get a summer job. One night as Joel and I were driving home after midnight, he took a shortcut through a closed service station in a rather rough neighborhood. Two guys looking for trouble yelled,

"Come back here and we'll teach you a lesson!" Joel circled around, stopped the car, and stepped out—all 6'6" and 263 pounds. Knowing this was going to be interesting, I, too, got out of the car.

"Well, if you were my size," the ruffian muttered, "I'd fight you."

"Here is someone your size—fight him," Joel said, pointing to me. With no time to negotiate, I could do nothing but fight. (I had just wanted to observe.) Fortunately, my first punch was a straight left jab which knocked him down. He got up—I knocked him down again—up again—and down for the third time.

"Please stop! You'll get my brother in trouble."

So we sat down on the curb and witnessed to him. I have learned since that this is not the best approach to soul winning—but I did get his attention!

Columbia, South Carolina, at this time in the late 40's, was distinctly separated into the "black" communities and the "white" communities, and since I worked several jobs to keep in school, I came in close contact with both. Collecting for a tire company, delivering newspapers, and working at "Terry's Drugstore" enabled me to see "the race of men go by." I happened one day upon a black brother and greeted him with,

"How's your church doing, Brother Ellis?"

"Oh, I'm leaving and going to another church—where they pay their preacher more."

Knowing him to be a man of God, I jokingly said, "But Brother Ellis, do you preach for money or do you preach for the Lord?"

"Oh, I preach for the Lord," he said,—"but you can't preach here on Sunday and board in Heaven the rest of the week."

I was fast learning that truth as a young Christian student, so eager to preach the Word. "You can't preach here on Sunday and board in Heaven the rest of the week."

# 5

# The Old Wedding Ring

*"When this old wedding ring was new,*
*And the dreams that we dreamed came true,*
*I remembered with pride, as we stood side by side*
*What a beautiful picture you made as my bride.*
*Even though silver crowns your hair,*
*I still see those brown ringlets there.*
*Love's old flame is the same,*
*As the day I changed your name,*
*When this old wedding ring was new."*

HOLDING HER LEFT HAND, I sang these words to my bride of 50 years, as our children, grandchildren, and a few other loved ones celebrated with us our 50th wedding anniversary.

Now, let me go back to the day "when that old wedding ring was new." We were married in the small stone chapel that basked in the sunlight of a large valley on Troublesome Creek. The Kentucky mountains rose around it, circling the grounds of Camp Nathanael, of the Scripture Memory Mountain Mission in Emmalena, Ky. where Mollie's parents were serving with the mission. I had purchased our marriage license in nearby Hazard, Ky. for $2.00. The guests at our wedding were mostly the children at the summer camp there and the missionaries. The flowers were the daisies gathered from the roadside that morning and entwined with some English ivy from Mollie's mother's flowerpots. Joel Ortendahl, my best friend from college, was Best Man. The songs we had thoughtfully chosen were: "I Love You Truly," "Savior, Like a Shepherd Lead Us," and "O Jesus, I (We) Have Promised." The message of these songs has been our prayer throughout our married lives.

Rev. Garland Franklin, founder and director of the mission, performed the ceremony. I slipped the "new" wedding ring on my bride's finger, and "the two became one." Inscribed in the gold of each of our wedding bands was the Bible reference of our own special verse: I Corinthians 3:9 which simply says, *"For we are laborers together with God." (KJV)* We didn't as yet know what that would involve—joys and sorrows, excitement, burdens, adventure, faith and lack of faith—but we trusted in the love and guidance of a gracious God.

As we stepped outside the chapel into the sunlight, an old wooden sled hitched to a dressed up mule was awaiting us for our wedding ride around the campgrounds, to the delight of all the camp children. Just before departing in my ("our" now) '39 Chevy, Rev. Franklin pressed into my hand a $10 bill, little knowing how very flat my billfold was. That kindness so impressed me that it began a pattern for me of seldom accepting money for the weddings I performed during my fifty-one years of pastoring.

The wedding was over, but the marriage had just begun. We climbed and circled the beautiful wooded mountains of eastern Kentucky until we crossed the state line into Virginia. The first little town was Pound, Virginia, where we found a small motel to spend our first night together. Attending the worship service the next morning in the little Baptist church there, the Reverend <u>Hawk</u> welcomed us. We were amused to hear that the pastor of the Methodist church in Pound was none other than the Reverend <u>Duck</u>. What a great place to spend a Thanksgiving—but this was only June so we left the Hawks and the Ducks behind and continued down the beautiful "Trail of the Lonesome Pine."

Since it was a week until I was to preach a revival meeting for my friend Joel Ortendahl in his church in Mt. Pleasant, South Carolina (and since I had almost no money in my billfold), I suggested to Mollie that we go by and see the Nesbits. The Scotchman Sandy Nesbit, the layman who was preaching when I was saved, was now in fulltime ministry, pastoring a small church in western Virginia. We were warmly welcomed, treated as "king and queen" in their home for a couple days—and even served breakfast in bed.

Leaving there we drove to Hiddenite, North Carolina, to the very humble home of Mollie's freshman roommate, Lorene Keever, whose parents were tobacco farmers.  Lorene had now taught school for a couple of years and dedicated her life to the great ministry of teaching children. Many years later she and her husband kept our four children on their tobacco farm for one month while we took Mollie's parents on their first and only trip to Europe. All of our children consider that experience a highlight in their young lives as they fed the pigs, tried milking the cow, "tied" tobacco, and learned to make biscuits every morning from scratch.

The following week I preached and Mollie used her chalk art ministry at Joel's church, Pleasant Hill Baptist, in Bethune, S.C.  Moving out for the week, Joel gave us his small two-room apartment at the top of some dark, creaky steps on the third floor of an almost condemned hotel in the little town. But to us, it was Paradise: one whole week with our own tiny kitchen and bedroom. We were excited: we were married and we were serving the Lord together. I remember little about that revival meeting except that the crowds were so good that we moved from the little church to the small rural high school auditorium.

And so began our life together.

# 6

# First Church

*"Bloom where you're planted."*

I AM SURE EVERY pastor has a "story" or two to tell of his first church! Because of my love and enthusiasm for the Lord's work, plus—my inexperience, I am one of those pastors. I was 21 years old, a student at Baylor University, having studied at Columbia Bible College for two and a half years. The many little Baptist churches dotting north Texas had no trouble finding a good pastor from among the many ministerial students at Baylor and the young men at Southwestern Baptist Theological Seminary in Ft. Worth. All were eager to get into the work to which God had called them.

West Shady Grove Baptist Church sat on the Collin County line adjacent to two other counties. My congregation was pretty evenly divided between the three: 15-15-15.

Forty-five in attendance was a good count on the best of Sundays. Behind the little white church, the hot north Texas sun beat down on the well-groomed cemetery that concealed the stories of generations: the young and the old, the righteous and the unrighteous. The black muck soil made the unpaved roads leading to the church completely impassable after a good rain. This was my first church field.

The fact that it was 163 miles from my dorm at Baylor was a challenge but not an obstacle, even though 15 of those miles were through the heart of Dallas because as yet, no expressway had been built to circle it. I drove up on Saturday night enjoying the love and hospitality in the homes of some members—some homes without indoor plumbing.

After a full day on the church field, I arrived back at Baylor at one or two a.m., ready for another week of classes. Many of those nights, I drove with my head out the window as I fought off sleep. A cold north Texas wind was an answer to my prayer.

Mollie had remained at Columbia to graduate, and after my junior year at Baylor, I headed back to Emmalena, Ky. to her parents' home, to marry the one for whom I had waited for two years. After our honeymoon, we began life together at the Baylor campus married student units, which actually were military trailers. Our unit consisted of only one room, with bed, dresser, and brick and board makeshift bookcase on one side, and a sofa and small table and chairs on the other. Between the two was a tiny kitchen space, opening to a small bathroom shared by another student couple who had a unit just like ours.

It was good to have Mollie join me in our work at West Shady Grove. The number of young people grew in attendance and we felt the need of having church service every week, rather than every other week as was the custom of the church. As a "half" time church with services on the first and third Sundays, it meant that if it rained one of those Sundays and made the roads impassable, we would meet only one Sunday a month. To me and to the young people, that was unsatisfactory! At the business meeting, the young people led in the vote to have "church" every Sunday.

At the end of our second year at the church, when we met for our annual meeting to discuss the issues of the church, a deacon stood to make a motion. I had never seen the man in church in the two years I had been there so was interested in his sudden "involvement."

"I make a motion that we go back to half time," he said. Another backslidden deacon seconded the motion.

"Why do you think we should go back to half time?" I incredulously asked.

"Well," he pondered, "I think we were more spiritual when we were half time."

With my tactless inexperience, I said, "We will take the vote now, but—I don't think anyone should vote who thinks he was more spiritual last year than he is now, because then he is backslidden, and no backslidden people should determine the policy of any church."

A man in the back stood up. "I think we should go back to half time, because we are $100 dollars in debt." Now these were cotton farmers, and I knew that the cotton was still in the fields, ready to be picked.

"I'll give the $100 dollars," I said, "Now we are out of debt."

Realizing that the next motion, no doubt, would be to relieve me of my pastoral job there, I resigned. What the church did not know was that I could afford to be bold, because I had already accepted the call, the previous week, to be the pastor of Liberty Baptist Church in Plano, Texas, where we would have some other exciting and wonderful experiences with the Lord. Oh, how young I was, and how much more I had to learn from Him!

However, in spite of such "deacon" experiences, our two years at West Shady Grove were good years: preaching and growing spiritually with my congregation. Lloyd and Suzie Withrow made us most welcome as they, along with others, made their homes regular Saturday overnight havens for their young pastor and wife. Sunday dinner tables were laden with fried chicken, potatoes, okra, and always a big banana pudding. When our baby Terry was born, the church women welcomed him with hand-crocheted booties, sweaters and bonnets, and cozy blankets. During the church services Terry slept in his little blue bassinet on the back pew, and it was from there one morning that we heard his first giggle out-loud, right in the middle of his daddy's sermon.

But let me tell you about the most unforgettable man in the church. His name was Mr. Burgess, one of my deacons. He was a man of God, who ate, slept, and lived his faith in his home, his church and his "world." Mr. and Mrs. Burgess lived with their three youngest children in a small frame house in Nobility, on the edge of Highway # 121 which runs between Bonham and McKinney. Nobility was no more than three or four houses and one store. Mr. Burgess worked for other people but also struggled to farm his own 26 acres of very unproductive lime rock soil, that stretched out behind their house. His only other buildings were a chicken shed and an outhouse.

The lack of material possessions did not affect Mr. Burgess' happy, laughing, joking spirit. One would not have to know him long to know that his "song" came from a close connection with, and trust in, the Creator of the universe. He could often be seen sitting in an old gray rocker on his front porch saturating himself with the truths from his well-worn Bible. On Sunday morning he would be opening that same Bible to share its marvelous message with his Sunday School class.

Mr. Burgess had another passion. That passion was to reach the world for Christ, and his "world" was the men and women, boys and girls, riding up and down #121 in front of his house. Posted there was his sign on which was printed a Bible verse or Christian phrase, which he changed frequently: "God loves you," "Except you repent, you will all perish," "The gift of God is Eternal Life." Long years after I left, Mr. Burgess died. The Collin County newspaper reported his death under the heading "The Sign Man Died."

As I thought back of him, I couldn't help but think of the oft-repeated phrase:

*"Bloom where you're planted."*

# 7

# Liberty

*"It's time to chop weeds."*

THE COWS WERE GRAZING just outside the living room window of our tiny house on Mr. Granger's large ranch. The "farmhand's house" served well for us as we began our ministry at Liberty Baptist Church. Working for Mr. Granger combining wheat, and also working at a service station in Plano, paid the expenses of our new family member, Timothy David, who joined his brother Terry. With farm living came a bit of excitement in our house one day, when we heard a strange squeaking coming from somewhere. Having very little furniture, we quickly traced the sound to our couch. With flashlight in hand, we pulled some tacks from the upholstery and discovered, tucked behind the springs in a cozy "bed" of stuffing, a nest of—was it 17 or 18—tiny pink mice! Our house was not big enough for them and us, so they had to go!

To save the church rent money, I felt a wise investment would be to build a parsonage next to the church, to accommodate us and any future pastors who would minister there. The church was in the country, north of Dallas, west of Plano, and had been in existence longer than the First Baptist Church of Dallas. It was almost entirely made up of farmers, with only three or four business people working elsewhere.

As we met to discuss the project of building a parsonage on the church field, one deacon questioned, "Where will we get the money? As for me, it would be impossible to raise even one hundred dollars." Being young and bold in my faith, I ventured, "Do you mean to say that if your daughter, whom you love dearly, were sick and demanded medical care that would cost $100, you would not be able to raise it?" The rest of the deacons, encouraged by my boldness, voted quickly to build—though there <u>was</u> a mention by one that the church may go bankrupt. Another thought the house should have a "path" instead of a bath since some in the community did not yet have indoor plumbing.

When deciding where to dig the well, the father of one of the deacons came to "witch" for the well, a rather common practice in those days in that area. It seems the stick he was holding would bend a certain way if water were available there for drilling. It's strange, I had already picked the spot for the well, the same spot that his bending stick confirmed!

As the work on the building began, excitement grew. All the work on the little house was done by the men of the church for the total cost of $2300 and was completely paid for when the last nail was driven and the last board painted.

When we last visited the church site many, many years later, we saw a lovely new church complex, beautifully landscaped and fittingly surrounded by a neighborhood of million dollar homes and polo grounds across the street. As Mollie and I reflected back, we knew in our hearts that no one in those exquisite houses was any happier than we had been in our little $2300 house, serving the Lord together with our church family. "Houses are built of brick and stone, but only God can make a home."

Since Mollie and I were often out preaching and doing her chalk art ministry in other churches, a great blessing was to have the Boydston family to help. Mrs. Boydston and their five children were always eager to feed and play with our two babies while we were gone. I wonder if Mrs. Boydston realized that *her* ministry was just as important as ours!

Again, we had a good number of young people in our church, but it grew dramatically when the Vest family moved into the area. Mr. and Mrs. Vest had 18 children, several of them teenagers, including two sets of twin girls. The Vests were sharecroppers, living on and farming someone else's land and getting a portion of the crop. It was quite an experience when the Vests invited us over to share Sunday dinner with them, and I wondered just how many chickens left the chicken house that day to fill the platter on the table.

In 1992, 38 years later, now living in Miami, I got a call from one of the Vest girls.

"Are you the Tommy Watson that pastored Liberty Baptist Church in Plano, Texas? I saw the article in the newspaper about a Christmas tree being put on Red Square in Moscow after the fall of Communism, and I knew it must be you."

Revivals in country churches in those days were always exciting times. Another pastor or a full-time evangelist would be brought in to preach for 10 days or two weeks. There would be special music, good gospel singing, and lives would be changed. There was always a big country meal for the preachers in a different home each day, so the waistlines were also changed.

For our Spring revival (we also had a Fall revival) I invited Bill Hinson, then my fellow seminary student and ping-pong competitor, to be our preacher. He stayed in our home, and since we were up half the night talking, we slept a little later in the morning. Leonard Young, one of my fine deacons stopped me one night with, "I passed your house this morning at 6:00 o'clock and it was still dark. You must sleep late."

"No," Bill said, "We were out visiting."

The next morning, Bill and I got up at 2:00 a.m. and drove over to Mr. Young's farm. Shep began to bark and the chickens in the henhouse stirred. A light in the back of the house came on as we stepped up on the creaking porch to the back door and knocked. Mr. Young came to the door with his shotgun.

"We were just out visiting and wanted to stop by and see your family," we explained. No matter the hour, Mrs. Young put on the coffee pot, Bill fried the bacon and eggs, I churned the butter, and we all ate and laughed and talked until the eastern sky announced the dawning of another day. Bill and I went back home and went to sleep, and Leonard Young and his family picked up their hoes and went to chop weeds in the cotton field.

# 8

# Pastor at Heart

*"I drove home and called my associate pastor
and jokingly said, 'Charlie, what's a can?'"*

I AM A PASTOR at heart. I loved my church. I loved my people. I loved my work. With all the experiences I have had outside the church, about which I write, it does not mean that these are one part of my life and my church was another. The fact is that my church family was involved in many or most of these experiences and together we grew in love, ministry, and sacrifice. Without them, their prayers and encouragement, I would not have been able to "color outside the lines" and accomplish what I feel God led me in doing during the 35 years Mollie and I served at the First Baptist Church of Perrine, now Christ Fellowship.

The pastor must wear many "hats," some which fit quite well and some that are not so comfortable. First and foremost, he must be a man of the Word and of prayer. But with the calling come also weddings, baptisms, burials, building projects, peacemaking, visitation, counseling, and much more. He must know how to work with the saint and how to win the sinner; how to call the "lambs" and how to care for the "sheep."

One new hat I donned while living in McKinney, Texas, pastoring Waddell Street Baptist Church, was that of part-time chaplain at the VA hospital there, with a Civil Service ranking of GS 11. It was a unique ministry, but was also God's provision for financing our two baby girls into our growing family. After car-pooling four mornings a week to Ft. Worth Baptist Theological Seminary, I would then work four hours a day at the hospital where I had varied experiences of counseling with every type of individual, from doctors and lawyers to street people. Let me introduce you to one very interesting person, Austin. One day while I was talking with Austin, a man walked by with cancer of the lip. With my very limited knowledge, I told Austin it was probably caused from putting the cigarette on the right side of his lip for twenty years. Austin then looked in the mirror and saw a brown spot on the right side of *his* lip. "What is that?" Not being a doctor, I could give him a quick diagnosis: "That's probably the beginning of cancer." The next day I came by.

"Austin, how are you coming in your smoking?"

"It's been the hardest thing I've ever had to do in my life."

"I'm so glad you stopped smoking," I said.

"Oh I didn't stop smoking. The hardest thing is to remember to put the cigarette on the left side of my mouth!"

COMING FROM MCKINNEY, THE county seat of Collin County, Texas, where we pastored our third church for six years, to a small church south of Miami and north of the Keys, was a major move. We consoled our children (who were 3, 5, 7, and 8) with a tank of tropical fish in the living room, instead of their pasture of American Saddlebred horses and three Argentina Shetland ponies, named Shadrach, Meshach, and Abednego. A new life and growing love for south Florida had begun.

Our church was situated between the southbound and northbound Highway #1 on a piece of land that offered no room for expansion, so, in 1963, we relocated our church to 5 ¼ acres of land where we built our worship center and education building. Thus, we were able to use the building on the highway entirely for the expansion of our work with migrants.

# Migrant Work

SOUTH FLORIDA WAS ONE of the world leaders in crop growing in the winter months, tomatoes being the major crop harvested. With five members of our church owning large tomato farms, I learned early of the plight of hundreds of migrant workers. Crowded together in migrant camps in the Homestead area, they lived in shacks during the harvesting time, and then moved with their families following the crops to similar conditions in central Florida. We learned that while the parents and older children were in the fields picking tomatoes, the four- and five-year-olds were watching the younger babies in the car.

God sent to us a young Cuban pastor, Rafael deArmas, who had the vision and burden for the hundreds of Mexican migrants. He and his wife Clysta set up a very efficient day care center for these babies and young children, using volunteers until we could afford to pay workers. All the children were bathed when they arrived each morning, dressed in clean clothes, and fed. They had a food and clothes distribution program and worship services to help meet the physical and spiritual needs of this ever-growing transient population.

I received a call one day from the county health office stating that we must have one worker for every two children under the age of two. Unless we complied, they would have to shut us down. I told them to let me know when they were coming, as I wanted to have TV cameras taking pictures as the babies were taken back, placed in cars and watched by one worker—a five-year-old. Sometimes, one must "color outside the lines"—especially when the lines are a bit distorted.

We met Chama and Angelita Gonzalez and their large family when they brought their twin babies to the migrant day care center. Some time later we hired them as the custodians at our church, where they worked for many years. (An extra blessing was the fantastic tacos she often prepared at noon for the church staff.) One of those twin babies grew up and graduated from Palm Beach Atlantic College, even getting a couple of her credits from Oxford University when we chose her and five other young people from our church to spend a semester in London, under the care of Jim and Connie Hill of our church.

## TV Ministry

IN THE EARLY DAYS of our television ministry, when networks sought to get permission for a station in a city, they were required to give so much free time for public service programming. To meet this requirement and to find favor in the community, Channel 10 ABC gave one half hour a week each to the Jewish, Catholic, and Protestant groups. Later when a form of deregulation came and the giving of free time was not required, I called the Executive of Channel 10 and asked why we were being cut off.

"You take three nights a week—too much of our production time," was the answer.

"What if we only take one night a week? One week tape two Catholic programs, and the next week tape two Jewish programs. And I will bring our Protestant program to you 'in a can.'" Channel 10 agreed and of course both the Jewish and Catholic leaders were greatly pleased. I drove home and called my associate pastor, Charlie Koch, and jokingly said, "Charlie, what's a can?" It meant we must set up our own studio in our church, do our own programming, and deliver the tape to the Channel 10 studio in downtown Miami. Therefore, for the next 18 years we had a free half hour of programming each Sunday morning.

Because I felt that outreach was and is the main mission of the church, and that television could reach more people with the gospel message than any other method, we purchased cameras and equipment and set up a studio in a large back room. James Srodulsky, a young man who grew up in our church, was brought on staff as the producer/

director. Volunteers were trained in camera work, building sets, and other facets of TV production, thus involving many people in this ministry. For some time, I interviewed people on our program "Christians in the Community."

An interesting big "high" in our broadcasting from our church studio happened rather unexpectedly—but it's good it happened! We had members of our church who were employed in U.S. Customs and, because they wanted to make our "set" look attractive, offered to give to us some large artificial plants from the U.S. Customs building, which were no longer being used. The painted backdrops (done by some of our ladies) were enhanced by this new array of greenery from Customs. One night before beginning an interview with a guest, one of our cameramen, who was a policeman, gave us a strong suggestion.

"I don't want to say anything, since I am new here—but I think you ought to take the marijuana plant off from behind Pastor Watson's head—and—off the set." Surprised and a bit embarrassed at our lack of botanical knowledge, I laughed, "We've had it there three months. If we take it off now, we'll lose half of our audience." But take it off we did.

## Graded Sermons

GOD'S CHURCH IS MADE up of all kinds of people—and I love them all. They come from all different backgrounds, in all different sizes, from all professions, with all different talents and abilities, with a variety of personalities, in different colors, young and old, and in our church— from many different countries.

With this type of congregation, you can expect the unexpected. Unexpected was the fact that I had one man who had been grading my sermons each Sunday on a scale from 1 to 10, with 10 being the highest. Now most pastors know when their sermons have been flat, and they definitely don't need someone to reinforce the fact, especially before reaching the back door! But I had adjusted and one Sunday morning jokingly mentioned the grading system.

We were invited to dinner at the home of a lovely Puerto Rican family, rather new in our church, and following dinner the father mentioned that his children had graded my sermon last week. They stood in a row in the dining room and the oldest son, a ten-year-old, turned his card over and showed a #10. (Bright boy, I thought!) The nine-year-old girl turned her card over to a #8. (She's grasping the message!) The next boy showed his card with a #7. (Not bad for his age!) Then the curly headed, black-eyed littlest boy turned his card over and in large black-crayoned letters was written "I fell asleep." The next week in church I asked the four children to come to the front and one by one show my grade cards—to the applause of the church family.

I am thankful that in reality we preachers have only one Person to whom we are accountable—but—we ARE accountable to Him! He tells <u>us</u>, as He told Timothy:

*"Preach the Word; be prepared in season and out of season; correct, rebuke, and encourage—with great patience and careful instruction. But you, keep your head in all situations, endure hardship, do the work of an evangelist, discharge all the duties of your ministry." (2 Timothy 4:2,5)*

*"Set an example for the believers in speech, in life, in love, in faith, and in purity. Until I come, devote yourself to the public reading of Scripture, to preaching and to teaching…Be diligent in these matters; give yourself wholly to them, so that everyone may see your progress. Watch your life and doctrine closely. Persevere in them, because if you do, you will save both yourself and your hearers." (1 Timothy 4:12b-13, 15-16)*

Lord, keep us faithful!

# II.   DOORS AJAR

# 9

# Cedars of Lebanon

*"You see, we had been to the top and would forever feel safe."*

NO TRIP IS EVER quite like one's first trip abroad. Our itinerary included Russia and Israel and the neighboring country of Lebanon, which stretches above the northern border of Israel. Its beautiful beaches on the Mediterranean and its gold-filled shops in Beirut make it an attractive adventure for any tourist. However, there was something else we wanted to see so Dr. Charles Stanley and Anna, Mollie and I left the tour group, hired a taxi and headed south to the ruins of the ancient cities of Tyre and Sidon. It was somewhere in this area where Jesus went one time, hoping He could escape the crowds, but it was impossible to be hidden from the public. It was here that a Syrophoenician woman had come to Jesus and begged Him to heal her little daughter. She was a Greek (a Gentile in religion), but Jesus saw her faith and told her to return home to her little girl who was healed. (Mark 7:24-30)

This was also the home area of our taxi driver who was very eager to show us his village. As we came over the small rise and entered the outskirts of the little village, we could have been entering it 2000 years ago. The scene was the same. There was a well; there were some women in the typical dress of Jesus' day, and they were bringing their water pots to the well. My mind immediately went to the conversation Jesus had with the woman at the well in Samaria. He was tired and He was thirsty, and He asked her for a drink. But very soon she was asking Him for a drink—a drink of the Living Water which He offered. *"But whoever drinks the water I give him will never thirst. Indeed, the water I give him will become in him a spring of water welling up to eternal life."* *(John 4:14)* And she drank deeply of this Living Water and shared it with her village.

But our taxi driver didn't stop at the well. He drove on. I wonder if these women at the well in the outskirts of his village were ever offered the "living water" that only Jesus can give.

I HAD OFTEN READ in the Bible of the "Cedars of Lebanon" and I wanted to see them.

David spoke of them when he said, *"The trees of the Lord are well watered, the Cedars of Lebanon that He planted,"* *(Psalm 104:16)* and again, *"The Righteous will…grow like a Cedar of Lebanon…they will still bear fruit in old age, they will stay fresh and green, proclaiming the Lord is upright, He is my Rock, and there is no wickedness in Him."* *(Psalm 92:12,14-15)*

Jeremiah writes: *"Woe to him who builds his palace by unrighteousness,—He says, 'I will build myself a great palace with spacious upper rooms.' So he makes large windows in it, panels it with cedar, and decorates it in red. Does it make you a king to have more and more cedar? Did not your father have food and drink? He did what was right and just, so all went well with him."* *(Jeremiah 22:13-15)*

David, I think, felt ashamed when he wrote, *"Here I am, living in a palace of cedar, while the ark of God remains in a tent."* *(2 Samuel 7:2)*

The "Cedars of Lebanon" were not a major tourist attraction so there was no tour bus to accommodate those who considered it a "must" to go to the height of the mountain where some cedars still stood. Actually, when we saw the small grove of tall and old trees that had weathered the years, there was nothing really impressive about them. The impressive thing, however, that we will never forget, was the ride up. We boarded our bus, which appeared to be an old school bus, and watched as the driver's assistant stepped up into the bus and placed a rock on the floor by his feet. The road was narrow and steep, one hairpin turn after another, and the cliff beside me went straight down for hundreds of feet. We quickly learned after the first treacherous curve why the driver's assistant had a rock. He carefully would place the rock under the back wheel as the driver, endeavoring to make a tight hairpin curve, backed as far as he dared without going over the cliff. We breathed deeply as we reached the top—until—I saw our driver reach under his seat for his pint of whiskey. Mollie, shaking in fear, said to me, "If he drinks that, I'm not riding down with him." I said, "If he *doesn't* drink it, I'm not riding down!!"

As the rest of the group gathered for refreshments before descending, we looked around at the vast vista above us, and Charles said, "Tommy, I want to go higher." Although it was spring, the ski lift was still running to satisfy the desire of a few adventurers like the four of us. We climbed into the seats with our feet dangling and fastened the bars across us. It was a slow ride and we could savor the beauty. Then we saw it, high up here above the grasslands below! It was a sheepfold, a rocky enclosure built of stones laid one upon another, for the safety of the sheep at night. There was an opening in the stone enclosure, and no gate. I looked—and I experienced God. I "heard" the words of Jesus when He said, *"I am the gate for the sheep. All who ever came before Me were thieves and robbers, but the sheep did not listen to them. I am the gate; whoever enters through Me will be saved. He will come in and go out, and find pasture. The thief comes only to steal and kill and destroy; I have come that they may have life, and have it to the full." (John 10:7-10)*

As we came down and rejoined our fellow tourists at the rest stop, we were ready for the school bus ride down. You see, we had been to the top and will forever feel safe in His sheepfold.

# 10

## The ’66 Trip

*"In Flanders Fields the poppies blow,*
*between the crosses row on row."*

WE WERE AWAKENED AGAIN by the rumbling thunder and the spattering raindrops on our pup tent. It was only minutes before it was a downpour and I wondered if our boys' tent was dry. No concern for the girls as they were tucked safely in their sleeping bags in the back of the Volkswagen. This was not the first night it had rained, nor the last, but rain would not stop us from enjoying an unforgettable vacation.

Having considered it for a short time, I approached the family at the supper table with my plan for this great adventure. It was early 1966.

"How would you like to go on a month-long camping trip across Europe this summer?" There was no need to ask the question a second time—and immediately we all began to plan. Since the girls were 9 and 11, and the boys were 13 and 14, we knew it would be an ideal *time* for such a trip, and camping would be the ideal *type* of trip. Of course, finances also definitely determined that it would be a camping trip.

Terry and Tim had experienced primitive camping excursions when they pushed their raft, and later, a little boat, loaded with supplies and a small tent, across the inlet to the tiny Chicken Key. I wonder now how we permitted such adventure in snake and alligator friendly waters. We certainly were not overly protective parents! As a family we had made a trip from Miami to San Francisco in our 13-foot travel trailer, as well as to Texas and North Carolina and shorter trips. But—this European trip would be like no other!

For the trip, I drew out all my money from the bank and ordered a $1600 Volkswagen square-back to be picked up when we arrived at the airport in Paris. Our gear consisted of two pup tents, a small clothes bag for each of us, and an old army footlocker. In the footlocker we stowed two pans, a few dishes, and towels. Upon arriving in France, we added a one-burner stove to its contents. Although it was low, the footlocker served as our table workspace as there are no picnic tables at European campsites. It is amazing how few are ones' necessities! We kept a record of our spending, which came to a total of $560 including the camping ($60), gas ($100), and airport tax ($30). We enjoyed lots of delicious ice cream—it was cheap!

The Wardenga family with their three children flew over with us and picked up their Volkswagen at the airport in Paris. Although we were not touring together, the children were always delighted when our paths crossed, as they did on the square in Venice and at the cathedral in Florence, and at several campsites. Both cars were together now, and it was 11:00 o'clock at night when we finally found, after much searching, a sign to a camp, high on a hill in Rome. We went into the little office, registered, and turned in our passports. Since none of us knew Italian, we assumed the man at the desk was telling us to follow him so he could lead us to two campsites. He got into his car, we into ours, and he started down the long, winding road up which we had just come. "No doubt," we thought, "there are some sites lower down the hill where he wants us to camp." We kept following him, though we were now getting down in the city traffic! But we couldn't let him get out of sight—because he had our passports! Speeding, then slowing down for traffic, circling a car accident, and finally getting away from the bright lights of the city—he finally stopped and as Hank and I got out of our cars behind him, in true Italian fashion, he motioned, "What—do you want?"

"Our passports," we said.

"I do not have your passports. They are back at the camp office. I'm going home for the night."

"Oh!" we said sheepishly. "We thought—." No need to explain. We laughed hilariously, got into our cars, and followed the weary man as he showed us the way back to camp.

No campers could possibly have seen more of Europe than we did in our 32 days in <u>all 12 countries</u> of western Europe, plus one night camping in Yugoslavia. A breathtaking scene of the cloud-circled mountains of Yugoslavia was captured in film and later on canvas as Mollie reproduced it in a large oil painting that now hangs on Tracie's wall. All but two nights we camped, eating soup or anything else we could fix on our one-burner stove. One night I opened a can with a picture of a cow on the label. Thinking it was beef, we were all disappointed when we discovered it was cow tongue—something we had never had or seen before, so we happily ate only our potatoes and the wonderful European bread. Food was not a priority when we had a whole new continent to explore!

A highlight of any European trip would be a visit to the Vatican with its history, its statuary, and the magnificent paintings in the Sistine Chapel. Hours were spent as we soaked up the beauty. We had seen pictures of the colorfully costumed Swiss Guards who for years had symbolically guarded the Vatican, and now, as we stood on the Vatican steps, we saw them close up. They were real people, handsome young men standing straight and motionless. But even Swiss Guards are "off guard" when they begin to talk with a beautiful young lady of eighteen like Susan Wardenga. She and Frank Schnyder, one of the Swiss Guards, corresponded some during the year, and the following summer when he had vacation from "guarding" the Vatican, he flew to America to visit the Wardengas. We and our children were also delighted to entertain a Swiss Guard at our dinner table.

Our children were intrigued as we visited five American military cemeteries, one of which was the burial site of General George Patton. The Luxembourg American Cemetery and Memorial, 50.5 acres, contains the remains of 5,076 American servicemen, most of whom died during the Battle of the Bulge. Two American flagpoles overlook the vast cemetery and between the flagpoles lies the headstone of General George S. Patton, Jr.

American Battles Monument Commission operates and maintains 24 permanent American burial grounds on foreign soil, in which are the graves of 93,242 servicemen of W.W.II. At the Ardennes American Cemetery, written in stone are the timeless words of General Pershing of World War I, "Time will not dim the glory of their deeds."

To Mollie and me, and our children, the Ardennes American Cemetery was more significant than Gen. Patton's because it was the burial site of a close friend of Mollie's from her high school days. The officer at the Visitors' Center helped us locate his grave among the hundreds of white crosses. It was a beautiful Sunday as our family sat quietly on some benches there and had our morning worship together, as I read and discussed with the children 1 Corinthians 15 about victory over death. They were meaningful moments for us all.

*"Where O death, is your victory? Where O death, is your sting? The sting of death is sin, and the power of sin is the law. But thanks be to God! He gives us the victory through our Lord Jesus Christ."*
*(1 Corinthians 15:55-57)*


Since we were all familiar with the poem "In Flanders Fields," by John McCrae, we also took the children to that First World War cemetery, Flanders Field, where still—"the poppies blow, between the crosses row on row."

On our last Sunday, with everything packed for our trip home, we found the American Church in Paris and listened to the message of the guest speaker, Dr. Daniel A. Poling, former chaplain in W.W.I, and now consultant with the Christian Herald. His sermon title was "Jesus Went a Little Farther." He told of his son who was one of the four chaplains in World War II who gave their lives when their transport ship, U.S.A.T. Dorchester, was sunk by a German U-boat torpedo on Feb. 3, 1943. When it was clear there were not enough accessible life jackets, the four chaplains gave their own to four young soldiers, then held hands, prayed, and began singing a hymn together as they went down with the sinking vessel.

"Before my son went away," Dr. Poling said, "he came to my office and asked for a talk. 'Dad,' he said, 'when I leave, I don't want you to pray for my return. Just pray that I will always be doing my job. I have great confidence in your prayers, Dad, and it may keep me from doing my duty if I knew you were praying for my safe return.'"

What a tremendous "closing" I thought as we left the church, for our family's month-long vacation in Europe. So listen, my children and grandchildren: Safety is not the ultimate goal of a Christian, but rather to keep doing your duty in loving service to your Savior and Lord.

# 11

## A Burden Passed On

*"Yes, Richard Wurmbrand, we're still hearing
the cries of the Persecuted Church."*

WE WERE GATHERED AT the Miami International Airport, forty of us. The large bags were stacked and tagged in one section, the small carry-on bags in another. Elderly and young, all sat waiting, eagerly anticipating their first trip to Russia.

"Do you have some Russian Bibles?" the white-haired lady whispered to the lady from Atlanta seated beside her.

"Yes I have. Do you think it's safe? Should we be doing this?"

As I looked around at the excited group, I thought back to a Sunday morning a year before, 1967. With Bible in hand, my guest speaker was about to step into my pulpit when he turned to me with soulful, almost pleading eyes, and his words jarred me.

"The trouble with you Baptists is that you don't believe the Bible."

Thinking that his words needed a response of some kind, I playfully quipped, "Why, I thought we were the only ones who do!"

"Doesn't the Bible say to go into all the world and preach the Gospel?"

"Yes," I said, "but it's impossible to get into the Communist countries now."

"Oh, you can," he challenged, "*if God leads you.*" And he stepped into my pulpit and shared his testimony and his burden. The guest speaker was Richard Wurmbrand.

A couple months after he had spoken in our church, I received a call from him.

"Pastor Watson, would you please write a letter of recommendation for me. I'm having difficulty getting into churches to share my testimony—and I *must* share it." I was so very humbled that God would ask of me, a little Baptist pastor, to give a recommendation for one of God's greatest saints of the 20th century!

BEING OF ROMANIAN JEWISH background, and following his conversion to Christianity as a youth, Richard Wurmbrand became a Lutheran pastor and missionary to Romanian Jews. When Communists came to power in post-war Romania, his ministry continued there, but "underground." He was arrested several times and spent fourteen years in prison, three of those years in a tiny solitary cell 30 feet beneath the earth, in total darkness. In order to maintain his sanity, he set a routine every day which included prayer and preaching. If there was no person to listen, he knew the angels were listening, and he practiced this routine for two years.

Then one day he heard a tap in his cell, followed by another. A prisoner in an adjacent cell had heard the muffled sound, and they began a Morse code type of communication which continued for a year. Realizing that his new friend was burdened with sin, Wurmbrand was joyful that God had given him the chance to minister to one person.

Years later while in a "death" room for those destined to die, Richard met the man who had been his single convert in solitary confinement. The man shared his testimony how a pastor had led him to Christ by tapping through the wall. Little did he know that the man next to him was that pastor!

Richard's wife, Sabina, also spent years in prison, in hard labor, with little food. Finally released in 1964, Richard Wurmbrand and his family were allowed to emigrate, after Norwegian Christians paid $10,000 ransom. In 1966 he appeared before a U.S. Senate panel, where he stripped to the waist before television cameras and displayed eighteen torture wounds suffered at the hands of the Communists. I, too, saw the torture wounds, as he and his wife were our houseguests. Who better than Richard Wurmbrand could plead, "Bibles, Bibles, they need Bibles, the only message that can change lives and promise Heaven."

And so began **our** efforts to smuggle Bibles to the spiritually-starved people of the Eastern bloc nations. "*Oh, you can—if God leads you.*"

In 1967, Pastor Richard Wurmbrand and Sabina sat in their kitchen and wrote a one page "newsletter" to those who had heard their testimony of persecution in Romania. "The body of Christ in America must be told what their Christian brothers and sisters behind the Iron Curtain were enduring," was their thought. Today and for over forty years, *The Voice of the Martyrs* has been that voice.

Today I leaned back in my comfortable recliner and picked up the latest copy of *The Voice of the Martyrs*. Here I read of Solihin of Indonesia, once a devout Muslim, but now a young man living and suffering for Jesus. When he became a Christian, neighbors surrounded his bamboo house shouting, "Burn this house! Kill him. Bury him alive!" Three times Solihin was brought before the village chief, beaten and threatened with death. Radical Muslims tried many tactics to convert him back to Islam, even offering him a good job and $2,700. Solihin told them, "I don't need money or a good job. I only need the Lord Jesus."

I turned the page in the *Voice of the Martyrs* and read of the growth of the Church in Iran in spite of oppression and the murder of Christian leaders. The fast-growing underground Church in Iran is finding that the power of Christ can erase hatred and replace it with love. The believers meet in apartments to read the New Testament and pray. Some even go out at night and lie on the floorboards of their parents' car and read by flashlight, since the Iranian *pasdaran* (special police) are always seeking to catch and arrest Christians. Satellite dishes are smashed to keep the gospel out of Iran, but that only works to advance the Kingdom, as the non-Christian seeks to find what it is that the government does not want the students to see.

Yes, Richard Wurmbrand, we are still hearing today the cries of the Persecuted Church and the voices of God's martyrs.

Footnote: Richard Wurmbrand died in southern California, February 17, 2001 at age 91. *Voice of the Martyrs*—www.persecution.com

Richard and Sabina Wurmbrand in our home in Miami

# 12

## The Strongest Grip

*"Working for the Lord doesn't pay much,
but the retirement plan is out of this world."*

FRAMED AND HANGING IN our bathroom is this motto which is read often. It's true, but we don't have to wait for the "retirement plan" because oftentimes God gives us an enormous "bonus" here in this world, also. One such bonus I received for the simple act of sharing a Bible. Since 1917 in the Soviet Union, across 11 time zones, *there was not a place to buy Bibles or Christian literature.*

The church was packed, people standing body to body, praying, singing, writing notes down on bits of paper, worshipping. Tears ran down the cheeks of babushka-clad women.

Somewhere in the mass of worshippers toward the front of the church there in St. Petersburg, Russia, I stood, crushed together with the others. Rushing to my mind came the words told us before we left: "Best not give Bibles to the pastors as they are required to turn them in." Silently, I pressed my small Russian Bible into the hand of the woman standing next to me. Quickly she dropped it into her purse, all time with her face straight ahead. AND THEN—in a couple of minutes, a grip on my arm. I'll never forget it. I'll feel it as long as I live! That grip said, "Thank you—thank you—pray for us."

That grip was my pay, my "bonus" for sharing His Word. "The retirement plan is out of this world" but His bonuses are surely good here.

# 13

## GUM, on Red Square

*"He appeared from nowhere and handed us the
contraband material, thanked us profusely and disappeared
into the darkness. We never saw him again."*

PERHAPS WE SHOULD HAVE been back in our hotel with the others in
our tour group, but instead we were standing in front of the huge GUM
Department Store on Red Square. It was a cool July evening like many
summer evenings in Moscow and perhaps we were a bit conspicuous,
standing there in our western attire and looking very American. The
year was 1969. Rev. Bill Hinson, a longtime friend from Southwestern
Seminary days, was with me when we were approached by a young
Russian man speaking broken English.

"You are Americans?" "Yes," we said.

"I am a Christian," he whispered. When he was assured of our
Christian kinship, he began to share with us his burden.

"My father was killed for his faith," he said, "but he had already
passed on that faith to me. Once when I was praying, a man approached
me and told me I needed to go to a mental hospital. 'A young man like
you,' he said, 'should not believe such lies.' I thought, 'Had my father
died for lies?' No! I was convinced he had died for the TRUTH. I made

up my mind that I would do all that I could to let the free world know what was happening here behind the Iron Curtain in Russia."

He paused—but seemed compelled to go on. He looked cautiously around and began again: "I have something I would like you to take to America when you return." His countenance showed his trust in us, and he guardedly whispered, "It's some documents, some film negatives and a tape, telling of the persecution of Christians here. Your country *must* learn what is really happening to your Christian brothers." He pointed to his watch.

"Tomorrow night at 8:30 I will meet you at the Central Baptist Church of Moscow, to give you the material."

"We'll be there," we promised, "8:30 tomorrow night." And we parted.

IT WAS DARK THE next night when we got into a taxi and told the driver our desired destination. My concern that night began the moment I saw his reaction. His face seemed to say, "You don't want to go there" and "I don't really want to take you there."

Few cars were on the streets of Moscow, and the streets and buildings were dimly lit as he wound his way to the church and dropped us off at the curb.

As the taxi drove off and turned the corner, our Christian brother appeared from nowhere and handed us the contraband material, thanked us profusely, and disappeared into the darkness. We never saw him again. I'll never know his name. I only know that he was doing what he felt compelled by God to do—to somehow convey to the West the message of the persecuted church. Would he too die for his faith as his father had? Someday we'll meet them both in Heaven and Bill and I will say, "Remember us? We met you in front of GUM Department Store."

Bill and I, now eager to get the material translated and see what we actually had in our possession, stepped through the side door into the dim light of the church office. A kind-faced middle-aged lady welcomed us and directed us to two worn leather chairs. Her hair was pulled back by a dark blue scarf knotted at the nape, and she wore a nondescript print dress.

"We were told you could translate something for us," we said as we handed her the packet our Christian brother had delivered to us. She glanced through the first papers, and a most alarmed expression came upon her.

"You don't want this," she said. "It is very dangerous for you to have it. This will get me in trouble and will get the two of you in trouble. Please, you must leave. Take it with you." Disappointed, yet barely understanding her fear, we thanked her and left through the same side door we had entered, and into the darkness, the documents and tape securely clutched in Bill's hand.

After walking a few blocks, we caught the first bus we saw, only to be encountered by a blurry-eyed drunk who tried to engage us in argument. A confrontation was the last thing Bill and I wanted. We changed buses, confusing anyone to whom we may have looked suspicious, and arrived at our Hotel Leningrad. The time was 11 p.m.

We crossed the spacious, but empty lobby, and stepped into the elevator. However, as soon as we stepped in, two large Russian men dressed in business suits and each wearing on his lapel a picture of Lenin, stepped in behind us.

"Floor #26," I said to the lady elevator operator. One of the big men nodded his head to the lady. (Obviously, he knew English.) Could it be that in this huge hotel, these men were on the same floor as we! At that moment I *knew* they were government agents, and here we were with illegal papers, a tape, and negatives, all condemning the Russian government. For a moment, I laughed inwardly, saying to myself, "Well, Watson, let's see you get out of this one." But it was a moment also when I knew the peace that Jesus spoke of when He said, *"Peace I leave with you, My peace I give you. I do not give to you as the world gives. Do not let your hearts be troubled and do not be afraid." (John 14:27)*

The elevator was slow. It was a long way to the 26th floor. We stepped out of the elevator. The two men stepped out behind us and followed us down the hall. Bill and I breathed a sigh of relief as we stopped at our door, turned the key, and the men passed by. We walked in and shut the door behind us. Were these government agents? It doesn't matter. We know that our God is greater than all of the forces of evil around us.

# 14

# Spinning Spokes, Europe on Two Wheels

*"This is the day that the Lord has made;
we will rejoice and be glad in it."*

THERE WE STOOD, ALL 49 of us, beside our bikes in front of the courthouse steps in downtown Miami. Mayor Chuck Hall officially greeted us, and the Miami Herald cameras flashed. For weeks the youth of our church had spent Saturdays biking to Homestead National Park, to prepare for a 20-day cycling trip through Europe. The Saturday rides were tough, but nothing like the experiences of climbing the hills of Luxembourg and biking against the strong north wind of Holland. Each evening in Europe found us 35 to 62 miles farther than our campsite of the night before.

On the lawn of the Youth Hostel in Luxembourg, each teen unboxed his own bike and assembled it, with the help of the boys who were designated as our mechanics. All of us ready, we began our biking, stopped for sandwiches of bread and salami we had bought the day before, and then on to our first campsite. But alas! When I called for the box with the pots and cooking utensils, it could not be found, having been left back at our church in Miami. No stores were open as it was Sunday. I breathed deeply and hoped none of the 49 hungry bikers would lynch me or our youth director, Richard Schinman. But we would not go to our sleeping bags hungry. We had the large #10 cans of beef stew which we opened with a pocket knife and set on our little two-burner camp stove. No pots necessary—until tomorrow when we would purchase some.

As we biked we tossed out hundreds of letters with a gospel message, wrapped in colored cellophane. A few months later a letter arrived from a 17-year-old Dutch girl who had seen our group pass her house and had read one of our letters. We responded with an invitation to come to America for Christmas, our youth paying her airfare. With our church bus loaded with our youth, we welcomed her and her 18-year-old sister at the airport for a two-week Christmas in Miami.

THIS BIKE TRIP IN 1970 was the beginning of annual Spinning Spokes trips for the next 25 years, our sons taking over as years went on. Mollie and the girls did the cooking those first years, which was soon made much easier with a cook wagon built by our creative missionary, Ray Hill. Several years we ran two groups a day apart: Ray Hill and family leading the second group with their cook wagon and vans (and we with ours), making it possible for as many as 150 young people to participate at one time. The bikes were stored each year at a farm in Luxembourg, and a couple of the boys went over early each summer to get all the bikes in shape.

There were three reasons why I started and continued Spinning Spokes.

1. Physical—I felt that most American young people are not sufficiently challenged physically. On a trip like this, they would accomplish feats they had never dreamed possible. Their bodies would be stretched to their limits.

2. Mental—There would be no better way to learn the history, geography and the culture of Europe than to bike through the hills and the valleys, wind through the village streets, eat the fresh pastries,

and visit the war cemeteries, monuments and museums. They would visit the 1000-year-old capital city of Luxembourg, with its massive medieval fortress; the burial place of General Patton, with hundreds of white crosses marking the graves of our dead; and the city of Trier, oldest in Germany, conquered by the Romans in 14 A.D. They would enjoy a boat trip down the Rhine to Cologne and bike into the Netherlands, visiting the hiding place of Anne Frank in Amsterdam. In Belgium, they would spend a day in delightful Brussels, then cycle to Waterloo, where Napoleon met his final defeat. They would experience the sights of history, traveling through the Ardennes Forest, where the Battle of the Bulge took place.

3. Spiritual—Young people are open and teachable. We trust that the examples of the leaders, as well as the truths of the Word taught, have impacted their lives for God forever. Each morning the bikers stood by their bikes and we sang together:

> "This is the day the Lord has made,
> We will rejoice and be glad in it."

I must say it was more difficult to sing it on the occasional mornings that they faced a cold and rainy day. I am sure this Bible verse, after so much repetition, was permanently implanted into their minds, and no doubt some morning five, or fifteen, or twenty years later, they found themselves singing that song as they began their day. I trust so!

Since campfires were not permitted in any European camps, our evening "Deely-Bop," as our son Tim called it, was a "no-campfire" circle of singing, skits, and a message from God's Word. Various church youth-group leaders led the nightly Bible devotional time.

Our bike route was about 550 miles through Luxembourg, Germany, Belgium, Holland, and a bit of France. Riding single file in groups of 6 or 7, the bikers knew to follow our strict rules for safety. On the trips on which I was able to go, my job was to drive up beside a lagging biker and encourage him with, "Come on, you can do it." "You're doing great!" "Rest stop is just ahead." All of the teens were working for their 100% biking patch, so very few yielded to the temptation to get in the van.

Our campsites were pre-arranged and always the camp owner welcomed us, as our kids were generally very well-behaved and left the camp cleaned up. I learned a lesson in camping there, however, that I have never forgotten. After repeatedly saying, "Somebody please get the water," or "Somebody empty the garbage," I learned that "*there ain't nobody named Somebody*." Jesus taught us that, as He called His disciples one by one, by name, and sent them out *not* by saying "somebody go and preach," but by saying "Go YOU into all the world and preach the gospel." "There *ain't* nobody named Somebody."

Spending 20 days with 14- to 17-year-olds can be a learning experience for both us and the bikers, but more than that, it can be a **comedy**. The bikers were camped at Polich, Germany along the Mosel River where, for miles and miles, the vineyards covered the slopes that seemed to go straight up. One of the bikers came to Tim one day and questioned, "How do they stand on those slopes to pick grapes? It is so steep."

"Well, when the first son is born," Tim began, "they cut off one leg so he will be able to stand on the steep slope and pick the grapes." Of course Tim didn't think *anyone* would believe such a tale. The next day we were in Berncastle, Germany, where we had a rest stop for the bikers, with time to wander around the beautiful old town. There happened to be that day in Berncastle a convention for World War II veterans. Of course there were several one-legged men among them. Back to their bikes to finish the biking day, some of the boys came to Tim, and in all seriousness said, "Tim, we saw several of the grape pickers." When on occasion I see a man with one leg, I think, "No, kids, they are not grape pickers. They are brave men who have sacrificed much in service for their country."

Because of limited space in our vans, each teen could only bring a sleeping bag and one small flight bag with personal items, biking shorts, and three bright orange Spinning Spokes t-shirts. The list of things to bring on the trip included "two half rolls of toilet paper," since half rolls seemed to pack easier in the bags. A brother and sister were with us whose mother had meticulously sliced the toilet paper roll vertically, end to end, leaving a pile of sheets on either side. I'm sure she must have pondered a long time to understand what she thought we meant, and struggled a much longer time as she carried out the tedious task. As I write this, I laugh again.

Crossing borders in Europe from Luxembourg to Belgium, to France, and to Germany were usually quite uneventful, except that too often we experienced a major verbal encounter at the French border.

"Where is your front license plate?"

"In Florida only a license plate on the back of the car is required."

"But you must have a front license plate also, to enter France."

"We don't have any."

Finally, unable to solve the problem, they would send our vans and cook wagon through the border crossing—but with a warning. Tim knew that I would soon be coming over to join him with our second group of bikers, so he struck on a brilliant idea.

"Dad," he said, "I'm tired of this problem we always have at the French border. You know those *'Arrive Alive'* plates that some people are putting on the front of their cars in Florida? When you come, bring me some of them." It worked! No more hassle at the border!

RAIN WAS A PROBLEM on some of the trips. It was no fun to get into a wet shirt, after sleeping in a damp sleeping bag, in a tent that sometimes leaked if the tarp had been improperly tied over the top. American kids, however, are resourceful even though they are not accustomed to taking care of themselves. Tim saw one boy in the tent, trying to dry his wet socks with a flashlight! Fortunately we had many more sunny days than bad days, and early upon arriving in camp, the clotheslines would be filled with washed t-shirts and shorts, underwear and socks. I do remember, however, one stormy, rainy day and night. The kids stayed in their tents, four to a tent, reading, playing cards, and wishing it would stop raining. But it didn't! Mud was everywhere; rivulets were flowing down the slopes. But—the van was dry! Mollie and I slipped in, leaned the front seats back a bit for a good night's sleep—at least for a dry night's sleep. We almost felt guilty for our favored spot, but before we could enjoy our dry comfort too much, the back door opened and Tracie and her friend Carol slid in out of the rain and positioned themselves under and on the back seat. We felt bad for all the wet campers, but what could we do! We laughed hilariously and said, "And to think they paid for this!!" And we dozed off for a few hours' sleep.

WELL ALONG IN EACH trip was the very foreboding mountain which had become the challenge of our bikers. Several days before we reached "Granddaddy Mountain" (the name Tim had given it), Tim began to describe it to our bikers: "It is high—steep in some parts—many curves—long—but all of you *can* make it. We're a team. We encourage each other. Our aim is to break the time record of any of our other groups." Each day he would remind them again of the challenge ahead of them, psych them up for the ultimate test, and when finally the day came, no one had to be told that *this* was the day. We positioned all the boys ahead and reminded them again that this was not a race to see who the winner or winners would be. Everyone who reached the top would be the winner! We lined up the girls at the bottom of "Granddaddy" to begin the climb they had feared and anticipated for days. There was a tremendous team spirit as some of the boys, after reaching the top, ran part way down and walked beside the girls, to encourage them as they struggled to reach the top in time to break the Granddaddy Mountain record.

Several times over the years, we have run across one of our former bikers, and when asked what trip they were on, the answer was: "the one that broke the record on Granddaddy Mountain." ( I'm going to let the secret out, bikers: Every group broke the record!)

There is always one in every group who either tries to show off his biking skills—or—will not abide by our biking rules. We had one boy who rated top in both areas. I'm glad I forgot his name, so I'll call him Sid. Sid was always complaining about the girls in front of him being so slow. (We did not permit passing.) They were not slow, but that was his continuous complaint. "Come on. Speed up. You're going too slow." After hearing this for several days, I had *had* it. When we came to one of our more challenging hills, I told Tim, our bike leader, to take it at "high speed" and placed Sid behind him. Tim had been all-district quarterback for his high school football team as well as the baseball team's best hitter. I knew he had enough athletic energy to be able to leave Sid way behind—which he did. He had also done this mountain several times before. Riding in the van behind him, I called out to Sid, "Come on! You're way behind! Speed up!" Never again did Sid complain about slow bikers. But on the other hand, Tim panted, "Dad, don't ever do that to me again!"

At the top of another high mountain, Tim warned all the cyclists of the very treacherous downhill ride ahead of them, with nine hairpin turns. He told them he would space them out, releasing one at a time to begin the descent. They must not "ride" the brakes, but keep their bikes in control, slow enough to make the nine tight corners. There would be no passing, which was always a "no-no." If broken, it would result in a dollar fine. Tim's final words were: "This hill determines whether you fly home in a seat or in a wooden box."

Sid listened, but did he really hear?? On about the fourth hairpin curve, he lost control of his bike, hit the gravel, skidded and flew off—not off the side of the mountain (for which I am grateful), but into a huge patch of nettles. Wearing only a t-shirt and riding shorts, he was covered with burning welts. Who says justice doesn't prevail?

# 15

## L'Abri: A Place for Answers

*"I wanted to see this man of God connect these
seeking young people with 'the God who is there.'"*

IN THE 60's AND 70's the Existential philosophy was being taught in the liberal universities and was becoming the rule of the day: there is no meaning or purpose to life. The hippy movement, beginning in California and spreading throughout America and Europe, grew upon that philosophy. However, this philosophy backfired. If there is no meaning to life then the "just do it" concept ran wild. "If it feels good, enjoy it." Four-letter-words became the accepted language. If there is no meaning to life, then disrupt all you like, be as vulgar as you want, cheat all you want, smoke pot, and turn on to anything. This produced not just dropouts from colleges but a dropout society. These hippies, who chose to break away from society and government and to reject conformity, did not realize that they created their own brand of conformity: looking alike, dressing alike, behaving alike.

Beneath all of this there developed a searching mind which said, "Surely there is more to life than this." For this reason, many traveled to L'Abri Fellowship, located in Huemoz, Switzerland, to seek answers from the world-renowned philosopher Dr. Frances Schaeffer. Dr.

Schaeffer's book *The God Who Is There* was giving credence to a theistic God who is alive and is not silent. This book, together with his *Escape from Reason* and *Death in the City*, had made him the number one guest lecturer at universities, theological colleges and seminaries around the world. His debates centered around the death of the rational in philosophy, art, music, and modern theology. His answer was: God *is* there and He *is not* silent. He has revealed Himself through Truth in the Person of His Son, Jesus Christ.

I wanted to see this man of God connect these seeking young people with "the God who is there" and lead them to a strong faith, so I came to L'Abri. As we sat around Dr. Schaeffer's dinner table, I realized not only his greatness but his compassion to give the truth of the Gospel to questioning young hearts.

UPON ARRIVING AT L'ABRI I met a handsome young man, who, since he had just arrived also, asked me to be his roommate. When we became acquainted he told me he was planning to go into the ministry, but he had come here to L'Abri to seek wisdom on a major decision in his life.

"I want to be used of God," he began, "but I have a critical decision before me. My girlfriend broke her neck in an accident and is permanently paralyzed from the neck down. We were planning to get married—but—." I waited for him to continue. "Do you think I could be fully used of God in my ministry, and still take care of her with the care she will always need?"

I hesitated before I gave the answer I didn't want to give. "I believe it would be a full-time job to care for a quadriplegic," I said. "In making your decision, you must consider that she, no doubt, would be able to contribute little to your ministry."

After that week in L'Abri, I never saw the young man again. But looking back over the years, I fully understand that she would not have hindered his ministry, but perhaps he could have hindered *her* ministry, which is now worldwide.

She has become an outstanding soloist, author, artist (with her teeth) and radio and television personality. Her name is Joni Eareckson Tada. During this time of physical tragedy and rejection, and the long and slow re-entry into the world, Joni had a very special friend by the name of Steve Estes. He helped restore her life, encouraging her spiritually and emotionally, helping her to find meaning and purpose in life—and he was co-author of her book *A Step Further.* Little did we know then that just a few years later, Steve Estes would become the youth director of our church in Miami, and he would greatly influence many more youth to find God's purpose for their lives.

# III.   BEHIND THE CLOSED DOOR

# 16

# An Impossible Door

*"Her only human contact was to see the knuckles of the guard as he pushed her tray through the slot, and hear him daily say, 'It is impossible for you to ever see your husband again.'"*

I WAS INTRIGUED AS I picked up the Miami Herald and read the story of three East German doctors who jumped ship off the Florida Keys in a daring attempt for freedom. East Germany at this time in the early '70s was the strongest of the Soviet bloc nations, separated from free West Germany by the notorious Berlin Wall. Having jumped impulsively from a Russian ship on its way to Communist Cuba, the doctors were rescued in the Gulf waters and brought to Miami.

Hearing of their escape, I immediately searched them out. Our church furnished an apartment for two of them, brothers, and helped them settle into life in Miami. For almost 2 years, Dr. Manfred Kupfer and his brother, Dr. Reinhold Kupfer, faithfully attended our church, worshipping with us and seeking our spiritual guidance. We hurt with them, knowing that there was little possibility of any reuniting with their families. Certainly no wives of men who had escaped would ever be permitted to join their husbands in their new-found freedom. To give such permission would only encourage others to attempt to flee to freedom. It would be *impossible*. This *impossibility* was especially valid, in the light of the fact that Gisela, the wife of Dr. Manfred, was also a neuropathologist. There were only 26 neuropathologists in all of East Germany at the time.

The day began as any other day. I was in my office, when Dr. Reinhold and Dr. Manfred walked in—with a request.

"Rev. Watson, we know that you are involved in smuggling Bibles into and documents out of Russia and other eastern bloc nations. We know you are concerned and burdened for the people behind the Iron Curtain, and we would like to ask you something."

"Go ahead Manfred," I said, almost fearing what the request might be.

"Could you—will you—help us smuggle our wives and children out of Leipzig? We have some contacts with an East German "underground" and have been led to believe that we could accomplish this with your help and 45,000 German Marks ($15,000 then).

"We must seek God's leadership in this," I muttered, as my heart pounded. "Could we have a time of prayer together?" and we bowed our heads and earnestly prayed. Certainly not fully understanding all that would be involved, I felt I heard God prompt me to do it. "Amen," I said and raised my head. "I'll help you."

With the help of Dr. Bill Hinson, then pastor of First Baptist Church of Ft. Lauderdale, and now CEO of Haggai Institute, we raised the 45,000 German Marks, in spite of the fact that we could make no public or private announcement of our plans for the use of the money.

Having raised the money, I must now fly to Berlin and personally meet with the underground smugglers to show them the money. We met in a very small hotel room, where seated a few feet from me and looking me straight in the eye, they began to interrogate me. They must be convinced that I was not an agent from the East German government seeking to entrap them. Once they were convinced, they told me to deposit the money in the Berlin bank under my name.

"We will call you in America when we are ready. We can give you just one day's notice to meet us here in Berlin, when the time is right."

We shook hands and I stepped out of the hotel into the sunshine, walked across the street and deposited 45,000 German Marks in the bank.

WEEKS—MONTHS PASSED. I WAITED. July came when I must take my Spinning Spokes cycling group through Europe. I called my daughter. "Tonie, you have the phone numbers of all our campsites," I said as I left. "You must call me *immediately* should I get a call from the East German underground while I am gone."

After several days of cycling down the Mosel River from Luxembourg, we had arrived at the beautiful campsite in Cologne, Germany, on the banks of the broad Rhine River. The tents were all set up. Some of the 45 campers were playing football, others were washing out a few sweaty clothes, all were hungrily awaiting the camp supper. It was 5:10 p.m. when the call came, and over the camp loudspeaker I heard, "Rev. Watson, come to the Bureau (office), you have a call from America."

"Dad, you must be in Berlin tomorrow morning or the deal is all off," said my daughter over the phone.

"What's wrong, Rev. Watson? May I help?" asked the camp director, having sensed my anxiety and overhearing my conversation.

"It is imperative that I be in Berlin tomorrow morning and that is an *impossibility* since it is after 5:00 and I am sure there are no more departing flights tonight."

"No it is not an *impossibility* as there is a 6:00 pm flight to Berlin."

"But it's 5:20 and the traffic on the autobahn will make it *impossible*."

"Look," she said, "sitting in that chair is my friend, who is a Cologne policeman, and he will be happy to take you and Dr. Hinson to the Cologne-Bonn airport—and you'll get there on time!"

We did. However, we lost rubber off the tires and years off our lives! There is no speed limit on the German autobahn! But Bill Hinson and I walked onto the plane at 6:00 p.m. with the plane door closing behind us.

AFTER A RESTLESS NIGHT and a speedy breakfast in Berlin, we drew our money out of the bank, put it in an Eastern Airlines flight bag we had brought for the purpose, and went to meet our contact men. They drove us through the bustling morning traffic of Berlin, through the outskirts, and then to a small old wooden farmhouse just north of the city. Here they were to count the money. I was a little apprehensive when we were told that the boss was in the next room and did not want to be seen. He would be the one to count the money.

"Could we have your flight bag please," and it was taken to the back room. As we anxiously waited, we scanned the simple room and noticed some antiques that interested both Bill and me. Bill bought a small table and I bought an antique wall clock.

After a lengthy time of mostly silence, they returned with the flight bag and set it at my feet. At that moment I had the strongest urge to look into the bag and see if I still had the 45,000 German Marks or if I had a bag full of old newspapers. But I must not show distrust. I knew that what I was doing was illegal and what the smugglers were doing was illegal. Were Bill and I risking our lives for the unknown contents of our Eastern Airlines flight bag?

Leaving the house we arrived back in the city, and for the next 4 or 5 hours, I clung to my bag, following our not-too-well-known companions, walking through byways and dark back alleys to a noisy disco. As we sat at a table, trying to eat heartily, no one would have known that under the table and behind the red table cloth, the strap of the flight bag was wrapped securely around my leg.

We were taken back to our hotel and told to wait. Dr. Reinhold had arrived from America and was there, hoping and trusting to see his wife and children. The call came shortly after 11:00 p.m.—they have crossed the border safely! We rushed to the street below and soon welcomed the sight of the smugglers' black car as it turned the corner and pulled up to the curb. The doors burst open and the wife and two children fell into the waiting arms of Dr. Reinhold. Only then did I turn over my precious flight bag to the smugglers.

"I thought I would never see you again, I thought I would never see you again," Dr. Reinhold's wife said as the tears spattered on the dusty walkway. My heart swelled with joy and thanksgiving. The car trunk had been their hiding place and a German guard at the border was paid off. But where was Gisela, Dr. Manfred's wife? It was my sad task to call him that night in Miami, to tell him his wife had not made the rendezvous.

Bill and I, weary from the strain of the day, entered our hotel room just as my new antique clock leaning against the wall struck midnight—but, alas, it struck 13 times.

"It's later than we think, Bill!" That clock still hangs on our wall, reminding us that it *is* later than we think.

WHERE WAS GISELA? WE learned later that she had deliberately missed the checkpoint when she realized she was being followed by the Secret Police. How did they know that she was planning an escape? The circumstances are strange. Her maid had secretly read in a letter from Dr Manfred to his wife the phrase that would be used as a signal for the escape. Although the signal had been changed, the phrase was used in a letter innocently. The maid reported to the secret police that the time was near for Gisela's attempt for freedom. The morning after her sister-in-law's escape, Gisela was arrested and held in a political prison in Leipzig, East Germany for five months, three of which were in solitary confinement. She was known only as #58. But she was not alone. "I had a strong belief in our Lord, and I knew He could help me get out of prison. I was not allowed a Bible but I had committed to memory many passages from the Bible that my uncle, a Lutheran pastor, had given me years ago."

Her only human contact in the prison was to see the knuckles of the guard as he pushed her tray through the slot, and see his eyes as he looked through the peep hole, and hear him daily say, "It is *impossible* for you to ever get out," and "it is *impossible* for you to ever see your husband again."

Learning that the United States government was working on establishing diplomatic relations with East Germany, I contacted our U.S. congressman Dante Fascell and asked for help. I requested that Gisela's name be brought up in the negotiations. Later he called and said, "In the negotiations regarding the diplomatic relationships with East Germany, Dr. Gisela's name was mentioned. But since she is an East German citizen, we were told that the U.S. had no right to interfere with their dealings with an East German criminal." Soon after this, however, Gisela and other political prisoners were released from prison, under an attempt to ease relationships with America and other free countries.

We continued to pray and work that Gisela could be legally permitted to be reunited with her husband in America. Neither East Germany nor the United States wanted anything to disrupt the attempt for diplomatic relations and the establishment of an embassy in Washington and East Germany. With this in mind, a State Department official called me. "Give up," he said, "Everything *possible* to get her out of East Germany has been done. It would be *impossible*, in as much as she is being closely watched."

Again, the word *impossible*. But we didn't give up. Our church family put feet to our prayers and stood at McDonald's, grocery stores, post offices, and shopping centers, gathering 32,000 signatures asking for the release of Dr. Gisela Kupfer.

When diplomatic relations with East Germany were finally established, I wrote to Gisela again. Certain that the East German government was reading our correspondence, I let them know that on the day their embassy opened in Washington, I would have busloads of our church youth there, marching around the embassy with signs saying "Let Gisela Go." Before our calendar year changed to 1975, many, many prayers had been answered, and Dr. Manfred Kupfer had received official word that his wife, Dr. Gisela Kupfer, would be released to join him in America. Gisela was free!

I flew with Dr. Manfred to Berlin to bring his wife home. As we sat down to breakfast in the hotel, she said, "May I pray?" In very broken English, I heard a most beautiful nine-word prayer, which I will never forget:

"Lord Jesus, thank you for making the *impossible, possible.*"

> *Jesus looked at them and said, "With man this is impossible,*
> *but with God all things are possible." (Matthew 19:26)*

GISELA AND HER HUSBAND Dr. Manfred Kupfer lived in Rochester, Minn., where he was engaged in research at the Mayo Clinic. They later joined his brother Dr. Reinhold Kupfer and family in West Germany where they began anew their medical work.

# 17
# A Delayed Flight

*"I know God's timing is always perfect!"*

A FOUR-HOUR FLIGHT DELAY in Tokyo was not welcomed by our tour group eager to get to Shanghai. However, we would soon learn that God's timing is much better than ours. From previous trips in Communist countries we had learned that workers under Communism do not give their best efforts when working overtime with no additional pay. It was late at night and hours past their time to go home!

Before leaving America we had packed 17 flight bags with 409 Chinese Bibles, and volunteers from our group agreed to carry one flight bag each. "Lord, please let us get these Bibles in," we prayed. If one bag of Chinese Bibles was found, all of our bags would have been searched, the Bibles confiscated, and perhaps our visas to China revoked. But it was late at the airport. The customs agents were more than ready to get home.

"Please, Lord."—Not one of the flight bags was opened for inspection!

With one miracle down, we were anxious to see how God would handle the next one. We had been given the name of a young Chinese lady who would be our contact in Shanghai to receive our Bibles. She would be doing this at the risk of her life, as China was a closed door to Christian literature. The young lady, "Lin Wang," knew only my name and the hotel where we were to be for two nights in Shanghai. Her problem was to find me. In China, a young lady did not ask for an American for two reasons. Either she was there soliciting for prostitution—punishable by death—or to collaborate with the enemy. How were we to meet? When our group walked into the huge lobby of the Hotel Shanghai, I saw that it was packed with tourists, many of them Americans. Crowds were standing at the check-in desk where I was standing. Being an impatient person, and since I had a large group, I thought perhaps I could speed up the process by going to the information desk to register.

Handing me a pen, the man at the information desk asked me to write the name of my group. As I began to write "Group-Watson," unnoticed to me, a young Chinese lady had entered the hotel lobby and walked directly to the small desk where I was standing. Seeing me begin to write "Watson," she said slowly and softly, "Are you— Tommy—Watson?"

"Yes, I am."

"I am Lin Wang," she said. "I left Beijing by bus 18 hours ago and—I just arrived." Amazed, I said, "I left Miami, Florida *36 hours ago* and—I just arrived."

God had taken two people, 7000 miles apart, and brought them both *to the identical spot* at *exactly the same time*. The airline thought they were four hours late. The pilot didn't know he was flying on God's time!

We wondered how this little Chinese lady would get these many Bibles from our rooms in the Hotel Shanghai to their destination. The next morning, we were surprised when she arrived at the hotel with a wheelchair. Three times she loaded it and departed, carrying her precious cargo—somewhere. In our short conversation, she told me of a town in central China where recently 10,000 people, mostly youth, had come to know Christ as their personal Savior. As she wheeled out the last load, Mollie said to me, "Since she came by bus from Beijing, I wonder where she got the wheelchair!"

"I don't know—but I am sure another miracle was involved."

I don't know how God works. Some say it was a coincidence that we met at the counter at exactly the same time, but *I know that God's timing is always perfect*, sometimes even using a delayed flight.

# 18

## Hidden Bibles

*"From Ray Hill's shop, thousands and thousands of Bibles were delivered to those bound under Communism."*

I RECEIVED A PHONE call one day from Germany, from Ray Hill, a long-time friend, asking if I would like to work together with him in the "Big Country" (which I knew to mean Russia). After sharing his plan with me, I went to my deacons asking for permission to put money in our church's monthly budget for a secret mission project that I could not even share with them. And so began a partnership in building vans for smuggling Bibles behind the Iron Curtain. I will ever appreciate the complete trust our deacons gave me to regularly fund this unknown project.

Ray, an engineering graduate from Le Tourneau University, his wife Pat, and their children Vickie, Daniel, and James had been living in Nuremberg since 1969. His plan involved setting up a garage in the outskirts of the city, where vans and campers could be modified to have secret compartments and storage areas. Combining his engineering skills and amazing creativity, he and his team built false floors in the vehicles, as well as roof racks with hollow walls and floors. Depending on the type of vehicle and size of the compartments, from 120 to over 2000

Bibles could be hidden and then smuggled into Communist countries. Much smaller secret spaces were also created to hide documents and manuscripts.

Because the shop was large, several vehicles could be worked on at the same time. Many young men from Europe and America served in the shop as mechanics, welders, wood workers, and painters. Steve Sutton, who a few years later became my son-in-law, spent one year living with Ray and Pat, doing mechanical work and painting in the shop.

After a vehicle had made a trip to and from a Communist country, it would be painted a different color prior to making another "run." Altogether, we had nineteen vans that made repeated trips across the borders into countries where Bibles were forbidden.

Young men, young women, and even families posed as tourists, entering Romania, Hungary, Poland, and other countries. Once safely across the border with the Bibles undiscovered, the "tourists" would meet secretly with Believers to unload the precious cargo. Yes, sometimes our "trippers" would get caught and the vans confiscated, but usually as they were leaving the country, after the Bibles had already been delivered!

I will be ever grateful for the privilege of ministering through Ray Hill's shop, from which thousands and thousands of Bibles were delivered to the people bound under Communism. I will be forever grateful to the young men who worked in the shop and to all those who endangered themselves to carry God's Word into the eastern bloc nations.

*"How beautiful on the mountains are the **feet** of those*
*who bring good news…"*
*(Isaiah 52:7)*

And in this case, how beautiful are the **vans**…

# 19

## But Pastor, an XKE Jaguar?

*"I'll let you have it for what I paid—$4000."*
*"What's the catch, Bill?"*

"Pastor Tommy, Bill Hinson is on the line." I knew there was a serious conversation coming up, because it was not the usual way Bill identified himself. Other times it was "Billy Graham calling for Pastor Watson," or "This is the sheriff's department."

"Tommy," Bill began immediately, "I have a deal you can't refuse. I have a two-year-old car, a 1973 V12 XKE Jaguar. It's a long silver bullet nose sports car of the elite; it has only 13,500 miles on it. It looks like new. I'll let you have it for what I paid—$4000." Remembering some previous tricks we had played on each other I asked, "What's the catch, Bill?"

"Well, I bought it for my son Billy, but when we went to insure it, the agent laughed and asked if I wanted to mortgage my home to pay the premium. I guess a seventeen-year-old is assumed to be a major driving risk!"

Knowing the value of the car was much greater, I said to Bill, "I'll give you the $4000, providing you give me a thousand dollars back to help build our specially-equipped vans for smuggling Bibles into Communist countries."

Deal done—sight unseen! A telephone transaction that pleased us both!

I enjoyed the comfort of the Jaguar, but I knew I was in trouble when I took it to the garage and the repairman came out in a white coat and with a stethoscope. I found out my car had 28 water hoses, and a replaced water pump cost me $248.00 (and that was in 1975). Realizing I was spending not only too much money but also too much time going to or coming from the garage, I soon sold the car and went back to my dependable Ford.

Many years later I wrote to Bill. "I owe you money on that Jaguar, Bill. That car is now selling for $40,000."

I HAVE OFTEN THOUGHT of the contrast in that super car with another super car that Ray Hill, our "creative missionary," modified in Germany. Ray was always anxious to help those who felt led of God to smuggle Bibles into the eastern bloc countries, but now he had run into a major problem. A very poor Christian man showed up at Ray's shop one day with an old, old coupe, asking Ray to convert it into a smuggling vehicle. The man wanted to fulfill God's call to him to take Bibles to Christians who had none. Ray looked at the coupe and rightly determined that if this man showed up at a border, the guard would look at the old coupe, identify the man as one of those zealous Bible smugglers, and proceed to meticulously search the car.

Ray, knowing that I was soon to come to Europe bringing a group of bikers, called me and gave me the strangest request I have ever received. "Tommy, would you buy for me two very fancy chrome stack mufflers—the kind that go up the sides of the cab of an eighteen-wheeler? Also, bring some expensive carpet to outfit the interior of a coupe." I brought it over and Ray creatively again went to work.

Much later Ray called and said "it worked." When the smuggler reached the checkpoint, the Communist guards all gathered around to look and laugh at this crazy little old coupe with two shiny chrome stack mufflers up the sides and a new blue carpet inside. They were still laughing as they motioned the little man through, with his chrome stack mufflers, and—*his hundreds of hidden Bibles*. I wish I had today—not my V12 XKE—but that coupe that God used to take the Word of God to the hungry and waiting Christians behind the Iron Curtain.

RAY HILL CONTINUED WITH his clandestine work in Nuremberg until 1978, when he lost his German visa, and so we set up shop in Coventry, England. However, we now had a different goal—or should I say, a somewhat different approach to reach our goal. Ray's plan was to take a Toyota truck frame and attach a recreation camper to it. The purpose was to have about thirty of these, stashed with thousands of Bibles in secret compartments, going into Moscow for the 1980 Olympics. We felt it would be easy to get RV's with American drivers into Russia for such a great event as the Olympics.

The Toyota company in London liked our RV idea and agreed to purchase 300 of them and give us one free for every ten we manufactured. This would give us the cost of production and salaries for our workers *and* 30 complete vans for our use. After Ray had made the first two prototypes in 1979, the British government put an embargo on the import of Toyota trucks. They were flooding the market and damaging the sales of the British-made trucks.

We were devastated, but our *amazing Lord* knew that America would boycott the 1980 Olympics in Russia. We would have no American drivers to transport in God's cargo! We were learning the meaning of Romans 8:28: *"And we know that in all things God works for the good of those who love Him, who have been called according to His purpose."*

# 20

## Behind the Iron Curtain

*"We waited but a few minutes—and then we saw him.*
*Dressed like a tourist with sunglasses, a camera slung over his shoulder,*
*he slowly walked by our van—a tourist, no. A slave, yes,*
*fearful that the secret police were watching."*

AFTER 10 DAYS WITH our 38 Spinning Spokes bikers, riding through Luxembourg, Germany, and Belgium, and camping at beautiful campsites along the Mosel River, we were about to separate. The bikers, led by our sons Tim and Terry, were preparing to travel now by bus to Switzerland, and Mollie and I and our dear friends, Pastor Don and Helen Houser would leave for Communist Romania. We left Luxembourg at 8:00 p.m. Thursday night in our rented yellow Hertz cargo van, which we dubbed "The Yellow Monster." How we appreciated "The Yellow Monster" as we used its roomy space for luggage and camping equipment and a place to take turns sleeping.

Having driven through Austria and Germany comfortably, we entered Yugoslavia and encountered thousands of Turkish people on the road headed for their two weeks vacation to the seashore or to their homes in Turkey. They worked in Germany and Italy, and took their vacations the first two weeks of July. It was bumper to bumper traffic on a two-lane bumpy road! How grateful we were that we were using diesel fuel, thus eliminating waiting in the long lines of cars buying gasoline.

It was 9:30 Saturday morning, July 2,1988, when we arrived at the border crossing from Yugoslavia into Romania. After being ordered to completely empty our yellow Hertz cargo van, we watched for three and a half hours as the guards meticulously searched every inch of the van and all its contents laid out on the ground beside it. We found out later that they were mainly looking for Bibles and pornographic literature since both were considered equally harmful. Intent on finding Bibles, which we were not carrying, they overlooked some other "treasures" we were taking in to help our Christian brothers and sisters.

BUT TO BETTER UNDERSTAND why we were there at the border, let me go back to a phone call I received some months before from a former member of my church, Jim Burton.

"Pastor Tommy," he said, "I met a man, John Moldovan, and heard him give his amazing testimony. He was released from prison, exiled from Romania under the Helsinki Accords, and received political asylum in the United States. Would you like to meet him and perhaps have him speak in your church?"

When he came to our church, and after hearing his testimony of faith and suffering, of being beaten 26 times with a rubber hose till his blood splattered the wall, I shared with him our involvement and work behind the Iron Curtain. Having experienced first hand severe treatment, he listened most intently. It wasn't until some time later that I understood the reason for his great interest. I received a call from him in Ft. Worth Texas, where he was in seminary, asking me that I pray about going to Romania to take some medicine to his sick and elderly mother. She was living alone, as John's father, a Baptist pastor, had been killed by the Communists in a planned auto "accident" (not an uncommon practice). I did not fully understand his request for medicine until I was in Romania and realized that even aspirin was not available to the general public. It could only be bought in special stores, using only American dollars. And who had American dollars?

"Your visit to Romania at this time," John said, "would be such an encouragement to the Christians there."

WANTING TO TAKE SOMETHING more into the country to help alleviate the desperate financial conditions of some pastors, as well as John Moldovan's widowed mother, John suggested that I smuggle in gold. Gold was sold high on the black market. Even the Communist Party members were eager to buy gold on the black market, in as much as they knew the lei (their currency) would continually devalue in their own country, and gold would always be of good value. For example, when I converted our dollars into lei I received 9 lei to a dollar. A few years later it was 45,000 to one dollar. The last time I was in Romania, I paid our hotel bill with a stack of 10,000 lei notes, about sixteen inches thick.

Wonderfully, God's hand led me to a gold dealer in Miami who had adopted a Romanian orphan. With his special interest in Romania, he sold me beautifully crafted gold necklaces and bracelets by the ounce rather than their crafted value. Though we were all unaccustomed to wearing such pieces of jewelry, Pastor Don and Helen Houser, Mollie and I donned them under our clothes, hopefully to be unnoticed by the guards at the border crossing. I was thankful that the next day I was able to give the most valuable gold bracelet I had to John's sick mother, the widow of a martyred pastor. She would now be able to get better medical attention from a doctor. Doctors were among the lowest paid of any workers in Romania.

But we also carried with us some other "treasures" for our Christian brothers in Romania. Before going into Romania, I asked Joseph, one of the Bible smugglers who had just returned from that country, "What else of value besides gold could I take in to help the people?"

"Coffee," he said. "One pound of coffee is worth one month's salary on the black market. Legally you can take in two pounds for your own consumption."

"Joseph," I said, "I'm going to take in 20 pounds, the gift of some young people in my church in Miami." On one occasion on a country road, when we were running low on diesel for "The Yellow Monster," we traded a truck driver ½ pound of coffee for 10 gallons of diesel.

Now LET US RETURN to the border crossing as the guards continued to search our belongings. Helen's address book was examined. She was asked if she or any of us had addresses of Romanian citizens, which fortunately, we did not. Each sheet of paper on Mollie's large drawing board was checked. We were permitted to keep our personal Bibles, but some of my sermon tapes were taken and also my book by William Murray, *My Life Without God.* (Surely God could use these in a guard's empty heart.) So with both faith and anxiety, we stood at the border crossing for three and one half hours. Mollie reminded me later that I was humming continually, "He Was There All the Time."

Finally released, we breathed a sigh of relief as we reloaded our van and drove on to Timisora, where we were to meet our contact the next morning—Sunday. We were tired, dusty, and eager to find a place to rest and bathe. Just as we parked the van on a side street, a gate opened in the wall and a lovely young lady came out. Although unaccustomed to seeing Americans, she was friendly and anxious to use her self-taught English. After being rejected at one or two hotels, with the help of this woman and her husband, we finally found a hotel. But why did the desk clerks not want to give us a room, we wondered, since obviously the hotels were nearly empty. We discovered later the reason for the delay—we were expected to give the clerk something "under the table," a common practice in Communist countries. So for the rest of our time in Romania, we had no trouble giving away the soap, coffee, and stockings we had brought along for gifts. It was a joy to see the gratitude that such simple gifts brought to people who had been deprived of so much for so long. We saw long lines of people waiting to buy bread and milk. Few cars were on the streets, but the buses were packed.

I AWOKE EARLY SUNDAY morning with great anticipation. What would the day bring forth? I only knew that we were to meet our contact, Vio, behind the orthodox cathedral at 9:00 o'clock. I drove slowly around the square and parked our ostentatious van behind the cathedral. The four of us sat in silence. It was exactly 9:00 o'clock. We waited but a few minutes—and then we saw him. Dressed like a tourist with sunglasses, a camera slung over his shoulder, he slowly walked by our yellow Hertz van—a tourist, no. A slave, yes, fearful that the secret police were watching. Vio was risking his life to be our guide and companion across Romania during his two-week vacation. All was clear, and he ducked into our van. We all immediately loved our new Christian brother. Although his English was limited, communication was no problem, as he carried with him always his Romanian-English dictionary.

We were directed to the First Baptist Church of Timisora, where Peter Dugulescu was pastor. It was a small building, very old and in a state of disrepair. We soon discovered that all of Romania was in a state of disrepair. The church appeared to seat perhaps 250 people. The 9:00 o'clock prayer service was still in session. As I looked in from the front of the church I could hear the continuous chain of short prayers, from both men and women, punctuated with the entire congregation's "Ah-men" after each prayer. I can still hear it.

The 10:00 o'clock hour was a Bible study in the same room, and following that, the 11:00-12:30 worship service. Don, Helen and Mollie were asked to "give greetings" from the churches in America. Mollie did a chalk drawing, as she did in every church we visited on the trip, and I brought the message from the Word. Looking up into the balcony I counted 34 violinists—what heavenly music! So for 3 ½ hours, in a packed, windowless, hot building, the people stood, or sat on hard benches—and no one left. The sun was beating down on the large walled-in courtyard where a couple hundred more were standing, children and babies included. No one knew we were coming. This was a usual Sunday morning. We were overwhelmed by their warm Christian greeting, "Pachi," meaning "Peace."

"This is a great day for Romania," Pastor Peter said to me. "Every evangelical church in our country will know that you in America are aware of our plight, and you have come to encourage us." "Behind the

Iron Curtain," was not just a meaningless term, but an intense isolation that the entire population of Romania and all eastern bloc nations felt. They were truly behind an iron curtain!

After the evening evangelistic service, we were invited to Pastor Peter Dugulescu's home for supper and fellowship. He had indicated that his house was "bugged," so as we left, he accompanied us to our van.

"Please," he said in a hushed voice, "would you come back tomorrow night to help celebrate our oldest daughter Lugia's 18th birthday? For several years, I have been invited to the American Embassy for its July 4th reception. This year," he said, "I had planned to take Lugia as a part of her birthday celebration since her birthday is July 4th.

I wanted her to enjoy Coca Cola, some American salami, and the chocolate candy that they serve at the Embassy." He paused and moved a little closer to me. "However, a State official called and instructed me not to attend."

"Pastor Peter, can these special foods be bought anywhere here in Timisora?"

"Yes," he said, "but only with American dollars."

"Tell Lugia she will have her party," and we promised to return the next night. And we did—with Coca Cola, American salami, and chocolate candy. Before the evening was over, we were touched as Pastor Peter put his arm around his daughter and lovingly spoke to her, reminding her (later interpreted to us) how very much she meant to him and her mother. When her mother was pregnant with her, she contracted measles and the doctor insisted on an abortion, which they refused. Lugia, now a lovely young lady of 18, had just graduated from high school, there completing her nurses' training.

Peter was a large man, with a much larger heart for God and his country, and he chuckled as he said, "We can't go to the Americans, so God sent the Americans to us." So with $100 and my little American flag as a centerpiece on their table, we celebrated the most wonderful 4th of July we have ever had!

Footnote: Lugia finished her education in America and now works with "Jesus, the Hope of Romania," an evangelistic association founded by her father. Peter Dugulescu went to be with Lord in 2008.

# 21

## Strong Coffee

*"We watched as a motley group of sweaty men started down from upstairs, hungry after a morning of work on the construction of their new church."*

FOR THIRTY YEARS, THE people of the small church in Timisora, Romania, had been praying for a much needed building. Absolutely *no* churches were being built in this Communist country and the struggle to get the necessary permission for building seemed an impossibility. But the body of believers prayed on. It is strange and wonderful how God, in His timing and in answer to the prayers of His children, accomplishes His purposes in spite of the Enemy, and sometimes, *through* the Enemy. Let me explain.

The government of dictator Nicolae Ceausescu was in the process of moving all the peasants from their hundreds of tiny farms and villages into eight-story apartment buildings in the city, because the government wanted better control of the people and the land. It was a sad time for these peasants to think of giving up their little plot of ground. Not because the government wanted to help the church, but because it wanted the church plot on which to build an apartment house, they offered in exchange a house on a corner lot in a respectable neighborhood. The stipulation was that it could not be torn down, only remodeled for the church. No problem! The church left only the steps and façade and tore down all the rest of the house. And the work to build began.

PASTOR PETER DUGULESCU WAS eager to show us the building in progress. We descended the concrete steps and found ourselves in the unfinished basement of the future home of the First Baptist Church of Timisora. Several long wooden tables had been put end to end to form one long table extending the length of the room. In a very small makeshift kitchen, opening to a corner of the basement, a woman was busily stirring huge pots of soup. Another lady was slicing thick dark loaves of bread, and another set the bread plates down on the long table. The soup smelled good.

We watched as a motley group of sweaty men started down from upstairs, hungry after a morning of work on the construction of their new church. They walked past the little kitchen area, picked up a steaming bowl of soup and stood at the table awaiting prayer. Pastor Dugulescu led in a prayer of thanksgiving for the food, the promise of this new church building, and the blessing of these friends from America. They joined in a song of thanksgiving, and as each one finished his meal of soup, potatoes, a small piece of meat, and applesauce for dessert, they rose to leave, and each one prayed again. It made me wonder if God is pleased with our sometimes hasty mealtime prayers.

It was a terribly hot day as the men had gathered to eat. One large burly man with a very concerned look moved over and spoke quietly to Pastor Peter.

"What did he say?" I asked, noting his concern.

"The water has such a bad taste that it is difficult to drink," Pastor Peter said.

"Oh, I can fix that," I said, as I leaped up the stairs, took from the yellow van three large cans, flew down the stairs and quickly made 20 gallons of cherry Kool-Aid. No Romanian had ever seen Kool-Aid! What a surprise to the men as they tasted the "water turned to wine," and they laughed as they thought of Jesus' first miracle. "You have saved the best until now." Needless to say, I left money to buy bottled water from a mineral spring—enough for the next two months of construction.

The men of the church were building this edifice with only one paid worker: the architect. They worked in three shifts, six days a week, some coming before or after their regular jobs, working as many hours as they could, and others without a job working all day. Elderly and young worked. In order to save time from traveling to their homes for meals, the women of the church cooked and served three meals a day. All were united in purpose. It reminded me of Nehemiah's men who "had a mind to work" as they rebuilt the walls of Jerusalem.

THAT SUNDAY NIGHT IN the evening service, again packed to capacity, I preached on the paralytic man who was let down through the roof of the house to be healed by Jesus.

I don't know why—I had never done it before—but I asked the question, "Do you know where those four men were the next day? They went to repair the man's roof! Wouldn't that be the Christian thing to do?"

Following the service, Pastor Dugulescu couldn't wait to talk to me. "It was not by coincidence that you said that the men came back to repair the roof. You see, the roof is the big hang-up on finishing this building. Because of the size of this building, designed to seat 600 people, it necessitates steel beams across the building to support the roof. But, there is only *one* crane in all of western Romanian that could lift and place those beams—and it belongs to the Communist government."

Having learned how things are done in a Communist nation, how everything is accomplished only by paying "under the table," I asked, "What would it take to get that crane over here to the church site?"

"Two pounds of coffee," Pastor Dugulescu said.

"Pastor, I have 16 pounds of coffee."

The next week the steel beams were up. You may think that a crane that size runs on diesel—but God enabled it to be run with *two pounds of coffee!*

*"Is anything too hard for the Lord?" (Genesis 18:14)*

Lunch after a morning at work

# 22

## The Escape

*"And how do you plan on doing this?" I asked.*
*"It's a dangerous venture, you know."*

As I WAS STANDING amidst the boards and bricks of the "church-in-progress" in Timisora, a young man moved towards me. He did not appear to be one of the working men that day because of his dress, but it seemed he had spent much time there, as he spoke to the men with familiarity. Perhaps he was on his way to his regular job and would return later when his job shift was over, to join hands with the laborers. At any rate, he introduced himself as George, and we briefly discussed the work that was going on around us. But obviously, he had something more he wanted to share with me. He hesitated for a moment and then began.

"We're planning to run," he said in almost a whisper. "My wife Emily and I are planning to run." I quickly understood him to mean they were planning an escape to the West. Their job situations had become very difficult, and pressure against Christians had become intense. They were young and they were determined to find freedom.

"And how do you plan to do this?" I asked. "It's a dangerous venture, you know."

My heart ached for them, but how could I help? I recognized the danger I could be in if I were charged with abetting an escape. I remembered the Cuban missionaries, who having helped people escape that Communist nation, spent seven long years in prison, suffering from hunger, disease and loneliness. Should I help?

"We know it's dangerous," George answered, "but we have made arrangements for our five-year-old daughter to stay with her grandparents until we are safe and can send for her. She will be happy and safe here with them. Our plans are to go by night to the Yugoslavian border, crawl under or through the barbed wire fences, and get into Yugoslavia. Once we get past the wires, there is a thorn hedge barrier. We'll get scratched and cut up, we know, but we will make it! We will purchase train passage from Belgrade, Yugoslavia to the coast of northern Italy. Then Emily and I will swim at night into Italy."

"I have two concerns about the train," I said. "First, when you step up to the ticket agent to buy your ticket, you will be recognized because of your language." (Romanian is a Romantic language and Yugoslavian is a Slavic language.) "As with Simon Peter, your speech will betray you. You will be identified as a Romanian and sent back to Romania.

"And you know what would follow. My second concern—how many Yugoslavian dinar do you have?"

"Enough, I believe. A friend gave me 8000 dinar."

"Not nearly enough," I said. "That seems like a lot in Romania, but not elsewhere. We have just driven across Yugoslavia, and I have 80,000 dinar left in my pocket, which I intended to use on my return trip through that country—but I have decided to give that to you."

I suddenly realized as I gave him the dinar that this was all the evidence the Romanian Securitate would need to arrest me. The Yugoslavian dinar was proof enough that I was not trying to help him meet his needs here in Romania, but was assisting in an escape. Someone said, "Fools rush in where angels fear to tread," but I had also said many times, "*the only place of danger is outside the will of God.*" Somehow, I felt this was what God wanted me to do.

"How will you survive in Italy without any money?" I asked. He told me he had two gold coins given to him by his grandfather, who had received them from an Englishman during World War II. "Please,"

George asked, "Would you take these for me, sell them in America, and wire us the money when we get to Italy?"

I gave him the name of missionaries in Rome and told him to call them if he and his wife made it to Italy. He was to call me collect from Italy if he had any problems and also to let me know where to wire the money.

ONE SUNDAY MORNING, A few weeks later, when I was sitting in my office before the worship service started, I received a collect call from George in Rome, Italy.

"We're in Rome," he said. "We made it, scratched up somewhat, but we're well."

"Oh, I'm so happy you are safe! How much did your train ticket cost across Yugoslavia?" I inquired.

"Eighty-eight thousand dinar!" he said with a "smile" in his voice. "It was the exact amount you gave me, plus the 8,000 dinar I had."

> *"Trust in the Lord with all your heart and lean not on your own understanding. In all your ways acknowledge Him, and He will make your paths straight." (Proverbs 3:5,6)*

FOOTNOTE: GEORGE AND EMILY stayed with our missionaries in Rome for about six months before migrating to the United States, settling for some time in Raleigh, N.C.

# IV.   WIDE OPEN DOORS

# 23

## Cathedral Square

*"When he said, 'Let us pray,' 200,000 people dropped to
their knees and prayed the Lord's prayer in unison."*

WHO WOULD HAVE THOUGHT that after 28 years, so suddenly, the Berlin
Wall would come down and the East Germans would breathe the
same free air as their West German brothers? Since August 13, 1961,
ninety-six miles of barbed wire barricade and concrete wall had been
the symbol of the Cold War. But it was opened by the East Germans
themselves in November 1989 and completely torn down by the end of
1990 as Communism collapsed and the Cold War ended.

When Poland and Hungary desperately reached for and tenaciously
clung to their first goals of freedom, our Miami Herald declared briefly
that Romanian dictator Ceausescu was "too deeply entrenched in
power that there is little hope of his following the other eastern bloc
counterparts." But what happened? The people, the soul of the country,
could tolerate bondage no longer! They filled Cathedral Square in
Timisora, Romania with young and old, shouting for freedom, and
asking for some pastor to speak for God. Pastor Peter Dugulescu took
a courageous stand and ascended to the balcony of the Opera House
across the Square. With microphone in hand, he spoke for freedom

and for God, and when he said, "Let us pray," 200,000 people dropped to their knees and prayed the Lord's prayer in unison. At that very same time, dictator Ceausescu was giving his last desperate address to the masses in Bucharest. The Romanian revolution had begun.

On December 22nd, Ceausescu declared a national state of emergency and ordered the army to use force to disperse the demonstrators. Defense minister Colonel-General Vasile Milea refused and was killed by one of Ceausescu's body guards. After a last attempt to address the crowd, Ceausescu and his wife Elena fled the building by helicopter, leaving it to the demonstrators.

The revolutionaries at this time had organized themselves into the National Salvation Front with the backing of the Army. The Securitate, however, remained loyal to Ceausescu and counterattacked in a campaign of terrorism. Heavy fighting took place in Timisora, Bucharest, and Sibiu. By December 25th, the revolution was all over. The Securitate threat had been largely neutralized by Army and National Salvation Front militia. The streets and Cathedral Square in Timisora were quiet now—though stained with the blood of the old and young who treasured freedom more than life.

It was behind that same cathedral eighteen months before that Don and Helen Houser and Mollie and I met our guide-to-be Vio, our inconspicuous friend and helper on our first trip to Romania. Take off your sunglasses, Vio, and call to us loudly across Cathedral Square. You're free! We'll meet you there.

How it progressed from the square in Timisora and the grassroots of Romania, to the corpses of Nicolae and Elena Ceausescu in the military barracks near the railroad station on Christmas Day, is history now. It all happened so quickly. Was it just a week? "Too entrenched in power?" Yes—but no power could withstand the surging drive for freedom that had begun to burst forth from the long-repressed hearts of the Romanian people.

THERE WAS ANOTHER PASTOR in Timisora whose church played a large part in the start of the revolution. I interviewed Pastor Lazlo Tokes of the Reformed Church when we returned to Romania two months later. His church members had been continually threatened, forced to run a gauntlet of Secret Police agents in order to enter the building each Sunday. When the service began, the agents stood at the door cradling machine guns. Simply attending church was an act of protest. I wonder, sometimes, how many of our church members would find a reason to absent themselves, if faced with such a "welcome." Meanwhile, Pastor Tokes was denied his ration book, without which he was unable to buy bread, fuel, or meat. His loving members shared their own slim resources, smuggling food and fuel to the family. However, fearing for his four-year-old son, he sent him to live with relatives.

There was reason to fear. The Secret Police told one of Lazlo Tokes' friends, an architect, to comply with their plans against the pastor. The architect refused, and a few days later his body was found in a Timisora park. The police termed his death a suicide. Then Tokes himself was attacked by four ski-masked men who burst into the pastor's small apartment, within the church building. The pastor and his wife and a few guests fought them off with chairs, and the intruders ran from the house leaving Pastor Tokes bleeding from a knife wound in the face.

The Secret Police had another plan. They would exile him to a small remote village outside Timisora. The court ordered his eviction from his house and his church, setting the date for December 15, 1989. This outraged the congregation of his church and many others and when they were threatened, they stood firm. The gathering crowd circled the church. Night was approaching. But there was a young boy named Danny, a member of the First Baptist Church of Timisora, who knew where the candles were kept. Gathering them up, he gave them to the ever-increasing crowd. He lit his candle and touched the next. One by one the candles were lit as the defenders marched around the church. Gunfire began. And then—a piercing pain shot through Danny's leg and he fell to the ground.

"I'm so sorry, Danny, that you lost your leg," Pastor Dugulescu said when he visited him in the hospital after that dreadful night.

"But, Pastor,—remember, I lit the first candle!"

*"I am the Light of the world. Whoever follows Me will never walk in darkness, but will have the Light of life." (John 8:12)*

Cathedral Square in Timisora, Romania

# 24

## The Beveled Glass Door

*"In one such house (church) where I noticed there were only women
and a few children, the pastor informed us that all the men in the
village were alcoholics. What chance do the children have?"*

GEOGRAPHICALLY, ROMANIA IS LOCATED in a strategic place, where
East and West meet. During the centuries, the great powers of the
world occupied the land of Romania: the Greeks, the Roman emperors,
the Turks, the Russian Czars, the Austrian-Hungarian Empire, Nazi
Germany, and in the last half of the century, the Communists. After 45
years under the latter regime, people lay hopeless, helpless, and hungry
for the Good News of Jesus Christ, but the resources for meeting this
need were not there. Help must come from outside.

Looking at a map of Romania, one can see two distinct areas. One
lies west and one lies east of the Carpathian Mountains. West of the
Carpathians are Banat and Transylvania, where 90% of the Baptists of
Romania live. The area east of the Carpathians covers almost two thirds
of Romania's land, but few Christians are to be found there.

Braila Comunitate (Association), where we began to minister,
covers nine needy counties. This is where Pastor Peter Dugulescu of
Timisora in the west urged us to go because of the great need. The

total population here was 5,500,000, which was almost a quarter of the population of Romania with a total number of only 1,800 Baptists. There were 29 Baptist churches and ten pastors. Two churches had over 400 members, four had between 100 and 200, and the other twenty-three had small congregations. These figures began to change immediately after freedom. In the first two years after the revolution, ten new churches were planted. Before the December 1989 revolution, Pastor Joseph Stefanuti had an underground "seminary" in Braila with 23 students, with some ready to step into new churches when freedom came.

ON OUR FIRST TRIP to Romania, prior to the revolution, we followed Peter Dugulescu's advice to go to the east. We headed for Braila, close to the border of Moldova and Russia. On poorly maintained roads, winding many times back and forth across the (not so beautiful blue) Danube, we arrived at Pastor Joseph Stefanuti's church, too late for the service, but not too late for the warm welcome from Joseph and Mary. We climbed some steep steps to their tiny apartment above the small church, where they lived with their three children. Only God knew at this time the great plans He had for them and His church there in Braila.

Also on this short trip to the east of Romania, I preached in Pastor Ovi Ghita's church in the adjacent city of Galati. After the revolution, when we returned, he told us that because he had let me preach in his church, his salary from his government engineering job was cut in half. However, because of that, after the revolution the mayor sought to compensate and gave him and his family a new apartment in a choice location. Mollie and I were the first to sleep there, even before the family moved in. (By the way, I gave Pastor Ovi the money I caused him to lose on our first visit.)

As SOON AS COMMUNISM fell, both of these pastors, Joseph Stefanuti and Ovi Ghita, immediately began building two beautiful church buildings with the gifts of Christians in America. I was happy that our church in Miami was the first to send a financial gift for the Braila church building. The Romanian Orthodox Church, upon looking at its unusual plans, said it would never get off the ground. However, eighty-seven architects from all over Europe viewed its unique design with amazement. It's dome rises above a beautiful circular worship center and classrooms that house the Bible School. Tucked beside the church on very limited space are buildings that house a dental and health clinic and a dormitory for the students of the Bible School. It is the center for training young men and women for the Lord's work and sending young preachers out to start new churches in many of the little villages of eastern Romania. In every single village there is an Orthodox church which is always in opposition to the Baptist church in the community.

On a later trip to the same area, we loaded Mollie's drawing board on top of a small car and went each night with a different pastor to his village church. There we shared God's message in word and picture, with many people or a handful, crowded into a small house or church building. In one such house where I noticed there were only women and a few children, the pastor informed us that all the men in the village were alcoholics. What chance do the children have?

KAY ARTHUR, FOUNDER OF Precept Ministries, had a love for the people of Romania, and immediately after the revolution told Pastor Joseph and Mary Stefanuti to find the most beautiful house in Braila so she could buy it for them. Several times we have enjoyed Mary's hospitality there. It is a grand old house with large rooms, high ceilings, and six beautiful twelve-foot high carved cherry or walnut doors with unique beveled glass. It wasn't until Pastor Joseph and Mary and their family had lived there several years that Joseph noticed his initials, "J.S." engraved in the beveled glass on the huge front door of their beautiful old house. It's yours, Joseph Stefanuti, by God's design!

Sometimes God's "extras" amaze me!

# 25

## Boxes to Go

*"God wants us to give more than a cup of cold water in His Name."*

FOLLOWING THE REVOLUTION IN Romania, with its people having gained freedom from the madman Ceausescu, *Time* magazine stated that the first ones at the border bringing aid into the country were the Bible smugglers. That was true—and we were among them. It is hard to describe the feeling I had as we drove across Hungary in March, 1990 and were passed by truck after truck from various Christian organizations, loaded with humanitarian supplies. Yes, Christians care! Jesus said, *"I tell you the truth, whatever you did for one of the least of these brothers of mine, you did for Me."* *(Matthew 25:40)*

For weeks our church was alive with excitement as moms and dads, children and teens, began packing boxes for families in Romania. Boxes of uniform size were picked up at the church and taken home to pack with various items such as coffee, canned meat, powdered milk, Tylenol, hosiery, and ballpoint pens. We were well aware of the many needs and deficiencies of the Romanian market—and it was not hard to get our church families excited and involved. As we reached the deadline, we counted 418 boxes, each containing about $65 worth of "blessings" for our fellow Christians in a very poor, but now free, country.

The above family boxes, however, were just a portion of the gifts included in the approximately 17,000 pound shipment. Only in America would you see a company like Texaco stop its refinery to refine for us 300 cases of non-detergent oil as part of our humanitarian deliveries. Texaco knew that oil was so expensive and so scarce in Romania that people drove forever without changing the oil. This produces a great deal of sludge in the engine which breaks up, clogging the engine, if detergent oil is used. We delivered the oil to 3 or 4 churches to be distributed to their people. They treated it like "black gold." Thank you, Texaco.

Other contents of our shipment were:

2000 lbs. of medical supplies
350 pairs of blue jeans
300 jumpsuits, 300 sweaters
18,000 needles and syringes
30,000 penicillin tablets
20 cots taken to an orphanage
300 Bibles & 200,000 Gospel tracts

I took with me two of our church staff to help in the distribution of the cargo: Bill Baggett and James Srodulsky. We picked up in Vienna two new vans and a truck, which we loaded with the 17,000 lbs. of cargo from the plane. Operation Mobilization told us of a Christian doctor in one Romanian town who was in charge of the medical supply distribution among doctors. God was providing just what we needed.

Before getting to Romania, while in Vienna, we heard of the Christian rallies going on in Romania that weekend. "But," they said, "we have no literature to give out." How thankful we were that we had packed those 200,000 Gospels tracts (in the Romanian language) to share the Good News with 200,000 people. It is hard for us to think— it's hard for me to think—that most of these were people who had never had a piece of Christian literature, many had never read the Bible— and certainly never owned one. They were a spiritually deprived and spiritually hungry people. We later learned that the Romanian Church in Hollywood, Florida, who had supplied us with the tracts, and whose address was on them, had to set up a committee to answer all the letters coming to them from Romania.

Constantly busy with delivery, we still had time to preach several times to crowds in packed churches and to 5000 people in the Sportatorium in Timisora, the first such meeting outside a church building in 40 years. There I preached on the passage: *"So if the Son sets you free, you will be free indeed." (John 8:36)* James and I interviewed Rev. Lazlo Tokes of the Reformed Church in Timisora, the humble figure whom God used to spark the revolution.

WE DISCOVERED WHEN WE arrived in Vienna in June of 1990 to begin our second humanitarian - evangelistic mission to Romania, that some of our 27000 lbs. of cargo had been mistakenly shipped to England. (It arrived in Romania a few days later.) We loaded what we had into the seatless yellow bus obtained by Operation Mobilization, totally filling it and overflowing its contents into our two rented vans—one red, one white. The bus and the two vans traveled together. Our team of six from Florida consisted of Dr. Pat Anderson and his son Chris from Lakeland, Linda Reed and Jan Kyzer from our church in Miami, and Mollie and me. Chris and Nico from Holland waited and drove the truck with the London load later. On the bus were Mike, the driver, three others who were connected with Operation Mobilization and Lee from the U.S. Embassy. Our destination was the eastern Romanian cities of Braila, Galati, and Tulcea.

Since we didn't get started for Budapest, Hungary till 3:00 p.m., we drove till 11:30pm, and being exhausted, found a motel in Szeged, Hungary where we rented 4 rooms (8 people) for a total of $110 with breakfast. Two of our men thought it best to sleep in the bus and the van to keep an eye on our loads.

As we arrived at the Romanian border at 12:00 noon the next day, we wondered what it would be like this time. No need for visas now. The border officer invited us in and graciously served us mineral water. What a change from two years ago when Don and Helen Houser and Mollie and I waited for three and a half hours at this same border, while the guards scrupulously searched and totally emptied our van, looking for Bibles or any kind of Christian literature. Now it was a new Romania.

Our drivers were tired so at 1:00 a.m. they pulled over by the side of the road for the night—only to discover that they had stopped next to many bee hives. Driving on another hour, and getting into the mountains, they decided it was enough for one day. Someone found a box of blankets in our cargo, threw a blanket to each of us and we all bedded down on the seats of the vans and front seat of the bus, for five hours of well-deserved sleep.

The sound of cowbells awakened us as a little tousled-haired boy herded the cattle across the road in front of us. I wonder if he recognized what a breathtakingly beautiful morning it was, as the sun was just coming over the hill causing the damp clover to sparkle like diamonds and the pine trees to be silhouetted against its brightness. I gave him a tract and some candy and watched him as he thanked me and put one piece in his mouth and pocketed the rest. We all scattered to our own "green" bathrooms and washed up in the tin basin set on the flat stone wall at the edge of the road beside us. The wall was also our breakfast table. We enjoyed hot coffee, orange juice, cheese, bread, jelly and peanut butter (that someone from OM had thoughtfully packed for us). It was a good start for a good day ahead, and we asked God's blessing upon it.

The travel was slow as our loaded bus led the way over very bad roads, through rundown villages tucked between the hills, and sometimes stopping for a herd of goats to cross or a stray cow to decide on which side of the road she wanted to graze. The sunflowers in the fields welcomed the hot day, brightening the landscape.

AFTER ARRIVING AT BRAILA, Pastor Stefanuti led us to a church member's house where we transferred our cargo to his courtyard, a little shed and a tiny kitchen. We were thankful that the load that went to London had not yet come. What in the world would we have done with it all at once? However we were pleased when it did come, as Mollie's drawing board lights had taken the London route also, and therefore were not there to be used in our crusade meetings the first few nights.

The heat was terrible in the small packed church this Sunday morning, where some of the people had been since 7:30, but with no complaint. The forty-voice choir, which we brought by bus from Timisora in the west, sang and our own Jan blessed us all with "Amazing Grace," one verse sung in the Romanian language. None of us there that Sunday morning could have imagined the huge new church building that God would provide in a few short years. (We were happy that our church in Perrine was the first to give to make that new edifice possible.)

But for now, Sunday night through Wednesday night, our meetings were held in the former Communist Party Hall, now the first time used for a Gospel meeting. The beautiful mandolin orchestra played, songs were sung, poetry was dramatically quoted (which was often a part of a Romanian worship service) and the Word of God was proclaimed. I could almost hear the angels joining in song, as we sang together,

"He is Lord, He is Lord! He is risen from the dead, and He is Lord!

Every knee shall bow, every tongue confess, that Jesus Christ is Lord."

We watched and listened as these hungry people personally partook of the "Bread of Life" as it was proclaimed.

TAKING TOYS AND BABY supplies for the orphans—and there are six orphanages in Braila—was a highlight of our Romanian experience as we saw each little child receive his own stuffed toy, the first he had ever had or held. I noticed that one wide-eyed little boy had been given a very small gray doggie, and he hugged it tightly. "Surely," I thought, "there are bigger and brighter toys in the boxes than that one," and I pulled out a big black and white spotted dog with a collar around his neck. When I offered to exchange it, the child held tightly to the first one. It was already his, and he wasn't about to let it go.

The Director of Orphanages had her office in a former mansion which now housed the 15 or 20 smallest babies. All the little babies were lying in wet clothes on wet sheets in their cribs. Although we saw stacks of diapers in the supply room, we were told they were so rough "like paper" that they would cause a rash, and with no medication, this would be a real problem. (Wait till they opened one box and saw the 800 good soft diapers!) Two of these precious babies had cleft palate, some were sickly, two of them were rocking themselves from lack of touch and holding, and they were all just three or four months old. One beautiful tiny baby was born to a 13-year-old mother.

The nurses helped us unload our boxes of supplies for all the orphanages into the basement storeroom there. Their thanks could be felt as these items were unpacked: eight hundred soft diapers and pins (they had never seen diaper pins), baby soap, lotion, powder, vitamins, 2500 lbs. powdered formula, 1000 lbs. of concentrate detergent, boxes and boxes of coffee—and *strawberry shampoo!* A large part of our supplies were given to us by Publix and Eckerds.

When we finished our week in the east, and with a much lighter load, we headed back to western Romania, zigzagging many times as we crossed the muddy Danube River, finally arriving back in Timisora. Our mission trip was over, and we will never be the same.

Two weeks after arriving home, we sent Dr. Boeru, a Romanian doctor from our church, to the First Baptist Church of Lakeland, Florida, to publicly thank them for their enormous help in supplying much of the above cargo. He told them of our visits to the orphanages and how a nurse there said the children would scream as they got the old lye soap in their eyes when shampooing. "Now," she said, "they beg to have their hair washed—with the new strawberry shampoo."

After the service that night, our doctor, puzzled, spoke to the pastor. "Who was that man about the fifth row back who seemed very moved emotionally, especially when I told the story of the strawberry shampoo?"

"Oh," said the pastor, "that is Mr. Hollis, president of Publix supermarkets. He gave the shampoo."

Thank you, Mr. Hollis. *"I tell you the truth, whatever you did for one of the least of these brothers of mine, you did for Me."* (*Matthew 25:40*)

Just one more BOX story. Can you listen to it?

I WAS STANDING IN the lobby of Miami International Airport with 45 boxes each weighing about 50 lbs. I went with a credit card in hand, but a prayer in my heart that I wouldn't have to use it to pay for shipping. (Forty-five boxes at $125 each would be $5625.00.) I was waiting my turn when a young man in his 30's rushed up to me with "Rev. Watson!" I did not know him and I waited for him to identify himself.

"I went with you on Spinning Spokes to Europe about fifteen years ago. Good to see you, and where are you traveling today?"

"Well, I'm on my way to Russia to take these boxes of vitamins and medicine to the Christians at the Second Baptist Church of Moscow."

"Could I help you?" he asked as he looked at the "mountain" of boxes, so I told him of my dilemma.

"No problem. I work for this airline and I'll handle it." And he did. No cost, no trouble.

*"Do you not know? Have you not heard? The Lord is the everlasting God, the Creator of the ends of the earth. He will not grow tired or weary, and His understanding no one can fathom."* (*Isaiah 40:28*)

# 26
## Up to "H"

*"I saw it coming and I knew it was not an accident!"*

WE HAD JUST COMPLETED a two-week crusade with Pastor Peter Dugulescu across Romania from Timisora in the west to Braila in the east. We preached in churches, a theater, and in large rented cultural halls which previously housed the voices of the atheistic government, but today, the voice of Jesus. It was 1991. After 75 years of religious persecution, closed church doors, government control, and the dark atheistic ideology, the people were hungry for something more.

ON SUNDAY PETER HAD arranged for the rental of a beautiful theater for a meeting for people by special invitation—doctors, professors, and other professionals. The theater was full, some even seated in the second row of box seats. The full orchestra and choir from the Timisora church had driven by bus all night across Romania, to sing and play at the crusade meetings in Braila. They presented over an hour of very excellent music. Peter interpreted as I preached, and Mollie drew. As he did each night, Peter recited some of his original dramatic poetry—a beautiful custom in the Romanian churches. Although I could not understand a word of it, I could "feel" it by its dramatic presentation, and I know it moved the listeners, because it moved me.

My heart rejoiced as we saw many people respond to the invitation to be followers of Christ. It was an exciting time in Romania. After these 75 years of darkness, the lights were coming on, and God was letting *us* experience it. Yet, the sinister forces of the evil ideology that had smothered the nation for so long were still at work in the hearts of many—and it would not be long before we tragically would better understand that.

BESIDES MOLLIE AND ME, three others were in the new white Mitsubishi van—Pastor Peter, Pastor Stefanuti from the Braila church, and John the driver. The van was a gift from Franklin Graham's ministry to Pastor Peter's new organization, "The Hope of Romania." We had gotten an early start from Braila so now, at ten o'clock, we were on the outskirts of Bucharest. Later that day I had an appointment in Bucharest with the Minister of Transportation to get papers to send our cargo from Miami for free, via Romanian ships. The next day Mollie and I would fly home.

Just then I saw it. A red government car parked on the side of the road ahead of us slowly pulled out and, as we passed, with deliberate precision turned his front bumper into the right rear wheel of our van, causing it to flip, end over end and three times sideways. The police arrived and said, "How many are dead?" Though all of us were bruised and battered, miraculously, only one needed hospital care— Mollie. Before we left America, we had been warned by a Romanian doctor friend, recently come from the country, to avoid riding in a car with a Romanian. "They will kill you," he said. The target was Pastor Peter Dugulescu and it was the fourth attempt on his life by the Securitate (Romanian secret police). One of those attempts was also a car accident.

The next day on the other side of Romania in Timisora, the "New Communist" paper said the fault was the driver of the Mitsubishi van (though John, our driver, had been completely cleared at the site of the accident). No, the new government established·after the bloodshed of December, 1989 was not Communist, but it had failed to prosecute those responsible for the bloodshed; thus, much economic power stayed in the hands of shadowy figures of the old regime.

I knew I must quickly get Mollie to a hospital, but how? When a truck driver offered to take us, I helped Mollie step up three feet to the first step of the truck. "Mollie," I said, "now we'll see first hand a Romanian hospital." A few days before, Peter had taken us to see a hospital in Timisora, and we had been amazed and so very moved as we saw the pitifully inadequate facilities and equipment with which these dear medical people had been forced to work for so many years.

Now, on the long bumpy road to the hospital, I knew she was in much pain, and I voiced my fear: "Mollie, are you okay?"

The answer was barely audible. *"I'm up to H."* I knew well what she meant. And I knew she was okay. You see, Mollie has a "dictionary" full of Bible verses in her mind that she has memorized over the years since childhood. She was quoting in her thoughts all the verses she could think of that begin with "A," then "B," and she was up to "H." She often does this, and I knew she was thinking clearly.

Although the X-ray machines and other equipment were antiquated, Mollie's doctors, Dr. Andrei and Dr. Christina were excellent. Finding five broken ribs and a broken scapula, they bound her tightly from waist to neck. The director of the hospital, Dr. Juliu Suteu, came to her bedside in Intensive Care on Wednesday.

"I am sending you to a private room," he told her, "and you *must* stay in the hospital till Friday."

The private room where they took her was very narrow with a high ceiling. An old white iron bed with clean sheets and a night stand were the only furnishings. Almost immediately, two workmen entered with their tall ladders, fixed the broken window shades, and put a lightbulb in the dangling fixture. They wanted to give their best on this very rare occasion of having an American woman in their hospital. It would be Mollie's home for a few days, and we were at peace. The first day in this room, kind Dr. Suteu came and sat down on the bed to talk.

"You're happy, aren't you ?" he said.

"Yes I am."

"Because you have Jesus in your heart?"

"Yes I have—do you?" Mollie asked.

He spoke with ease and trust. "For many years when things were very hard and I could not say anything to anybody, *He* was there."

For five days we stayed in the Ambassador Hotel in Bucharest, till Mollie was able to travel, and it was a time ordained of God to receive the love and prayers of compassionate Christians from all over Romania and to share the message with our dear doctors who came to the hotel to see us.

"I would like you to come to our flat for dinner tomorrow night. Would you?" Dr. Andrei asked. They lived on the 6th floor of a very typical old apartment building, and as we walked into the small entrance, Dr. Andrei was happy to see that the elevator was working. But with Mollie's fear of elevators, and since this one had been broken down earlier in the day, we opted for the stairs—and took them very slowly to the sixth floor. We commented on the outstanding meal his wife Alice had prepared, and his response was, "Yes, like Christmas." Their pretty little sixth-grade daughter listened quietly, in awe.

"You are the first aliens we have had in our home," Dr. Andrei said, wanting to make us feel special. (I suddenly visualized myself as this little green man with long ears and big round eyes. However, Mollie looked the same as usual, so I assumed I did.) Dr. Andrei said they had no friends, partly because of his profession, and also because it was expensive to have friends. The love shown among the Christians and their love and care for us now must have made a big impression upon him. His one question and perhaps the main reason for having us to his home was to find out *why we were different*.

"I have treated hard, rough gypsy women with similar hurts as your wife, who screamed out in pain. Your wife was calm however, even without a shot. When I told you she was in shock, you said, 'No, she is not in shock,' and I wondered how she could be so tough through it all."

"Her strength is from above," I said. "The verses from God's Word, which she was quoting in her mind and heart were sustaining her, and when she said she was up to 'H,' I knew she was not in shock."

DR. ANDREI WENT WITH me to a meeting of the National Baptist Congress there in Bucharest. "I've never been to a meeting like that before!" he said. "May I call the Pastor?" He did, and I heard he was attending a class for the "seeking" at a Baptist Church there in Bucharest. God was at work with Dr. Andrei.

*"I planted the seed, Apollos watered it, but God made it grow."*
*(1 Corinthians 3:6)*

# 27

# Only Gypsies

*"We may never know what one act of obedience can accomplish."*

WE DROVE ACROSS A narrow wooden bridge on the outskirts of the village of Ciucurova, then parked beside the only building on the slope. It was a small four-room building, the headquarters of the Forestry Department, where we were to have our meeting.

Ciucurova was a village in eastern Romanian, one of many without any Christian witness. That is until the mayor, shortly after freedom from the bonds of Communism, was able to make a trip to California to visit his brother. There he met Jesus as his Savior and came back eager to change his worldly business practices and make a difference in his village. But the people, under the leadership of the Orthodox priest, were not ready for change, and in fact, fired the mayor. He continued with his job working for the Forestry Department. In spite of opposition from the Orthodox Church, however, his main burden now was to start a church here in his village, where the message of salvation by grace through faith could be offered to all.

Boards had been laid across boxes to form benches, perhaps six rows, and a small speaker stand was in front. It was past six o'clock starting time; it was getting dark—but no one was there. It was cold in the building and I shivered as I stood looking out the back window toward the wooden bridge—and I prayed. "Lord, please don't disappoint this man; bring people out to hear Your Word." A few began to come; we sang a song or two, the young preacher I had brought along preached. Just as he was about to finish, more people came in. Then more. The benches filled and he extended his sermon again. It was a wonderful and encouraging evening as we were assured that God had plans for these people, and we prayed for the future of a church here in Ciucurova.

SOME MONTHS LATER BACK in Miami, we were notified of a small house in Ciucurova that could be renovated for a little church to accommodate the group of new believers. The cost would be impossible for them but as I stood in my pulpit, I told the story of their need. It would cost $2000 to buy the house and $1000 to renovate it into a church building. Before I got to the back door of my church I had $3000 in my hand and had to turn down the next money that was offered.

A COUPLE YEARS LATER, we were back to minister to this church in Ciucurova. (I wished the two donors could have been with us.) The pastor led the choir of fifty beautiful black-eyed gypsy children who made up half of the congregation that now overflowed the little church. How they could sing!! Without a movement, they listened intently as I told the story of the Prodigal Son.

"But they are only gypsies!" The words stung me as I remembered hearing them from the mouth of a prejudiced Romanian on another day. "Only gypsies," but people whom God loves—people for whom Christ died!

I REMEMBER OUR FIRST contact with gypsies on our first trip to Romania in 1988 before the fall of Communism. We had been told to not give money to the begging gypsies as it only encouraged more begging. We parked our yellow Hertz van in front of the hotel where we were to stay and where only two or three other cars were parked, so we knew the hotel was about empty. As we opened the van door, the gypsy children "attacked" us, begging for money and trying to take anything they could reach in the van. At a very small restaurant nearby, the gypsy women and children scurried to the tables, grabbed the scraps, stuck them into their bags and dashed out before the waiter could stop them.

ARE THERE ANY GYPSIES living in your town—or mine? Probably not! But there are people just as needy that I pass every week or every day. They are the poor, the lonely, or the ones "not like us." I am more comfortable to ignore them—until in my mind, I hear again the music of the gypsy children's choir.

*Who brought these children to Jesus?* The pastor-choir director, the two men from my church in Miami who gave the $3000 for the little church, the mayor who was fired because he had become a Christian, his brother in California who had led him to Christ… on and on it goes. We may never know what *one act of obedience* can accomplish.

*"How. then, can they call on the one they have not believed in? And how*
*can they believe in the one of whom they have not heard? And how*
*can they hear without someone preaching to them?"*
*(Romans 10:14)*

# 28

## Calarasi

*"It was time for the preaching—but—the one
who was to translate for me did not show up."*

IT WAS A COLD, crisp night. Snow thinly covered the ground as we
pushed open the iron gate into the courtyard of a large, once elegant
old house, now the Baptist church of the city of Calarasi, Romania.
Travis Young, one of my deacons in Miami, had recently paid $6000
to complete the purchase of this building for the church. We were
welcomed into the tiny make-shift apartment by the young pastor and
his beautiful but timid wife. A single bed dominated the room, and
a baby bed, small table, and two chairs completed the furnishings. A
heater near the entrance made the room more than comfortable as we
talked as best we could, in two languages. As always we felt the warmth
of Christian love. When it was time for bed, Mollie and I were taken to
a large room that was perhaps the living room of the old house, where
now stood only a bed. Although it was heaped with many blankets, I
remember it as the coldest sleep of our lives.

The next morning we saw that a heavy snow had fallen, covering
the courtyard and street and whitening all the trees and bushes and
buildings into a winter wonderland. A stove was in the middle of the

room which was the "church," and people began to come, warm their hands and feet, and find a chair a comfortable distance from the stove. Hymns were sung, some tunes being familiar to us, followed by a time of prayer. Again, each prayer ended with a united "Ahmen." It was time for the preaching—but—the one who was to translate for me did not show up. Finally, as a last resort, a deacon went out into the street to find someone—anyone—who knew English well enough for the task. A lovely 23-year-old lady, not a Christian, was finally found and brought in to translate the sermon for me. Her name was Muriel. My text was Ephesians 2:8-9.

*"For it is by grace you have been saved, through faith—and this not from yourselves, it is the gift of God—not by works, so that no one can boast."*

Trying to explain in a simple way the meaning of God's grace, I said, "There is not one thing you can do to save yourself." Muriel stopped translating and turned to me and said in English, "There's not?" Realizing this was an entirely new truth to her and perhaps others there, I shared the incredible truth of Titus 3:5.

*"He saved us, not because of righteous things we had done, but because of His mercy."*

God was at work in Calarasi.

IN APRIL OF 1991 we returned to Calarasi, traveling and preaching with Peter Dugulescu. There were now fifteen members of the church and fifteen more who were being instructed and awaiting baptism. For a special Saturday night meeting, the church had rented the government cultural building facing the beautiful park that stretched along the Danube. At 5:00 o'clock starting time, there were only about 10 people inside. A small group who came in a van from Braila began singing on the street and inviting people to come. We started late but soon the place was full. Peter interpreted for me, and Mollie drew one of her chalk art pictures, "The Way of the Cross." As Peter gave the invitation, scores of people, including at least one gypsy, came up on the platform to make public their decision to receive the Christ of that cross. No, to all the "Muriels," there is not *one thing* you can do to save yourself. It is all God's grace—"everything for nothing, to those who deserve the exact opposite." We must come by the way of the cross.

Lord Jesus, I know that I am a sinner and I need your forgiveness. I believe that You died for me on the cross and rose again from the grave. I turn from my sins, and I invite You to come into my life. I receive You as my Savior and Lord. Thank You for making me a child of Yours.

*"Yet to all who received Him, to those who believed in His name, He gave the right to become children of God." (John 1:12)*

They came by way of the Cross

# 29

## I Touched a Leper

*"Yes, with my hand, but more with my heart!"*

I HAD NEVER SEEN a leper nor touched one, but I knew Jesus had. I would have liked to have been with Him when He came down from the mountainside and saw the mass of people waiting for Him, crowding around Him, and begging for His touch of healing. Had I been in the crowd, I'm sure I would have noticed the leper, dirty and repulsive, kneeling in front of Jesus. Why was he bothering Jesus? But then I would have heard his desperate cry, *"Lord, if you are willing, you can make me clean."*

> *"Jesus reached out His hand and touched the man. 'I am willing,' He said. 'Be clean!' Immediately he was cured of his leprosy. Then Jesus said to him, 'See that you don't tell anyone…'"* (Matthew 8:1-4)

Did Jesus really mean for him to tell no one? Did He really expect him to be silent about this, the most wonderful thing that could have happened to a leper? It was too good to be contained, but now Jesus had to stay outside in lonely places. Still the people came to Him from everywhere.

Leprosy is a chronic bacterial disease of the skin and nerves in the hands and feet and in some cases, the lining of the nose. It is an infectious and painful disease, which although curable, leaves sufferers deformed and crippled if left untreated. Since there was no treatment in Biblical times, the disease was not uncommon and is mentioned many times in the Old and New Testaments. Dr. Luke tells of ten lepers who came to Jesus for help. They had been put out of the city to fend for themselves or survive with the donations left by their families. It was a miserable life, but our compassionate and loving Lord saw them and healed them. It is hard for me, however, to understand why all ten didn't fall at their Healer's feet and thank Him and worship Him. Only one did. We are much too much like them. We receive and receive, but where are our "Thank you's"?

WE WERE ON OUR way to Tichilesti, the leper colony in eastern Romania. Arel Gacea, pastor of Tulcea Baptist Church, was our driver. He made this long and dusty drive every Sunday afternoon to minister to a handful of lepers. We were eager and excited to go with him, but also apprehensive. A little wooden church building stood at the end of a short street, along which were doors opening into a long barracks-type structure. Each door represented one man's or woman's simple abode. A man or two, seated on a bench in front, showed us there was life here. A dining room, kitchen, and other utility buildings were nearby.

A few men and women, no more than eight or ten, with distorted faces and crippled hands, sang as Arel played his keyboard, and they listened intently to the message I brought to them from God's word. It puzzled me, however, that no more were in attendance since there certainly was nothing else to do in this leper colony. Had their hearts also been hardened to the Lord's voice as their bodies had been slowly deteriorating? Following the service, those who attended were delighted with the balloon animals we created for them and the candy we dropped into their laps—*and our fingers and hearts touched.*

"Tommy," Arel said, "let me take you to see one man who is unable to come anymore to the chapel for worship, though he would like to." As we entered his little home I saw seated in a chair a man with what they call a "melon face," his mouth, eyes, and nostrils being only openings in the melon-shaped head. He was a Believer and ready for his new home in Heaven as soon as the Healing Savior would call for him. In the meantime, in his small simple room, he waited—*and our hearts and lives touched.*

Years have passed—and he is no longer living at the leper colony in eastern Romania, but he has taken up permanent residence in Heaven—where there is no more pain, or loneliness, or leprosy—*because Jesus touched him.*

# 30

# A Tree "Glows" in Moscow

*"It was late afternoon in Moscow, dark and cold, snow was falling—as we threw the switch and the 4300 lights on the giant tree glowed in the frosty air."*

THE YEAR WAS 1991, shortly after the fall of Communism in the Soviet Union, when I was driving along a stretch of US #1, thinking. Now, it is difficult on treacherous US #1 in Miami to drive and think at the same time, so therefore one treasures any positive thoughts that may enter one's head. I remembered the times I had stood on Red Square in Moscow. The flash went through my head of the many times on television we had seen Khrushchev, Brezhnev, and other dictators viewing the troops, the tanks, the missiles of the mighty Soviet army. I remembered a time when we had stood in a long line to visit Lenin's tomb beside the Kremlin wall on Red Square. Having in previous years been in contact with the "Underground Church," and knowing of the religious deprivation of the dear people of Russia, I wanted to make a positive contribution now—and where better than on Red Square! A huge lighted Christmas tree on Red Square! I couldn't wait to get home to tell my wife.

"God gave me the best idea, Mollie, as I was driving down Highway #1. I'm going to put a Christmas tree on Red Square."

"You are going to do—what?"

"Mollie, it's going to be as tall as the tree on the White House lawn. It will be glowing with hundreds of lights, the first time in 75 years that Red Square has seen Christmas."

"And how—are you going to do this?" she incredulously asked.

"Deneen is in Moscow now, and she is singing in a Christian crusade with evangelist John Guest. I'll call her and ask her to start the process."

Deneen Alexandrow was the Miami-born daughter of a Russian father and Ukrainian mother and had grown up from a child in our church. She was young and attractive, fluent in the Russian language, and I knew she was the one who could help make the project a success. She was already known in Russia as a contemporary Christian singer whose tapes had circulated among Christians in several cities there. Within a few days she had met with members of the Moscow Trade House, similar to our Chamber of Commerce, though operating as an official government agency and answering to President Yeltsin.

Some days passed, and then the phone call: "Pastor, although there is no official answer, there is excitement here about the possibilities. So let's proceed with the Christmas tree plan."

Working the plan was difficult. Praying was intense as we had to raise $60,000 to have the 60-foot tree, made in California, shipped across the Atlantic and constructed on Red Square. Only God could work this miracle! The artificial tree was in two containers on a ship in the middle of the Atlantic before we had received official permission from the Moscow Trade House that the tree could go up. This was done in an eleven-page document, signed by President Yeltsin, not only giving permission to erect the tree on Red Square, but also making Christmas a national holiday in Russia.

Christmas tree on Red Square, the first in 75 years

IT WAS LATE AFTERNOON in Moscow, dark and cold. Snow was falling as Yuri, our Russian friend, and Deneen, drove us from the airport to Red Square for our first glimpse of the tree, standing majestically between the historic St. Basil's Cathedral and the wall of the Kremlin. We were shivering and breathless, and then, in a moment, the darkness changed as Deneen and I threw the switch and the 4300 lights on the giant tree glowed in the frosty air. On top of the tree a six-foot star shone brightly, just a few hundred feet from the red star above the Kremlin. That red star, for years, had projected fear to the nations of the world. Our star, for centuries, has symbolized the Peace that can come to the hearts of all who receive that One, Jesus, who was born beneath the star of Bethlehem of Judea, over 2000 years ago. That wonderful story was depicted by a manger scene that someone beautifully had set up down the slope from the tree.

On a large platform beside the tree, the Russians presented a special program with professional singers and folk dancers. Then appeared the Russian Father Winter and Santa Claus.

"Thank you, Santa Claus," said Father Winter, "for putting this beautiful tree on Red Square."

"I didn't put the tree here," Santa replied. "The Christians of America put it here."

The Russian television, during station breaks, showed the tree throughout all of Russia and referred to it as "The Tree," a term with reverence. Thousands of people came by bus, foot, and subway to see the tree.

One day as I was standing on Red Square I was approached by a team from the U.S. State Department. They had been sent to Russia to measure the results of companies now participating with the newfound Russian freedom. They were interested in seeing what their contributions were to promote industry and goodwill. One member of the team said to me, "I was stationed in Moscow for 12 years during the Cold War. When I walked on Red Square today and saw the tree, I wept. This has been the most positive influence for goodwill for Moscow that we have seen."

We were interested in "goodwill," but we kept to our primary mission of sharing Christian literature and Bibles under the tree so that the real message of Christmas could penetrate the hearts of the spiritually-deprived and hungry. For 75 years and across 11 time zones, there had been no place to buy Bibles or Christian literature. Christians were persecuted and imprisoned if they chose to speak to their children about Christ or try to share their faith outside of a "registered" church.

For the next two years, we took groups with us to share gospel literature, candy, and balloons on Red Square.

*"And suddenly there was with the angel a multitude of heavenly hosts, praising God and saying, 'Glory to God in the Highest, and on earth PEACE, GOODWILL to men.'" (Luke 2:13-14 KJV)*

Although we had the vision, and some thought it to be an unrealistic vision, I was encouraged by the faith and trust of George and Carolyn Sprinkle. After sharing with our church my desire to put a tree on Red Square, George came to me and simply said, "I'll help you." Knowing George to be a man of his word, God assured me with George's statement that it was more than my dream. It was God's will. If you are a lay person, you never know what one word of encouragement could mean to your pastor or to a fellow Christian. It was only natural for me to invite George and Carolyn to accompany Mollie and me to Moscow, as the Christmas lights lit up Red Square and were seen by television around the world.

*"Jesus said, I am the Light of the world. Whoever follows Me will never walk in darkness, but will have the Light of Life." (John 8:12)*

# 31

## The Miracle of Multiplication

*"Little did we know that our simple vision of starting a camp for children would result in the establishing of fifteen churches in the Ukraine."*

I COULD NEVER HAVE imagined what God was going to do behind another door that He was opening! This time it was in the former Communist country of the Ukraine. It was such a privilege to see God use Johnny Reeves, a layman in our church, to spearhead a ministry that would multiply many times over.

In the city of Odessa on the shores of the beautiful Black Sea, a Young Pioneers camp had been established and used for many years to train Russian children in the atheistic Communist ideology. It had been the showplace of all such camps in the Soviet Union. But now, in 1995, it was the site where the First Baptist Church of Perrine conducted a camp for 65 precious orphans from around Russia. Mollie and our grand-daughter Lorna, who had just graduated from college, were among the group. After the camp, the Russian director said, "If someone had told me three years ago that Americans would be teaching Russian children about Jesus Christ in this camp, where once Russian children were instructed in the doctrine of Communism, I would have told them they were crazy."

In 1997, the camp was moved to Nizhyn, Ukraine and conducted in conjunction with the Nizhyn Prayer House, an affiliate of the Ukraine Baptist Union. We worked with the local mayor, social workers, children's hospital directors, director of the school board, the health department, and other government officials. By 2008, camps had been conducted in over 20 different former Young Pioneer camps, schools, and churches throughout the Ukraine. Fifteen buildings had been purchased in different cities and villages, and churches now meet in these renovated buildings.

Lena S. and Oxana, college students, were translators in our first camp. They became convicted, received Christ and were baptized in the Black Sea during our second camp. Lena was very instrumental in moving the camps to Nizhyn and became the Ukraine director of the camps. Her husband Oleg became a Christian and is now the Ukraine Director of the Gideons. Oxana brought Tolek to the camp as the sports director and he soon found Christ as Savior and was baptized. He married Oxana, and they moved to Chersky and began taking college students and teachers to camp. Oxana also brought her high school sister Yulka to the camp to work with the music program and she soon accepted Christ. Through the testimony of Oxana and her sister Yulka, their mother has accepted Christ and is now the children's director in her church.

In 1998, at the age of 16, Lena Z. came to her first camp. She later married Giana, the son of the pastor of the Nizhyn church. She became the camp director, trainer and writer/translator of all the programs for the camps, and continues in that role, growing the program every year.

I wish you could meet Mila, who came to her first camp when she was 5 years old. In 2007 at age 15, she took six other young people to the town of Mana to hand out 500 invitations to attend a new camp to be conducted in a school there for the first time. Twenty children signed up for the camp, but ninety attended! There was no Christian children's program of any kind in Mana, so the Sunday following camp, one of the Ukraine youth counselors, together with five other youth, returned to Mana and started a weekly Bible class for children. In 2008, over 100 children attended the camp there.

From one camp with sixty-five children, there have been many years when there have been four camps in different locations, because of the Christian growth of the children who grew up in the Christian camps. There they learned to become directors, teachers, and leaders in sports, music, drama, and crafts.

The camps are Ukraine Christian Camps conducted by Ukrainians through their churches. Little did we know that our simple vision of starting a camp for children would result in the establishing of fifteen churches in the Ukraine, with many of those saved at the camps continuing to carry on the work as leaders. This is the *miracle of multiplication*, and I believe it is the method God used in the early church for the spread of the Gospel—and the method He will use until He comes again. Are you a part of it?

# V.  MIAMI MISSION DOORS

# 32
## The Dolphins

*"The Dolphins had set a new record by playing in three Super Bowl games and winning the last two. I flew with the team from Miami to Oakland."*

ARRIVING UNEXPECTEDLY IN MY mailbox one day was a copy of Coach Don Shula's new book, *Everyone's a Coach*. Opening it to the cover page I read, "To Tommy Watson, Thanks for your help," and signed, "Don Shula." Here is, I believe, the greatest football coach ever—certainly the coach with the most winning games ever—saying to me "Thanks for your help." How many of those games did I help him win? None. How many plays did I draw up for him? None. How many suggestions did I give to him during the 14 years I served as the chaplain of the Miami Dolphins? None. Then what did he thank me for? Coach Shula knows that there is more to life than the physical—there is the spiritual—and he was thanking me for helping to meet the spiritual needs in the lives of his players.

Three and a half hours before the game, I would eat with the team at the Miami Country Club. Always, Coach Shula would stop by the table where I was sitting and thank me for coming. Only once did I get up from the table and talk to him outside the dining room. The Dolphins had lost 2 games in a row, and I noticed he seemed somewhat distraught. "Coach," I said, "there's nothing that a good win can't correct." "Oh no, Tommy, that's not on my mind. My son David's wife is in the hospital and about to give birth." It was then I saw his human side, apart from football.

"Tommy, I have something for you," Coach Shula said one morning before chapel, and he left to go to his car in the parking lot, to bring back parking tickets for me. Here was a man four hours before the game, set on winning, yet thoughtful of others. This is a side of Coach Shula of which reporters never speak

Step back with me in time and read what was predicted of me on the "Prophecies" page in my Craddock High School yearbook. It was predicted that I would return some day to my high school as a football coach. God called me to a higher calling but still gave me the joy of working with the best of the best in the football world.

THE YEAR WAS 1974. The Dolphins had set a new record by playing in three consecutive Super Bowl games and winning the last two. They also held the record as the only professional team with a perfect season, something that perhaps will never be repeated. Now this year, we had just won our division and were to play the Oakland Raiders in Oakland for one last crack at playing in a fourth Super Bowl, which would set a new record.

I flew with the team from Miami to Oakland, and after breakfast and the chapel service on the morning of the game, I headed toward the stadium with my hand in my pocket, clutching my ticket. I, and everyone else, knew well the reputation of the Oakland fans: they were vile and hostile and ugly. For all games, the Dolphins gave me a couple choice seats, but for this game there was a mix-up. My tickets placed me in the midst of some very rowdy and fierce-looking Oakland fans with *no* Dolphin colors in sight. All I could see as I looked around was a sea of silver and black and ugly painted faces. I am normally a loud and verbal participant at football games, but—very aware of my location, I said to myself that this was one game where I would keep my mouth shut.

My seat was about thirty rows up on the ten-yard line, at a good angle to see well the entire field. The Dolphins won the toss and chose to receive. The kick went deep and was taken on the goal line by #89, Nat Moore. Although Nat had been a running back at the University of Florida, he was now a wide receiver for the Dolphins. With the Dolphins, he also returned kickoffs. I had a clear view of seeing the ball go to Nat. I watched him as he hit the 30-yard line, the 40, then the 50. There was a hush in the seats around me. Now Nat crossed the 40-yard line and impulsively I leaped to my feet and shouted with all the gusto I had, "COME on, Nat, COME on, Nat!" I heard myself yell, and fearfully, I suddenly realized that the ugly painted faces around me were not looking at Nat crossing the goal line, but were focused on me.

I HAVE THOUGHT MUCH about that parenthetical experience at the Miami-Oakland game. Why did I jump up and yell in that very hostile crowd? Why didn't I just enjoy it in my spirit and keep quiet? Because I had something to yell about—something too good to keep to myself, even though the crowd was hostile. As Christians we have so much to "yell" about.

—We have a message of salvation for the lost. *"'COME now, let us reason together,' says the Lord. 'Though your sins are like scarlet, they shall be as white as snow; though they are red as crimson, they shall be like wool.'"* *(Isaiah 1:18)*

*"The Spirit and the bride say, 'COME!' And let him who hears say, 'COME!' Whoever is thirsty, let him COME; and whoever wishes, let him take the free gift of the water of life."* *(Revelation 22:17)*

*"Christ Jesus came into the world to save sinners—"* *(I Timothy 1:15)* That is worth "yelling" about!

—We have a message of comfort and hope for all the hurting, lonely, and suffering people in the world. Jesus said, *"COME to me, all you who are weary and burdened, and I will give you rest."* *(Matthew 11:28)* This too, is something to "yell" about!

—And we have the wonderful message of the promise of Christ's coming again. We hear John as he was exiled on the isle of Patmos, after he had received the marvelous revelation of future things, calling out, *"Amen. COME, Lord Jesus." (Revelation 22:20)*

It is worth yelling about even though the crowd is hostile! "Come on, Lord Jesus. Come on, Lord Jesus."

Two "Hall of Fame" players: Dan Marino
and Dwight Stephenson

# 33

## The Game Plan

*"This was the day that I was a prophet!"*

As usual on game day, after the chapel service, I sat down to eat with the Dolphin team. The menu was always the same: a big thick steak, baked potato, canned peaches, pancakes, orange juice, coffee, and bread.

Following breakfast, the defensive team went to one room and the offensive team went to another, and only in those rooms was the game discussed. But today, before separating, Coach Shula stood and asked for their attention. He needed to speak to both teams at the same time, as the game plan was being changed. The change would involve some of the players from both teams. Some of the defensive players would move into position to block for the kicking team. One of the players was defensive end Vern Den Herder.

"We have been watching films of the Colts and noticed that both their defensive ends slashed toward the inside to block the kick." Shula continued, "So here is the game plan. We are going to fake the field goal and I want Den Herder in the flat, to take the pass."

I took my usual seat in the Orange Bowl. In the third quarter, the Dolphins lined up for a field goal. On the 4th down, with about eight yards to go for the 1st down, it was very evident to the 75,000 seated in the stands that they were going for a field goal. No, it was evident to only 74,999—because I knew the game plan.

To those seated around me I said, "The Dolphins are not going to kick a field goal. They're going to fake a field goal and go for a touchdown with a pass to Den Herder in the flat."

"No way," they laughed. The ball was snapped—the ball holder faked placing the ball down and did as Coach Shula had instructed. He turned and threw it to Den Herder in the end zone for a touchdown. I didn't tell them that I knew the game plan, but when it happened I simply said, "I'm a prophet." No, the secret was: I knew the game plan.

Today we are participants in the game of life. We are on the 4th down with just a few yards to go. The time clock is ticking away and we have only so much time to accomplish our coach's game plan. Some of us are quarterbacks, some tight ends, but all of us are under the orders of the same Coach. His game plan is stated clearly in His Word:

*"Go into all the world and preach the good news to all creation."*
*(Mark 16:15)*

*How* you obey that command is between you and God. He is the Coach, you are the player. He knows your abilities, your strengths and your weaknesses, but He also knows your potential and your heart. The command is simple: "GO."

Jesus used the word "Go" quite often:

| | | |
|---|---|---|
| Matthew 28:16 | "Go to the MOUNTAIN" | to see the resurrected Christ |
| Matthew 20:4 | "Go to the VINEYARD" | to work |
| Matthew 22:9 | "Go to the STREET CORNERS" | to invite people to the banquet |
| Matthew 28:19 | "Go into ALL THE WORLD" | to preach Good News to all |

The command is clear and simple: "GO."

It's so simple—even a caveman can do it. I read about that caveman in Mark the 5th chapter. Jesus met him in the tombs, which were caves on the east side of the Sea of Galilee. The man was possessed by many demons, but was healed by Jesus. When the crowd went out to see what happened, they saw him *"sitting there, dressed, and in his right mind, and they were afraid."* Why afraid? They had never before seen a miracle! The "caveman" wasn't afraid—because he *was* the miracle! He begged to go with Jesus but couldn't, as Jesus the "Coach" was calling the plays.

*"Go home to your family,"* Jesus said, *"and tell them how much the Lord has done for you, and how He has had mercy on you."* He not only went home to his family to tell, but he went to all of the ten cities of the Decapolis and told what God had done for him.

The Coach has the game plans.
Lord, I'm listening—and, yes, I will GO.

# 34

## Jail Ministry

*"She did not finish her prison term. She died in prison, and the angels transferred her to her new Home—not because she deserved it—but because Christ paid for the transfer."*

MANY YEARS AFTER I had graduated from Craddock High School in Portsmouth, Va., I was invited back to my school to speak in an assembly program. Coach Hogan, my football coach, now the assistant principal in the high school, stood up to introduce me. "This is the meanest boy that ever came to this school," the principal said.

The entire student body laughed, but he repeated, "No—this *is* the meanest boy that ever came to this school."  I am thankful, however, that God saw me as I was, loved me as I was, changed me from the inside out, and set me on a new path.

Could it be perhaps that because of that "mean" sinful nature that I had, when God saved me, He gave me a very compassionate heart for the mean, the lonely, the suffering, the lawbreakers, and the wayward? I could see myself as one of them, and I knew that if God could change me He could change them. But where did I find the mean, the lonely, the suffering, the lawbreakers, and the wayward?  I found them in jails, in correctional schools, and in rehabilitation homes.

My opportunity to begin to serve these kinds of needy came when Chaplain Hosea Hernandez of Miami-Dade County Corrections came to me with a burden on his heart.

"Tommy," he said, "we have seven detention centers here in Dade County and I am the only full-time chaplain. Would you consider becoming the chairman of an organization that would help meet the need in these detention centers? We could call it *South Florida Jail Ministries*." Realizing that the need was great, I accepted the challenge, and this led to an exciting ten years of recruiting ministers to volunteer their services as chaplains in these detention centers. Now, rather than having just one chaplain, we had some twenty volunteers who would regularly visit the jails, preaching, teaching, and distributing literature and Bibles to the incarcerated.

Our church took the responsibility of providing a woman, Shirley Blando, to become the full-time chaplain of the Women's Detention Center. Shirley, realizing that some of the inmates, as juveniles, had been neglected or abused by their fathers, requested that I visit often, thus helping them to learn to trust someone who could become a positive father image.

## On Death Row

DEE C., IN PRISON on death row, was awaiting her execution for an extremely heinous crime. She and her lover had killed her boss. When the boss's mother continued to question the absence of her son's visits, their solution was to kill her also and bury her in her own back yard. When I first visited Dee she was witnessing on death row about her newfound faith in Christ. Later she was granted a new trial, was sentenced to twenty-five years, and was taken off death row to a cell in the general population of the prison, where she was permitted to attend chapel and sing in the chapel choir. As she gave her testimony in the prison chapel at Broward Correction Prison for Women, other women prisoners heard it, saw her changed life, and also gave their lives to Christ. Dee also had a giving heart and a gifted hand and used her spare time in prison to create gifts for others. Mollie was the recipient of two of her beautiful, brightly colored hand-crocheted sweaters and two cloth dolls. The dolls have four faces: a smiling face, a crying face, a sleeping face, and a yawning face. Mollie has often used these dolls in her devotional talks to women, describing the "Four Faces of Motherhood." As I think back of Dee, I think of a person whose witness for Christ, in word and action, was not hampered because she was in prison—where, I am sure, it would not be the easiest place to be a bold witness. I believe that God has given to each of you a job that only you can do. Dee was doing her job well. Are you?

On a Sunday morning, a group of Christians visited the chapel service in the prison and heard Dee give her testimony.

"Dee, do you remember me?" asked one of the men in the group after the service.

"It seems like I do—but I can't place you."

"I am the judge who sentenced you to the electric chair."

And they hugged.

Dee did not finish her prison term. She died in prison, and the angels transferred her to her new Home—not because she deserved it—but because *Christ paid for the transfer.*

> *"But God demonstrates His own love for us in this: While we were still sinners, Christ died for us."* (Romans 5:8)

## Residential Treatment Centers

Working in the jail and trying to follow up on those who were released created a new work for us. We started the Agape Women's Home, a residential treatment center for those being released from jail who needed help overcoming their drug addictions. Most of these had been involved in prostitution to keep up their drug habits. Since it was our drug rehabilitation program, these ladies were brought to our church every Sunday morning for worship and sat in the second and third rows in the center section. I know Jesus was pleased, because He too had some of the same kind of recipients when He spoke. Didn't He take time at the well of Samaria to share the living water with a woman who had five husbands and was then living with another man? Jesus said that He had come to seek and to save those who were lost. In 1992 when the devastating Hurricane Andrew hit and destroyed our area of Miami-Dade, the Agape Home had to move elsewhere, where God was continuing to transform the women into "vessels of honor, fit for the Master's use."

Manny Alvarez worked in our Agape Women's Home. Seeing the good results of this sixty-day residential program, Manny came to me and asked me to become chairman of a new board to help male addicts. Thus, New Hope was started. Our church gave the first $5000 for this project, which soon outgrew the small ten-man facility we had. A motel in Homestead was bought, making it possible to help more men. Today, the forty-bed facility is kept full with recovering drug addicts and alcoholics whose lives are being restored by the power of God and the love of His servants

## At the TGK facility

AFTER MY RETIREMENT we had some new opportunities to work in the prison system of Miami. The women's chaplain of the TGK facility asked us to come at Christmas to do some programs with Mollie's chalk drawings. After doing several services with them, the chaplain mentioned a real need for someone to come and work with the incarcerated boys. The need grabbed our hearts, so we went through the required preliminaries to get our passes for this facility. At 7:00 o'clock each Tuesday night for the next 18 months, we waited in the TGK lobby with a few visiting moms, dads, wives, husbands, and children of the prisoners until our turn came to go through the five electronic gates to get to our unit #24. I had a Bible study for boys ages 15-18 who, because of the seriousness of their crimes, were being tried as adults. Many of these were up for murder, awaiting their trials. Since the Bible study was voluntary, we were especially moved as we saw these boys choose this, rather than watching television or playing cards with the majority. They always showed great respect for "Miss Mollie," perhaps because usually the mother figure in their homes was more dominant.

One challenge "Miss Mollie" gave the boys was to learn the twenty-six Bible verses she gave them—one for each letter of the alphabet. Only one boy learned them all and to him she presented a certificate of honor. But whether they learned one verse or twenty-six, or whether they came to one Bible study, or every Tuesday night, these young men who had already terribly messed up their lives were *listening* to God's Word.

> *"So is My word that goes out from My mouth: It will not return to Me empty, but will accomplish what I desire and achieve the purpose for which I sent it." (Isaiah 55:11)*

After one Tuesday night Bible session with the boys, we discovered when we went to our car that my cell phone had been stolen. As I went to pick up my newspaper the next morning, I saw that our car had been stolen from our driveway, just inches away from our front steps. With the police and our On-Star, the car was located. However, all of Mollie's drawing equipment was taken out of the trunk including the board, lights, chalk, and CD player. In invisible phosphorous chalk, on the board, was a picture of Jesus. Could it be, maybe, the thieves switched on the black light (maybe in their garage)—and saw *Him*—the One who died for their sins? And maybe—just maybe, their hearts were changed?

## Kirby

Mollie and I stopped by "The Colonel's" to pick up a bucket of chicken and some drinks and headed for Kirby's house. Kirby was an 18-year-old African American young man who was released from TGK to his home while awaiting his trial. But—he was not free. On his right leg he wore an ankle bracelet, monitoring his location, limiting him to the interior of his house—not including the patio. For this limited freedom, his parents must pay $75 a week. He eagerly invited us in and meticulously set the table for our lunch. His parents were at work and his younger sister was at school, so having finished eating, we sat in their neat and comfortable living room to talk. I never asked the boys in jail what their crimes were, but now Kirby wanted to share. He said he was in for robbery, kidnapping, and sexual abuse. After an encouraging visit, we had prayer together in the living room. When Kirby prayed—a sincere, profound, concerned, long prayer from his heart—I was moved to tears. I have never heard a better prayer! Kirby had told us that his mother went to church. Now I know a little more about her—her prayers are being answered for her son. Mothers, Dads, keep praying for your "prodigal."

## Lead Me to the Rock

Before leaving Miami, I had the privilege of visiting one-on-one each Tuesday night with a 14-year-old boy who had made national headlines for luring his best friend into a restroom in their middle school in our area and stabbing him forty-two times. When he was arrested in his classroom, a notebook was found in his backpack telling of the plan for his next victim to be his sister. After our first hour together in jail, I suggested he begin to read the Bible through, starting in Genesis. Certainly he had plenty of time as he was kept in a solitary cell, not permitted with the other juveniles, which was as much for his protection as for theirs. During the hours we spent together, we discussed the passages in the Bible he had been reading the previous week. When we left Miami, he was about half way through the Bible. It was not a new book for him, for you see—he had been a student in our church academy from first grade through sixth, where the Word of God had top priority in our curriculum. Who can explain? Who can understand? Where do I turn?

> *"Find rest, O my soul, in God alone; my hope comes*
> *from Him. He alone is my ROCK and my salvation;*
> *He is my fortress, I will not be shaken." (Psalms 62:5-6)*

## "Character Endures"
## O. J. Simpson

IN 1980, ONE OF America's most popular celebrities quoted Horace Greeley's *"Fame is a vapor, popularity is an accident and money takes wings. The only thing that endures is character."* His name was O. J. Simpson. Of course, that was before his court case for the murder of his wife.

Following his trials in California, O. J. moved to Miami, close to our church. Standing in an elegant shopping mall one day, Mollie and I saw O. J. Simpson coming out of the large movie theater. Since he was alone, I approached him and introduced myself.

"I'm Tommy Watson—I was chaplain of the Miami Dolphins for fourteen years." His face lit up. "Oh yes, Doc Eshelman," he said. (Doc Eshelman had been the man largely responsible for starting the chapel services among the National Football teams.) We talked about Doc Eshelman and it was evident that O. J. had attended the chapel services with his teammates at Buffalo.

"I am on the board of Pro-Athletes Outreach," I said, "an organization of ex-National Football League players as well as active players for the NFL and Major League Baseball. We have conferences each year with some outstanding speakers, presenting programs to help athletes understand the importance of spiritual values in their lives. We would love to have you attend one of our conferences." I saw immediately that O. J. had missed my point entirely. I was not asking him to be a speaker at a conference but was offering a conference where he could find forgiveness and help for the future. As he was seemingly oblivious to his need, I gave him my card—"If ever you want to talk to a minister, call me." No, he never called—maybe he never felt the need.

As he walked away, I glanced back at the theater and noticed one of the movies then showing was entitled "Catch Me If You Can." He has been "caught" and now O. J. Simpson is in prison. If only he had lived up to his words of 30 years ago: "The only thing that really endures is *character*."

Young people, remember that.

# 35

## Alex, of Cuba

*"I have been a hard core Communist. I cannot tell all*
*the crimes I have committed in the name of Communism."*

HAVING BEEN A PASTOR in Miami for 35 years, I have learned to love the Cuban people. I have heard the stories of their deprivation and suffering in Cuba. I have felt the aching heart of a mother who is separated from her children by 90 miles of water. I have ached with the widows of those young men who were lost in the Bay of Pigs Invasion as they sought to take back their country. I have listened to the cries for religious freedom, I have watched thousands of Cubans who have fled to America and have built new lives for themselves. And I wanted to help.

The opportunity came when Mollie and I were invited to go to Cuba in October, 1993 with Pastor Comesanas, the pastor of a large Hispanic church in Miami. We were to visit his relatives and preach a week of meetings in a Baptist church in Havana. Although the United States government had requested that Americans not visit Cuba, we found ourselves on a flight from Miami to Cuba, yet without visas for entrance. At that time it was difficult to get into Cuba directly from America, so some went via Canada or Mexico.

We carried some medicine, gifts, clothes, Mollie's drawing equipment and four gallons of medication for lice treatment. These four gallons were beautifully gift-wrapped in colored paper and ribbons. Perhaps the lice medication was the most appreciated—the need was great. When going into a Communist country, one always fears Customs, so we said a "Thank You, Lord" as we went through a Customs check without paying any duty. God wanted us there.

Some weeks before this trip, I was talking to our Spanish mission pastor and dear friend, Carlos Armenteros. I casually mentioned my desire to go to Cuba some day. Little did I know that he had a burden on his heart and had his church in prayer that we would be able to get into Cuba in order to share Christ with his unsaved father. Upon arriving and before the first service of the week's meetings, I found Carlos' father and gave him a new pair of shoes and some medicine from his son. When the invitation was given that first night to accept Jesus as Savior, Carlos' father was the first one to step out. We should not have been surprised. Had not Carlos' mission family been praying for this night?

As we walked around the neighborhood in Havana, visiting some of Pastor Comesanas' relatives, he often whispered to me, "You may bless her" or "You may bless him," which meant that I could share one of my many $20 bills I had brought along for such a purpose. ($20 was almost a month's salary.)

We met a doctor on the church steps with very sore looking eyes. He told us that he had pink eye but had no medicine for it. The only place to obtain the medicine was a special store where everything must be paid in American dollars, which he did not have. Since he had pink eye he could not go to the hospital to work, and since he could not go to work he could not get paid. With the $20 we gave him, he bought the medicine, a chicken, and 3 eggs. We visited in his tiny apartment one night and met his beautiful wife and precious little 4-year-old girl. Some paper and crayons we gave her was a treasure. The doctor works only till 1:00 p.m. at the hospital—thus saving the hospital the expense of the noon meal.

The people are spiritually hungry as well. The church was full every night, and God worked in the lives of many. One man peddled a bike carrying four people for ten miles to get to the night service, and then he peddled back to his home afterwards.

> *"Blessed are those who hunger and thirst for*
> *righteousness, for they shall be filled." (Matthew 5:6)*

THE STORY I AM about to share was told to me by "Alex" near the end of our week in Havana, as we sat together in his small upstairs apartment in the same building that housed the church.

"I've heard you preach this week here in the Baptist church, Tommy, and I trust you so I am going to share my story with you. I have been a hard core Communist. I cannot tell all the crimes I have committed in the name of Communism. I have killed in the name of Communism. I have done ungodly things in Angola with the Cuban army, in which I served as a Major. Everyone knows that I have been completely dedicated to the cause of Communism." Alex shifted in his chair, and continued.

"It was on the second day of the Bay of Pigs invasion when I took prisoner a young 19-year-old Cuban American boy, Jose, who had left the Florida shores and come to help take back his homeland. I laughed at him and cursed him. In order to humiliate him, I took his camouflage shirt from off his back and paraded around waving that shirt. I have taken the shirt with me wherever I have gone these past 30 years, as I have fought for Communism. 'Look, we will conquer,' I said, waving the shirt. 'We have overthrown those who have tried to invade us—we are Communists.' I have had important people ask me for this shirt—have had them try to buy this shirt from me."

Again Alex shifted in his chair, hesitating, contemplating how to continue.

"Two years ago, I became disillusioned with Communism, and I recognized that it was taking from our people and it was destroying our country, and—I became a Christian. But now, Tommy, my conscience bothers me for what I have done. When you go back to America, find

Jose for me—he should now be in his early 50's. And please tell him three things.

First, would you tell him I was wrong? Communism is not the answer.

Second, tell him that I am sorry.

And third, would you ask him to please forgive me? And, then, Tommy, will you give him back his shirt?"

So I brought out of Cuba this old camouflage shirt, and after several months I found Jose, now a medical doctor on Key Largo. We went before the brigade, his battalion 2506, in Miami and I watched those rugged men, who still long for the freedom of their homeland, weep as I gave the good doctor his shirt back.

I can't help but think that Alex's story is like many of ours. We, too, are going in the wrong direction and have the wrong goals. We must come to Christ with our empty lives and say to Him:

First, "I was wrong in not wanting Your will for my life."

Second, "I am sorry for my sins."

Third, "Please forgive me."

And then, with Christ in our lives, we go out seeking to give some shirts back—seeking to do things that will honor our Lord.

Dr. Jose receiving back his shirt

# 36

## Shave the Beard

*"How good and how pleasant it is for brethren to dwell together in unity."*

CAN YOU IMAGINE MY paying $30 for a videotape of a young pastor's installation service? Mark Coats was a very close personal African American friend of mine who had started the fast-growing Grace of God Baptist Church in an elementary school in Goulds, Florida. His father, the Rev. Joe Coats, pastor of the large and growing Glendale Baptist, was an early leader in bringing many other black churches into our Miami Baptist Association. Mark and I had become close friends as a result of our working together in Miami Dade County while I was chairman of Mayor Penelas' Committee on Religion. Mark was employed as Special Assistant to the Mayor.

When Bishop Malone, the main speaker for the installation service, mounted the platform and stepped up to the pulpit, I knew I was in for a treat. He opened his Bible to Psalm 133:1-2 and with his bellowing voice read these words:

> *"Behold, how good and how pleasant it is for brethren*
> *to dwell together in unity.*
> *It is like the precious ointment upon the head,*

*that ran down upon the beard, even Aaron's beard:*
*that went down to the skirts of his garments." (KJV)*

"The Head," he said, "is the PASTOR, the anointed of God." The oil runs down on the beard, which represents the DEACONS. The deacons need to be anointed and mature in the Word of God, men of faith. "If you have a problem in the church," he said, "you don't cut off the head—you shave the beard. You know," he added, "you can grow another beard. Groom the leadership. Check their tithing record. Are they committed to the head?"

Bishop Malone continued, "The oil flows down on the garment, which represents the CONGREGATION. Most ministries die in the beard, not in the congregation. If the vision never reaches the people, it is because the DEACONS are killing it—."

"Mark, stand on the Word of God, even when your sheep start looking like wolves. Stand on the Word of God."

Why did I buy the videotape? Because of Bishop Malone's interesting interpretation of the passage on "how to keep unity in the church." You don't cut off the head—you *shave the beard*. I have said many times that I would be a much better preacher if I had the wisdom, imagination, and descriptive language of my many black pastor friends. I'm not sure of his exegesis, but I know one thing: it surely got my attention and was well worth the $30 and the four hours spent at the service. Even Mayor Penelas stayed till the end.

# 37

# Taking a Stand

*"When wrong is wrong and right is right, take a stand."*

SERVING IN THE GROWING, changing, multicultural city of Miami for 45 years, I had several exciting and challenging encounters with the Miami-Dade County Commissioners. One such story follows.

I was seated in the chambers of the Miami-Dade County Commissioners for the first reading of an ordinance that would levy a 3% assessment against all church property in Dade County. The commissioners knew that they could not tax church property but they thought, that perhaps, they could get away with an assessment.

I stood up to speak against the reading.

"Rev. Watson," the Chairman said, "no one can speak now because this is just the first reading. If this committee votes it, there will be a second reading one month from today, at which time you may speak on the motion."

"Sir," I said, "I know why I am here. I've been coming to these meetings for years. One night I spent the whole night here on one issue that I and my church felt strongly about. I'm here today to ask you what you are going to do about the rumor that you will be closing black churches."

There was a breathless pause.

"The other day, I spoke in a small black church that was on some very valuable property. Your 3% assessment against that church property would close that church. So the rumor is out there that you are closing black churches—and I know it's out there—because *we* started the rumor."

There was a bigger gasp. And although no one was to speak on the first reading, and because there had been a riot in a black section the night before, (though not on this issue) the Commissioners voted 13 to 0—right then—to not have a second hearing, thereby killing the 3% assessment.

I received a call from Mayor Penelas that afternoon. He asked me, as the new Chairman of the Religious Committee for Miami-Dade County, to speak that night at a town hall meeting with the thirteen commissioners and some prominent black leaders. He requested that at the meeting I inform them that I would be appointing four or five outstanding black leaders to my committee, thus assuring them a strong voice in the affairs of Miami-Dade County.

When wrong is wrong and right is right—take a stand!

# 38

## Sister Louina

*"That may not be what he believes, but that is what I believe."*

IN THE 1960's, WHEN few Baptist churches were integrated, I received a call from Sister Louina of the Catholic Children's Home, adjacent to the large Catholic church in our neighborhood. I knew from her accent that she was from the Netherlands.

"Rev. Watson, we have six children here in our Home who are Baptist. We like to see our children in church and were wondering if you would be willing to have them come to yours. By the way," she said, "they are black."

"Willing?" I said. "We would be most happy and excited to have them."

The next Sunday I announced that we would have six black children in our Sunday School and worship service. "We are *not* voting on it. I know our church would not want us to be less Christian than the Catholics in caring for all people."

This opened a door for dialogue with the Sisters as I often went by to visit with them. On one occasion Louina's brother, a Catholic priest and professor of Thomas Aquinas' teachings at an Amsterdam university, came to visit her here in America. She brought him to one of our worship services and we invited them to our home, along with a young seminarian who was traveling with him.

"I would have been afraid to invite you in," I said jokingly, "if you had said you were a professor of Ignatius Loyola's teachings." I remembered having visited a church in Rome and seen a statue of Ignatius Loyola stepping on the neck of a Protestant.

We discussed theology, and of course that involved the grace of God. We shared our differences, noting that the Catholic Church teaches that it is the "custodian of grace," bestowing grace by baptism, confirmation, etc. One hopes that in the end, he has received enough grace to get into heaven.

I shared that we believe that grace comes freely as a gift when one accepts Jesus as Savior and Lord.

*"Yet to all who received Him, to those who believed in His Name,*
*He gave the right to become children of God." (John 1:12)*


*"For it is by grace you have been saved, through faith—and this*
*not from yourselves, it is the gift of God—not by works,*
*so that no one can boast." (Ephesians 2:8-9)*


"That's what I believe," the young seminarian said, after listening to our discussion.

"No, no," I stopped him, and turning to the professor I said, "Tell him that is *not* what he believes."

"That may not be what *he* believes," Sister Louina interrupted, "but that is what *I* believe!"

ON ONE OF MY visits to the Children's Home, I was offered a drink of wine. I thanked them, but said that I do not drink, and of course they wanted to know why.

"I do not drink—not because the Bible tells me not to drink— but because all of my life since I became a Christian, I have tried to protect my testimony. Suppose I had been drinking, and on my way home I had an accident. The police would stop and check me, and the next day's paper would read, 'Alcohol involved.' I choose to not be a stumbling block to any one." They understood and appreciated my conviction.

On another visit with the Sisters, Louina began, "When I visited your church, I noticed that you had no crucifix anywhere. Why? A crucifix is very important to us."

"Christ's death on the cross is very important to us, too," I said. "He died for our sins, but He arose for our justification. Therefore, we don't display a crucifix, but an *empty* cross. He died, yes, but He is alive forevermore." At this, Sister Louina jumped for joy.

"Oh, how beautiful that is!"

I don't know where Sister Louina is today, or where her brother is, after these many years. But I think she would be happy to know that on the 2000th anniversary of Christ's birth, Pope John Paul II bestowed upon me the gold medal BENEMERENTI.

# 39

## 2000th Jubilee Year

*"The Catholic Church wants to do something good for you."*

In a pastor's home, the phone rings often: people sharing burdens, requests, joys, and thanksgivings. The phone call I received this night was different, perhaps the most puzzling call I had ever received. It was from the archdiocese of Miami, requesting that I please send my resume to the Archbishop of Miami. A strange request! I was certain that he did not want me for a priest—I was married! "Why," I thought, "should I send my resume?" The answer came, "The Catholic Church wants to do something good for you." So I mailed it. A few months later, I received the letter from the Archbishop of Miami, announcing that the pope was to bestow on me the Benemerenti Medal.

Being a Baptist pastor, I did not want to offend any of my fellow Baptist brothers. How would they feel about me accepting the invitation and the honor from the Catholic Church? After some thought, Mollie and I decided that I should accept it as it could be a platform for relating with our Catholic friends in the future. Certainly I was in more agreement with them on abortion, homosexual lifestyle, and gay marriages, than many of the "main line" Protestant denominations.

The heading of an article in the Miami Herald read, "Papal Awardees include those outside the faith. Five non-Catholics receiving the honors." Little did I know of the high honor until I read that the award is only given out during a Holy Year or during a special Jubilee. This was the 2000th Jubilee year of the birth of our Lord.

# The Papal Medal
## *Benemerenti*

*"A papal medal entitled Benemerenti was first awarded by Pope Pius VI (1775-1799) and intended to recognize military merit. Other such medals have continued to be bestowed by subsequent pontiffs on men and women who have distinguished themselves by special service or accomplishment.*

*The Benemerenti Medal instituted by Pope Leo XIII in 1891 was meant to be a permanent honorific and has in fact been confirmed as such by the subsequent pontiffs.*

*The award of the Benemerenti is usually made during a Holy Year or during special Jubilees."*

"A Funny Thing Happened on the Way—." When we first arrived at the Cathedral of Saint Mary, I was ushered into a large side room with a crowd of people. Each year the Archbishop gives awards to the faithful of his diocese for their various accomplishments and service for the Church. Since this was a Jubilee year, the Archbishop not only made his awards, but presented the Papal Medal, *Benemerenti*. Men led us to the assigned seats according to the merit of the award. This was a rehearsal seating for our seating in the main Cathedral. Since the man did not recognize me as a leader in the diocese there, and since I was not wearing a Roman collar, he looked for my name in the back row of the assigned seats. Since it was not there, he went row after row until, with great embarrassment, he seated me in my chair in the front row.

I am humbled and grateful for the award, and I am blessed to be able to use it in breaking down natural religious barriers with my Catholic friends.

Latin Proclamation from the Pope

# 40

## Homeless Centers
## Community Partnership
## for the Homeless

*"I know very little about the homeless,
but if we start with a prayer and ask for God's guidance
and miracles, we will have a better chance for success."*
*Alvah Chapman*

FEW PEOPLE KNOW OR understand the influence of the Bible in our communities—specifically in our Miami area. Alvah Chapman was the former CEO of the thirty newspapers of the Knight Ridder chain. He and his wife Betty attended a very intensive Bible study at the First Methodist Church of Coral Gables in the fall of 1991. The group met Sunday evenings when they focused for three hours on what they had learned the previous week. The study was in the book of Romans, the 13th, 14th, and 15th chapters, emphasizing the practical aspects of our faith. As the 37th week ended, they were asked to make a promise to serve God with a stronger commitment because of their deepened insight into the Word.

"Rather than do many things for the Lord, why don't you find *one* thing God wants you to do, and do it well," the teacher challenged.

Following the class, Alvah and Betty Chapman prayed much and agreed that the one thing they would both like to do was to help the homeless in Miami-Dade County. It was an immense commitment and undertaking, involving the approval of the state as well as the county commissioners and local leaders. When Governor Lawton Chiles officially appointed Alvah Chapman as chairman of the Governor's Commission on the Homeless, Alvah accepted with these words:

"I know very little about the homeless, but if we start with a prayer and ask for God's help and God's guidance and *God's miracles*, we will have a better chance for success," and he led them in a prayer. All of the board meetings have opened with prayer, and—God *has* abundantly brought success.

The center in downtown Miami was opened in October of '95 and reached its capacity of 350 a few months later, until more space was made available for another fifty. The South Dade Community Partnership for the Homeless center was opened in October, 1998, at the site of the former Homestead Air Force Base and also stays full at 350 capacity. What was so amazing from the very start was the number of *families* that were coming.

WHEN ALVAH CHAPMAN FORMED his board for this immense project, now named "Community Partnership for the Homeless," he enlisted me to serve on the board as the Chairman of the Religious Committee, which included a black minister, a Catholic priest, and a Jewish rabbi. Our task was to help meet the spiritual needs of the homeless population served by this ministry. One of my job commitments was to enlist eighty churches who would provide and serve the evening meal once a month or every other month for the 350 people in the center. Our church in Perrine has never missed serving their monthly meal to both the downtown and the South Dade centers since their beginning, for these many years. We also enlisted different churches in the community to be responsible for worship and Bible studies in the centrally-located chapel at each of the Centers.

The management of the Homeless Centers consists of a partnership between churches, Miami-Dade County Schools, the Health Foundation of South Florida, and the Veterans Administration. All of these work together to meet the needs of the men and women, boys and girls who make their homes there for the maximum of sixty days. The children and youth are bussed to the public schools and have a well-equipped study room and playground when they return. The adults learn culinary art, computer science, custodial management, etc. to prepare them to enter back into society with a marketable skill.

As the chairman of the Religious Committee of the Centers, I received a call one day from Alvah Chapman asking if I could come with him to tour the downtown center with Bill Bright, founder of Campus Crusade, who had heard of the great success of our program. Having had Bill Bright speak in our church, I was happy for the opportunity. It was a very humbling experience as I stood by these two great visionary servants of God, one reaching out hands and heart to the lost and needy on college campuses—the other to the lost and needy on the streets of Miami-Dade County.

When I left Miami and resigned from the board, we had raised, mostly through Alvah's contacts, over $12 million for the downtown homeless center, $10 million for the South Dade facility, and about a $13 million endowment.

Also at that time, when I left, our two centers had served 43,000 people, many staying for sixty days. Of the 43,000 that entered our doors, we successfully out placed 23,000 (found jobs for them outside), which is a 58.5 % success rate. This caused us to be called the "model program" for other large cities of America.

Alvah Chapman died Christmas Day, 2008, in Miami, Florida. How special it was for me to receive a Christmas card from him just two weeks earlier, in which he told me he had made a contribution to the Homeless Centers in my name. Alvah's commitment to his Lord, and his great love for others, will leave a lasting legacy for thousands of people.

"WE NEED TO BUILD a dog kennel for the Homeless Center." It was Alvah Chapman speaking to the board—so we all listened, although the "need" was puzzling to us all.

"There are some people who remain on the street because they have dogs," he continued, "and of course we have no provisions for dogs. This was brought to my attention by one of our large contributors. He said someone had approached a street person, inviting him to come into our program in order to help him get back into society, but the homeless man said he could not. He had a dog and he would not leave his dog."

In telling the story to Alvah, this large contributor said, "I will give you another million dollars if you will build a dog kennel for the Center." Needless to say, the vote of the board was *immediate*—and *unanimous*!

I haven't checked the *Guinness Book of Records*, but I believe I would be correct in saying that I am the only Baptist preacher who has given a prayer of dedication for a $40,000 dog kennel at a homeless center.

# 41

# Project Teamwork

*"Hurricanes do open doors of opportunity for service."*

MOLLIE AND I WERE just finishing our visit to the Ukraine, celebrating its first anniversary of freedom from Communism. As we entered our hotel a phone call from America was awaiting us.

"Dad," Tracie said, "Hurricane Andrew has hit Miami. The church is in shambles and no one knows if your house is still standing." We caught the first plane home!

"Well, Mollie, I guess this settles that we are not to retire this year. God still has a job for us to finish in Perrine." (Three years later we retired.)

No one who has suffered through a hurricane and its aftermath would choose to go through one again. But *it does open doors of opportunity for service.* Two of God's visionary servants, Rick Englert and BJ Behnken, partnered to organize a relief effort at our church. They worked hard and efficiently, hosting 50-100 volunteers every week.

We housed volunteers on cots and air mattresses in our fellowship hall, the only room in the church that didn't have major damage.

A few months later Project Teamwork was organized, a non-profit Christian relief organization for recruiting volunteers and rebuilding homes. It was then that they asked me to be chairman of the Board of Directors, a position that I held for the next sixteen years. We were off with a bang. The Florida Senate and the Florida House awarded Project Teamwork a ten-million-dollar grant. This catapulted us into a major rebuilding program, called Operation Rebuild, as we aggressively assisted those in need. As chairman, I watched this fledgling little response team grow to a major contributor in the recovery efforts in South Florida, ministering to thousands.

Project Teamwork's portion of Operation Rebuild resulted in a $27 million project, with 900 homes rebuilt and a volunteer base that exposed 18,000 people to the love and action of the gospel.

And then came Hurricane Mitch in Honduras. Within a few days following this hurricane, we immediately began sending relief supplies. Several planeloads of food, water, and basic supplies were flown into Honduras and distributed by helicopter, truck, horseback, and hand-to-hand by local Honduran church members.

When Honduran government officials were asked their biggest need after the hurricane, the response was "housing!" I accompanied Rick and BJ to Honduras, along with the Festus Stacy Foundation, and my heart broke. We saw villages with only rooftops exposed, where men, women and children had been buried alive in the mud. We visited the orphans, and talked to surviving families living in cardboard boxes on the side of the road. We knew Project Teamwork had to respond.

In two short years, Project Teamwork leveled and tiered the mountainside, dug a large well to accommodate the area, built sixty homes, and partnered with the Red Cross to bring in electricity. For those two years, Project Teamwork led team after team to Honduras to work on the completion of the village. Each family was charged a small fee of $35 a month for its home, and additional resources were raised through volunteers to complete the village. In less than five years, all the families paid off their mortgages and owned their own homes. Recently, an elementary school was completed, and the people of the village named the school "Project Teamwork."

The winds blew again and wiped out whole areas of the Gulf Coast of Louisiana and Mississippi—and they called her Katrina. Within a few weeks we were contacted by other ministry leaders, and Project Teamwork was off again to assist hurricane victims. In Biloxi, with the partnership of the Salvation Army, we established a "volunteer village" located under the bleachers of an old high school stadium. This volunteer village was a great success. Because of its availability to volunteers, many teams from hundreds of organizations and churches were able to return over and over again. The village was able to accommodate 140 volunteers a day with both food and lodging.

We didn't forget the needy children. Members of a very large Christian foundation accompanied us to Honduras. When they returned to south Florida, they approached us about starting a foster care agency. With full support and funding of this foundation, the Board agreed to address foster care, and Project Teamwork started the task of becoming a licensed Christian foster care agency. It was a difficult struggle, but God once again cut through the choppy waters of bureaucracy, and Project Teamwork 4KIDS was established in Broward County.

After working side by side for a year, Project Teamwork turned the entire foster care division over to Calvary Chapel. 4KIDS is the leading foster care agency in Broward County, with over 90 licensed Christian foster homes, Safe Place, six group homes, and His Caring Place, a home for pregnant teens. The budget is about $3 million a year.

After serving sixteen years as chairman of Project Teamwork, I have stepped down, but my heart will remain with this exceptional ministry. This has been a very exciting God-driven adventure.

# 42

## Dark Chocolate

*"One piece of dark chocolate a day, please."*

I GAZED DOWN AT the dense green jungle below from my seat behind the pilot of the single-engine Cessna. As far as the eye could see in all directions, the jungle met the cloudless blue sky. Norm Evans, the all-pro offensive tackle of the perfect season Miami Dolphin football team, and his daughter Tina, were with me. I was eager to show them the mission work among the Kuna Indians on Ailigandi, the central island of the string of San Blas Islands off the coast of Panama. I knew the most exciting part of the flight would be the landing—because I had experienced it before. The crosswind over the ocean was very strong and the runway was very short. The stall button was screaming, and I knew the flaps were the only thing that kept us up in the air. I breathed a sigh of relief as we touched down and stopped at the very end of the runway. The pilot turned to me with a smile from ear to ear. "Thank you for asking me to fly you here, as I needed the reassurance that I could land on this short strip. The last time, I ran off into the ocean."

PRIMARILY BECAUSE OF MALNUTRITION, the Kuna Indians are the smallest people in the world, except the pygmies. They live in huts on the islands, and they fish, grow jungle gardens on the mainland, and harvest coconuts as a money crop. Ailigandi is an eight acre island with 2000 Indians.

Dr. Daniel and Jane Gruver had gone to the Canal Zone in 1961 for Daniel to do his internship at Gorgas Hospital, where he could study tropical medicine. In 1965 he arrived on Ailigandi and began his work there in a "clinic" that consisted of two rooms, four cots, no equipment, no medicines, no water, no electricity, and no helpers. In the next ten years he turned the clinic into a sixty-bed hospital. As the only doctor for the 35,000 Kunas, he covered all the different services, including dentistry. He trained his own Kuna nursing assistants and lab technicians. Because of the need, Dr. Gruver began to do cleft lip and palate surgeries even though he was only a general surgeon. While at the hospital, he did over 100 cleft lip repairs, as such babies died because they could not nurse or were deliberately left out to die. A doctor was located who agreed to take the hospital for a few years while the Gruvers returned to Miami for a plastic surgery residency. Panamanian leader Torrijos assured them that they could return to the hospital after the schooling. However, when Manuel Noriega came to power, he prohibited any American doctor from practicing in Panama.

BECAUSE OF THIS PROHIBITION, the San Blas Medical Mission was born with its main objective being the education of Kuna doctors. So far the mission has educated five Kuna doctors, who have developed into great Christian leaders. The mission also offers high school scholarships to Kuna children. Education on the islands only goes through the eighth grade, and children must go to Panama City if they want to finish school.

One of the major problems in San Blas was protein starvation of babies. This is different from general starvation as it is almost impossible to reverse, so the hospital started a children's feeding center where 400 children were fed once a day. With the improvement of the health of the children over the years, the center in Ailigandi was reorganized to feed only children that the hospital diagnosed as malnourished. The center still feeds 100 per day. A third program, besides educational scholarships for doctors and students, and the feeding centers, is aid to the Kuna pastors, especially to those who are bi-vocational on the smaller islands. Some of the older pastors have attended seminary on the mainland.

A great deal of the money for the mission today comes from the sale of molas, which Jane Gruver, known as the Mola Lady, buys and sells. What is a mola? It is the hand- stitched art of the Kuna Indians. They are panels of decorated material made in pairs for the front and back of the Indian women's blouses. The designs are geometric, fish, animals, Kuna customs—or anything as varied as the women who create them. It is a unique backward appliqué, with no two molas being alike. Jane travels to San Blas once a year, buys the blouses, then sells the molas to art collectors or art lovers. To own a mola is to own a piece of the San Blas.

Our Perrine Baptist Church in Miami became the "mother church" of San Blas Medical Mission, and though I became president of the board when the mission was incorporated in 1984, I take little credit for its accomplishments. All credit goes to the Gruvers whom God used to work miracles there. One of our medical school scholarship students, Dr. Gregorio Martinez, was part of an interesting research project. Curious as to why Kuna Indians have little age-related hypertension, he partnered with a Harvard research team to solve the riddle. They discovered that the Indians' use of raw cocoa in all their cooking could quite possibly be the secret. So the world is enlightened to the fact that we can enjoy dark chocolate because it may assist in lowering blood pressure. So let's "eat up"— one piece of dark chocolate a day!

# 43

## Pass It On

*"Here are a few good things we have passed on to our children."*

IN THE EARLY 1970's a very meaningful Christian chorus became popular among youth groups and adults alike, entitled simply "Pass It On." The meaning was clear: we are to "pass on" the message of Jesus to others. First and foremost, we have passed on that wonderful message to our children, who have in turn, passed it on to their children. Here are several other good things that I feel we have "passed on" to our children.

Lack of Prejudice: While living in Miami, the world south of us became very much a part of our world as Cubans, Mexicans, South Americans, and people of the islands moved into our peninsula, coloring our culture. Our son Terry chose a career in social work in a school in Georgia, giving his life working mostly with black underprivileged youth and writing grants for public school programs to engage and stimulate young people to better their lives.

Love for Sports: There would be no baseball game or football game in which our boys played, from Little League to Westminster Christian

High School, that I was not seated in the bleachers, if at all possible, cheering on their teams. Our sons and our daughters have "passed on" that love and enthusiasm for sports to our grandchildren. We know! Mollie and I have yelled and sweated watching Brittany dash down the basketball court in the hot gymnasium in Mobile, and we have nearly frozen as we wrapped up in blankets yelling for Brady's soccer team in Fayetteville, Georgia.

Joy of Giving: Early in my Christian life I learned that tithing was not an option: it was a command. But it also brought tremendous satisfaction. God speaks through the prophet Malachi saying: *"Will a man rob God? Yet you rob me. But you ask, 'How do we rob you?' In tithes and offerings." (Malachi 3:8)*

Mollie and I have found tremendous joy in giving, knowing from experience the meaning of Jesus' words when He said, "It is more blessed to give than to receive." The more we give the more we want to give. We have "passed on" the joy of giving to our children, for all of our children are tithers to their churches and give beyond that. I have always felt that somehow, if one tithes, he will not get too far away from regular worship in his church. No one can know the joy of giving until he has practiced giving. In a father-son conversation in the car one day, young Tim asked, "Dad, do you ever get hurt in giving?" "No, Son, you might get burned but you never get hurt."

Heart for Missions: Every Wednesday night our boys were in RA's (Royal Ambassadors) and our girls were in GA's (Girls Auxiliary) learning about, and doing, missions. As adults in their various churches, they found themselves for years teaching the RA boys and the GA girls, "passing on" the vision and burden of missions to others who will "pass it on" here and around the world.

When Tracie was fourteen, we sent her with a group of several young people from our church to work for a month on the island of Ailigandi off the coast of Panama. There, missionary Dr. Dan Gruver had built a small hospital serving all the Kuna Indians on the inhabited San Blas Islands. The teen boys worked days on the mainland, clearing and working the farmland, helping a man whom our church had sent over for a year. The two girls in the group, Tracie and Denice, worked in the hospital, sorting medicines, taking vital signs, etc. They all slept in different extended family huts, sleeping in hammocks that were hung to the side during the day.

On a previous trip to the San Blas Islands, I had taken with me Adon Taft, then the Religious Editor of the Miami Herald. We were flown in a small plane from the Panama City airport to the small island airstrip that serviced Ailigandi. When we landed, a group of Indians was there to welcome the plane, including a boy wearing a t-shirt with the words "The Devil Made Me Do It," perhaps left by another American visitor to the island. Returning home I read Adon Taft's interesting newspaper story of the Kuna Indians and his experiences on the island. I cut out the article together with a picture of the boy with "The Devil Made Me Do It" shirt. Before Tracie left for her summer in the San Blas, I had given her the picture. "If you see the boy with this shirt, give him the picture. He'll enjoy a picture of himself."

One day as Tracie was winding through the narrow paths between the huts, she saw the boy wearing that t-shirt. "Stop, don't move. Wait right here—I'll be back"—and she ran back to her hut, picked up the picture, brought it back, and gave it to the delighted boy. After her day's work and supper with the mission group, Tracie trudged back to her hut. There, to her surprise, was the boy wearing the shirt! He was one of the extended family with whom she had been living for two weeks in the large one-room hut. It was the shirt that identified him. (The thought came to me: what am I "wearing" that identifies me as a Christian? A smile? A forgiving spirit? Godly love?)

Because we "passed on" the heart for missions to our children, they in turn are passing that on to their children. No sacrifice is too great in order to give their children the opportunity to see and experience missions, at home and abroad.

<u>Love for People, Especially the Hurting</u>: This was so exemplified as we heard the story of an experience our daughter Tonie had in helping a "hurting" person. I am quoting it verbatim from the story as we received it from her.

"After living in south Florida for nearly all of my life, our family had moved to a large city in Alabama. We started attending a church in the area and I had decided to join the choir. Upon entering the beautiful stained glass windowed choir room, I noticed a very large woman sitting with an empty chair on either side of her. As soon as I seated myself beside her, the smell of her body odor nearly overwhelmed me. It was obvious why the chairs were empty next to her. I remembered thinking to myself, "This is exactly what I expected, moving to Alabama." However, the Lord had a definite mission in mind for me that continued for the next ten years, and this woman sitting next to me became my friend.

Anna was only 38 years old, but because of her weight, greasy unkempt hair, and missing teeth, she looked much older. She still lived with her ailing parents and had never had a job. It was a pretty rough situation for her at home, and several months later she found herself homeless. She told no one of her plight and found refuge in the bushes at church. She got a bit braver and decided to make the inside of the church her home. This was one of the largest churches in the state and had a pretty high-tech motion detector sensor throughout the building. Somehow, she managed to live in the choir room for several days unnoticed. Because of the motion detector in the corridors, she knew not to venture out to the restrooms after hours. She used the plastic-lined garbage can as her toilet.

The church secretaries knew I had befriended her, so it was me they called when she was found. Anna never had been taught proper hygiene. To be quite honest, it was difficult to even stand next to her. It took a little coaxing to get my family to buy in to the fact that Anna was coming to live with us until we could find her a place to live. For the next six weeks, I gave her every health and beauty tip I could think of. She went to the dental office where I worked, and I cleaned her teeth. We had some dental work done for her and got her an electric toothbrush. My hairdresser even volunteered to cut her hair for free. Then we went to the dress shop for extra large women and tried to put together some kind of wardrobe. The following Sunday was quite interesting! People from all over the church noticed the remarkable change. She was clean and presentable.

Now came the hard part. How does one teach an obese, self-conscious woman how to go out and get a job? It is just not that easy. Anna needed a job desperately in order to be able to afford a low rent apartment. She had never driven a car, so she needed to find a job within walking distance from an apartment.

Scores of people from the church had now joined the "Anna Mission" and we had "showered" her with things that she would need in her apartment. But before she could get an apartment, we needed to get her a job. The church had agreed to pay her first and last month's rent when she found work.

Here was the plan. I told Anna to wait in the car as I walked into McDonald's. I had put on a dress suit, the very one I had worn when I went to my own job interview as a dental hygienist. The cashier greeted me and I asked to see the manager. The manager came out and greeted me with a smile as I asked her if she were hiring. She obviously thought that I was the one looking for employment. For the next ten minutes, I proceeded to tell her about Anna. I told her that if she hired Anna, she would have an employee for life. Anna would be working there when every other employee in the whole place was gone.

It has been several years since I have seen Anna, as we have once again moved to another state. I do know that Anna still works at the McDonald's. The last time I spoke with her, she had only missed one day of work and that was to bury her mother.

It would be wonderful to be able to tell you that after these many years, Anna has worked her way up the corporate ladder in the company. That is not the case. However, this hardworking woman is successful. She is not MY success story. I am hers. You see, it was through her that the Lord showed me what true giving is. From the start I didn't necessarily feel like pouring my life into this woman. We are not to give for what is to be gained. Obedience was my motivation. It was this giving, out of obedience to the Father, that brought me more joy than I could have imagined."

# VI.   DOORS ALONG THE WAY

# 44
# Along the Way

*"The road was twisting, treacherous, and narrow."*

I BOUGHT A BUS ticket for as far as my money would go, and then someplace in Louisiana I found myself beside the road hitch-hiking. It was Christmas break at Baylor University where I was a student, and I was eager to reach Columbia, S.C. to see my bride-to-be, who was a senior at Columbia Bible College. It didn't take long till a young army officer pulled over and invited me to ride with him.

"Where are you headed?" I asked.

"To Columbia and on up to Virginia."

"Good. I'm headed for Columbia, also."

A little later: "Would you mind driving for me? I've been driving most of the night."

So the officer slept—and I drove his new car across Mississippi, Alabama, Georgia, and all the way to the door of Mollie's dormitory in Columbia, S.C.

Through those early years, I often picked up hitch-hikers "along the way," knowing that they, like myself, had no funds. I always made it a practice to use it as an opportunity to share my faith in Christ. On one occasion, I picked up a young man, about 28, who, not knowing

I was a minister, began to share his life with me. He had been a school teacher, making a comfortable living, enjoying life, but then he began to drink—at first, just a drink now and then. He lost his job. His wife and family left him. He became despondent and his future seemed dark. I knew I had the answer—but did he want the answer?

I used an approach I had never used before, by asking a question I had never asked before: "What would you say are the two most important things in life?"

"Peace and security," he shot back, without blinking an eye.

"You are exactly right, and you have told me that your wayward, sinful life is completely void of peace. The Bible says, '*But the wicked are like the tossing sea, which cannot rest, whose waves cast up mire and mud. There is no peace...for the wicked.*'" (Isaiah 57:20-21)

"The second important thing in life, you said, is security. Here you are on the highway, alone, hitch-hiking, jobless, without family and with a dim future. Little security! The Apostle Paul also had very little, was often on the highway, or in prison, without family, but he had a bright future. Real security! He wrote to the believers in Rome: '*For I am convinced that neither death nor life, neither angels nor demons, neither the present nor the future, nor any powers, neither height nor depth, nor anything else in all creation, will be able to separate us from the love of God that is in Christ Jesus our Lord.*' (Romans 8:38-39) That is security, my friend."

I wish I could say that this young man who saw his need for peace and security turned his life over to Jesus, the One who could give him those things. But he didn't. He, like millions of others, rejected Him—or ignored Him. Is there a difference? I doubt it.

WHEN I SEE A woman "along the way," standing beside a malfunctioning car, I am compelled to stop and see if I can help her. I stopped one night as darkness was approaching and changed a lady's tire. She told me she was a journalist for the Homestead News Leader. The next day a friend called, informing me there was an article in the News Leader about this "Rev. Watson, the Good Samaritan." A few weeks later, "along the way" to our home on a country road, again a car was broken down. Another lady! Since it was more than a flat tire, we left the car and Mollie and I drove her to her home in Homestead. In our conversation, she mentioned she worked for the Homestead News Leader. Yes, you're right! The next day, another Good Samaritan article in the paper! I called the News Leader, thanked them for the good publicity for our church, but added, "Please, if anybody else from your staff breaks down, and I happen to stop to help, don't write it up—your readers will think that all I do is ride "along the way" and pick up women!

You HAVE GATHERED FROM the above "along the way" story that we lived far out in the country, known as the Redlands. Houses were scarce and scattered between farm land, groves, and nurseries, and ours was tucked in the middle of an avocado grove, almost beyond civilization. I had been through a long day on my church field, and now nearing 11:00 pm, I was happy to be almost home. I hoped Mollie was still awake. It was a starless night—and then I saw him: A black man, in a black leather jacket, pushing a black motorcycle. (I tried to think of a story in the Bible—and then—.)

"Are you out of gas?"

"No, my battery is dead and I'm not able to kick-start it."

"I'll help you," I said. "I'll push by hand, but get it up as fast as you think I can push, and then let out the clutch. But don't stop—keep going." I was in my late 60's and I gave it all I had—and he took off! The problem was that he took off *so* fast, that I didn't get my hands off the back luggage rack till he had dragged me a few feet down the asphalt.

"Mollie, I'm home," and she saw my dirty, bloody shirt. And, oh yes. I just thought of the Bible story: The Good Samaritan who helped the beaten up man "along the way." Only I don't remember the Good Samaritan being bruised and bleeding!

It wasn't the best road to take from Jericho to Jerusalem, and I don't believe it was the shortest, but our tour group chose to take it because it is called the "Old Jericho Road." A small rock building "along the way" marked the general spot of the old inn of the parable Jesus told in Luke the tenth chapter. The road was twisting, treacherous, and narrow. It appeared from the bus seats, as we turned each curve, that the bus was extending over the edge of the cliff and there was no return. Easily I could picture the Samaritan man with his little pouch of necessities for a short visit to Jericho, coming around the curve and seeing the crumpled form of a man, bruised and bleeding, alone on the edge of the precipice. The Bible says, "He had compassion on him," or "He took pity on him." He was the Good Samaritan.

Everyone lives according to one's philosophy of life. It doesn't have to be written down or intellectually profound. In fact, mine is very simple: "Do something, even if it's wrong." Since I love the Lord and love God's Word, you may wonder where I get that philosophy! I get it from this parable, the parable of the Good Samaritan. Let me explain. Anyone who knows anything about first aid realizes that *everything the Good Samaritan did for this poor man by the road was wrong.*

1. First of all, the Bible says that he had compassion on him. It is best to not get emotionally involved with the patient. Tommy Brown, the Chief of the Paramedics of the Fire Department of Miami-Dade County, and a member of my church, told me that in his forty years of giving first aid, only once did he put the blood pressure cuff on incorrectly, and that was on his own grandmother. Being emotionally involved may mar one's actions.

2. The second thing the Samaritan did wrong was to pour a foreign substance into the wound, not knowing if the patient were allergic

to it. He put in oil and wine. As I was growing up, my grandmother with her 17 children and us kept a big bottle of iodine handy at all times. She generously spread it on every big or little scratch. I thought that was a good plan to follow, until one day when I was directing a children's camp at Florida City Baptist Camp, a boy was brought to me somewhat scraped up. I reached for the iodine bottle and his nine-year-old brother stopped me. "You will kill him with that! My brother is highly allergic to iodine!"

3. The third thing he did wrong was to move the patient. The Bible said that this man was "half dead." Can you imagine moving a man that could have several broken ribs and draping him across a donkey's back for a ride up a rocky road to an inn!

4. The fourth thing he did wrong was to make himself liable for the debts of a stranger. In the morning he gave the innkeeper two silver coins and said, "Look after him, and when I return, I will reimburse you for any extra expense you may have." Logically speaking, that was very unwise. The writer of Proverbs had a strong thought on this also: *"Do not be a man who strikes hands in pledge or puts up security for debts."* *(Proverbs 22:26)*

ALTHOUGH EVERYTHING THIS GOOD Samaritan did was wrong, yet his heart was right—and that makes all the difference. In America we have what is called the "Good Samaritan law." It is a legal principle that prevents a rescuer who has voluntarily helped a victim in distress from being successfully sued for wrongdoing. Its purpose is to keep people from being reluctant to help a stranger in need, for fear of legal repercussions if they make a mistake in treatment.

IN ANOTHER PARABLE (MATTHEW 20) Jesus spoke to some men waiting for work in the vineyard and He said, *"Why have you been standing here all day doing nothing?"* And I would have added, "Do something, even if it's wrong!" Jesus wants action. Yes, we will make mistakes, and yes, people may misjudge our actions. But I think we often miss out on seeing miracles because we don't step out on faith. God has a way of guiding us if we are not sitting still. <u>When God opens a door, *drive* through it, because God can't steer a  parked car.</u>

# 45
## Pulpit Exchange

*"There Mollie and I stood on the dock, by the Rock, thinking of that great venture and the price the Pilgrims paid for their religious freedom."*

WOULDN'T IT BE INTERESTING to exchange pulpits with another pastor for a couple weeks? I got the opportunity when R.T. Kendall, pastor of Westminster Chapel in London and a long time friend, called and asked if I would like to exchange pulpits with Rev. Ian Coffey. He was the current pastor of the church that cared for the Pilgrims before their departure, now the Mutley Baptist church in Plymouth, England. Arrangements were made, and Rev. Coffey, his wife and their three boys flew over and stayed at our place on the "Poor Farm" (as we had named it). They enjoyed our five-acre avocado grove (between Homestead and the Everglades), as well as fishing off the Florida Keys. He would preach in our church, in Perrine, for two Sundays.

Mollie and I, in turn, would enjoy life in Plymouth, England while we ministered in the church there, staying in the Coffey's lovely old narrow three-story house, with our bedroom being the sole room on the third floor. Their high-fenced backyard was beautifully filled with flowers and a small protective fabric-covered vegetable garden, which received the light but kept out the possible cold. I enjoyed watering both the flowers and the vegetables. A trickle of water flowed into a tiny stone pond, almost hidden by the yellow flowers that surrounded it, making both the frogs and the butterflies happy.

The Mutley Baptist Church had many young people, especially now, since a group from YWAM (Youth With A Mission) was here helping in some ministry in Plymouth. The church was warm and friendly and very receptive to God's Word.

An older couple, but rather newlyweds, entertained us royally, taking us to many sights around the area. Special to us was the expansive Dartmoor, the last great wilderness of southern England, where nothing seemed to exist but purple heath, waving grass, rocks, sheep, and wind—always the wind. It was a strange and mystical beauty that one could also feel and hear. Now and then, around a hill, was a village with a few unique shops and red and pink geraniums in every window box..And there was a bridge across a rushing—or a trickling—stream. Always a bridge, always a stream, and always the wind.

This morning Mollie and I were to walk down to the port—down to Plymouth Rock—the symbol of the spot from which the Pilgrims set sail in 1620. There had been 110 pilgrims—44 who called themselves "Saints" and 66 others, whom the Pilgrims called the "Strangers." It had been a long, cold, damp trip—65 days before they sighted land on Nov.10th. Many had died on the trip. There also had been much disagreement on the ship between the Saints and the Strangers, which was resolved in the Mayflower Compact, which guaranteed equality and unified the two groups.

The first winter in their settlement, which had been named "Plymouth," was devastating. Of the 110 Pilgrims and crew who left England, less than 50 survived the first winter.

There Mollie and I stood on the dock, by the Rock, thinking of that great venture and the price the Pilgrims paid for their religious freedom. I think of a far greater price that was paid for our freedom from sin—the blessed and sacrificial blood of our Lord.

*"From the ends of the earth I call to you, I call as my heart grows faint; lead me to the ROCK that is higher than I." (Psalm 61:2)*

W E TOOK A BUS back to London and found an inexpensive room at the Salvation Army, just across the street from a beautiful four-star hotel. As we ate in the small breakfast room, we looked across at the spacious hotel.

"Mollie," I said, "that's where I stayed on my last trip here to London."

"Wow!" She reflected for a moment—and then—"I'd rather be staying here. We can sit here at breakfast and look across at the beauty of that hotel. But if we were staying there, we would be looking out their window—and see only this little place." Contentment! It's a great virtue. Oh, we've stayed in the best of hotels, but we have also slept, two on a cot, in the sitting room of a humble Romanian couple.

We readied ourselves for the morning service at Westminster Chapel, just a short walk up the same street, where I was to preach this morning in the absence of Dr. R.T. Kendall. The stately old church was sandwiched between much less significant looking buildings, but with broad, welcoming steps leading up to its entrance. There in the vestibule, we were warmly greeted by two deacons. I had preached here before, but was again awed by the spacious interior, the high pulpit and ornate organ. I recalled that this church had been blessed for many years through the ministry of Dr. G. Campbell Morgan, the renowned pastor, theologian, and author of many books.

This morning, I mounted the high pulpit and preached from the text: *"Joseph is no more and Simeon is no more, and now you want to take Benjamin. Everything is against me!" (Genesis 42:36)* It certainly seemed like all of Jacob's valuables were being taken from him. Now they had sent for Benjamin, his only son left at home. Things were bad but not as bad as they seemed, because Jacob didn't yet know the end of the story.

Seemingly, at an earlier time everything was going against Jacob's son Joseph. He had been thrown into a pit, he was sold into slavery; he was lied about by the wife of one of Pharaoh's rulers, and he was thrown into prison, where he spent years. Was Joseph feeling the same as his father Jacob, when Jacob said, "Everything is against me!"? I think not, although, I'm sure he questioned at times, but Joseph used those years in prison as a training ground and a trusting ground. Things were bad, alright, but not as bad as they seemed.

Trials and hardships come to all of us. How do we handle them? From where is our strength? Can God help us through our troubled times and *use* us in spite of the trials?

And then I told the story of Johnny. Johnny was a nineteen-year-old grocery bag-boy with Down Syndrome. He had been challenged, with the other employees, to find something to do to bless the lives of the customers.

"Mother," Johnny pondered, "is there something special I can do to bless the lives of those who come through my line at the store? What can *I* do?"

"Johnny, you know, you like to collect quotations. Why don't you type these on small pieces of paper and drop one of these in the grocery bag of each shopper." And that's what Johnny did, working long into the night. Each day, a longer line stood at the check- out counter where Johnny was bagging than at any other counter. All were anxious to get their "quote for the day." One man said that he used to come shopping once a week for groceries, but now he stopped by every day—in order to get his quote.

As I finished my sermon that Sunday morning at Westminster Chapel, a lady whom I had not noticed before came to speak to me. Beside her was her young son—who had Down Syndrome.

"This is the first time I have been in this church," she said. "I had come to my wits' end and thought, maybe coming here today, I could find hope and strength. The sermon gave me that. And by the way, this is my son,—and his name is Johnny."

I have never seen Johnny or his mother since that day. He is older now. Perhaps he too, is standing at a grocery counter handing out quotations or Bible verses to London shoppers as they pass by.

LONG YEARS AGO I read the fable of the chicken who was lying on her back in the middle of the road with her feet pointing straight up. Walking down the road came a man, and upon seeing the chicken lying in the road with her feet pointing straight up, he asked, "Little chicken, why are you lying in the middle of the road with your feet pointing straight up?"

Replied the chicken, "I heard the sky was going to fall."

"But, little chicken, you know you couldn't hold up the sky!"

Replied the chicken, "Yes, but one must do what one can."

Are you doing what you can for the Kingdom of God? Am I?

# 46

## Prejudice Comes in All Colors

*"No, I'm not going to tell you—because you're a Jew."*

IN THE EARLY '60's, Perrine was a small, sleepy suburb fifteen miles south of downtown Miami. Here was our church field. Although it was south of Miami, many of our people were from south Georgia and had brought with them some of the south Georgia prejudices. Prejudice can lift its ugly head even in churches that strongly proclaim that Jesus loved and died for all people. God has His special ways of dealing with His children in teaching them that all people are equal in His sight. I know, because I grew up as a very prejudiced person in Portsmouth, Virginia. While attending a revival meeting, as a young man of twenty, I watched police come in and ask African Americans to move from the first floor to the balcony. A strange feeling ripped my heart, and I was thankful that I was seated in the balcony.

One Sunday morning, early in my ministry in Perrine, Dr. Jim Plinton visited our Sunday morning service. Jim Plinton was an African American, a fine Christian gentleman, and a vice president of Eastern Airlines. After several visits, he told me he would like to join our church, but he noticed there were no other black members.

"When the vote is taken, will the people accept me?" he questioned.

"Mr. Plinton, if they don't accept you, we will both walk out that back door together."

Baptist pastors are not supposed to have "best friends" in the church, but everyone soon learned that Jim Plinton was my best friend.

Jim was very articulate, having been an instructor of the all-black 99th Fighter Squadron of the Army Air Corps. He was the personal instructor of Gen. Daniel "Chappie" James who always visited with Jim when he was in Miami. I learned much from Jim Plinton as he was a world traveler and acquainted with a great number of the presidents of the African nations, having been in Africa sixty-five times helping to set up African airlines.

I also learned from his wife that Jim spent hours on his knees in prayer. I knew him as a man who laughed a lot and loved much and many. I heard him sing in the choir and share his testimony. What a great man of God!

Because of my stand on the race issue, my congregation often said of me that I didn't have a prejudiced bone in my body. I emphatically corrected them, by telling them my plans for my funeral. I told them that I wanted four pallbearers: one Asian, one African American, one Latin, and one Anglo.

"By this you will think I am not prejudiced," I told them. "But PLEASE, don't let a Cuban drive the hearse! We'll be late for the funeral, and he'll blow the horn all the way." My Cuban members laughed the loudest. I loved my church family and my church family loved me. We know from years of experience that there can be unity and fellowship even with a church family from fifty-eight different countries.

I WAS AMONG FIFTY Miami pastors in Jamaica preaching revivals. All of Jamaica was excited, not because of our upcoming revivals, but because Haile Selassie, the emperor of Ethiopia, was visiting Montego Bay. The people who were most excited were the Rastafarians, who believed that Haile Selassie was the "lion of the tribe of Judah" and took his pre-emperor name, Ras Tafari, as theirs. Crowded on the square that day were 40,000 people, many on rooftops, to get a glimpse of the man whom they worshipped. Some of the Rastafarians had a distinct appearance: long, matted, unkempt hair, wearing bright-colored clothes, and smoking home-grown marijuana. They spotted me as the only white face in this sea of black humanity. They circled me and continued their chant, "Haile Selassie is God—Haile Selassie is God." It was an uncomfortable and lonely moment! Right then, I made a strong determination that if I ever saw a black person standing alone in a sea of white faces, I would go and stand beside him, letting him know that he had a friend. For the adventure of it, early the next morning, I joined the crowd at the airport to see Haile Selassie off. The crowd consisted only of the Rastafarians and Tommy Watson.

I EXPERIENCED ANOTHER, MOST surprising, encounter with prejudice, as I stood at the Damascus gate in Jerusalem. It was not black against white—nor was it Muslim against Jew, or Jew against Muslim.

I approached a very sophisticated, lily-white, blond-haired, normal-looking woman, and asked what I thought was a normal question. Here is the conversation:

Me: "Do you know where the Post Office is?"
Her: "Yes."
Me: "Where is it?"
Her: "I'm not going to tell you."
Me: "Why not?"
Her: "Because you're a Jew."
Me: "No, I'm not a Jew."
Her: "What are you then?"
Me: "I'm a Baptist. Do you know what that is?"
Her: "No."
Me: "I'm not going to tell you."

Prejudice will keep her out of heaven, for you see, Jesus was a Jew.

*"After this I looked and there before me was a great multitude that no one could count, from every nation, tribe, people and language, standing before the throne and in front of the Lamb. They were wearing white robes and were holding palm branches in their hands. And they cried out in a loud voice: 'Salvation belongs to our God, who sits on the throne, and to the Lamb.'"*
*(Revelation 7:9-10)*

# 47

# An Unusual Baptism

*"She was handed red roses as she stepped into the baptismal waters."*

I KNOW *I* HAVE never had a baptismal service like this one in my forty-five years of ministry, and I wonder if anyone has! The setting was perfect. The congregation was seated in the sanctuary of the beautiful historic Central Baptist Church in downtown Miami, where I was interim pastor, and where once Dr. C. Roy Angel saw a thriving ministry. The membership had dwindled now, with young families moving to the suburbs and the faithful few struggling to keep up the building and the ministry. But some things had not changed: the people loved the Lord and one another, the organ music still swelled through the sanctuary, and today, the May sunshine was beaming through the gorgeous stained glass windows, brightening the pews and the people. Yes, it was a perfect setting!

Today the congregation of Central Baptist Church unexpectedly became the wedding guests of Don and Cally during the baptismal service. The bride, in a white baptismal robe and carrying a lovely bouquet of red roses, and the groom, also in a white robe, joined me in the baptismal pool as the wedding song was sung. I announced the couple's intentions to the surprised congregation.

"These young people have received Christ Jesus as Savior and Lord," I explained. "They have decided that to have a right relationship with God—and—a right relationship with each other, they need to get married before they are baptized."

The Antigua natives recited their vows, exchanged rings, and were pronounced husband and wife. The marriage was then sealed with a kiss, to thunderous applause from the congregation, assuring the young couple of their prayers and support. Then I baptized the newlyweds.

I think of another unusual baptism that I read about in Acts the 8th chapter. I don't know his name—nobody does. He was simply identified as *"an Ethiopian eunuch, an important official in charge of all the treasury of Candace, queen of the Ethiopians." (Acts 8:27)* The meeting of this Gentile with Philip, the evangelist, was surely orchestrated in heaven!

Here was a God-fearing Gentile proselyte who had gone to Jerusalem to worship and was on his way home to Ethiopia in his covered chariot. As the horses stirred up the sand, the man blew the dust off the scroll he was reading and puzzled over its meaning. He read aloud, as the ancients often did, or maybe he was reading to also benefit his driver.

The scroll from which he was reading was Isaiah's description of the Messiah. *"He was led like a sheep to the slaughter, and as a lamb before the shearer is silent, so He did not open his mouth. In His humiliation He was deprived of justice. Who can speak of His descendants? For His life was taken from the earth." (Acts 8:32-33)*

God sent a qualified teacher, Philip, who had just come from a revival in the city of Samaria. An angel of the Lord had told him, *"Go south to…the desert road that goes down from Jerusalem to Gaza." (Acts 8:26)* This was a divine appointment.

*"'Tell me, please, who is the prophet talking about, himself or someone else?' Then Philip began with that very passage of Scripture and told him the good news about Jesus. They came to some water and the eunuch said, 'Look, here is water. Why shouldn't I be baptized?'" (Acts 8:34-36)* Perhaps it was a small wadi in the desert, or a small ditch beside the road with a little water in it, (I've seen that) or it could have been a pool especially prepared by God for this very special occasion in the desert, but Philip baptized him, and he went on his way south to his home in Ethiopia.

After the Six-Day War in 1967, Israel began bringing back to their homeland thousands of Jews scattered in many countries around the world. One of those countries was Ethiopia. Recently found there was an ancient replica of the arc of the covenant. These Jews who were brought back to resettle in Israel, were, however, Jews who believed that the Messiah was Jesus. When they were brought back, Israel made them go through rituals to reconfirm their Jewish faith.

"But," they said, "We are more Jews than you, because we have kept all the Jewish laws and rituals, but *also* believe that the Messiah was Jesus." They insisted, "You can implant these things in our heads, but you can't take them out of our hearts."

Could it be that this Ethiopian eunuch that Philip baptized was the first one to bring the story of Jesus, the Messiah, to the African continent?

# 48

# Marriage Is Not For Children

*"A successful marriage takes work—hard work—but the more you put into it, the more you will get out of it."*

"I'D LIKE TO BRING my husband over to talk," I heard her say as I picked up the phone in my office, and in 20 minutes I heard them coming down the hall. I opened the door, and yes—she was "bringing" him. She was 6 feet tall, towering over his 5'8" frame. As I welcomed them in and offered them chairs, I heard her say, "Sit down." I did! And so did Chuck. She was thirty and he was twenty-two. I realized quickly that I was about to engage in an interesting session and decided that I would begin with some non-directive counseling.

"Yes, uh huh. Is that so? Uh huh." She did all the talking and most of it was a deluge of words which were verbally destroying him. He, in his chair, seemed to be sinking lower and lower, until I felt I must rescue him.

"Chuck, have you had time to analyze your problems?" Now I have heard many great and profound statements in my life. I have read Socrates, Plato, and Aristotle. But never have I heard more descriptive words than when Chuck answered me. He looked at her, starting at her feet and moving up the 6 feet to the top of her head—and muttered:

*"Pastor, I just think I bit off more than I can chew."* I had to agree with Chuck—but silently.

Chuck and his bride-to-be were probably happy as they walked down the wedding aisle months before. Almost all *weddings* are happy—it's the living together after the wedding that causes the problems. And why is that? Because too often the couple does not know the three essentials to bring to the marriage altar.

What are those three essentials, those vital characteristics which too many couples ignore?

1.  MATURITY   According to sociologists, there are five stages that a person goes through before he is ready for marriage:
    a.  Love for self: This is evidenced when a baby awakens in the middle of the night, hungry and wanting to be fed. He wants what he wants when he wants it.
    b.  Love for a parent: A baby is totally satisfied by the cuddling and love of the parent.
    c.  Love for the gang (friends of the same sex): A child's world has enlarged. He has playmates, friends and team members and has learned that he cannot always have his own way.
    d.  Love for <u>persons</u> of the opposite sex.
    e.  Love for one girl or one boy, who is put above everyone else, even one's self. Having experienced and understood each of these stages, someone ready for marriage realizes that self, parents, and friends cannot be put before the one true love. Marriage is for the mature.

2.  PURITY   Is it old-fashioned to come to the marriage bed a virgin? Is it possible in this day and time? Are there still young people who save their most personal and precious gift for their husband or wife, for their wedding night? Yes. And what are the benefits? There is no guilt, no fear of pregnancy, a trust in your mate to be faithful after marriage, and a peace in your heart that you are not disobedient to your Lord.

3.  FAITH   If going into partnership in a business requires faith in one's business partner, how much more does going into a

marriage relationship require faith, or trust, in one's marriage partner! This faith is best experienced when each has a personal faith in the Lord Jesus Christ and is growing closer to Him through the Word and prayer. Picture it this way: at the top of a triangle is the Lord. At the bottom left is the husband. At the bottom right is the wife. As each grows closer to the Lord, the two grow closer together. It always works!

It is true that marriage is a very beautiful relationship, because it was created in the heart of God for the joy of His greatest creation. There is nothing—business, other people, or self interests—that should come in to mar or disturb that relationship.

I think of a multi-millionaire who flew in a couple times from the Caribbean with his wife for marriage counseling. He told me of all his assets and how people depended on him for their livelihoods. His business demanded so much of his time that he had no time for his wife and she was "dying" of loneliness.

"I live out in the country, in the Redlands south of Miami," I said to him. "You remind me of what I saw on the way to work today. There is a very dilapidated house that I pass on my way to my church, with a broken down fence surrounding a small piece of barren land, on which a few chickens and ducks were pecking around for survival. The owners had thrown their cans, garbage, and scrap wood into a pile in the middle of the yard. And there, on top of that pile, was their billy goat. You know, you remind me of that goat. You are the king of your mountain."

As I said that, his wife began to cry. "I grew up on a farm in the north, without indoor plumbing," she said, "but I would rather live like that than without love and harmony in our home."

Most of you who read this are not living like this multi-millionaire, but there is always the danger in a marriage of putting business, other people, or self-interest ahead of your relationship with your spouse. May I give you four phrases that I beg you to use often:

"I love you."

"I was wrong."

"Please forgive me."

"May I help you?"

Then add the final words: "Let's serve God together."

A successful marriage takes work—hard work—but the more you put into it, the more you will get out of it. I am reminded of an experience I had as I stood behind a lady at an ATM machine in Miami. She put in her debit card and requested $10.00. A slip came out stating "insufficient funds." She turned to me puzzled and said, "It looks like any bank would have $10.00 in it." No, my dear lady, whether it's a bank or a marriage, you must put something into it to get something out—and the *more* you put into it, the more you will get out of it.

# 49

## Abortions or Adoptions?

*"We have always talked of adopting an Asian baby, even
before we had our own Devery and Kiley."*

IT WAS A WEDNESDAY night in early April of 1989, when our prayer
meeting group was engrossed in a big discussion on abortion and the
pro-life demonstrations at several abortion clinics in Miami. A young
Jamaican nurse suggested that if Christians are really serious about
stopping abortions, they ought to be willing to pay for moms to have
their babies and even help some families with the financial burdens of
adoption. "Would we—would you—be willing to do that?" Having
never had that particular question asked of me, although my church
family knew where I stood on abortion, I paused, and then answered,
"Yes, I believe we should be more willing to help, and I for one would
be willing to help pay the money necessary for someone else to adopt
a baby."

Little did I realize how soon I would commit myself to put action
behind those words.

I did not know that the previous Sunday night after church, our
daughter Tracie and husband Steve had been talking to Dr. Ted and

Pat Place on the parking lot as they were leaving. Ted was a Christian counselor and also arranged for many adoptions.

"I was talking with another nurse at South Miami Hospital," Tracie began, "and was telling her that we were not planning on having any more children. She said that she and her husband had also decided the same, a few years ago, but now had changed their minds and were trying to adopt."

"Yes," Ted began, "I offered that couple an Asian baby that is due soon, but they are really only interested in adopting a white baby. However, I have another couple who is planning to adopt the Asian infant."

"We have always talked of adopting an Asian baby, even before we had our own two girls, Devery and Kiley. Keep us in mind if you ever are working with another Asian family," Tracie said.

Although I knew nothing about that Sunday night conversation, Thursday I got a call from Ted Place asking me if I thought Tracie and Steve were serious about adopting an Asian baby. Remember, it was just *the night before* in prayer meeting when we discussed supporting more adoptions! Ted had just gotten a call *that morning*, he said, from the family who was planning to adopt this baby, saying they were backing out. (Could it be just "coincidence" that Tracie and Steve had unexpectedly talked with Ted just four days earlier?) I called Tracie, and of course her first response was, "Daddy, you know that there is no way Steve and I could afford the thousands of dollars involved in an adoption!"

"Tracie, if the Lord wants this baby to be in your home, then five thousand dollars—or five million dollars—would not be an obstacle."

Tracie, Steve, Mollie and I all agreed that we could not make this awesome decision literally over night—but it had to be made soon because the baby was due in a month. We tentatively set up the lawyer's meeting for Monday morning, feeling that we needed the weekend to think and pray earnestly about this decision. We all prayed and discussed and planned. Steve and Tracie wanted Mollie and me to be just as involved in the decision as they, since we would be putting out so much financially. After church on Sunday, we and Ted and Pat Place and the "children" went to a Chinese restaurant where we were able to talk together and find out a little more about the baby's history.

On Tuesday the Lord gave Tracie a wonderful assurance that He was really with them, guiding them and listening to their earnest prayers of the last few days. When she went to the mailbox, she found a beautiful note from friends of their high school years. Basically it said that each week they pull out one of the Christmas cards from all they received, and then they pray for the family that sent that card.

"Daddy, this very particular week, they chose *our* card and were praying for *us*, whatever special needs we might have," Tracie said. "What a beautiful way for the Lord to show that He is guiding us."

BRADY IS NOW A student at Georgia Tech, a leader in his church youth group, and a grandson any granddad would be proud of. I don't know what the future holds for him but the Psalmist said, "*If the Lord delights in a man's way, He makes his steps firm; though he stumble, he will not fall, for the Lord upholds him with His hand.*" *(Psalm 37:23-24)*

Most grandparents cannot be involved in their grandchildren's lives from before the beginning, as we were in Brady's. However there is one way, regardless of distance or family relationships, that all of us grandparents can make an indelible mark in our grandchildren's lives. That is by prayer. We *must* pray for them daily and let them know that we are praying for them. In the world they face, their only hope is Jesus.

# 50

## Bernadette

*"Just because he opened a door for you,
it doesn't mean he wants to marry you."*

I WANT YOU TO meet two of the most beautiful people I have ever known. I first saw them one Sunday morning seated halfway down the rows in our church, she in her wheelchair and he on the bench beside her. Immediately following the service I went to meet them and made an appointment to visit in their home the following Thursday. From our first visit, Mollie and I and Jeff and Bernadette Todd became "forever friends." She was born in Jamaica with infantile muscular dystrophy and when she was five years old she overheard her parents talking and crying behind a partially closed door. The doctor had told them that their little girl could not live beyond eight years old, and so day after day, year after year, she lived with this secret—and dreaded to see her eighth birthday.

"Bernadette," I said to her one day, "you have a testimony that needs to be shared. I would like for you to speak to our church family, and I want you to be on our television program on ABC channel 10 for me to interview you." After that program, I knew she had not only a tremendous testimony but a God-given gift of communication.

Having been seen on television, and having given her testimony in our church, she began receiving calls from churches, schools, and clubs, asking her to speak and share her testimony. And that is what she does: <u>simply shares her testimony</u>. Over the years we have watched her disease progress as more and more of her muscle strength leaves, till today she has only the use of one finger that can move the lever on her wheelchair. But, her ministry has also progressed. She faithfully continues doing what God has called her to do. As she tells her story again and again, she always gives an opportunity for people in the audience to pray a prayer of commitment of their lives to Jesus, the One whom she loves and so faithfully serves.

Just as gifted is her humble, godly husband Jeff, who joyfully cares for her in loving and sacrificial service. Never, never have I seen such beauty! Never have I seen such a servant's heart. Hours before daylight he begins his job of cleaning and purifying swimming pools, and then he is home by 11:00 to get Bernadette up and dressed for the day. She plans the meals—he prepares them and feeds her. Always her hair looks nice, her nails are polished, and their small house is always clean and in order. As he pushes her for their evening walk, they are a "breath of fresh air" to the neighbors.

Jeff and Bernadette met at Dade Junior College when he *opened a door* for her to get her wheelchair through. She went home that day and told her mother she had met the boy she was going to marry, but her mother said, "Bernadette, just because he opened a door for you, it doesn't mean he wants to marry you!" When she asked him to go out to eat with her and three girlfriends for her birthday, he said he would, if she would join him for church on Sunday. She did, and there she met the Master.

Her heart has long been for missions. The long plane trips and full ministry schedules are very difficult for her, but in the past few months she has given her testimony in Brazil, Bolivia, El Salvador, Peru, and Argentina, at schools, pastors' conferences, women's meetings, churches, and orphanages. She often gives toys to the children and shares tears with the hurting. And always she tells what God has done for her.

Bernadette and Jeff have been especially blessed by Tony, a young man from Bolivia who serves with them as cameraman, translator, and right hand to Jeff. Thank you to those three for *rolling through* the doors that God is continually opening.

*"The Lord is my strength and my song; He has become my salvation. He is my God, and I will praise Him, my father's God and I will exalt Him."*
*(Exodus 15:2)*

# 51

## South Africa's Pastor John

*"We heard of Pastor John's vision for the future
and gradually that vision became ours."*

HE WAS A TALL, soft-spoken man, with a graying beard and a kindly smile—and I knew at once that I wanted to know him better. The Miami Baptist Association and the Baptist churches of Cape Town, South Africa had formed a partnership in prayer and ministry. Today we were hosting the Cape Town pastors in a get-acquainted luncheon in downtown Miami. When the host home assignments were made, I was tremendously pleased that this man, Pastor John Pascoe, was assigned to me to be our houseguest. I would also shuttle him to the various appointments during the week.

In our conversations around the table at home, Mollie and I were fascinated as John told of his church, Westridge Baptist in Mitchell's Plain, of its multifaceted ministry in the community, and of its mission outreach to other countries in Africa. We heard of the small home for orphan boys, the house provided for three widows, and the weekly dinners provided for the hungry. He told us of the gymnasium, called the F.R.O.G. Center, built by a group from North Carolina. This structure was built not next to the church, but a short distance away, across from an elementary school and next to a Muslim grocery. It was a building for the community, housing also an office, a kitchen, and three rooms for day care children.

We listened as he told us of the racial and cultural makeup of South Africa, and particularly of Cape Town. There are three very distinct groups: the *Blacks,* who are in control, the *Whites,* who are second in status, and the *Coloreds,* who are at the bottom socially. It was these latter ones with whom we would soon be privileged to work and share Christ's love.

We heard of Pastor John's vision for the future and gradually that vision became ours.

"What could we do," we inquired, "to help your work in Mitchell's Plain?" His first response was the need for Vacation Bible School, not for the church, but for the children in the community. This could be held during the public schools' spring break the last week of September. Since the F.R.O.G. Center was open to all, Muslim and Christian alike, and since there was a good working relationship with the elementary school across the street, Pastor John told us we could use the F.R.O.G. Center for the assemblies and the public school for the classes. (Often the public school used the F.R.O.G. Center for its large programs as the school facility had only classrooms.)

Pastor John Pascoe went back with the other pastors to Cape Town, South Africa, but he left us with a vision and mission that would forever change us and the lives of many others. The year was 2002. Certainly now, we must apply to ourselves the meaning of F.R.O.G. (Fully Relying On God) if we were ever to do the task that God was leading us to do in Cape Town. To reinforce that in our minds, ladies in Miami made 400 stuffed calico frogs for gifts to the children in Bible School. We must "fully rely on God."

After months of preparation, and with all of our Vacation Bible School material with us, seventeen of us made the long trip from Miami to Cape Town, to teach the Word of God to children from first grade through teens. Year after year we return, always with some new workers, but also with many of the same workers, who are compelled to return by the drawing chords of love for the hundreds of beautiful children who desperately need to hear the stories of God's love. Two of those workers are our daughters, Tonie and Tracie, who every year return to teach the third and fourth graders in classrooms that are overflowing, sometimes without room for desks, but with 70 children sitting on the floor.

AN ORPHANAGE FOR CHILDREN affected by AIDS became a burden for Pastor John and his church. Thousands of young people in South Africa have parents who have died of AIDS or are too sick to care for them. The church bought a small house adjacent to the church, with room for eight children. The remodeling was almost finished when our 2003 mission team arrived for Vacation Bible School. Mollie and I and our daughters joined in furnishing the little house, and the youth of Miami Springs Baptist Church, where I was then Interim Pastor, made quilts for the four bunk beds. The next year we were surprised to hear they had named it "Molly's Place," and I held the first baby girl, Molly, who came when she was just eight days old.

WHEN PASTOR JOHN AND his wife Evelyn came to visit us at our new home in Penney Farms Retirement Community in north Florida, I showed him the PET (Personal Energy Transportation) shop here. Some of us who live here enjoy working to build carts for people who have lost their legs, mostly by land mines in war-torn Third World countries. John became very interested in the carts and realized that many in South Africa and neighboring countries could benefit from them. His next visit to Penney Farms was for the specific purpose of learning in the shop how to construct the PET carts.

Because of the generous gift of $15,000 by a couple on our mission team, Pastor John took it as a leading of the Lord to go into production of the carts there in Cape Town. With the help of a few of his men, he made a fiberglass mold and began production in a corner of the F.R.O.G. Center.

Pastor John presenting the carts to the First Lady of Mozambique

Pastor John had, for sometime, a burden for the neighboring country of Mozambique, which had suffered through years of war. More than 120,000 people of that country had lost a limb to land mines, and he saw an opportunity to help. He contacted the Consulate of Mozambique in Cape Town, requesting a visa to the country, so he and his helpers could deliver these carts. The Consulate was thrilled. "You need no visa as I will personally meet you at the border and will take you and your men to deliver your carts to the First Lady of Mozambique." The National Television of Mozambique filmed this presentation for the entire nation to see, as the carts were presented to the first eleven recipients. With the myriad of benefits from independent mobility, these recipients now have a new purpose for living.

*"THIS IS A TRUSTWORTHY saying. And I want you to stress these things, so that those who have trusted in God may be careful to devote themselves to doing what is good. These things are excellent and profitable for everyone."* (Titus 3:8)

MY FATHER LOST BOTH legs to diabetes and was unable to work. I remember that someone made him a little flat board with skate wheels on it, intending for him to sit on Main Street in Portsmouth, Virginia and receive donations. He became too sick to do this, dying at the age of forty-eight, when I was a junior in high school.

# 52

## Greater Dreams

*"May your dreams be greater than your memories."*

I FIRST HEARD THOSE words from Pastor John Pascoe, but it became our prayer when Mollie and I moved from Miami to Penney Farms Retirement Community in north Florida in December of 2005. We have had wonderful memories, some of which I have written about in this book, but there will be many more which lie ahead that I will never write about. We will yet experience God, yet see miracles happen, yet taste new "food" from His Word, and yet encourage fellow travelers on the road. He is a living God, yesterday, today, and forever.

When I was a young pastor at Waddill Street Baptist Church in McKinney, Texas, I directed one summer a countywide youth camp at Lake Lavon. I have always felt that young people and children can perhaps be reached for Christ easier in a camp setting than in a church. One of my young fellow pastors, Wilson Davis, was playing softball with the youth. He hit the ball, ran to first base, second base—and he died on third base. Yes, he physically died on third base.

I don't want to die on third base. I'm running for Home base. You may be saying, "I'm tired—I've done my work—I'm not well—I taught kids in Sunday School—I don't have time—I don't know what

I can do." As long as you are on third base, there is still more "running" before you get Home. The "running" may be from a rocking chair with a prayer list in front of you, but keep "running." It may be from a chair by your phone inviting people to your church or Bible study, but keep "running." It may be in a restaurant with a word of encouragement to a weary waitress. "We always have prayer before our meals," I said to our waitress one evening. "Do you have something you would like us to pray about?" "Yes," she responded, and she shared a burden of a sick daughter. So if you are on third base, keep "running"—until your foot touches Home plate.

One of many quotations written in the front of one of our Bibles is this: "*Life has many disasters and reversals, but only one tragedy: to grow old without growing up; to die a withered acorn, without ever having known what it is to be an oak tree.*" But many who read this book *are* oak trees, strong, sturdy oak trees that have weathered many seasons and many storms. So since you are an oak tree, keep producing acorns (little as they may seem) that will grow into more oak trees—that will produce more acorns.

"*MAY YOUR DREAMS BE greater than your memories.*" We wondered just how God would answer that prayer that had become ours. What would God have for us to do here at Penney Farms and in the "world" around us? We loved young people. Would the Lord still give us some other opportunities to influence young lives—or were we too old? We did not have long to wait. A couple weeks after we moved into our cottage, there was a knock at our door. We had never met him, but when we invited John in, he excitedly told us about FLYCA (Florida Youth Challenge Academy), thinking we might be interested in looking into it. It is a program for at-risk young people between the ages of sixteen and eighteen, high school drop-outs who lack direction about their future. The Academy is operated, he told us, through a cooperative agreement between the National Guard and the Governor of Florida. Each class of 100 to 140 cadets spends 5 ½ months at near-by Camp Blanding in a strict military environment where all will work towards a high school diploma or GED. After the graduation here, there is another 12 months in the off-campus placement that each cadet has chosen, working with his mentor. He or she will get a job, go to college or technical school, or join the military.

We were immediately interested, and we enlisted helpers for a ministry every other Saturday night. Each session includes one hour of Bible study and one hour of worship with music, chalk art, and a message or testimony. It later became my responsibility to staff every Saturday night with leaders and workers (including youth) from near-by churches. Our reward is to pray with many hurting kids and see lives changed, as many receive Christ as their Savior and follow that decision with baptism in a near-by church.

SOMETIME LATER, ANOTHER MINISTRY opened to us, this time in another age bracket.

"I have an idea for a ministry to senior citizens that I think the four of us would enjoy and which would be an inspiration and encouragement to many." These were Dolly Koch's words as she laid out the plan. Charlie and she, Mollie and I discussed and prayed about its possibilities. Years ago in Miami, when Charlie had been my associate pastor, Dolly had begun the monthly associational senior luncheons in different churches, which is still a very successful program there in Dade County. We began now by sending out letters and brochures, and soon we were getting invitations from churches all over north and central Florida to come to their senior luncheons. As "Seniors Serving Seniors," we present a one-hour program including humor ("old folks" need to laugh), Charlie's piano playing, Dolly's inspirational singing, my brief devotional, and Mollie's black light chalk art.(www.seniorsservingseniors.org)

MANY CHURCHES TODAY AFFORD the opportunity for senior adults to participate in both local or distant mission opportunities. After two days of travel in our church minibus from north Florida, about twenty senior citizens in our mission group arrived at our destination. Ambassadors for Christ Camp is a beautiful retreat tucked away in the mountains of lovely West Virginia. We led a three-day revival at the local Baptist church in Huntersville, and we held a meeting in the men's prison, with the inmates participating with their prison chapel choir. Across the street is another prison, of sorts, but with no fence around it and no locks on the doors. It is called "The Birthing Center," a place where a woman prisoner can stay with her newborn baby until the child reaches eighteen months of age. These months are credited as part of the woman's sentence. After the eighteen months, if the mother's prison term is not finished, she goes back to complete it, and the baby is cared for by a family member. There is no need for fences or locked doors in this prison, since the mother and baby "bonding" is all the security that is necessary.

Our ladies' quilting club in our home church supplied beautiful and colorful baby quilts, one for each mother to choose. She could also choose clothes and other baby supplies. Our men were busy cooking hamburgers and hot dogs on the grill in the backyard of the Birthing Center. It was a special day for them and us as we concluded it with a song and a short message from God's Word.

HOW BLESSED MOLLIE AND I are, as octogenarians, to continue daily the exciting adventure of following our Lord. As long as doors keep opening, we plan on running through them as fast as our legs will carry us!

*"'For I know the plans I have for you,' declares the Lord, 'plans to prosper you and not to harm you, plans to give you hope and a future.'"*
*(Jeremiah 29:11)*

May *your* dreams be greater than your memories.

On to greater dreams

# Anti-Blackness at School

Creating Affirming Educational
Spaces for African American
Students

Joi A. Spencer and Kerri Ullucci

Foreword by Tyrone C. Howard

## TEACHERS COLLEGE PRESS

TEACHERS COLLEGE | COLUMBIA UNIVERSITY
NEW YORK AND LONDON

Published by Teachers College Press,® 1234 Amsterdam Avenue, New York, NY 10027

Copyright © 2022 by Teachers College, Columbia University

Front cover design by adam bohannon. Photo by tomertu / Adobe Stock.

*Library of Congress Cataloging-in-Publication Data is available at loc.gov*

ISBN 978-0-8077-6756-6 (paper)
ISBN 978-0-8077-6757-3 (hardcover)
ISBN 978-0-8077-8133-3 (ebook)

Printed on acid-free paper
Manufactured in the United States of America

*To our dear friend and teacher, Mike Rose, who passed away as we were writing this book: Your fingerprints are all over our work. We stand on the shoulders of a giant. We love, miss, and thank you.*

# Contents

# Series Foreword

This book is being published at a time when there is a backlash against the national reckoning on race that took place in the United States after the killings of African Americans, including George Floyd and Breonna Taylor, by police (Cobb, 2020). In *White Rage: The Unspoken Truth of Our Racial Divide*, the historian Carol Anderson (2016) poignantly describes how after every period in which African Americans made racial progress—such as the Civil War, the Emancipation Proclamation, and the civil rights movement of the 1950s and 1960s—White rage emerged to halt the gains that Blacks had made. One manifestation of White rage today is the organized movement by conservatives to halt the teaching about race in the schools by labelling these efforts "critical race theory" (Kendi, 2021). Christopher F. Rufo, a conservative scholar at the Manhattan Institute, envisioned a way to mobilize parents against teaching about race in the schools by deliberately and misleadingly calling these lessons "critical race theory" (Fortin, 2021; Wallace-Wells, 2021). Rufo's strategy has been effective in mobilizing parents, school boards, and state legislatures against teaching about race in the schools (Cineas, 2020). Republican-dominated legislatures in many states have passed laws that ban or restrict the ways in which race is taught in the schools. Thirty-seven states considered bills or took other steps to restrict the teaching of race in the schools between January and June 2021 (Schwartz, 2021). One hundred and seventy-five bills have been introduced or pre-filed in 40 state legislatures that restrict how teachers and students interact about topics related to race and sex since 2021. Thirteen of these bills have become law in 11 states (New York Times Editorial Board, 2022).

During the current resurgence of institutionalized racism and White backlash, this book provides an in-depth and exhaustive depiction of anti-Blackness in U.S. schools. Spencer and Ullucci make a persuasive and compelling case that anti-Blackness is institutionalized and pervasive within American schools. They distinguish *anti-Blackness* and *racism*: "We want to be clear that racism is a different, although related, phenomenon to anti-Blackness. Racism is a system of advantage based on race. Racism is a wider concept, under which anti-Blackness falls" (page 3). "Anti-Black racism is a particular form of racism that is historic, systemic, and rooted in antipathy towards the *Black* community" (page 3). The authors provide readers with explicit, egregious, and telling examples of how anti-Black racism differs from other forms of structural and cultural racism because of the ways it victimizes and dehumanizes African Americans.

Spencer and Ullucci describe, in complex and meticulous detail, the ways in which anti-Blackness is manifested in the institutional and cultural structures of schools and in the attitudes and behaviors of teachers and administrators. The manifestations of anti-Blackness in schools portrayed by the authors include the ways in which the school curriculum marginalizes the history and culture of African Americans; the deficit views of African American students and families that many teachers and school leaders internalize; the characterization of Black students as having abundant athletic skills and abilities but low levels of academic knowledge, skills, and capabilities; and what the authors call the "adultification" of Black youth, which means viewing and treating Black students as adults rather than as children. The authors point out, for example, that Black preschoolers (age 4) made up almost half of out-of-school suspensions for their age group in a report published by National Public Radio in 2014 (p. 56). Spencer and Ullucci describe how the adultifiction of Black youth results in the overpolicing of Black bodies, including their hair, clothing, and behavior.

The major purpose of the Multicultural Education Series is to provide preservice educators, practicing educators, graduate students, scholars, and policymakers with an interrelated and comprehensive set of books that summarizes and analyzes important research, theory, and practice related to the education of ethnic, racial, cultural, and linguistic groups in the United States and the education of mainstream students about diversity. The dimensions of multicultural education, developed by Banks and described in the *Handbook of Research on Multicultural Education* (Banks, 2004), *The Routledge International Companion to Multicultural Education* (Banks, 2009), and the *Encyclopedia of Diversity in Education* (Banks, 2012), provide the conceptual framework for the development of the publications in the Series. The dimensions are content integration, the knowledge construction process, prejudice reduction, equity pedagogy, and an empowering institutional culture and social structure. The books in the Multicultural Education Series provide research, theoretical, and practical knowledge about the behaviors and learning characteristics of students of color (Conchas & Vigil, 2012; Lee, 2007), language-minority students (Gándara & Hopkins, 2010; Valdés, 2001; Valdés et al., 2011), low-income students (Cookson, 2013; Gorski, 2018), multiracial youth (Joseph & Briscoe-Smith, 2021; Mahiri, 2017), and other minoritized population groups, such as students who speak different varieties of English (Charity Hudley & Mallinson, 2011) and LGBTQ youth (Mayo, 2022).

Anti-Black racism, which is a form of *institutional and structural racism*, is the conceptual and organizing framework for this book. Other books in the Multicultural Education Series focus on institutional and structural racism and ways to reduce it in educational institutions. These books in the Series reinforce and amplify the messages conveyed in this book: Özlem Sensoy and Robin DiAngelo (2017), *Is Everyone Really Equal? An Introduction to Key Concepts in Social Justice Education* (Second Edition); Gary Howard (2016), *We Can't Teach What We Don't Know: White Teachers, Multiracial Schools* (Third Edition); Zeus Leonardo (2013), *Race Frameworks: A Multidimensional Theory of Racism and Education*; Daniel Solórzano and Lindsay Pérez Huber (2020), *Racial Microaggressions: Using Critical Race Theory in Education to Recognize and Respond to Everyday Racism*; and Gloria Ladson-Billings (2021), *Critical Race Theory in Education: A Scholar's Journey.*

The introduction and the first three chapters of this book consist of extensive documentation and discussion of the ways in which anti-Blackness is manifested in the curriculum and institutional culture of U.S. schools. Chapters 4 through 6 describe actions that teachers and administrators can take to respond to anti-Blackness in schools by creating what Spencer and Ullucci call *Black-affirming spaces*. Using a concept adapted from bell hooks (2001), Spencer and Ullucci describe *homespaces* as spaces that "provide safety and nurturance to Black people" and "do not ask Black students to choose between being educated or being Black" (p. 89).

The authors provide readers a comprehensive and compelling example of Black-affirming spaces by describing the STEM Summer Academies, 1- or 2-week-long programs for middle and high school students focused on academic achievement in science, technology, engineering, and mathematics. Spencer and Ulucci document how the Summer Academies use students' funds of knowledge and cultural resources to create robust, motivating, and culturally affirming STEM learning experiences and opportunities. A noteworthy component of the Summer Academies is descriptions of their STEM journeys by the counselors in the program who have similar cultural backgrounds to most of the students. Teachers, curriculum specialists, and other educational practitioners will find the authors' discussion and examples of Black-affirming possibilities and spaces, such as the vivid and engaging descriptions of the STEM Summer Academies, welcome and powerful examples to emulate in their own schools and communities.

—James A. Banks

## REFERENCES

Anderson, C. (2016). *White rage: The unspoken truth of our racial divide.* Bloomsbury.
Banks, J. A. (2004). Multicultural education: Historical development, dimensions, and practice. In J. A. Banks & C. A. M. Banks (Eds.), *Handbook of research on multicultural education* (pp. 3–29). Jossey-Bass.

Banks, J. A. (Ed.). (2009). *The Routledge international companion to multicultural education*. Routledge.

Banks, J. A. (2012). Multicultural education: Dimensions of. In J. A. Banks (Ed.), *Encyclopedia of diversity in education* (vol. 3, pp. 1538–1547). Sage Publications.

Charity Hudley, A. H., & Mallinson, C. (2011). *Understanding language variation in U. S. schools*. Teachers College Press.

Cineas, F. (2020, Sept. 24). Critical race theory, and Trump's war on it, explained. *Vox.* https://www.vox.com/2020/9/24/21451220/critical-race-theory-diversity-training -trump

Cobb, J. (2020, June 14). An American spring of reckoning. *The New Yorker.* https:// www.newyorker.com/magazine/2020/06/22/an-american-spring-of-reckoning

Conchas, G. Q., & Vigil, J. D. (2012). *Streetsmart schoolsmart: Urban poverty and the education of adolescent boys*. Teachers College Press.

Cookson, P. W., Jr. (2013). *Class rules: Exposing inequality in American high schools*. Teachers College Press.

Fortin, J. (2021, Nov. 8). Critical race theory: A brief history. *The New York Times.* https://www.nytimes.com/article/what-is-critical-race-theory.html

Gándara, P., & Hopkins, M. (Eds.). (2010). *Forbidden language: English language learners and restrictive language policies*. Teachers College Press.

Gorski, P. C. (2018). *Reaching and teaching students in poverty: Strategies for erasing the opportunity gap* (2nd ed.). Teachers College Press.

hooks, b. (2001). *Salvation: Black people and love*. Perennial.

Howard, G. (2016). *We can't teach what we don't know: White teachers, multiracial schools* (3rd ed.). Teachers College Press.

Howard, T. C. (2014) *Black male(d): Peril and promise in the education of African American males*. Teachers College Press.

Joseph, R. L., & Briscoe-Smith, A. (2021). *Generation mixed goes to school: Radically listening to multiracial kids*. Teachers College Press.

Kendi, I. X. (2021, July 9). There is no debate over critical race theory. *The Atlantic.* https://www.theatlantic.com/ideas/archive/2021/07/opponents-critical-race-theory -are-arguing-themselves/619391/

Ladson-Billings, G. (2021). *Critical race theory in education: A scholar's journey*. Teachers College Press.

Lee, C. D. (2007). *Culture, literacy, and learning: Taking bloom in the midst of the whirlwind*. Teachers College Press.

Leonardo, Z. (2013). *Race frameworks: A multicultural theory of racism and education*. Teachers College Press.

Mahiri, J. (2017). *Deconstructing race: Multicultural education beyond the colorbind*. Teachers College Press.

Mayo, C. (2022). *LGBTQ youth and education: Policies and practices* (2nd ed.). Teachers College Press.

New York Times Editorial Board. (2022, March 19). America has a free speech problem. *The New York Times.* https://www.nytimes.com/2022/03/18/opinion/cancel -culture-free-speech-poll.html?searchResultPosition=1

Schwartz, S. (2021, June 11). Map: Where critical race theory is under attack. *Education Week.* https://www.edweek.org/policy-politics/map-where-critical-race-theory -is-under-attack/2021/06

Sensoy, Ö., & DiAngelo, R. (2017). *Is everyone really equal? An introduction to key concepts in social justice education* (2nd ed.). Teachers College Press.

Solórzano, D., & Huber, L. P. (2020). *Racial microaggressions: Using critical race theory to recognize and respond to everyday racism.* Teachers College Press.

Valdés, G. (2001). *Learning and not learning English: Latino students in American schools.* Teachers College Press.

Valdés, G., Capitelli, S., & Alvarez, L. (2011). *Latino children learning English: Steps in the journey.* Teachers College Press.

Wallace-Wells, B. (2021). How a conservative activist invented the conflict over critical race theory. *The New Yorker.* https://www.newyorker.com/news/annals-of-inquiry/how-a-conservative-activist-invented-the-conflict-over-critical-race-theory

# Foreword

As more energies have been centered on antiracist efforts across the country, many educational advocates have applauded the long-overdue push to get serious about engaging with and, ultimately, dismantling racism in U.S. schools. As the nation's school-age populations continue to become increasingly diverse, there is a desperate need to finally get real about race. Getting real about race means recognizing the unprecedented racial and ethnic demographics that are present in today's schools and that will only increase in the foreseeable future. So, in short, we are tasked with teaching more students of color and fewer White students. Getting real about race means acknowledging systemic racism, examining the effects of White supremacy, and realizing how power and privilege manifest in schools and society at multiple levels. Getting real about race also means going beyond superficial antiracism efforts that are cloaked in the rhetoric of colorblindness and protected by institutional silence in the face of blatant mistreatment of students of color. We have to recognize that one-size-fits-all interventions do not work; they fail to interrogate racism at individual and institutional levels. To be clear, addressing and examining racism has the potential to radically transform the way that students of color experience schools. However, antiracism efforts alone cannot suffice in this moment. What is frequently absent from the antiracism framework is the perniciousness of anti-Black racism. Education scholar Chezare Warren describes anti-Blackness as "an invisible cultural logic that urges a deep disdain for blackness and Black life. It actively shades how one *reads* Black bodies, and no one is exempt from having internalized anti-blackness. . . . Anti-blackness casts Black people as inhuman, lacking emotion or intellect" (Warren, 2021, p. 8). It is this deeply ingrained logic of Black being bad, Black being less than, Black being unworthy of time, love, care and attention, that Joi Spencer and Kerri Ullucci take on in this important work. To be clear, data across the educational spectrum unpack the deeply troubling manner in which Black youth experience schools. Black youth are more likely to be overpunished and overdisciplined, more likely to be placed with inexperienced teachers and in overcrowded classrooms, less likely to graduate from college, and less likely to be placed on career and college tracks (Howard, 2020). Needless to say, anti-Blackness is alive and well in schools all across the country. The challenge is dismantling anti-Blackness and uncovering the insidious way in which it is ingrained in public life, everyday thinking, policies, and procedures in the wider society, and in practices, policies, and curriculum in schools. It is essential to note that anti-Blackness is birthed, fostered, and maintained in homes, neighborhoods, courtrooms, playgrounds, boardrooms, lending institutions, and schools all across the United States. If antiracism advocates are serious about eradicating racism, there needs to be an explicit and unapologetic focus on anti-Blackness. Spencer and Ullucci boldly lay out a blueprint based on theory, research, and solutions that offer us a path forward. Just as anti-Blackness is learned, it can and must be unlearned. However, the challenge in unlearning anti-Blackness rests with the sobering reality that the overwhelming number of today's classroom teachers are White; the majority of school leaders, board members, and superintendents are White as well. To ask or expect anti-Blackness to be dismantled in a White-dominated culture is to demand something nearly impossible. According to Yancy (2016), Whiteness is oppressive and serves as the culprit of exclusion, derailment, segregation, policing, surveillance, and brutality toward Black Americans. In essence, Whiteness thrives in the midst of anti-Blackness, and often schools are the breeding grounds for this state of racial discontent for countless Black children.

The fact that the mere presence of Black bodies poses a fundamental threat and fear to many educators is vexing in this moment. The impulses to police, scrutinize, surveil, and control Black bodies in many schools and classrooms across the country are manifestations of anti-Blackness. The irony to this reality is rooted in the idea that schools (at least in theory) are supposed to serve as places that nurture, care for, protect, and affirm all students who enter schools on a daily basis. However, far too many Black children experience just the opposite at the hands of the very adults who are supposed to be there as educational protectors and providers of safety, nurturing, and care while in school.

Spencer and Ullucci make it crystal clear at the outset of this book that "Anti-Blackness is all around and unseen. It is clear as day and carefully hidden" (p. 1). It is this fact that must be confronted if we are truly committed to creating antiracist learning environments. Talking to Black students about how they often feel seen as "Others" highlights the depth of anti-Blackness in many schools. Talking to Black students in predominately Black schools who lament the lack of resources, funding, and adequate materials to learn speaks of the breadth of anti-Blackness. Talking to Black students in racially mixed schools where they are the minority and understanding how their language, bodies, hair, and ways of expression constantly are under the White gaze that tells them they are different and "less than" demonstrates the deep harm of anti-Blackness. Noting how academic "slide" has harmed Black students most during the COVID-19 pandemic demonstrates how anti-Blackness manifests itself when it comes to who has the least opportunities to learn

(Horsford et al, 2021). The dimensions and displays of anti-Blackness are often obscured, even invisible, to many, but painfully part of the day-to-day realities of many Black students as they seek to merely experience joy in the name of learning. The courageous stance that Spencer and Ullucci take is laudable because they make it abundantly clear that the diversity, equity, and inclusion efforts that have become widespread in schools across the nation are not enough in this moment. Moreover, they contend that until power imbalances and White supremacy are front and center of our reform efforts, schools will continue to uphold anti-Blackness. In short, nibbling on the edges of what ails millions of Black students becomes part and parcel of the problem. A refusal to listen and learn from the persistent ways that Black youth are deemed "problems," how they are frequently adultified, how their excellence is often labeled as "surprising," or flat-out apathy from "caring" teachers, keep anti-Blackness alive and well. As readers engage in this work, there will be obvious disbelief or dismissal from some, or there will be minimizing of the concepts, examples, and iterations that are beautifully highlighted in this work. As is to be expected, when anti-Blackness is highlighted, often Whiteness manifests in order to deny its existence, victim-blame, or offer class-based explanations. The type of behavior that Luke Wood and Frank Harris (2021) call "racelighting" is another manner in which anti-Blackness manifests in schools. Let's tell Black students that what they are experiencing is not real and does not exist, that they are overreacting, and that the real problem is their behaviors, attitudes, and efforts, or even worse, just made up in their minds. A different discourse must unfold, a more robust set of efforts have to be put in place. How do we act with courage and conviction? How can education scholars, practitioners, and policymakers recognize the complicit role that their silence plays in the maintenance of anti-Blackness? Moreover, there is a need for more of our White colleagues and coworkers to play a more important role in being vocal, active, and outspoken about the damage anti-Blackness does to everyone in schools, Black and non-Black students. Will Smith and colleagues (2011) have spoken about how racial battle fatigue does extensive damage to people of color in education spaces. Spencer and Ullucci call for action in this work, and not merely superficial action, but deep, structural change action that examines policies, practices, procedures, and people in school settings that frequently do irreparable harm to Black children. Let us be clear: This work is not for the faint of heart, not for the thin-skinned, and not for those who are closed to healthy, honest self-reflection about the roles that they may play in creating or maintaining harmful environments for Black students to learn. The summer of 2020 has been labeled a "racial reckoning" in this nation's history, as millions of people nationwide engaged in protests around the deaths of George Floyd and Breonna Taylor. Chants of "Black Lives Matter" were heard not only in the streets, but in organizations and institutions alike. The commitment to end systemic racism was also a call that many made. Schools can play transformative roles in this effort to create something different, or they can be complicit. Which path will we take?

—Tyrone C. Howard
University of California, Los Angeles

## REFERENCES

Horsford, S. D., Cabral, L., Touloukian, C., Parks, S., Smith, P. A., McGhee, C., Qadir, F., Lester, D., & Jacobs, J. (2021). *Black education in the wake of COVID-19 and systemic racism: Toward a theory of change and action*. Black Education Research Collective, Teachers College, Columbia University.

Howard, T. C. (2020). *Why race and culture matter in schools* (2nd ed.). Teachers College Press.

Smith, W. A., Hung, M., & Franklin, J. D. (2011). Racial battle fatigue and the Mis-Education of Black men: Racial microaggressions, societal problems, and environmental stress. *Journal of Negro Education, 80*(1), 63–82.

Warren, C. A. (2021). *About centering possibility in Black education*. Teachers College Press.

Wood, L., & Harris, F. (2021, February 21). Racelighting: A prevalent version of gaslighting facing people of color. *Diverse Issues in Higher Education*. https://www.diverseeducation.com/opinion/article/15108651/racelighting-a-prevalent-version-of-gaslighting-facing-people-of-color

Yancy, G. (2016). *Black bodies, White gazes: The continuing significance of race in America* (2nd ed.). Rowman & Littlefield.

# Acknowledgments

From the outset we leaned on teachers and colleagues to provide us with feedback on our writing; we wanted so much to get this right! We were fortunate to have many people reading with us as we wrote. We thank Princess Bomba, Jennifer Raphael-Guzman, Elsa Wiehe, Barbara Spencer Dunn, and Derek Michael for their time, ideas and encouragement.

A special thank you to Tyrone Howard, who has been watching out for us for over 20 years. We value your work, your mentorship and your support.

A thank you to Bruce Marlowe, for his support and feedback on our book proposal. He is an expert editor and a kind friend.

## FROM KERRI

A thank you to the Foundation to Promote Scholarship and Teaching at Roger Williams University, which provided me with time to write in the midst of a pandemic.

To Andre and Atticus, who knew how important this was and are old enough to give me time. I hope you will grow into men who see the harm of racism and work against it.

## FROM JOI

Thank you to my family, my foundation. You taught me to value education and to treasure it as freedom itself. Thank you for giving me the time and space to pursue my dreams. I offer gratitude to the National Science Foundation for their funding of our STEM and STEAM work as well as to the University of San Diego and the San Diego Foundation for investing in this work. I am deeply grateful to my research partners, Drs. Odesma Dalrymple and Perla Myers. When you love what you do, you never work a day in your life.

To you, Mom. You are our roots. May this offering in some way honor your many sacrifices. To Marques, Myles, Maliyah, and Myah, you are our wings. May these words remind you of all that has been given for you to live free, and encourage you to go and do the same for others. To the Rock of Ages. There are simply not enough words to express my thanks.

# Where We've Been
# (We've Been Here Before)

We watched the inauguration of President Joe Biden and Vice President Kamala Harris together, with MSNBC and texts closing the 3,000 miles between us. With Kerri in Rhode Island and Joi in San Diego, we witnessed history inch ahead. We were struck by how plain it is that for every step towards racial justice (the elections of President Barack Obama and Vice President Harris), we take many steps back (a racially fueled insurrection, the violence in Charlottesville). While we cheered the effervescence of Amanda Gorman's poetry and appreciated seeing people in power who look like us, we were also aware that the National Mall was *empty*. Military personnel ringed the grounds, a silent reminder of the racism that had overwhelmed Washington, D.C., the week before. White supremacy was on display again, this time via an insurrection at the Capitol, showing yet again how anti-Blackness operates throughout our society.

And so it goes in the United States.

Anti-Blackness is all around and unseen. It is clear as day and carefully hidden. Black excellence endures and gifts us moments small and large that speak to possibility and hope. But racism remains.

The deaths of George Floyd and Breonna Taylor highlight the ongoing violence Black communities face in the United States. Combined with the recent normalizing of racial hatred by the former U.S. president and outright attacks on multicultural initiatives, the events of the last years have underscored the many faces of anti-Blackness. While schools are often framed as places of neutrality and fairness, many U.S. schools have either harmed Black children or been silent in the face of their struggles, undereducation, and mistreatment. While there are undoubtedly adults in these spaces who work to support Black children, many others ignore Black families, minimize Black youths' concerns, and believe that taking a colorblind stance will solve the problem of inequity in education. None of these tactics will help to undo the damage exacted upon Black children in schools.

Anti-Blackness in schools is a well-entrenched component of American life. Almost 100 years ago, Black scholar and historian Carter G. Woodson argued, "The thought of the inferiority of the Negro is drilled into him in almost every class he enters and in almost every book he studies" (1933/2009,

p. 6). Anti-Blackness is a very particular kind of racism, one steeped in a refusal to acknowledge Black humanity and a disdain and disregard for Black lives (ross, 2020). We fully acknowledge that many communities in the United States face challenges, and that those challenges (e.g., sexism; antisemitism; transphobia, discrimination against immigrants, refugees, and Spanish speakers) are real and need attention. However, the United States has a 400-year relationship with anti-Blackness (Baptist, 2016; Kendi, 2017). It is this particular phenomenon and its effects on schooling that this book addresses.

## WHERE WE ARE GOING

Our work charts the contours of anti-Blackness in schools. We seek to achieve four main aims. We want to (1) *illuminate the ways in which anti-Blackness affects education*. From the normative to the procedural, examples of anti-Blackness can appear in all corners of school. We seek to call out the ways in which school policies, programs, belief systems, and customs are particularly hostile to Black youth. We seek to (2) *explore the ways in which diversity work is not synonymous with antiracist work*. Our model focuses on justice and equity as endpoints; we explore how being intentional about goals is key to working against anti-Blackness in schools. We seek to (3) *provide concrete, doable, and meaningful ways in which teachers and administrators can work against anti-Blackness* in their schools. We sketch out readings, activities, lessons, and concrete techniques to talk about anti-Blackness, inventory its presence, and take steps to unpack the harm it causes. Finally, we (4) *catalog resources*. As teacher educators, we are mindful of having reliable, accurate materials that will allow teachers to do anti-Blackness work in schools. We curate easily accessible resources that will allow readers to keep these issues on their agendas consistently, in ways that challenge racism and uplift Black youth in their care.

We are mindful of (and thankful for) the many important books already written about Black youth and education. Books such as *Sing a Rhythm, Dance a Blues* (Morris, 2019), *We Want to Do More Than Survive* (Love, 2019), *For White Folks Who Teach in the Hood* (Emdin, 2017), *Black Male(d): Peril and Promise in the Education of African American Males* (Howard, 2013), *We Dare Say Love* (Nasir et al., 2018) and *The Guide for White Women who Teach Black Boys* (Moore et al., 2017) address similar topics and greatly advance our understanding of how to better educate Black youth. We gratefully acknowledge these works and build upon their foundation.

This book offers a new path for teachers who wish to create Black-affirming spaces. To do this, we deliberately attend to our intellectual ancestry by highlighting the Black lineage that forms the foundation of our work. At the same time, we always have our eyes ahead, demonstrating how anti-Blackness manifests and how it can be disassembled. We focus solely on African American youth, rather than minoritized youth more broadly. This single focus allows us to explore the particularities of Black youth experiences. Our effort to highlight the nuanced and persistent ways in which anti-Blackness operates in schools at every level while suggesting practical means to oppose it is what makes this contribution stand apart. This book is for educators who seek to move beyond colorblindness and "neutrality," and, for the unconvinced, demonstrates why it is urgent to do so. Providing resources for schools to locate where bias and inequity surface is the first step in doing better by Black youth. We hope to spur this self-awareness.

This book is for those concerned with action, who want concrete, practical tools for immediate use in schools. We imagine this work as a jumping-off point for professional development about issues of equity, justice, and anti-Blackness. The resources and materials can be used for teacher book groups, with teacher leadership teams, as part of new teacher mentoring, and with administrative groups as they are charting new ways to support Black youth in their schools. As former teachers, we understand that educators want to do something with their knowledge. This book provides readers with those options.

It is important to unpack the idea of *anti-Blackness* before going much further. We want to be clear that racism is a different, although related, phenomenon to anti-Blackness. Racism is a system of advantage based on race (Wellman, 1993). Racism is a wider concept under which anti-Blackness falls. For a fuller discussion of racism in its numerous forms—systemic, institutional, individual, historic, and so on—we suggest the following sources: *Why Are All the Black Kids Sitting Together in the Cafeteria?* (Tatum, 2003), *Stamped from the Beginning: The Definitive History of Racist Ideas in America* (Kendi, 2017), *White Fragility* (DiAngelo, 2018), *Caste: The Origins of Our Discontents* (Wilkerson, 2020); *A Kids Book About Racism* (Memory, 2019), and *Racism Without Racists* (Bonilla-Silva, 2017). Anti-Black racism is a particular form of racism that is historic, systemic, and rooted in antipathy towards the *Black* community. When we lack attention to the specificity of anti-Blackness, we allow it to "[reinscribe] Black students' hyper/in-visibility, uneducability and their always already necessitating discipline, punishment, and policing more broadly" (ross, 2019, p. 2). While other communities of color experience racism as well, anti-Blackness has its own particular history, contours, and consequences. Anti-Black racism is *foundational* to the United States; thus, building consciousness of anti-Blackness is key for educators hoping to thwart it.

As we mentioned earlier, in no way do we seek to minimize the pain that trans communities, immigrant communities, and refugees (among others) have faced, particularly during the recent Trump years. We hold to Ladson-Billings's stance that we need to do all we can to minimize inequality, and as she does, we have chosen race as the focus of our attack (Ladson-Billings,

2021). We write about anti-Blackness because this is the work we can do; this is where our experience and agency lie.

We are cognizant that within the U.S. context Black people were considered property and their genealogies documented on the ledgers of landowners next to cows, chickens, furniture and kitchen utensils. We offer two brief vignettes to introduce how Black people are and have been dehumanized. Wilkerson shares the following story in *Caste: The Origins of our Discontents* (2020). In 1951, a Little League baseball team won their city's championship game. As a reward, the boys were allowed to celebrate in the city swimming pool. The one African American child on the team was not allowed to get into the pool, so he had to watch as his friends played. Feeling sorry for him, the pool manager agreed that the young boy could be placed in an inflatable boat and pulled around the swimming pool one time. He was cautioned sternly that at no time was he to let any part of his body touch the water. The rest of the children looked on as the boy got into the boat and was pulled around the pool (Wilkerson, 2020).

The boy could not touch the water, of course, because he was considered polluted. It is important to unwind this vignette, as it is critical to see the layers. The child was not included because he was considered dirty. He would foul the water, highlighting the degree to which he was not seen as *human*. A child, who should be celebrating a baseball game victory, was instead considered a kind of pathogen, one that would harm the White people in the pool. We are deliberately repetitive here because this form of racism is just so basic, and the timeline is just so recent. This is not a sly, quiet jab at intelligence. This is not the omission of a Black author. It is the most foundational judgment that this Black child is not only unlike White children, but that he himself is toxic. The boy himself learns a lesson about racism. The White boys around him learn lessons, too, about how you treat Black people.

A second vignette. On March 3, 1991, motorist Rodney King was finally pulled over after an 8-mile pursuit by the Los Angeles Police Department (LAPD). Over the next 15 minutes, King was shot twice with a taser gun, kicked continuously and beaten by multiple officers with a police baton, and had his neck and back stepped on at least six times. Later, it was discovered that attending police officers and judicial officials within Los Angeles had invoked the term "NHI" to describe the King case. NHI is the abbreviation for "No Humans Involved." It is a term Los Angeles officials had created to describe cases involving young, Black males of LA's central city.[1] In Sylvia Wynter's open letter to her colleagues (1994) after the King uprisings, she highlights this use of "NHI" as a way of classifying Black males as the least equal of all (Wynter, 1994). While we are not declaring anti-Blackness as necessarily more harmful than other traumas, we do believe that the classification of Blacks as nonhuman is foundational to the United States as a nation and central to its functioning. Black Americans are the nation's "conceptual other" (Wynter, 1994, p. 43).

An additional point of clarification: authors use various names to catego-rize peoples in the United States, the Americas, the larger African diaspora, and Africa. We find these discussions both important and rich. How people of color (POC) refer to themselves, and how White people refer to folks of color, differ considerably. The use of African, African American, Black, Jamaican, or Kenyan all confer different meanings both to the person describing their identity and to non-POC who are trying to discern the nuances. For example, Joi uses the term African American intentionally to convey the experiences of Black Americans who are descendants of enslaved Africans in the United States. She sees the term as giving place and historical roots to Blacks in America. Here in Rhode Island, Kerri hears "African American" being used as a more formal alternative to "Black." In her experience, the term gener-ally is not used to capture history or specific identity when used by White people. The choice to use Haitian versus Black versus African American is deeply personal and steeped in story, history, and interpretation. We see this. Recognizing both their affordances and constraints, we use the terms African American and Black interchangeably to describe children of African descent living in the United States. We use the term anti-Black (vs. anti–African American) because we believe Black casts a larger net. We capitalize both White and Black to clarify when we are speaking of people groups. We use the terms "Black boys" and "Black girls" when we are speaking about youth. We do this because using "males" and "females" to refer to children adultifies Black youth in ways that are both damaging and dangerous.

## ON OUR COLLABORATION

This effort is the culmination of two careers. Twenty-plus years each into our work as teachers and professors, we are stunned by the reality of now. The election of a Black president brought the backlash of Trumpism; trainings similar to courses we teach have been challenged by the government;[2] in the midst of a global pandemic, violence against Black people continues. We have been gathering stories, working with families, and conducting research for years, slowly building this book through a long and purposeful collaboration. We now bring our work to fruition.

Our collaboration is unique in several ways. First, the authors have been in the field of education for a combined total of 44 years. We see the com-plexities of this work through many different vantage points, including those of classroom teacher, professor, parent, school designer, auntie, math special-ist, and researcher. Our experiences teaching youth span a wide variety of set-tings and demographics. We have taught emergent bilinguals, in multiracial classrooms, in schools for refugee and newly arrived youth, in mostly Black spaces, in mostly White spaces, in urban schools, and in public and private settings. We have both attended and taught in private and public institutions.

Most importantly, this book is an interracial collaboration. Joi Spencer is a Black woman from California; Kerri Ullucci is a White woman from Rhode Island. We bring with us all the positionality and insights that come from doing equity work with a wide variety of audiences. We find this dual set of perspectives particularly valuable right now.

Breaking with the conventions of academic writing, we share our backgrounds in first person. Positionality matters. Owning who we are and how this shades our experiences is key to being honest about how we contribute to this work. Each of us speaks for herself.

**Joi Spencer**

*I am an African American woman from South Central Los Angeles. I grew up in a Black-centered working-class/middle-class Black community (if you want to know what a Black working/middle-class community looks like, I suggest reading the book* Black Picket Fences *by Pattillo-McCoy, 2013). My neighbors were sanitation workers, teachers, cooks, soldiers, librarians, police officers, factory workers, mechanics, and engineers. I grew up reading Malcolm X, Martin Luther King Jr., and Marcus Garvey. My dolls were Black, and my mother went through great lengths to ensure that I had a strong Black identity. As a very young person, I attended a multiracial church (Black and White). As a preteen and teenager, I attended the oldest church founded by African Americans in the city of Los Angeles. Our church bulletins highlighted the lives and achievements of Black people every Sunday, and our pastor was central in Los Angeles' civil rights causes.*

*I am a descendant of enslaved people in the United States. My maternal family migrated from Georgia and Florida to Wisconsin in the 1940s, finding life in the South completely intolerable. Before their move to Wisconsin and amidst the travails of Southern life, my maternal family members built a strong community, served in the church, voted, learned to read, and raised children. My mother and her siblings attended an elementary school in Florida where every teacher, principal, and parent was Black and focused on the success of every child. These stories of her early schooling and community in Winter Park, Florida, have been passed down to me. My mother migrated from Wisconsin to Los Angeles in the 1960s on the second wave of the Great Migration. My paternal grandparents and their siblings lived full, rich lives in Texas. Their story in Texas is documented in the book* Claiming Sunday: The Story of a Texas Slave Community *(Snider, 2018), and their community, Monte Verdi Plantation Family Slaves, has an official Texas Historical Marker.[3] My paternal grandparents left Texas in the 1950s and came directly to Los Angeles. My dad served in the Army and later worked as a truck driver. My mother was a teacher's aide in Los Angeles public schools and later a receptionist.*

*Like Kerri, I have loved education, teaching, and learning all my life. I attended public schools in Los Angeles, learning alongside students from a large variety of racial, cultural, linguistic, and religious backgrounds. I began tutoring mathematics in junior high school and was involved in various programs providing support and instruction for kids throughout my community. After college, I spent a summer running a Freedom School and later taught middle school mathematics for several years in Northern California, in a community with many similarities to South Central Los Angeles. I have always been concerned about and focused on improving the educational opportunities of Black people. My undergraduate thesis, master's thesis, and dissertation all attest to this commitment. I have studied race and racism (and have seen it play out) for many years in my own life, in the lives of my family, and in my community and nation. I see learning (with a particular focus on mathematics learning) as emancipatory and am deeply troubled by the kind of education that many Black youth receive today.*

### Kerri Ullucci

*I am a White woman from New England. My grandparents are French-speaking immigrants from Quebec, and second-generation immigrants from Italy. I grew up in a White ethnic community with lots of Italian people, attended mostly White schools, was part of an Italian church, and was raised in part by an Italian grandmother. I grew up with two parents, in a mostly middle-class home. I am the first in my family to go to college.*

*My grandfather was a janitor. My grandmother did piecework at a jewelry factory located in what is now a neighborhood where many Guatemalan and Central American families live. My family was doing the newly-arrived-to-the-US-and-at-the-bottom-of-the ladder reality not so long ago. I remember.*

*I began my teaching career early (at 16) through Summerbridge, a program designed to get underserved kids into intense summer academic programs, while getting high school students interested in teaching. It worked. I never left schools.*

*I have been either a teacher or a student every year of my life since that summer. Summerbridge was multiracial by design. Students, teachers, and administrators represented all kinds of folks: newly arrived immigrants from Liberia, families from Laos and Cambodia, teachers who were Sudanese and Nigerian and Mexican, kids from Cape Verde and Thailand and Vietnam. This establishment of my baseline—of working with people different from myself—set the pattern for my career. I spent my 1-year, full-time student teaching placement with a Black mentor teacher, who shaped how I understood my profession. I taught a subsequent year of Summerbridge for a Black director and at a summer school in Providence under the direction of a Black man. My academic advisor and dissertation chair for my PhD program is a Black man. In coteaching courses and in conducting research and writing with him, I learned to see differently. I share this list because my understanding of how to teach was and is shaped by these Black mentors. I understand that this is rare for a White educator. My professional life has been largely inflected by the tutelage of Black educators.*

*In 16 years of teaching courses on race and racism, of working with teachers, of collaborating with Joi, I keep learning how to be conscious. It is a never-ending effort. I am never done or complete. I do not have this all figured out.*

*I am not a person of color. Racism is not directed at me. My experiences and the knowledge that I have gathered along the way do not emerge from a lived experience of being the subject of racism. I contribute to this work by listening, by reading, by paying attention to who is in the room and who is not, by teaching, by leading difficult conversations, and by listening some more. I understand antiracism as a group effort, one White folks have an ethical obligation to show up for and engage with urgently.*

## ACKNOWLEDGING CONCERNS

We want to be plain about potential concerns readers may bring with them to this book. In anticipating roadblocks, we wish to be real about the many legitimate critiques that exist when doing this work.

### Concerning the Perils of Integration

We feel that it is important to name that this book is about supporting Black children and youth in mainly non-Black spaces. This is the legacy of integration. We will explore this concern in further depth in Chapter 2, when discussing the complex legacy of *Brown v. Board of Education*. However, at this juncture, we appreciate that integration has had negative consequences, including the loss of Black teachers and administrators who were dismissed, disempowered, and often delegitimized after *Brown v. Board of Education* was decided. We acknowledge that the work of integration happens almost exclusively on the backs of Black and Brown children. We recognize that countless scholars have placed their energies in working to figure out how to make White schools better for Black kids. Numerous Black scholars have critiqued this work (see, for example, D. B. Martin's 2007 article "Beyond Missionaries or Cannibals: Who Should Teach Mathematics to African American Children?"). We see the complexities of assuming that White spaces will ever truly be safe and uplifting to Black children. We recognize that the ultimate solution is that Black youth need an opportunity to learn from individuals who love and cherish them, and who respect their cultural practices (Boykin, 1994), social realities, and heritage.

We also want to be clear that in our focus on Black youth in schools, we are in no way suggesting that they as a group are broken, damaged, or need to be fixed. Instead, we are saying that the systems, policies, and beliefs that surround Black children are often broken, damaged, and need to be fixed. Black children are brilliant, capable, and worthy. Our work is grounded in these truths.

## Concerning the Focus on Anti-Blackness

You can look at any component of schooling—curriculum, pedagogy, coaching, discipline, family interactions—and see anti-Blackness in action. The fact that this is invisible to many White people is important to note. White people are not reliable narrators of whether or not racism is occurring because racism is not directed at them. If there is one critical truth that we can help to surface in schools and with people doing this work, it is simply that *just because something has not happened to you, it does not mean that experience does not happen at all.*

Race, and specifically Blackness, is rarely named in schools. School policies reflect what is seen and acknowledged. For example, in California, migrant education supports students whose parents are migrant workers. Likewise, states are mandated to provide particular services to students learning English. In New York and many places on the East Coast, we have newcomer education. Federal Title I supports K–12 students living in poverty, while Title IX defines and supports the opportunities afforded to women. These policies name needs by commonality, shaping what we are able to address, place on our agendas, form initiatives around, and fund. Anti-Blackness is not acknowledged as a phenomenon that shapes and stymies the learning and development opportunities of Black youth. Anti-Blackness is not seen as the culprit for the challenges that Black youth face in schools. We cannot realistically hope to support kids if we refuse to see them, name their pain, acknowledge that it is real, and subsequently invest time and resources into undoing harm. Colorblindness is not serving schools. Refusing to speak, name, or acknowledge Blackness or anti-Blackness leaves us exactly where we are currently, spinning yet again without making much traction towards real change.

## Concerning the Role of White People

Anti-racism is a multiracial effort. There must be a role for White people. That role may be different than White educators imagine. Schools that serve members of White communities are often highly resourced and possess the most valued forms of social capital. Their PTAs raise thousands of dollars each year and their property taxes support the hiring of additional teachers (art, music, engineering), school nurses, and school psychologists, and they

fund a long list of extracurricular activities and opportunities. These are resources that many Black students and their communities can only imagine. It
also reflects one of the primary reasons why Black parents place their youngsters in non-Black schools or schools outside of their immediate communities.
They are hoping to provide them with better opportunities and recognize that
those opportunities come with the historical wealth of White communities.
In this regard, the non-Black teachers in these integrated school spaces hold
the responsibility of stewarding Black parents' hopes and dreams. Thus, the
role for White administrators, teachers and other educators is to learn from
parents, listen to their hopes for their children, and then become committed
to partnering so that these hopes can be realized. This will certainly mean
doing things differently and letting go of uninformed beliefs about what is
best for Black kids. Humility and non-defensiveness need to be our guides.
White people can show up, be uncomfortable, feel out of place, but still per-
sist in this work.

## ORGANIZATION OF THE BOOK

Chapter 1 turns to some of our foundational vocabulary in doing anti-racist
work, as well as an explanation of the difference between multicultural work
and anti-racist work. Through this chapter, we establish a shared language
in which we will build our subsequent chapters. We also begin by looking
back and tracing some of the intellectual work that has preceded us. We look
at pre- and post-*Brown* scholars and their efforts towards describing and
ameliorating anti-Blackness in education. This acknowledgment is a critical
component of our work. In academic systems that are often mired in racism
and sexism, we want to state clearly the accumulated wealth that we draw
from in writing this book. Chapters 2 and 3 begin our efforts to chart anti-
Blackness. Here we look at policies, procedures, content, and practices that
harm Black youth. Chapter 4 turns to imagining what Black-affirming spaces
might look like, drawing from a successful case study of a summer STEM
program. Chapter 5 moves into the practical sections of the book, providing tools with which schools can assess themselves as they work to unveil
anti-Blackness in their programs and policies. We then look at ideas for addressing anti-Blackness through lessons, professional development, activities,
and other concrete ways to raise these issues in Chapter 6. The final chapter
provides resources for doing this work.

We too were teachers, and appreciate the desire to flip to the tools
at the end of this book, skipping the ideas and commitments that lead to
them. Please stick with us, though! The initial chapters help provide valuable anchors for readers that will allow them to do this work with depth
and nuance. For school administrators, we understand the pressure to produce results immediately. This often means addressing demands to raise test

scores, lower suspension rates, and improve graduation outcomes. Given that such urgent calls for immediate change have largely served to stifle progress, we hope that you will appreciate the wisdom of the long game. Building learning communities that can recognize and then undo the racism that is embedded within the systems, practices, and policies of our schools is the best route forward.

## NO PLACE AT THE TABLE

We want to share a small but meaningful experience that shaped this book as we wrap up this chapter. While the phrase "no place at the table" can be interpreted in many ways, in this iteration, unfortunately, the meaning is literal.

All 4th-grade students at one of our local schools were engaged in a unit-long exploration of culture and diversity. At the culmination of the unit, all students were required to bring a dish representative of their cultural background to a gradewide food celebration. The explicit purpose of this event was to highlight diversity; that was the very goal. When the family of one of very few Black children arrived with their contribution of sweet potato pie, they walked throughout the auditorium looking for the appropriate place to set their dish. Flags from across the world sat on the tables and served as markers for where families should place their foods: the lasagna next to Italy and the matzo ball soup next to Israel. Unable to find a marker for their food, the family asked one of the grade-level teachers where to place their dish. She replied, "Just put your pie on the Mexican table." There was no place on the tables allocated for them.

While at first blush this omission may seem like a minor oversight, it is an important place to shine light. It signals the larger set of mindsets (Black people do not have a rel culture. They aren't really from anywhere in the world. What flag would I use for them anyway?), slights, and erasures that Black chilldren face as they endeavor to learn and succeed in school. We want Black children and their families to have a dedicated seat at the table and to be able to ask for, and receive, what they need to succeed.

## OUR INTENTION FOR THE READER

To White people and non-Black POC who care about these issues, this is the time to redouble our efforts. We know there are dedicated educators who want to do the work and are committed to change. Our intention here is to provide support to imagine concrete ways to rupture anti-Blackness that moves beyond words. Stick with it, fight for change, know you have many allies, have faith that your work is valued and needed. We ask you to keep these issues on your agendas consistently, in ways that challenge racism and support Black youth in your schools.

In setting our intentions for Black readers, we want to give particular praise to Black principals, teachers, coaches, cafeteria workers, custodians, librarians, district leaders, social workers, superintendents, families, and communities who have been fighting this good fight for so long. We see you and appreciate the countless ways that you support and love Black children every day. For all readers, we hope to assist educators with the initial steps of reimagining schools so that they become humanizing and actualizing institutions for Black students.

# Part I

# FOUNDATIONS OF ANTI-BLACKNESS

# Foundations

## Anti-Blackness Defined, Ancestry, and a Common Language

Many books address diversity and equity in education, each with its own set of goals and assumptions. Being specific about where we are heading and who can do this work are critical steps in this process. Our goals in this chapter are to be transparent about how we engage in this work, explicit about our definitions, and inclusive about who can work towards antiracist goals. We introduce anti-Blackness in schools, explore the differences between diversity, equity, social justice, and tolerance, and clarify how teachers in all settings can engage in antiracist work. We trace our intellectual roots and introduce the Black scholars who have created our foundation. Together, these pieces provide the framework upon which we will build the subsequent chapters.

### RACE AND RACISM: SOME FOUNDATIONAL IDEAS

Part of the confusion over issues of race stems from lack of clarity over terms used to describe social identities. Is Egyptian a race? Is racism defined by those obvious examples of hatred, like physical attacks? Or do jokes count, too? We open this chapter clarifying some of the key terms we will use in the book.

When we refer to *race*, we mean the shorthand term used to sort and categorize people into groups based on skin color and physical features (National Museum of African American History, 2014). Wilkerson (2020) explains race as a "signal of rank . . . the division of humans on the basis of appearance. In America, race is the primary tool and the visible decoy, the front man, for caste" (p. 18). She goes on to argue that "the use of inherited physical characteristics to differentiate inner abilities and group value may be the cleverest way that a culture has ever devised to manage and maintain a caste system" (p. 20). Ladson-Billings argues that race is a *project* (2021), one that does *work* in schools as it reinscribes hierarchies and inequalities.

Despite not being a valid biological concept, race categories have significant impact on peoples' lived experiences. This is often hard to sit with, as something *not real* should seemingly have no impact on one's life. But while race is not something that biologically separates us—there is no gene that all Black people have that no White people have—the consequences of the *story* we tell about race remain (see *Race: The Power of an Illusion* [2003], a documentary series produced by California Newsreel, for an insightful treatment of this topic). We have been telling inaccurate stories, stories filled with misinformation about intelligence, capability, and biology. We seemingly have not been able to put down these stories, or even recognize them as *just stories*. The consequence of telling race stories for 400+ years is that they have spun out their own realities. Peoples' life chances—their abilities to stay safe from harm, rent an apartment, or secure a loan—are inflected by race. Wilkerson conveys this story-like feature of race when she recounts a conversation between herself and a Nigerian playwright: "There are no black people in Africa," relays the playwright (2020, p. 53). The playwright goes on to explain that Africans have other identities, for instance Igbo or Yoruba (referring to Nigerian ethnic groups), but that they don't become Black until they go to America or the United Kingdom. Thus what the United States uses as "common sense" in the assigning of racial categories *does not exist* the world over. It is a system of *caste-making*. It is a *story*. Race is not something we have always had, a permanent component of humanity. Instead, it is a concept created by people for a specific purpose. We are not destined to exist like this. We could choose another way.

Relatedly, Coates maintains that "race is the child of racism, not the father" (2015, p.7). This is a critical realization. Racism spurs race. The practice of inhumane treatment creates the necessity of race. In this light, race is an artifact created as a means to an end: to justify the ownership of some people by others. As we said earlier, racism is a system of advantage based on race (Wellman, 1993). This is a twist on the typical definition of racism as a system of disadvantage. This flip draws White people into the definition by focusing on the benefits they receive through this system. For example, as a White person, Kerri can navigate airports and stores without being surveilled. No one asks her how she got her job or her spot in a PhD program or her scholarships to college.

In its most simplistic version, racism is seen as a personality flaw ascribed to a handful of people or "bad apples." In this view, racism is located at the individual level and one is either all racist, OR a good person; we don't imagine that people can be a little bit racist. Rather, to be a racist is to be "an inhuman monster" (Demby, 2014, p. 9). But this kind of thinking does not help us either. Racism happens at the systems or institutional level (think school discipline policies) AND at the individual level (an individual student writes a slur on a Black student's notebook). People can do "quiet" things that are racist (refusing to rent an apartment to a Black family) and loud and public things (marching in a White-power rally). Moreover, people can be consistently racist, or racist once in a while, or engaged in something that was passively racist last Tuesday that they are currently ashamed of but that nevertheless still happened. By this we mean that racism manifests in many ways, and we do not have to be a 100% hateful person to engage in racist practices and behaviors. It is pretty much impossible to grow up in the United States and not be influenced by racism. White people are poisoned by the racism we see and hear, and none of us escapes untouched. Rather than White people vehemently denying that racism exists, it is a better use of effort to identify where, when, and how racism flourishes. This is a shared consequence of our socialization in the United States. Negative stories and images infect our beliefs (prejudices) and, at times, our actions. While you personally may never take part in a KKK rally or shout a racist slur, there are covert ways that racism crops up: in the split-second judgment of the Black man walking on the street, in questions about intelligence and who merits college acceptance, in our general lack of knowledge of any African people group/history/contribution. Relatedly, White people can consider what they *do not have to deal with on the day to day*. This is an equally valuable and often overlooked avenue of understanding racism. White people generally do not have people petting our hair (this happens), or teachers telling us to visit the writing center for editing before even reading our work (happened) or taxi drivers refusing to pick us up at the airport (that happened, too). Our takeaway here is that (a) racism can be both individual and systematic, (b) racism is ubiquitous and not confined to "bad people," and (c) we are all influenced by racist thoughts, beliefs, and practices.

## BUILDING ON THE PAST: ANCESTRY

Black scholars and teachers have been fighting against anti-Blackness for hundreds of years. Our work builds on decades of efforts by African American scholars, educators, and community members who have seen education as a tool for Black liberation. In this section, we delineate Black thinkers who have influenced our work. This intellectual heritage includes a mix of elders (those born into a pre-*Brown* context) and contemporaries (scholars from the post-*Brown* and beyond generation). We build upon these ancestors' work to highlight the sustained and substantive intellectual work that has always existed in the Black community. There is a lineage to our writing.

Black people have always been teaching and learning, always been uplifting, often in hidden and fugitive ways (Givens, 2021). These Black scholars, including Fanny Jackson Coppin, Carter G. Woodson, Frederick Douglass, Mary McLeod Bethune, James Baldwin, Bettina Love, Christopher Emdin, Ibram X. Kendi, Kimberlé Crenshaw, Gholdy Muhammad, Monique Morris, Tyrone Howard, Lisa Delpit, Na'ilah Nasir, Gloria Ladson-Billings, Geneva Gay, James Banks, Asa Hilliard, Vanessa Siddle Walker, and Isabel Wilkerson, created the foundation on which we write. We are grateful for the ways they have shaped the lines of inquiry and argumentation woven through this book.

We call out four specific Black educational ancestors to center our focus: Frederick Douglass, Mary McLeod Bethune, Carter G. Woodson, and

Gloria Ladson-Billings. Why do this? First, as we are building our foundations in this chapter, it is important to understand the intellectual heritage of
the Black community. Understanding that an intellectual heritage exists, specifically one related to learning and education, resituates Black youth within
the educational/intellectual/academic space rather than outside of it. The
Black community is and has always been deeply invested in the learning of its
children and the educating of its communities. Educational historian James
Anderson (1988) relays the stories of Black enslaved and free communities in
the South that prior to the Civil War ran schools undetected by White people.
At the risk of torture and death, these educators taught Black children to
read, write, and compute (Anderson, 1988).¹ Wollenberg (1976) relays accounts of the African American families in San Francisco who in 1872 filed
the first school segregation court case in California's history. Prior to this case,
Black people in California established private schools, formed organizations
such as the Colored Citizens Convention (which artfully agitated for educational opportunities), insisted that public schools be created to educate their
children, funded prominent Black educators to come to the state and teach,
and, when the time was right, worked to end legal school segregation in their
state. Vanessa Siddle Walker (1996) documents with expert detail the commitment of Black educators, parents, community members, and youngsters in
Casewell County, North Carolina, to the highest-quality education available
anywhere in the United States. These stories are not unique or anecdotal, but
existed throughout Black America. In each case, African Americans saw education and freedom as inseparable and symbiotic. For the sake of acquiring
literacy and education, they were tortured, maimed, and dehumanized; some
even lost their lives. Their churches, schools, and businesses were destroyed;
they lost their jobs; they were driven off their land and had to flee for their
safety (Curry, 1996). They paid taxes that built White children's schools in
districts that refused to use public monies to educate the descendants of the
enslaved (Anderson, 1988). Then, without hesitation, they gave donations
from their meager wages, held bake sales, hosted fish fries, wrote letters to
solicit funds, and donated resources and raw materials. Despite their poverty,
they endured a system of double taxation so that the generations after them
could have the hope of liberation (Anderson, 1988). The narratives of Black
underachievement, the Black–White achievement gap, the school-to-prison
pipeline, the overidentification of Black children for special education, and
the burden of acting White would be foreign to them. They did not see being
Black and being intelligent as oppositional states, and they would be struck
to encounter educators who believed such ideas.

These ancestors are important for another reason. They sit at the nexus
of freedom fighter/activist and educator. In other words, they understood that
education work was freedom work and that the liberation of Black people
was contingent upon what they were able to learn. Education and African
Americans' existence have been uniquely tied. Their historical status as

unprotected, nonhuman, and noncitizen made the need for access to information critical. Forging freedom documents, reading a map, deciphering a sharecropping labor contract, passing a literacy test at the polls, interpreting the equal protection clause of the Constitution to gain access to a needed resource, and obtaining a passing score on one of a litany of IQ exams (including the Army IQ test, SAT/ACT, GRE, etc.) have all been crucial tools in their dangerous, slow, and painstaking acquisition of freedom. Black people's quest for humanhood via literacy has existed alongside an active, formal, and legal denial of this asset. The quest for humanhood and citizenship has brought profound purpose to literacy. Rather than reading for leisure, we see African Americans reading with the goal of liberation. Frederick Douglass is therefore an appropriate first archetype.

## Frederick Douglass

Frederick Douglass was born in Talbot County, Maryland, less than 72 miles away from the United States capital. When Frederick was born in 1817, the United States was engaged in systematic conquest of indigenous lands and in the throes of an intracontinental slave trade. When transporting Africans from their continent was outlawed in 1808, American slavers' options for free human labor were now limited to those already in the states and their progeny. The American slave complex was held together by an endless slate of laws and practices dictating and limiting the physical movement and access to knowledge of the enslaved. Narratives attest to the severe punishments of enslaved Africans who were caught possessing any forms of literacy. In the *Narrative of the Life of Frederick Douglass, an American Slave* (1845), we find him as a young boy tricking neighborhood White children into teaching him the alphabet. Later, upon learning that his wife has taught Douglass to read, Douglass's owner rebukes her, stating, "Learning will spoil the best n—— in the world. Now," said he, "if you teach that n—— (speaking of myself) how to read, there would be no keeping him. It would forever unfit him to be a slave. He would at once become unmanageable, and of no value to his master. As to himself, it could do him no good, but a great deal of harm. It would make him discontented and unhappy" (Douglass, 1845, p. 33).

As Douglass pointedly reflected on the exchange between his owner and his owner's wife, he explained, "I now understood what had been to me a most perplexing difficulty—to wit the white man's power to enslave the black man. It was a grand achievement, and I prized it highly. From that moment, I understood the pathway from slavery to freedom" (p. 33). While Douglass was far from being the only slave to learn to read, his story holds particular significance. Douglass was an especially noncompliant and resistant slave. He ran away often and spoke back to his owners on numerous occasions. His resistance resulted in physical altercations with his owners and eventually with him being sent to a "slave-breaker." The goal of the slave-breaker was to so diminish the spirit and will of an enslaved person so as to render them wholly subjected and obedient in all forms. But Douglass could not be broken. He fought the slave-breaker and eventually secured his freedom through a daring escape. In insisting that his humanity be respected, Douglass experienced a particular kind of physical and psychological brutality from his owners. Slave-breaking represented the most pernicious racism that America had to offer. The goal was to break the body and spirit. Literacy was a means of reclaiming his humanity and dignity, as well as an actual way to deliver himself from bondage. Literacy was a beacon and a tool.

The knowledge that Douglass was able to acquire throughout his life, including job skills and literacy, formed a throughline to his liberation. It meant life in all of its forms, including self-determination, self-actualization, and physical and mental safety. This is true today for many Black youth in our schools. Racism in many forms, has confined them physically to underserved and divested neighborhoods and communities, limited their access to green spaces and recreation, and shortened their life expectancy. Their ability to acquire the language of power, contemporary job skills, and critical literacy could turn the tide of their lives. In short, education could signal their liberation, as it did for Douglass. It is with this spirit and this backdrop that we hope teachers will teach Black children and youth. Education can be emancipatory.

## Mary McLeod Bethune

Mary McLeod Bethune was a powerhouse of a woman who worked to improve access to the United States's bounty for African Americans in general and African American women and youth specifically. We do not attempt to capture the full measure of her civic and social efforts here (because the breadth of her work, quite frankly, is stunning), but instead focus on her education-based work. Bethune's parents were formerly enslaved. Like Douglass, she learned to read and write as a young person and understood and voiced the clear connection among education, literacy, and the liberty of Black people. In her lifetime, she took on a variety of jobs in order to achieve her greater goals of Black liberation, opportunity, and social equality. Apart from her leadership in education, she worked on her parents' farm and picked cotton, raised money by providing food for workers at a local dumpsite, sold insurance, and fundraised aggressively amongst White progressives.

Many would like to place Bethune as an integrationist, perhaps even aligning her with Booker T. Washington (a Southern educator who often employed an accommodationist stance with White segregationists). However, unlike Washington, Bethune urged protest and active agitation against Black American discrimination. She argued, "We must challenge skillfully, but resolutely, every sign of restriction or limit on our full American citizenship" (Bethune, cited in McCluskey & Smith, 1999, p. 4), and that Black people "should protest openly everything in the newspapers, on the radio, in the

movies that smacks of discrimination or slander" (p. 26). Likewise, she did
not seem to engage in the endless debates about whether Black people needed
a liberal arts education or a vocational one (Du Bois, 1903; Washington,
1903). Bethune advocated for Black youth and Black women to have access
to the highest-quality education *and* to economic and job opportunities. The
first school that she founded and ran for young girls (in Daytona, Florida)
answered that question easily by simply integrating both. Students learned
how to cook, sew, and clean in the morning and learned literature, foreign
languages, and mathematics in the afternoon and evening. Likewise, Bethune
pushed for youth job opportunities. She worked ardently to ensure that services and funds within the National Youth Administration be extended to
Black and minority youth. The significance of this should be underscored.
Operating from 1935–1939, the NYA had an annual budget of $580 million,
with a major portion of the funds granted to college youth to engage in work-
study projects and job training. As with other federal allocations, had there
not been advocacy for the Black community, the vast majority of these funds
would have gone to White citizens. Her pragmatism is evidenced by the enormous energies that she devoted to both formal education and work opportunities for Black youth. Her background as a working-class Black woman
meant that she was deeply acquainted with the economic struggles of Black
people. When she founded the Daytona Educational and Industrial Institute
for Negro Girls in 1904, she built desks and benches from old, discarded
crates, and the students used elderberry juice as ink in their pens (Bethune-
Cookman University, n.d.). She was college educated (at Scotia Seminary and
Moody Bible College), but her college degree did not grant her immediate
access to middle-class White America, and she likely knew that this would be
the case for her students.

Bethune is a beacon to us for several reasons. She was unapologetic in
her pursuit of the "unalienable rights of citizenship for Black Americans"
(McCluskey & Smith, 1999, p. 3). Her particular care for Black girls, both
through her opening of a school specifically for them and in her example as
a leader when she was head of Bethune-Cookman College (the only HBCU
opened by a woman), was remarkable. Her example should guide educators
of African American youth to care for the entirety of the students in front of
them and to protect the dignity of Black children. When the Ku Klux Klan
threatened to burn down Bethune-Cookman College, Bethune walked out
to meet these night riders. They stood down. She was not messing around!
She, like Douglass, understood that education and freedom were intimately
linked. Education and voting were key concerns to Bethune, and she fought
mightily to ensure voting rights for Black people. She also opened a hospital,
opened a library for Black Floridians, was personal friends with Eleanor Roosevelt, headed a government agency, and was a leader of many boards and
groups. We admire her fearlessness, moxie, ability to see further, and tireless-
ness in pursuit of equity. She was a force of nature.

## Carter G. Woodson

Woodson was born in New Canton, Virginia, in 1875 to parents who were both formerly enslaved. His father, James Woodson, was a carpenter and a Civil War veteran. While Woodson experienced extreme poverty, his family and community were strong and intact. He worked on his family's farm, supplementing his father's meager earnings. Despite his inability to attend grade school regularly, he excelled in his studies. He was able to learn the necessary foundational subjects and complete primary school. He was a nontraditional, overage secondary student, having to work in the coal mines of Huntington, West Virginia, as a teenager. Undefeated by the series of setbacks he faced, Woodson matriculated into Douglass High School in Huntington at the age of 20. Only two years later, in 1897, he received his high school diploma. Woodson's journey to higher education would unwind in a circuitous fashion over the next decade and a half, a reflection of the ways in which racist structures shaped and impeded the lives of Black people in America. He graduated from Berea College in Kentucky in 1903, where he earned a bachelor's degree in literature. After serving as a school principal in the Philippines, Woodson attended the University of Chicago, earning both his bachelor's and master of arts degrees. By the time he obtained his doctoral degree in history from Harvard University (only the second African American in the United States to do so), Woodson had completed two bachelor's degrees and written his dissertation twice. (His dissertation advisor forced him to rewrite his thesis, claiming that Woodson's findings were fabrications.) Carter G. Woodson is the only individual whose parents were enslaved in the United States to obtain a PhD (National Park Service, 2021).

Even after receiving his PhD from Harvard, Woodson struggled to find academic work, as universities would not hire Black historians. Woodson's passions unfolded in a lifetime commitment to correcting the historical record to demonstrate the vast contributions of Black people. Until that time, African-descent people were virtually invisible in the U.S. historical record. Likewise, the role of Black people in the history of other cultures was missing. White historical organizations, including the American Historical Association, not only refused to acknowledge Black contributions in the American historical record, but also did not allow Black people to attend their conferences, even though they paid dues. Woodson worked to correct these omissions. In 1915 he established the Association for the Study of Negro Life and History, an important step in opening the field of Black history to the world.[2] One year later, the Association's *Journal of Negro History* became the first academic journal to publish research on the historical contributions of Black people. Perhaps one of Woodson's most profound contributions was the founding of Negro History Week in February 1926. Later becoming Black History Month, observances across the globe have promoted growth in public knowledge of Black advancement, thought, and achievement.

Unlike most academics, Woodson wrote for a variety of audiences. His life working on his family's farm, in the coal mines, and as a public school teacher formed him as a people's historian. Perhaps most importantly for the sake of our discussion, Woodson centered much of his work on the education of teachers and young students. His *Black History Bulletin*, aimed at providing K–12 educational resources for the teaching of Black history, continues to be published today.[3]

We highlight Woodson, then, for several reasons. Foremost, like many African American youth, he endured significant challenges in his quest for a formal education. The economic poverty of his community was a direct result of the system of racism in America. He persisted. He found dignity in education. He created an organization that documents the contributions of Black history to this day. Woodson's insistence on correcting the historical record by presenting an accurate picture of the contributions of Black people is a legacy that endures. He forced people to see what they had been overlooking. We endeavor to follow his model.

## Gloria Ladson-Billings

Gloria Ladson-Billings is a professor, researcher, and scholar. Born in West Philadelphia in 1947, Ladson-Billings began her career as a schoolteacher. She went on to get her master's at the University of Washington and her PhD at Stanford University. She spent the majority of her academic career at the University of Wisconsin–Madison, retiring as the Kellner Family Distinguished Professor in Urban Education in the Department of Curriculum & Instruction.

There are many reasons why we have selected Ladson-Billings to highlight here; we will focus on three areas in particular. First, we value that Ladson-Billings compels researchers to look at the academic successes, rather than failures, of African American students. She is plain in her book *Dreamkeepers: Successful Teachers of African American Children* that her work was not about despair but about "keeping the dream alive" (2009, xvi). *Dreamkeepers* was pivotal to us as young doctoral students in that it was telling another story about Black children, one that refuted the dominant narrative. Hers is a story of success, of what does work, of what is possible.

We are also indebted to her work on culturally relevant pedagogy. Ladson-Billings (1995) outlines culturally relevant pedagogy (CRP) as having three core notions. First is the focus on academic achievement. Children are expected to achieve academically. This achievement goes beyond success on standardized tests. Children are challenged and asked to stretch. Their teachers believe in their capacity. The second core notion is cultural competence. Ladson-Billings argues that "culturally relevant pedagogy must provide a way for students to maintain their cultural integrity while succeeding academically" (1995, p. 476). They do not give up their Blackness. They are not asked to deny their culture. Academic success is not equated with "acting

White." The third and final core notion is a sociopolitical critique. This includes a concerted effort to address social inequities and providing children with the tools to affect change. Culturally relevant pedagogy has been critical to us both as professors and as researchers in that it underscores the cultural role in learning, reminds us that our work is always political, and reiterates that all children are capable, can learn, and can succeed, if given the right context.

Finally, we also model our approach to writing on Ladson-Billing's work in *Dreamkeepers*. In her methodology, Ladson-Billings uses Patricia Hill Collins's framework, which is based in Black feminist thought, to organize her research. Collins's work includes four propositions, each of which Ladson-Billings incorporates in her work with teachers of African American children. We have adopted two of those components in our work: *concrete experience as a criterion of meaning* and *an ethic of personal accountability*. With this proposition, importance is given to lived experience and expertise. Hands-on experience matters. We draw on this approach in honoring the work of teachers and in drawing from personal stories. The second proposition maintains that "Who makes the knowledge is as important as what those knowledge claims are" (Ladson-Billings, 1995, pg. 474). Individual positionality matters. We try to be very explicit about who we are and how that influences our work.

Methodologically, Ladson-Billings also weaves her research with her personal, lived experiences as an African American child in school. She expressly acknowledges that this approach can be seen as messy and subjective. As she writes, she moves back and forth between personal remembrances of being a student, juxtaposing them with her research. In this way, Ladson-Billings integrates "scholarly tools" (typical writing features of academic discourse) with "personal experiences" as a way of incorporating her "necessary subjectivity" (2009, xvii.) We will follow a similar method here. Joi in particular will echo this kind of knowledge-building, drawing on her own experiences as a Black girl in Los Angeles schools.

The four educational ancestors whom we have chosen here are simply the tip of an ever-expanding iceberg of Black educator/freedom fighters. Each educator demonstrates the unique manner in which literacy and education have been tied to the identity and liberation of Black people. Their work reinforces that racism is a fixture of American education (embedded both in its practices and in its policies); racism must be acknowledged and confronted by educational practitioners; and educational practitioners can productively work towards undoing racism.

## THE COMPLEXITIES OF ANTI-BLACKNESS

In the Introduction, we framed our understanding of anti-Blackness in the broadest sense: an antipathy to Black people and a failure to value their humanity. Anti-Blackness shows up in overt, violent manifestations and in more covert ways. While reading a piece of research for this book (research conducted by a widely published, nationally known Black scholar), we found that instead of "professor/academic/researcher" as his descriptors on Google, his profile comes up as "basketball player." Despite several attempts to change it, the description remains.

In the same way that anti-Blackness infects the larger U.S. society, it also impacts the functioning of schools. As we are writing this chapter, the governor of Texas signed the "anti-critical race theory bill" (Texas HB 3979, 2021). This bill dictates:

> (4) a teacher . . . may not (A) be required to engage in training, orientation, or therapy that presents any form of race or stereotyping or blame on the basis of race (B) require or make part of a course the concept that: (i) one race or sex is inherently superior to another race (ii) an individual, by virtue of the individual's race or sex, is inherently racist, sexist, oppressive, whether consciously or unconsciously . . . (vii) an individual should feel discomfort, guilt, anguish, or any other form of psychological distress on account of the individual's race or sex; (viii) meritocracy or traits such as a hard work ethic are racist or sexist or were created by members of a particular race to oppress members of another race; . . . (C) require an understanding of The 1619 Project.

There are currently 21 versions of this kind of bill across the United States. To clarify, *the New York Times*'s 1619 Project seeks to "reframe the country's history by placing the consequences of slavery and the contributions of Black Americans at the very center of our national narrative" (Silverstein, 2019, para. 4). This is explicitly being omitted, by name, in this Texas bill. Through these bills, governors further muzzle teachers on an already fraught topic. By not allowing teachers to address systemic racism, or privilege, or merit, schools extend the protections of Whiteness. The explicit banning of the 1619 Project highlights anti-Blackness on an institutional scale.

On the interpersonal level, last spring a group of Texas high school students engaged in a slave trade thread on a Snapchat group in which they assigned selling prices to their Black classmates (Pietsch, 2021). When the principal was questioned, she called the incident "bullying" rather than racism.

So, to step back, we see anti-Blackness functioning on a variety of levels, affecting people in large and small ways. The remainder of this book will address the concrete ways anti-Blackness shows up in schools. But we want to lay out a few complexities first that muddy the waters of anti-Blackness work. Despite a belief that schools are neutral and fair, schools are manifestations of the communities they inhabit. They are not insulated from racism or bias; they reflect the norms and beliefs of the community. The idea that schools are free from bias is quite pernicious. In our college classes, students occasionally bring up the notion that schools are "neutral" and "apolitical" and it is the *bringing up* of topics such as racism or colorblindness that is the problem. We wish to counter this mindset from the start. Schools are sites where power dynamics are constantly at play. What we teach, who teaches, who learns which subjects, how we push or constrain students, how teachers are rewarded and assigned, and what is omitted all reflect who is valued, deemed worthy, and privileged. The decision to teach Columbus through a Eurocentric interpretation of colonialism is not neutral. It is just traditional.

Neutrality is a myth that helps to cover the functioning of anti-Blackness. But Pearman (2020) lays out a wide array of ways in which anti-Blackness shows up in schools from teacher beliefs, to pedagogical methods, to lack of cultural studies and the inability to see Black children as gifted. However, instead of seeing the consequences of racism, schools often point to the imagined deficits of Black culture, Black values, or Black intelligence. We agree with Lopez and Jean-Marie (2021) when they argue, "This lack of success for Black students must be understood within systems of oppression instead of pathologizing of Black bodies and marginalization of communities" (p. 51). The central focus of this book will be the many ways in which anti-Blackness manifests in schools. At this juncture, understanding that it is real and consequential is the first step.

We suggest a particular self-check at this point, based on our experience as professors in schools of education. As we mentioned in the Introduction, many White folks let a lack of personal experience with racism shadow their empathy. We see this manifest when students say, "I've never noticed racism in my _____ (school/neighborhood/church)." This thinking seems to follow that since racism does not happen to them, they cannot imagine racism is happening at all. Many students that we both work with are White. Many are from suburban, racially homogenous neighborhoods. When asked to identify how or if racism persists, sometimes students are at a loss. When we take into account that we live in hypersegregated neighborhoods, and many White people do not interact with people of color daily, part of this lack of awareness makes sense. Racism is not directed towards White people. That said, helping our students see that *their reality is one model of reality* is absolutely key. Because White people do not see, acknowledge, or experience racism does not mean it is not there. Just because I (Kerri) was not pulled over by the police or stopped at the airport, or told that I speak English so well (!) does not mean others do not go through this. Glaude writes, "It is exhausting to find oneself, over and over again, navigating a world rife with deadly assumptions about you and those who look like you, to see and read about insult and harm, death and anguish for no other reason than because you're black" (2020, xiv). When White people read interpretations like this, instead of defensiveness or disbelief, we could honor the perspective that is being shared.

On the other hand, we sometimes work with students who have been to more integrated schools. For example, maybe they attended schools in Southern California where perhaps a handful of POC attended. Often these are private schools, or schools in well-to-do neighborhoods. The students do not see themselves as racist. They think that the mere fact that a Black person was at their school is evidence that racism in *not* in effect. However, they should question why, in a district that is 60% POC, there was only one student of color in their school. We want students to keep pushing beyond mere representation. Having various people groups represented is an important step in this work, but it is not the end goal. While the one-Black-student-in-8th-grade example can be used to show integration, instead, let's ask:

- Why is representation so sparse in a city with so many POC?
- Why aren't White children bused to Black neighborhoods?
- Why do Black children not find themselves represented in honors courses in this school?

A final point of contention arises over whether claims of anti-Blackness are opinion or reflect facts in the world. Many people who do race-focused work are accused of dealing in opinions rather than well-established evidence. For example, the idea that race matters in the United States is chalked up to *an individual's opinion*. This is untrue. This would be akin to someone saying that the law of gravity is a personal opinion. We have literally hundreds of years of evidence, collected from every area of society (education, law, health, banking, the arts, entertainment, mental health, etc.) that show disparate outcomes based on race. Moreover, the outcomes are always similar.

We are tempted to provide the reader with a laundry list of evidence here, to provide overwhelming confirmation that racism is everywhere. How Black people in middle-class neighborhoods still deal with racism (refuting the belief that class is the only issue that impacts peoples' lives). How racism happens at both the micro level and macro level. Overtly and covertly. By institutions and individuals. Let's engage in a thought exercise instead. Can those who question whether racism is real prove that racism is *not* in effect? That race does not matter? That people are not impacted by racism? What if we flip the question and ask those who deny racism to substantiate their points? What would they offer? What if the burden of proof were theirs? Can they prove that the United States is a race-neutral meritocracy where access and opportunities are fairly distributed and our social identities have not historically and do not contemporarily interfere with our opportunities?

What would happen if we just admitted that racism is real?

The oft-repeated maxim that "everyone is entitled to their opinion" turns out to be treacherous. When students say, "Black people don't value education" or "Black people only get into college because of affirmative action" and then cover themselves by asserting, "I am entitled to my opinion," they are missing two critical points: Opinions can be wrong (that is, contrary to observable fact), and holding them can have consequences. As educators, we feel like we are called to help students disabuse themselves of the notion that just because they have an opinion on something, that must make it true. This is dangerous for students, and it is dangerous for our country. We can have the opinion that we are mermaids (not true, sadly), or residents of the moon (alas, not true). Holding an opinion is not insulation against lies. Opinions in and of themselves are not facts. Thus, a colleague's opinion can be that racism does not exist, or that slavery was not that bad, but it does not make it true. Facts make it true. Evidence makes it true. Triangulation makes it true.

Finally, because something is an opinion also does not shield the believer from consequences. Opinions are not magical. Opinions do not trump other peoples' right to live with dignity. For example, if an undergraduate says, "The Black kids in my dorm are ghetto (I am entitled to my opinion!)" and then one of those Black kids cusses them out, we gently point out the phenomenon of cause and effect.

Our takeaways regarding opinions as they pertain to race can be summarized with these points:

- Everyone has opinions.
- Some opinions are based on fact and evidence. Others are not.
- Words have power. When we introduce our opinions to others, they can have ramifications.

Thinking about how we know what we know, and what might be clouded by stereotype, is a critical self-check. We do not need to weigh in on everything. One of the key hallmarks of maturity is knowing when we do not have anything to say, because we do not know enough. Not having an opinion on something does not make one wishy-washy, or a flip-flopper, but is instead an indication that one knows the limits of their own understandings.

### HOW CAN RACISM BE COUNTERED?

Schools and colleges of education have worked to counter racism, Eurocentrism, and bias in a variety of ways. There are many routes to doing this work, called many things: diversity, multicultural education, inclusion, social justice, tolerance. However, anti-racism is not the same as tolerance or acceptance; inclusion or representation are not the same as justice. All of these terms convey different approaches and end goals. For the sake of this book, *equity* and *educational liberation* are our goals when thinking about how we mark progress in this work. While the difference in terminology might seem minor, the differences between the terms are critical.

Said another way, representation (having physical manifestations of diversity in spaces) and inclusion (ensuring students of different backgrounds cross paths) are not our ultimate goals. This is an important distinction because these notions limit much of the conversation about diversity in schools. In imagining Black-affirming educational spaces, we need to reach beyond heroes and holidays (Lee et al., 2011) and other physical manifestations of diversity. There is nothing inherently wrong with a focus on diversity. However, diversity is not the destination, but rather a stop along the way. We fear that many schools see diversity as the ultimate apex; in including Black baby dolls or books on Sonia Sotomayor, they have completed their work regarding equity and inclusion. Representation and inclusion are parts of the solution. But equity is a higher bar.

Throughout this book, we hold antiracism as a core goal. We believe that an antiracist is "one who is supporting antiracist policy through their actions or expressing an antiracist idea" (Kendi, 2019, p. 13). Kendi argues that antiracism is a *nametag* rather than a *tattoo*. This is a critical distinction. One does not "do" antiracism on Monday and become permanently an "antiracist." One acts in antiracist ways consistently. Tokenism and inconsistency are the enemies of antiracism. Antiracists strive for depth and breadth and urgency.

As was mentioned earlier, multicultural education often gets defined by a more basic understanding of diversity. We see teachers adding a chapter on Buddhism, or poetry by Black authors. Again, this is a needed and valuable step. Students need to see themselves and others in the materials they read, toys they play with, and examples they see. However, we support Gorski's caution (2020) that "we must avoid being lulled by popular 'diversity' approaches and frameworks that pose no threat to inequity—that sometimes are popular because they are no real threat to inequity" (para. 1). In a particularly cogent manifestation of the superficiality of some diversity initiatives, Gorski (2019) shares his recollections of a typical "celebration of diversity": taco night at his school. In attending this event Gorski points out that he learned:

> (1) Mexican culture is synonymous with tacos; (2) "Mexican" and "Guatemalan" are synonymous and by extension all Latinx people are the same and by further extension all Latinx people are synonymous with tacos (as well as sombreros and dancing cucarachas); and (3) white people love tacos, especially in those hard, crunchy shells, which, I learned later, nobody in Mexico eats. (p. 1)

Despite being a cheeky example, the recollection gets at the heart of an important matter. While this event was no doubt planned to be inclusive, what it yields in many ways is a retrenchment of stereotypes. While Mexican people do indeed eat tacos, there is more to understanding Mexican-ness, yes? So we need to push further. There is simply too much work to do in service of justice to stay fixed at "diversity" as a goal for schools. Instead, the work is much more urgent and wide-reaching.

## ANTI-BLACKNESS AS MORAL FAILURE

The work of Glaude (2020), Miles (2021), and Wilkerson (2020) is instrumental in the way we conceive of our work. In his deeply important book, *Begin Again: James Baldwin's America and Its Urgent Lessons for Our Own*, Glaude states about contemporary America: "I hoped that one day white people here would finally leave behind the belief that they mattered more" (2020, p. xvii). He goes on to explain this as the *value gap*: the persistent belief that Black people matter less. This gap is a form of *the lie*, "a broad and powerful architecture of false assumptions" that suggests that "black people are essentially inferior, less human than white people and therefore deserving of their particular station" (Glaude, 2020, p. 7). He goes on to explain other components of the lie, the falsehoods we tell about American history and about our place as a moral beacon to the world. Glaude is making a deeply ethical case. He insists that suffering and despair continue in this country because the United States continues to replicate the lie; "white America refuses to change" (2020, p. 55). This is a moral failing. The inability of White people to witness and reckon with the lie is a spiritual failure. We wish to stop here to let this point resonate. The argument Glaude makes is not that racism is mean. Or unfair. Or an issue of misunderstanding. He is saying that racism is a *persistent moral failure*, one that is life-threatening to Black people and morally debilitating to White people.

This failure can be seen in a family keepsake shared in the book *All That She Carried* (Miles, 2021). A simple sack, inscribed by the granddaughter of an enslaved woman, echoes the trauma of the lie. Miles shares the hand-stitched testimony of Ruth Middleton in 1921:

> My great grandmother Rose
> mother of Ashley gave her this sack when
> she was sold at age 9 in South Carolina
> it held a tattered dress 3 handfuls of
> pecans a braid of Roses hair. Told her
> It be filled with my Love always
> she never saw her again
> Ashley is my grandmother
>
> Ruth Middleton
> 1921

In this object, White people see a side of slavery and racism that is most often glossed over in their history books: the perspective of Black people. The trauma of families torn apart. The legacy of loss that Ruth conveys when she stitches "It be filled with my Love always." This is the legacy of moral, ethical, and spiritual failure.

Wilkerson (2020) is making a similar claim. She compares racism to a rampant pathogen, one that is ever-present, able to mutate and highly contagious. She goes on to clarify that slavery, in particular, "was not merely an unfortunate thing that happened to black people" (p. 44). Slavery, and its daughter racism, are *evils* that *dehumanize* Black people.

Gholson, Bullock, and Alexander (2012) come to the same conclusion as Wilkerson and Glaude: Exposing moral failure is where antiracist work must focus. In their piece on the brilliance of Black children, they argue: "We can no longer afford to make equity arguments on evidentiary grounds, we have learned from those before us that no amount of evidence or proof will be sufficient to mandate systemic change—there is no silver study. We believe that forceful moral argumentation is the way forward for systemic change under the axiom of brilliance" (p. 6). Nxumalo (2021) reiterates that we are awash in anti-Blackness, intense and unrelenting. Citing Benjamin (2016, in Nxumalo, 2021, p. 1191), "We are drowning in the facts of inequality and injustice." It is not for lack of knowing. Combining these works, a critical pattern emerges in identifying the scope of the issue at hand: Racism is central, dire, persistent and an issue of morality. How do we begin again?

Is it by dressing up as "Indians" for Thanksgiving? Listening to a clip of MLK? Coloring a picture of Rosa Parks? Inclusion cannot do the job here alone. The response to this moral failure, to this ethical disaster, is not taco night.

In general, schools, do not focus on racism. Research by Kohli et al. (2017) showed that educational research is eight times more likely to include words such as *diversity* or *multicultural* over *racism*. However, to overlook racism in all of its forms yields an incomplete view of school communities and renders invisible how racism infiltrates our practices, policies, and outcomes. The antidote to moral failure is not representation. It is the radical uprooting of racism.

## PUSHING AHEAD: ADDRESSING QUESTIONS AND CONFUSIONS

As we have worked with teachers, both practicing and preservice, for over 20 years, several misunderstandings have arisen persistently regarding how to move into conversations about race and racism and how we can best guide students. Here we unpack some common questions and confusions.

### Isn't the Goal Colorblindness?

In undergraduate classes, our suggestion that teachers NOT aspire to colorblindness is often met with suspicion. In one particularly tense interaction, a student was incensed with Kerri's suggestion that we notice race. The student was upset with the entire line of thinking. Isn't the goal to treat everyone the same? We see similar justifications in the "outrage" over the teaching of critical race theory that is happening across the country during the writing of this book. Here in Rhode Island, a community member in June 2021 filed 200+ public record requests, challenging the district's teaching students about race. In her opinion, schools should be "treating students without regard to race" (Doiron, 2021, para. 13).

We reject this rationale. Ignoring race does not make people antiracist. It may make (White) people more comfortable, but it does nothing to remedy the problem. It buries the problem. We simply don't live colorblind lives, despite often espousing that we do. We need to check our motivation for aspiring to colorblindness. Colorblindness is often used as a form of rhetorical "armor." When we say we are colorblind, it is often as a move to demonstrate our lack of racism. But innocence is not gained by an individual claiming colorblindness. Colorblindness is not protection. Apart from being dishonest, colorblindness ignores people of color and their experiences. It denies the historical realities of Black communities in service of White innocence.

Take this (improbable) scenario: Kate, a White person, is meeting Barack Obama. Upon meeting him, does Kate really not notice he is Black? Is it really unknowable? In all honesty, nothing registers regarding race/culture/ethnicity? Nothing is clicking consciously or unconsciously? Kate looks at Barack and thinks, "You are just like me. I thought you were White." None of this seems very plausible, does it?

Ignoring his Blackness does not make Kate anti-racist. What if she looked at him and *simply acknowledged who he is?*

Thus, in schools, instead of being colorblind (or unconscious), we instead suggest being color-conscious. This is both out of respect for the child and family and simply because it is more humane. When we say we are colorblind, what we are really saying is, "I am going to ignore who you are, and treat you like a White person because it makes me uncomfortable to acknowledge that you are Black. If I notice you are Black, then I have to deal with my erroneous beliefs about Black people. It forces me to face a reality about how Black people got here and what their experience has been. If I default to you being White (despite this being disingenuous), then I don't have to deal with all the messiness that stereotypes and habituation to racism has wrought."

What would happen if we treated the child like the Black person they are? Honestly, with care and dignity, not using Whiteness as the standard or default?

## We Already Had a Training on This. Can't I Just Read a Book and Fix This? I Feel Like We Talk About These Issues Too Much.

Sure, you can read a book to learn more about the experiences of Black folks, their history, culture, and so on. In fact, we encourage you to do so. Kerri's PhD advisor used to tell her, "The less you know about people, the more you make up." We strongly agree. The more we know about each other's lives, the less we stereotype. Read all you can: histories, biographies, books for children, Black poetry, plays. Some favorites of ours that we have read over the last 6 months include: *Stamped: Young Reader Edition* by Jason Reynolds and Ibram Kendi, *What Doesn't Kill You Makes You Blacker* by Damon Young, *The Vanishing Half* by Brit Bennett, *We Were 8 Years in Power* by Ta-Nahisi Coates, *We Are the Ship* by Kadir Nelson, and *Fugitive Pedagogy* by Jarvis Givens.

But when we think about the scope and duration of racism, that it is something we have been carrying for over 400 years, we cannot credibly think that a 2-hour training will remedy the problem. We are socialized into racism. A critical problem in doing this work is that there is a sense with some audiences that this is a one-and-done event. You are trained in "inclusion" and then 2 hours later you are no longer impacted by racism or bias. As educators, we all know that this is not how people learn or unlearn. We know that it is difficult to unlearn something that we have become habituated to, and most of us have been raised up in the smog of racism (Tatum, in California Newsreel, 2003). If we have been slowly poisoned by the smog for 20, 30, or 40 years, the antidote can't be delivered in 2 hours, right? It will require a consistent, focused remedy.

**My Family Was Treated Badly Too, and They Are White.**

Without a doubt, White families can struggle with all manner of hardships and obstacles. Poverty, alcoholism, substance abuse, and mental health issues affect White families. White families can be hindered by their lack of education, lack of fluency in English, and lack of stable housing. White people can be treated poorly because they are immigrants, or because they are gay, or because they have a disability. The important distinction, though, is that *being White is not causing the problem*. Something else is the bearer of the hardship (poverty, immigration status, homophobia). Folks doing this work should not equate being White with having an easy life because it simply is not true. That said, racism is not the reason White people struggle. Families of color can be impacted by all the obstacles above, PLUS racism.

**Is Black a Race or a Culture? Do All Black People Have the Same Culture? I Have Taught Black Kids Before and Understand Them.**

Culture and race are not synonymous. Like all labels, "Black" tells us something, and covers up much more. Black people share an experience of Blackness. They do not have a monolithic culture. This only makes sense. When referring to those Black students, which Black experience are we speaking about?

- Kreyòl-speaking immigrant children from Haiti?
- African American youth with family that have been in the United States for 200 years?
- Refugee children from Somalia?

- Afro-Caribbean children who speak Spanish?
- Muslim children from Nigeria?
- U.S.-born children from Louisiana?
- Black kids from Chicago?
- Deaf Black youth from Massachusetts?

Any and all of these children could be in your classroom. Black children can speak English, Spanish, French, Creole, Igbo, Swahili, Amharic, or other languages; be from the South, Los Angeles, Bermuda, or Senegal; practice Islam, Christianity, Judaism, or no religion at all; or be the kin of refugees, immigrants, or a granma who arrived from Liberia in 1978. Which culture are we speaking of?

With labels, instead of seeing them as definitive, it is better to see them as a clue that requires more research. You have a Black student in your classroom. Their Blackness matters. Black people in the United States are racialized and share this lived experience. However, keep digging. The child is uniquely themselves, too. Learn more about the individual and what they need. It is important for teachers to learn and understand about the many cultural backgrounds of their Black students, while seeing the connecting thread of Blackness.

## These Issues Are a Total Land Mine. It Is Better to Stay Away From Them. It Is Easier to Maintain the Status Quo.

We get it. Right now, in the midst of split-second judgments on social media, we understand why many people feel that it is safer to stay away from these conversations. There are times when we feel this pressure. It is particularly hard when criticism arises from unexpected quarters—other women, folks of color, people you feel a kinship with or with whom you are fighting a similar fight.

But who is the status quo easier for?

Every time we make a choice to conform or refute, maintain tradition or go rogue, we prioritize. What we prioritize changes. In not protecting your colleague who is getting heat for the Black Lives Matter flag in her classroom, perhaps we prioritize our own comfort over the inclusion of others? Or maybe the priority is staying out of the fray? But this potentially comes at the risk of Black students feeling like we don't understand or protect *them*. We all have our own bandwidth for risk and how much we are willing to risk can change over time and place. However, it is disingenuous to think that maintaining the status quo is neutral.

## IN CONCLUSION

We return to Baldwin in thinking through whose work antiracism should be. Glaude (2020) explains that Baldwin believed writers were "a kind of conduit" (Glaude, 2020, p. 53). Said another way, writers are a kind of witness, who "tell the story, make it real for those who refuse to believe that such a thing can happen/has happened/is happening here" (p. 53). Baldwin, like so many other Black intellectuals, has been making racism real for White people for generations. We have an overwhelming amount of evidence. There is no surprise. There is no credible way to feign ignorance. The "conduits" have been connecting White people to Black folks' realities for far too long. They are not being heard, understood, attended to, believed.

According to Glaude, Baldwin believed "White Americans . . . had to save themselves" (2020, xxiii). White people have to do the work now. Racism cannot end without this step. Baldwin explains, "All that can save you now is your confrontation with your own history, which is not your past, but your present" (Glaude, 2020, p. 68). *Your present*. Right now, the moral failure continues.

In a similar vein, Love (2019) argues that "racism does not exist without Whiteness" (p. 143) and that White people need to grapple with Whiteness and colorblindness if they want to be true allies (which she labels co-conspirators). This is multiracial work. It is not the sole work of Black people. It is the responsibility—indeed, the moral obligation—of White people to address the harm of racism.

We have chosen to wrap up this and the next three chapters, the ones that are most saturated with content, with some reflection questions. We hope these will allow you to connect your own experiences with the focus of these chapters.

### REFLECTION QUESTIONS FOR CHAPTER 1

- How do you see anti-Blackness manifest in the educational setting you work in?
- Teachers often strive to be colorblind. Have you experienced this? What are the shortcomings of this approach?
- What are the goals for diversity-focused work at your school? Is representation the focus? Justice?
- What are the cultural backgrounds of the Black families at your school?
- How familiar are you with Black scholars and their work? How could you build on your knowledge?

## CHAPTER 2

# Anti-Blackness in Schools
## Overt Hostility and Ignoring Black Intelligence

In this chapter we provide readers with specific examples of how schools enact anti-Blackness and discuss the contexts that allow such enactments to occur unchecked. We begin with the most straightforward instances: overt, no-need-for-interpretation incidents of racism in schools. This is an important place to start, as it serves as a critical self-check that these totally-over-the-top, in-your-face acts of racism are plentiful and nationwide. The United States is not past them yet. While we frequently hear claims that the United States is "post-racial" (see Dawson & Bobo, 2009) and "this isn't us," acts of blatant racism still occur often and from coast to coast.

However, our focus will quickly change. Rather than an extended presentation of the numerous egregious acts of racial intolerance that occur on K–12 campuses each year, our later examples will draw on *sanctioned* and *embedded* school practices and policies. These practices and policies are operationalized by trained educators and paid for by taxpayers. As such, they are part of the very structures of schools.

We then explore how Black intelligence is imagined and defined. An array of *stock stories* (Bell, 2010)—stories that uphold the status quo about racism—suggest Black antipathy towards education. The image of an underachieving Black child is frequently normalized and expected. But as with many stories we confront in these chapters, this one is inaccurate. We share the stories of parents who must fight to get their children tested for gifted education. We hear about youth who are questioned by teachers and fellow students about whether or not they belong in honors courses and then must prove themselves, while White students are assumed to be prepared for them. Time and time again, Black intelligence is seen as something out of the ordinary. This racialization, then, becomes the lens through which non-Black children encounter African American youth. These early experiences of Black youngsters as inferior, unimportant, and even dangerous become the foundation for a society in which Black people are routinely marginalized. In other words, *we teach non-Black youngsters how to treat Black youngsters in school every day*. That treatment then becomes a societal pattern, materializing in subsequent generations. The caste system that we see in American society is largely set in early school experiences.

To counter these stereotypes, we weave academic research and theory together with first-person stories in this chapter. This draws from Gloria Ladson-Billings's use of personal story in her book *Dreamkeepers*. We include these stories because they are largely absent from research and the American metanarrative (Perry, 2005). We appreciate that this approach breaks with academic "rules" about writing. However, part of our goal in this book is to highlight the real, experienced, painful consequences of anti-Blackness in schools. We have tried to be plain about our own positionality and how it dovetails with our work. In this chapter, Joi will share her experiences as a talented, but overlooked, Black girl in schools. She was far ahead of her peers, she had an engaged and tenacious mother, but teachers were unwilling to see her as academically advanced.

## OVERT RACIAL HOSTILITY

Much of this section is filled with absurdly racist actions that are hateful and tiring. We are mindful of what we include in this book; we do not want to give space to hate, and we caution folks to wade carefully through this subsection. We feel it is critical, though, to address overt, hostile acts of anti-Blackness in educational settings. We cannot pretend they do not exist, as it only takes a minute to find many examples of them in the news and on social media. Our intent is not to injure Black readers; however, to skip over how anti-Blackness manifests overtly in schools would leave out a key piece of this reality.

1. September 2021. In the early Fall, several Black student organizations at University of Massachusetts (UMass) Amherst received a common email, written by the "UMass Coalition for a Better Society." On *The Grio*, Magee (2021) shared part of the email:

   We look down upon you, we instantly know in all manners from your language which most of you still speak in some broken form of Ebonics or to ghetto-speak to where your [sic] from (third-world sewers in America bought and paid for by the u.s taxpayer) to how you live (like hoodrats) to how you appear (fro hair, big lips, black skin) you are different. (para. 4)

   The letter says that Black students did not get into UMass Amherst on merit. It goes on to suggest Black students should "consider doing the human race a favor and get sterilized" (Magee, 2021, para. 2). As the email shows, places of learning, even of higher learning, are sites of blatant racism.

2. September 2021. High school students at Park Hill South High School in Missouri recently circulated a petition to bring back

slavery (Johnson, 2021). Screenshots of the incident include comments "I love slavery" and "I hate Blacks" (Hays, 2021, para. 3).

3. September 2021. Students at Salinas High School in California deface a Black baby doll, then take a TikTok video of them stomping the doll. The doll is marked up with big lips and an ankle monitor (Rodriguez, 2021).

4. September 2021. In Bennington, Vermont, local sports news reports students being called the "N-word," "monkey" and "terrorists" during a soccer game, by the opposing team and spectators (Huntley, 2021).

5. October 2021. A teacher in a North Carolina school had her Black students raise their hands, then told them they would all be her "field slaves" if it weren't for the Constitution. At the same school, a parent shared that "A White student had called a Black student a monkey. . . . When the Black student educated him on that being racist and him not liking it and not to call him that and asked the teacher for support, the teacher turned around and said to him, 'Oh, it's OK. We're all a little bit racist.'" (Forman, 2021, para. 6)

6. October 2021. A teacher in Houston is fired after becoming upset that he cannot use the n-word. According to WKRC (2021) the teacher complained to his students, which they recorded, "'And why is it 'cause I'm a White guy, I can't say that? I can't say the N-word?' The teacher goes on to question why there isn't a White history month along with comments about other ethnic groups." (para 3–4)

7. July 2021. In Palmdale, California, a teacher goes on a 30-minute racist rant after meeting with a Black mother, Katura Stokes, via Zoom call. The teacher failed to disconnect after the call, and Zoom captured her telling her husband that they are "'Two kinds of pieces of s***. They're black, he's black." She then goes on to say that Stokes's son has learned to lie to everyone and make excuses and that 'this is what black people do.'" (Schwebke, 2021, para. 15).

8. In a 95% Black and brown school in the Bronx, a principal recently banned the teaching of Black History Month lessons. When a teacher at the school went ahead and taught the Harlem Renaissance to her students anyway, the principal confiscated student-made posters (Branigin, 2018a). While the incident itself is worthy of attention, the follow-up thread that was posted on The Root (a website that highlights African American news and happenings, founded by Henry Louis Gates Jr.) really struck us. A response to the original article was written by Branigin (2018b):

So, when are we going to start talking about how White women, as a force, are the first perpetrators of direct and personal racism against Black and Latino people? As the dominant demographic in our educational system, I would bet my house that a significant amount of folks, if not the majority, *first experienced racism at the hands of their White female teacher.*

(Posted by Just passing through 2/14/18 at TheRoot.com; emphasis added).

Also happening concurrently:

9. September 2021. A Black principal in Texas is suspended for supposedly supporting critical race theory (Howard, B. L., 2021).There is no evidence that he is, nor is it clear why that would be a punishable offense.
10. June 2021. A teacher at Robert E. Lee High School in Jacksonville, Florida, is fired for displaying a Black Lives Matter flag and agitating for Black students' well-being (Kaur, 2021).

*Let's hold one moment.*
Let's acknowledge that *Black children go to a high school named for Confederate general Robert E. Lee. In 2021.* There is also a high school in the same district (Jacksonville, Florida) named for Andrew Jackson, the slave-owning U.S. president. The high schools are 72% and 81% Black, respectively. (Robert E. Lee High was renamed in August 2021 to Riverside High. The name of Jackson High remains unchanged.)

Across these examples that take place in a very small window of time, we see blatant racism in schools from California to New York. There are countless other incidents that we did not include. You are almost sure to find examples in your own home communities. We encourage readers to do a Google search of "racism in schools" along with the name of your state to see what comes up.

We highlight this overt racism for a simple reason: to reiterate that it exists. Black children continue to go to schools in spaces where they are called the N-word, where other students refer to them as slaves and monkeys, and where their intelligence is explicitly questioned and undermined. On top of this must be added all the more quiet and hidden ways that bias can be conveyed, the beliefs that frame Black children as not intelligent or committed to education. It is this stereotype we turn to next.

## IGNORING BLACK INTELLIGENCE

In Gholson et al.'s (2012) important editorial exploring Black brilliance, readers are called to reflect on their beliefs about Black children. The authors ask,

"What do I really believe about Black children and their abilities? How does my work reflect those beliefs?" (p. 4). Basing their editorial on the work of Danny Martin (2011), math education scholar, the authors press their readers to consider *whether we expect Black brilliance*. Or are educators wed to a White standard of academic excellence? Martin argues for a new baseline when working with Black youth.

> We must accept, and insist on, the brilliance of Black children as axiomatic. We must avoid the trap of having to prove that Black children are brilliant. We must avoid generating arguments, logic models, and counternarratives requiring proof that Black children are not brilliant. (Martin, 2011, in Gholson et al., 2012, p. 3)

The idea that Black children are inherently less intelligent, less capable, or in need of the most support is yet another outgrowth of the stories we tell that have taken on a life of their own. Looking again at the history of Black education in the United States, we turn to the work of Jarvis Givens. In his truth-telling book *Fugitive Pedagogy* (2021), we see the historical refutation of this story. Black people have always sought education in the United States. Despite laws that expressly forbade Black people from becoming literate (beginning in 1740), Givens estimates that 10% of enslaved Africans learned to read and write (2021). This is a stunning fact. Despite their bondage, and considering that their access was barred, materials were withheld, and slaveholders explicitly fought against any education (not to mention, again, the illegality), literacy was still considered a key to freedom. We have seen this example already with Frederick Douglass. Because Black learning was a fugitive act, "outlawed and defined as . . . criminal" (Givens, 2021, p. 3), early enslaved Africans learned in the shadows, hidden and covertly.

Givens also describes the communal nature of Black education: "Literacy was never primarily an individualized, antisocial endeavor in the context of Black life; it was largely a social act at the center of Black political struggle" (2021, p. 39). Givens explains that Carter G. Woodson was hired as a reader by coal miners, who paid him with fruit and sweets for reading to them. As he read (often the daily newspaper), the coal miners would discuss and argue the relevant issues of the day. Reading was a community endeavor, communal work, a way for Black people to strive together. But Woodson was clear back in 1901 that White people neither saw nor respected the long history of Black learning and community uplift. In an effort to push back on "the dominant narratives of Black pathology" (Givens, 2021, p. 44), Woodson had students participate in oratorical performances for the public, to allow White people to see the intelligence of Black youth. Argues Givens (2021):

> Woodson also critiqued the implicit message that black people were incapable of thinking for themselves. The idea that black people lacked the capacity for reason—what the Cameroonian philosopher Achille Mmembe refers to as the

"Western consciousness of Blackness"—was used to justify White paternalism and the persistence of racial domination. (p. 103)

These public performances were a way to push back on this. However, despite how successful his students were, White folks still found a way to undercut Woodson. Some gave credit to the White superintendent as the "real" explanation for their success (Givens, 2021). This "whitewashing of Black genius" (Black, 2020) is a consistent feature in White storytelling about Black intelligence. When the biracial Frederick Douglass engaged in debate with a White doctor in 1850 over whether Black people *were a different species*, his convincing arguments were chalked up to the influence of his White (slave-owning) father; those in attendance declared that none of his intellectual ability could have come from his Black (enslaved) mother (Black, 2020). Poignantly, Douglass specifically and forcefully credits his intellect entirely to his mother in subsequent comments, entirely rejecting this notion of Black inferiority.

This theme—that Black learning is neither new nor exceptional—is echoed by Gholdy Muhammad (2020) in her restorative book, *Cultivating Genius*. Muhammad reminds the reader that the history of Black educational excellence in the United States reaches back to the early days of this country. Black literary societies, founded in the 1800s, were convened with the aim of "advancing the condition of African Americans" through opportunities to build reading, writing, and speaking skills post-slavery (Muhammad, 2020, p. 26). Her work shows a rich and expansive history of education advancing the well-being of Black communities. For men and women, old and young, Black literary societies were built on a collectivist ideal that one's individual knowledge must be shared with the community; not to do so would be considered selfish (Muhammad, 2020). During the 1800s, groups of people would meet together to share texts, debate, and engage in educating one another. This was a form of community uplift.

Stephon Alexander, a Trinidadian professor of physics at Brown University, provides a contemporary example of how the Black community supported education in places like New York. He shares this story about growing up in the Bronx in New York City. He would take the city bus back and forth to high school, and while riding, do his homework.

And one day a guy said to his friend: "This guy is doing supreme mathematics." And from that point on, they basically protected me. Treated me as one of their own, and so I always felt welcome in my community. This is the same group of guys that encouraged me to go to college. They were like: "You need to go to college, get that knowledge and come back." That sentiment stuck with me. I've always wanted to bring my knowledge back to the community in whatever way that I could. I never held this idea of a conflict between being authentic and being smart and seeking knowledge. These ideas were never paradoxical growing up in the Bronx. Now, the media portrayed that differently—that our culture was anti-intellectual. But that was not the case where I came from. Being smart has always been a part of being from the streets. (Ogbunu, 2021, question 3)

There is a long history of Black intellectual work. Black academic excellence has always existed. Intelligent Black people, Black people learning, Black people succeeding in schools-
And yet.
The stereotype remains.
Muhammad recalls asking White teachers to tell her about their Black students. They responded that such students were "unmotivated, they can't read or they have discipline problems" (in Ferlazzo, 2020, p. 5). There is a pattern of ascribing pathology to Black children and their intellect when we should be ascribing the gaps to lack of learning opportunities. Let's use math as an example.

There is clear and consistent evidence that Black students receive a different kind of education than others in mathematics. What Gutiérrez (2008) names our "gap-gazing fetish" (i.e., spending resources and energy documenting differences in the test scores of Black students on the one hand and White and Asian students on the other) obfuscates a pernicious reality, that Black students often receive an embarrassingly subpar learning experience. Mathematics education researchers have begun to document this truth more and more over the past couple of decades (Flores, 2007; McGee & Martin, 2011; Oakes et al., 2004; Spencer, 2009; Strutchens & Silver, 2000). We look at mathematics performance among Black students in particular, as mathematics is far too often seen as a proxy of intelligence and capacity. While it has shed light on differences in learning opportunities, documenting the differences in mathematics achievement scores between U.S.-born Black and White students has become a national obsession, with roots in societal beliefs about the intellectual inferiority of Black youth (Spencer & Hand, 2015). A quick Google Scholar search of the terms "black white mathematics achievement gap" and "race differences in mathematics achievement" produced 310,000 and 795,000 sources respectively. Test scores so easily confirm what is already believed to be true. But what do they actually mean? The student achievement to which we as educators have been compelled to give our attention is in fact a social construction. The finely disaggregated test data that we pore over during our monthly meetings (carefully demonstrating student performance by race, gender, language, disability status, and the like) so often points to the low performance of Black children. But this is more a symptom of poor teaching than it is a representation of Black children's ability. In other words, Blackness does not produce low achievement scores; rather, racialized experiences, like those that Joi navigated while in school, shape, funnel, and siphon off the learning opportunities of Black students.

Flores's (2007) study deconstructed the mathematics "achievement gap" to lay bare the mathematics "opportunity gap" that Black students face. His work demonstrated that African American students experience limited opportunities to learn mathematics on a number of fronts, including limited access to experienced teachers, frequent exposure to low expectations, and inequitable per-student funding. Like us, he asks:

> What kind of images do we form about the students who lag behind after reading such statements? What kind of assumptions, conscious or subconscious, do we make about their capacity for learning? Do we ask why their performance is worse? Stopping with only an examination of the symptoms often leads too easily to a focus on student characteristics as the cause. (p. 30)

His work goes on to show that African American students are less likely to have teachers who emphasize high-quality mathematics pedagogy, including those who employ "reasoning and non-routine problem solving; computers; and, teachers who use computers for simulations and applications" (p. 32). Likewise, his work reveals the high percentages of out-of-field and inexperienced mathematics teachers that Black children often face.

In her examination of qualitative NAEP data, Lubienski (2002) presents the mathematics classroom experiences of Black youth. Rather than focus on racial achievement differences between Black and White students, she asks: What kind of mathematics instruction do Black students have access to? Her research provides compelling evidence that 4th-, 8th- and 12th-grade Black students received different kinds of pedagogical inputs than their White counterparts. For example, Black students were "more likely to be assessed with multiple choice tests," while White students more often had instructors who put "heavy emphasis on the reasoning skills needed to solve unique problems" (p. 272). As she explains:

> According to NAEP data, Black students were more likely to be tested on finding the single correct answer to problems (on a multiple-choice test) without the use of a calculator, which suggests basic fact computation as a major instructional focus. White students were more likely to have teachers go beyond computation skills as evidenced by the use of calculators and the emphasis on reasoning to solve unique problems. (p. 272)

Mathematics is a microcosm of larger trends in the learning of Black students. However, the fingerprints of low expectations are evident across the country. ProPublica produced an open-source application in 2018 aimed at locating and exposing racial inequalities in U.S. school districts. Their database, *Miseducation* (Groeger et al., 2018), allows people to access data on local schools and how they support, or interfere, with equity. A sample of their findings:

- White students are 6.9 times as likely to be enrolled in at least one AP class as Black students in Bladen County, North Carolina.
- Black students are, on average, academically 3.8 grades behind White students in DeKalb County, Georgia.
- Black students are, on average, academically 3.5 grades behind White students in Alachua County, Florida. (Groeger et al., 2018)

Data from the Office for Civil Rights expands on these deficits (2016). Their work found that Black children have less access to high-level mathematics and science courses, are underrepresented in gifted and talented programs and AP courses, are more likely to be retained, and are more likely to be taught by inexperienced or unlicensed teachers.

Skepticism towards Black intelligence and buying into deficit views of Black youth are clearly still with us. This is a contemporary problem. What shocks us is that instead of considering the consequences of context and history, people instead lean into pathological explanations that posit low performance as something wired into Black people.

Let's look at Virginia as an example. According to the *Miseducation* database referenced above, Virginia has some of the widest education gaps in the United States. The gaps between White and Black students have *widened* since 2005 (Waldman & Green, 2018). Fifty percent of Black children cannot read on grade level in the city of Charlottesville, VA, compared to 10% of White children. In an audit conducted in 2019 by the Equity Collaborative, researchers in Loudoun County, VA, found students who reported that the teachers "treat us like we are super dumb" (p. 11); students reported widespread use of the N-word, a word teachers explicitly did not condemn; students asked, "When a kid who is misbehaving and is Black—why do you hear 'that kid's going to end up in jail someday'—but you don't hear that about the White kids who mess up?" (Equity Collaborative, 2019, p. 12). Parents reported children being called "liar" by principals when they reported being called the N-word.

Schools were under no pressure to desegregate in Virginia until the *Brown v. Board* case in 1954. After the case, Virginia defied the court's mandate to integrate "with all deliberate speed." Loudoun County's Board of Supervisors voted in 1956 to allow public funds to pay for private schools, allowing White children to avoid desegregated schools at the county's expense (see *An Apology to the Black Community of Loudoun County*, Loudoun County Public Schools, 2020). The same year Loudoun voted to suspend paying for public schools if they were desegregated. In 1958, Virginia Governor J. Lindsay Almond shut down two White schools in Charlottesville rather than integrate them. Charlottesville went on to add testing requirements for Black children who wanted to attend majority-White schools. Two additional court orders, in 1963 and 1967, filed by U.S. federal courts tried to compel Virginia to desegregate their schools.

Loudoun County Public Schools, *in 2020,* released a public letter to the Black community apologizing for rampant racism (2020):

> There was significant resistance by the School Board and Superintendent to integrate our schools during the era of Massive Resistance and several other inequities persisted as a result, such as:
>
> - inequities in teacher salaries, recruitment, on-going professional learning, as well as administrative leadership development for principals and staff;
> - inequities in recruitment for college and advanced placement preparation for students;
> - a lack of diversity among applied and admitted students to the Academies of Loudoun;
> - disproportionate discipline of Black students;
> - school names and a school mascot named after or potentially named after Confederate figures and plantations;
> - the facilitation of lessons and activities that do not reflect cultural responsiveness and instead reinforce subservient gender and racial roles;
> - failure to teach students about the Black Post-Civil War communities that existed into the mid-century. (p.1)

A historic self-check is important here. While, as we have shown, Black youth have employed many underground ways to access education throughout history, schools across the United States were not compelled to desegregate until 1954. Even after the *Brown v. Board* case, many districts continued to refuse Black children admittance, dragging their feet for decades. Loudoun did not admit them until 1967. It is important to point out that these obstacles were intentional. All the dimensions listed in the apology letter above were designed to maintain the racial and economic status quo. For example, let's look at inequities in teacher salaries. Returning to Chapter 1 for a moment, this is not simply an issue of one person being mean to another. This is a system-wide policy. The choice to underpay Black teachers was a district-wide decision. Consider the further accrual of benefits afforded to Whites who received those larger salaries, attended those private schools, or experienced the tax benefits of the unfair laws. While disadvantaging Blacks, the laws were simultaneously advantaging Whites. The legacy of this arrangement lives on today. While Loudoun is our first example, they are hardly alone.

A note to readers: While we cite the *Brown* case here as a marker of improved educational opportunity for Black children, we call out that pre-*Brown* African American "segregated" schools were often incredible spaces of Black learning and liberation (Walker, 1996). While these schools were ruthlessly underfunded and Black communities endured double taxation to maintain them (Anderson, 1988), the schools nevertheless affirmed Black student identity, promoted high achievement, and produced generations of

African American leaders and thinkers. There is an unsupported assumption by liberal educators that *Brown* was a natural solution to inequitable schools. Ladson-Billings's *Landing on the Wrong Note: The Price We Paid for Brown* (2004) and her speech at the North Carolina Law Symposium, *Can We at Least Have Plessy: The Struggle for Quality Education* (2006) are both critical to understanding the shortcomings of integration as it was enacted post-*Brown*. What *Brown* has demonstrated is that simply sitting Black children next to White children does not solve longstanding challenges of inequity. Derrick Bell, famed civil rights attorney, called *Brown* "a magnificent mirage" (2004, p. 4). In their work on Black critical theory, Dumas and ross (2016) argue that there are many ways in which desegregation negatively impacted Black communities, including making them more unstable, interfering with the mental well-being of Black children, and impeding the development of healthy racial identities. They cite Ladson-Billings's claim that this was a "deal with the devil" (Dumas & ross, 2016, p. 432), one that sent Black children to hostile environments, often far from their families, with no curriculum or pedagogy put in place to support them. This concern is echoed in Ashley Woodson's (2021) work. She writes that desegregated settings "devastated the Black educational infrastructure" (p. 17). Woodson argues that early Black Southern teachers were concerned that desegregation would be harmful to Black children, in that it would undermine Black children's pride, displace Black teachers, and destroy community connections. Fast-forwarding to 2021, Ashley Woodson states, "We can't honestly argue that post-*Brown* learning conditions have ameliorated Black subordination in any meaningful way. . . . Trauma is now apparent in the historical insistence that Black children's wholeness was only accessible through forms of schooling designed to serve White middle class children and sustain White supremacy" (p. 17).

We acknowledge that the road to integration has been long and winding; that Black children must overcome many obstacles to attend integrated schools; that the Black community gains and loses with desegregation; and that all schools have lost due to the deprofessionalizing of Black teachers and administrators.

Returning to post-*Brown* realities, Boston was also exceedingly slow in desegregating their schools. In 1972, Black parents sued the Boston School Committee for maintaining segregated schools, almost 20 years after *Brown v. Board*. Judge W. Arthur Garrity ruled in 1974 that schools were indeed segregated:

> The court concludes that the defendants took many actions in their official capacities with the purpose and intent to segregate the Boston public schools and that such actions caused current conditions of segregation in the Boston public schools. . . . Plaintiffs have proved that the defendants intentionally segregated schools at all levels, built new schools for a decade with sizes and locations designed to promote segregation, [and] maintained patterns of overcrowding

and underutilization which promoted segregation. (*Morgan v. Hennigan*, 379 F. Supp. 144, 146; in Delmont, 2016)

This ruling put into motion a busing plan to integrate city schools. Busing, however, was met with widespread outrage and violence. Garrity and his family received death threats. The first day of school in 1974, the National Guard was called in to counter protesters who were breaking windows and throwing bottles at school buses transporting Black children. Violence and protests continued for years. In 1976, an anti-busing protester, Joseph Rakes, assaulted a Black lawyer with an actual American flag. The image was captured in the Pulitzer Prize–winning photograph "The Soiling of Old Glory," taken by *Boston Herald* photographer Stanley Forman. The truly surreal image shows a well-dressed Black man reeling back as a White teen, using a large flagpole as a pike, prepared to lunge at him. The American flag itself ripples with the movement.

Again, this is 1976. In Boston. In the widely believed to be "tolerant" North. Mass protests against integration and violence consistently menaced Black children. Giving an interview in 2021, Cedric Turner, a Black student at English High School in the Fenway (a Boston neighborhood), remembers attending football games where rocks were thrown, the N-word yelled, and windows broken by White students and families (Woolhouse, 2021). At one game, White families took out guns to intimidate the football team, a memory that brings tears to Mr. Turner's eyes when sharing it almost 40 years later.

Garrity himself oversaw the desegregation plans through 1982, when the task was turned over to the State Board of Education. Stunningly, in marking the 30th anniversary of the original Herrigan case, a *Boston Globe* reporter argued:

> On the 30th anniversary of the Boston school desegregation case, Boston schools are racially segregating once again. Many factors, including the continuing migration of White families from the city and segregated neighborhood housing patterns, undoubtedly contribute to increasing segregation in Boston schools. However, the elimination of voluntary racial fairness guidelines in school assignments and the inability to take race into account in making admissions decisions in the exam schools further exacerbate the difficulty of maintaining a racially diverse school system. Boston, it seems, is no example to follow. (McArdle, 2004, para. 8)

Advancing to 2021, Boston is still accused of not providing equitable education for its Black youth. Massachusetts overall is widely considered to have one of the best public school systems in the United States. Boston, however, is a different story. Boston's city population is 22% Black and 44% White. According to a damning report from the Massachusetts Department of Elementary and Secondary Education, "Opportunity and achievement gaps abound in the district" (2020, p. 2). In a district profile, the Commissioner of Education for the state highlights the following Boston data:

> On the 2019 MCAS English language arts assessment, just 25 percent of African American/Black students and 26 percent of economically disadvantaged students met or exceeded expectations, while 63 percent of Asian students and 62 percent of White students met or exceeded expectations.

> Similarly, on the MCAS mathematics assessment . . . only 21 percent of African American/Black students and 23 percent of economically disadvantaged students met or exceeded expectations, while 73 percent of Asian students and 62 percent of White students met or exceeded expectations. (pp. 1–2)

Black and brown children in Boston public schools do not experience the same education as their White suburban classmates. Over the last 20 years there has been no movement in integrating schools. Remember that Boston's population is 44% White? Boston public schools are only 13% White (Ciurczak et al., 2020). The evidence of segregation is quite clear. Where are all those White children?

Looking across these two places (Virginia and Boston), we see a pattern. Pre-*Brown v. Board*, Black children often attended schools that were separate and not equal. They did not have the same resources, facilities and funding. The education of Black children, by the government, was not a priority. Post-*Brown*, these districts intentionally took great pains not to change the status quo. They created obstacle after obstacle to maintain segregation. This persisted through the 1970s and even into the 1980s with continuing court orders. That was just 40 years ago. 40 years. There has never been a point in time where the education of Black children has been a persistent, urgent, nationwide issue that was well supported and well funded. And let's add this historical reminder: Slavery ended only about 150 years ago. In the span of human existence, both the education of Black children and the ending of Black bondage happened just minutes in our past. As much as we in the United States seem to believe that these issues are so far behind us, that our racist past is so long ago, there are people alive today whose parents and grandparents were enslaved[1]. These observations together lead us to an obvious question: Is there something wrong with Black children, or is there something wrong with the way we *educate* Black children?

## SOME STORIES

I (Joi) was bused to a majority-White elementary school in an almost entirely White upper-middle-class community. It was clear to everyone (every teacher, parent, student, administrator, custodian, etc.) which students lived in the community (White) and which students were bused (Black). While rarely discussed, race sat just below the surface of conversations, decisions, and attitudes towards students. I was a quiet, academically minded student. My mother spent the majority of my elementary school years fighting for me to receive access to the resources that she believed I deserved. In the 3rd grade, at our annual student award ceremony, I was awarded with an "Outstanding Improvement" award instead of an "Outstanding Achievement Award," even though I had higher grades than many of the students who received the Achievement Award. I remember feeling insulted and hurt when students who were not as academically strong as me were rewarded for their achievements, while I was overlooked.

Also in the 3rd grade, I would come home often complaining to my mother that I felt that the teacher ignored me and that perhaps she did not even know who I was. My mother asked for a conference with the teacher. Before the conference began, the teacher shared, "I don't have any problems with Joi" (as if this were the only reason to pay attention to a student). As they sat and conferenced in our classroom, my mother asked, "Where does Joi sit?" The teacher could not recall where my seat was. She pulled out her seating chart and found that I sat in the back row of the classroom. My mother shared that I felt like the teacher did not know or like me. The teacher was alarmed and said that she would change my seat and try to pay more attention to me.

When I was in the 5th grade, my mother requested that I be tested for the gifted and talented program. The teacher informed her that not enough of my standardized scores were high enough to test me for the program. She did not say that she had tested me and I had not performed well enough on the exam to be admitted into the gifted and talented program. Rather, she refused to test me based on my performance on a standardized exam. I watched throughout all of elementary school as my classmates (many of whom I regularly outperformed academically) received gifted and talented services and programming.

In the 6th grade, we were assigned to write a report on a chosen country. When the teacher passed back our reports, she stated that two students had done a stellar job. She then revealed that I was one of the students, but that the other student (a White male student) had done just a little bit better than me. This student was highlighted in a school news story and given special recognition by the principal. I am not sure what made his report "a little better."

I was chosen to speak at our 6th-grade graduation. During our final dress rehearsal, I, along with each of the other student speakers (four or five students), recited their speeches. My speech drew applause from the small group of teachers and students gathered at the rehearsal, which made me feel really proud. The next day during graduation, one of the female students who had struggled greatly during the dress rehearsal gave a speech that now had several exact elements and phrases from my speech. This particular student was from the local school neighborhood. It was clear that our teachers had rallied around her after the dress rehearsal to ensure that she was not upstaged by one of the bused students.

By the time I reached 6th grade, I was reading at a 12th-grade level. Unable to deny me any further (and based upon my grades, academic performance, and standardized exam scores), I was immediately granted admission into one of our city's gifted and talented junior high school programs.

In my freshman year of high school, my history teacher returned my first essay of the school year. I had worked hard on it and had even spent time talking with my best friend, Daniel, about what I was planning to write. Daniel, an African American boy, was one of the smartest kids I had ever met. His vocabulary was powerful, and he was extremely well read. There was little question that he was one of the brightest students in our freshman class. Like me, he was enrolled in enhanced and honors courses where they were available. When I received my essay back from the teacher, written on the top of the paper in red ink were the phrases, "Wow! I'm surprised. Good job," followed by the grade A-. I worked to process what the comments meant and turned the phrases over and over again in my head. Was she surprised that I only did A- work, holding the expectation that I was capable of doing better? If so, then why the "Good job"? Was she surprised that I did well? Did the essay itself wow her or did it wow her, that *I* did well on it? As I sat there working to make sense of it,[2] I glanced over at Daniel, to see how he had fared. Catching a glimpse of him, I could see that he was quite upset. When we met at lunch to talk about the essay, I learned that his fate was perhaps worse than mine was. There was only one word written on top of his paper, "plagiarism," followed by the letter grade "F." I was stunned. He was incensed. The teacher had underlined particular words throughout his paper and written a series of notes such as "Use your own words," and "Do you know what this word means?" Over the next few weeks, Daniel met with the teacher several times trying to convince her that these were indeed his words and his essay. She never budged. She simply refused to believe that a young man such as Daniel had the capacity to write such an essay. It was heartbreaking, but Daniel had to begin his freshman year of history working his way up from a failing grade. Throughout the school year, this teacher demonstrated to us (through her comments, actions, decisions, and dispositions) a belief that the intellectual capacity of Black students was limited and inferior.

Daniel and I learned then that we had to take one of two approaches with our history teacher: Give in to her expectations of us and water down our work (making it palatable and in line with her beliefs about our capacity), or take things to the next level and work to "wow" her at every step of the way. We took the latter, outpacing and outperforming everyone in our class. As I would learn later, ours was a strategy that many African American youngsters decide to take. Ebony McGee and Danny Martin's (2011) work speaks to this phenomenon. Their article, "You Would Not Believe What I

Have to Go Through to Prove My Intellectual Value!," documents the experiences of Black mathematics and engineering college students as they navigate and manage the particularly negative stereotypes of Black performance in STEM fields. McGee and Martin use the term "stereotype management," described as "a tactical response to ubiquitous forms of racism and racialized experiences across school and non-school contexts" (2011, p. 1347), to help explain the sustained success of certain Black students. This is different from stereotype threat, which is characterized as "being at risk of confirming, as self-characteristic, a negative stereotype about one's group" (Steele & Aronson, 1995, p. 797). Unlike stereotype threat, which undermines and suppresses the success of those being stereotyped (Steele & Aronson, 1995), stereotype management propels achievement. Students are aware of the stereotypes that they are facing and are actively strategizing to overcome them. This strategizing gives them agency.

When I was in 6th grade, one day our teacher departed from her typical process of dismissing the class to go home at the end of the school day. Normally, we were dismissed based upon the table that had behaved or achieved the best in class that day. However, on this day, my teacher paused a bit before dismissal and then said, "Today, I want my blonde-haired, blue-eyed kids to go first." I watched as my friends Cory and Amy and so many more stood up and left the classroom. Let me unpack this experience, as its impact on me was great. As I stated, being dismissed first in our class was a daily ritual. It was a way for our teacher to communicate to us who and what she approved of and a moment for her to acknowledge the good job of students who had worked hard, paid attention, and succeeded. It was an honor that was (at least in my mind at that time) open to all students, as long as they worked hard and behaved. However, in this quick moment, the blinders fell from my eyes. For the first time, I realized that there were characteristics that my teacher paid attention to that I had absolutely no knowledge of, and that she was basing her judgments about us (about me) on criteria completely outside of my control. She had broken a sacred contract between student and teacher: that in the space of this classroom, the only things that mattered were hard work, achievement, and good behavior. Something more was broken that day: my understanding of the true relationship between my classmates and me. Until that day, I did not know what blond hair was. I knew that many of my classmates were "White." That was a term that I was fairly familiar with. However, I had neither language nor understanding that there was different nomenclature for describing the shades of hair color that my White friends had. If you asked me to name the colors of my classmates' hair, I would have described them in relation to the color brown, from very light to very dark. You can imagine my shock as kids from all over the classroom stood up, as if on cue, pushed in their chairs and happily left first for the day. You can imagine my surprise when a characteristic that I did not know existed was known and even lauded by both my teacher and my friends. Perhaps more importantly, you can imagine my hurt when children who had misbehaved, talked back to the teacher, done poorly on assignments, and failed to turn in homework stood up and accepted an honor that they did not deserve for characteristics that I would never have. It was as if my teacher were saying, "You can force busing on me, you can even place Black kids in my classroom, but my allegiance will remain with the White children who rightfully belong here." Likewise, to her Black students, my teacher was clearly saying, "You can behave well, you can even earn good grades, but you will never be truly accepted or enough by me. You will never be *my* blonde-haired and blue-eyed children." I changed that afternoon. And whether my classmates were cognizant of it at that time or not, they too were changed.

For those with blonde hair and blue eyes, they learned that they were favored, that the rules did not apply to them. For everyone else, we learned that the standard for beauty and favor (in the eyes of our teacher) was blonde hair and blue eyes. We learned that while she *said* that working hard, playing fair at recess, and completing our homework were what she valued most in us, what she truly believed and cared about was something entirely different. Her words and actions that day revealed her true loyalties. Her small act happened so quickly, almost invisibly, that afternoon. Her gentle grin as she acknowledged her special students standing and leaving for the day, the lowered eyes of the kids who remained sitting, and my realization that she too had blonde hair and blue eyes. It was simply dismissing kids to go home at the end of the school day, yet it represented the countless acts of spoken and unspoken, visible and invisible ways that racism shaped my life.

## THE PHYSICAL AND MENTAL TOLL OF THE DEFICIT VIEW

Like working one's way up from the bottom of a well (Bell, 1992), succeeding while Black in school can be a tiresome, exhausting climb. This aspect of anti-Black racism is rarely addressed in the literature. Yet it is real and has abiding effects. Epidemiologist Sherman James describes John Henryism as "a strong behavioral disposition to confront adversity with determined high-effort coping" (James, 2021, minute 19:57), where adversity is described as "undue hardship caused by laws, societal norms, and institutional practices (i.e., structural racism) that constrain significant upward socioeconomic mobility" (minute 20:26). His 12-item scale used to measure John Henryism detects high-effort coping with such items as, "When things don't go the way I want them to, that just makes me work even harder," and "It's not always easy, but I usually find a way to do the things I really need to get done" (Feldscher, 2021, para. 6). James's research demonstrates that (1) African Americans tend to score higher on the John Henryism scale than any other group and that (2) There are physiological costs related to prolonged exposure to societal stressors.

In American folklore, John Henry was an African American steel driver who gave his life hammering drills into solid rock to make way for the American railroad system. After the Civil War, Henry is placed into a competition where he competes against a steam-powered drilling machine to see who can most quickly hammer steel through solid rock. Henry outpaces the steam drill, tunneling rock across the entire American frontier. Soon after the competition ends, John Henry drops dead from exhaustion, having built the infrastructure for the nation, but giving his life in sacrifice. That his name would be used to describe the experiences of achieving African Americans (students, scholars, workers, etc.) is appropriate given the racism they must endure in our schools and the battles that they must fight against the rock of racism. However, as James's definition explains, this effort has consequences. The prolonged exposure to these adversities coupled with high-effort coping "can lead to a whole remodeling of the cardiovascular system and the onset of high blood pressure and organ damage" (James, quoted in Feldscher, 2021, para. 7). Thus, the allostatic load—the "cumulative burden of chronic stress and life events" (Guidi et al., 2021, p. 11)—weighs most heavily on Black individuals in American society (see Greenberg, 2020, for further discussion). There is no doubt that our schools contribute to this problem.

This deficit approach to Black youth spins off an additional phenomenon: the concept of Black exceptionalism. Black exceptionalism is "the notion that Black people who are educated, smart, articulate, poised, and basically every other positive adjective you can think of are atypical or rarities among the general Black population" (Agada, 2015, para. 7). Instead of seeing intelligent Black children as common and "normal," Black children who succeed academically are often seen as rare or even surprising. For example, in 2014, Akintunde Ahmad graduated from high school in Oakland, California, with a 5.0 GPA and an admission offer to Yale. He was featured on the *Ellen Show* and was celebrated as one of the rare Black boys who found academic success in Oakland (Getachew, 2021). Getachew, a Black graduate of the same high school, reminds us that in a city like Oakland, where most of the kids are Black, these "rare" events should not be rare at all. Black valedictorians should be the norm. Black kids going to college should be the norm. The trope (as Getachew refers to it) of Black exceptionalism injures Black youth. It sets underachievement as the norm. When Black youth succeed, instead of it being normalized as these talented students being part of the general community, they are framed as one in a million. In this way, Black exceptionalism confines Black excellence, making it not a day-to-day reality but a once in-a-blue-moon miracle.

## IN CONCLUSION

We began this chapter detailing several of the overt racist activities that have taken place in U.S. schools. We provided examples from 2021 to make the case that these realities are not bygone relics of some other age. We moved quickly to the legacy of Black intelligence and detailed the ways in which it has always operated. Black people are the only group in the United States for whom it was illegal to learn to read and write. Yet literary societies defined free Black and post-enslaved communities.

The narrative of Black intellectual inferiority lies at the root of anti-Black racism in schools. The story that Black youth and their communities are worth less and thereby deserve less is embedded deep within the policies, practices, and imaginations of those who run American schools. Our running picture of racism as evil White men covered in sheets riding horseback through an African American homestead works to shelter us from the current harms Black students endure. As long as we are not overtly keeping Black children out of White schools (flashback to a tiny Ruby Bridges walking through an irate White mob to enter the doors of the then all-White elementary school). we are shielded from the claims that racism is in action. But it is indeed, as we have begun to detail here.

It is not possible to neglect with such regularity and consistency someone whom we genuinely value. In our next chapter, we extend this thesis further as we explore the omission of the Black experience from curriculum, white-washing of history, and the valuing of Black youths' athleticism over their intellects. As we move into the next chapter, we offer some questions for reflection and wrap-up of this section.

## REFLECTION QUESTIONS FOR CHAPTER 2

- When you think of how racism shows up in your home community, where do you see overt racism in action?
- What is the history of school integration in your district/state? What obstacles (e.g., I want my kid to be able to attend school in our own neighborhood) have White families offered as to why integration isn't possible? If there are no Black youth in your district, what explains this?
- What is the status of Black education in your home community? Is there a difference in the quality of education that Black vs. White (vs. Asian, vs. Latinx) children receive? What accounts for the differences in instruction that we see between Black and White students?
- How would/do Black community members and youth explain their experiences in local schools? What obstacles did they face? Did they experience negative beliefs about their intelligence or limited access to academic programs and opportunities?

## CHAPTER 3

# Anti-Blackness in Schools

## Omissions and Whitewashing, Centering Athleticism Over Intellect, and Adultification

In this chapter, we continue to expand our discussion of how anti-Blackness manifests in schools. We reiterate that these are common, everyday occurrences that are normalized in the practices, policies, and even the culture of schools. These examples are not anomalies. For African American children, schooling is racialized: it is shaped, altered, and diminished by racism.

We begin with the content of what we teach, our curriculum. We look at anti-Blackness via *whitewashing* and *omission*, when we look at how Black history is included (or not) in the curriculum. A Texas social studies book recently was called out on social media for including the statement, "Millions of workers from Africa came to the southern United States to work on agricultural plantations" as a way of explaining slavery (Isensee, 2015, para. 2). There is so much wrong here. Workers they were not. To say they came to the Southern United States omits the fact that the North was complicit in slavery as well. Enslaved Africans worked in fields, AND in all other trades. Many of them became skilled artisans. "Came to work" conveys, incorrectly, that they did so willingly. "Kidnapped and made to work" or "forced to work" would be more accurate. A focus on "work" omits the "owning" part of slavery, which extends further than one's work life. The inability to identify enslaved Africans correctly, to tell the truth about our history, provides a skewed understanding to youth who learn of "workers" instead of stolen people. Here we look at the ways in which Black people and their history, literature, and art are missing, marginalized, or "adjusted" in ways that obfuscate the truth and minimize their contributions.

The centering of Black physical ability—mainly through sports—is an outgrowth of the stories that are told about Black people and their physical prowess. We look at anti-Blackness in its aspect of centering athleticism over intellect. Schools recruit and then invest in the athletic promise of Black students, ignoring important facets of these young people's identities and development. Black youth are seen as athletic and physically capable, the antithesis of intellectual and intelligent. As a result, their intellectual gifts are overlooked, and their bodies are placed in the service of schools' athletic programs. The consequences of this are numerous, including the academic underdevelopment of Black students and the codification (in the minds of non-Black students) that Black students' only contributions are to the athletic standing of their schools and communities.

We look at anti-Blackness via *adultification* when we look at the phenomenon of school discipline. Black preschoolers (age 4!) make up almost half of out-of-school suspensions for this age group despite only being 18% of the population (National Public Radio, 2014). This early association of Black children with deviance, combined with the inability to see Black children as children (playful, goofy, curious, beautiful), helps to set the conditions for the overpolicing of Black bodies.

Finally, as Black minds are constrained in schools, so are Black bodies. We will look at the way that Black youth are policed, be it their hair, clothing, or behavior, in ways that White children are not. Building on adultification, we turn to the disproportionate toll of school discipline on Black children. From dress codes, to rules on hairstyles, to the criminalization of minor school infractions by actual police, Black youth are the recipients of heavy-handed policies that overlook that they are *children*. As we see in the news, the consequences of this overpolicing are dire.

As we begin this discussion, we gently remind readers that each of these groupings of anti-Blackness represents different manifestations of racism: the deeply held beliefs that there are different kinds of humanity and that particular "groups" are superior (in morality, intelligence, etc.) than others. We highlight this point to demonstrate just how expansive, entrenched, and ubiquitous anti-Blackness is.

## OMISSIONS AND WHITEWASHING

When you were in grade school, you remember reading stories by African American authors such as Faith Ringgold or Walter Dean Myers, right? In history, you learned of the immense diversity in Africa, studying various people groups and some of the 2,000 African languages, and can point out South Africa or Kenya on a map. Throughout social studies, you consistently learned about Black people who were creating, resisting, and moving society forward, beyond Martin Luther King and Rosa Parks. You have taken field trips to local Black history museums.

In middle school you learned about the complex global trading systems and architectural feats that were present in ancient Africa. You learned that Africa is a continent, not a country, home to arguably the richest man in world history (Mansa Musa), and some of the earliest universities (University of al-Qarawiyyin, Morocco) and libraries (in Egypt and Timbuktu). You are knowledgeable about Black intellectuals, those authors, artists, poets, and scientists who helped build the United States. You learned about the kingdoms of Nubia *and* Egypt. In high school, you learned about race and racism, and how racist policies (redlining, gerrymandering) create economic and social obstacles for African Americans. You studied the Harlem Renaissance. You learned about Black women leaders, from Mary McLeod Bethune to Ellen Johnson Sirleaf.

You know about people and places in Africa.

You can point out African influences in American culture, from the banjo to jeans/denim to the cultivation of rice.

Your high school had Black students in AP courses, and in calculus and physics.

You know about Black scholars and thinkers, those born in the United States and those born abroad.

You have read Walker and Baldwin and Du Bois and Angelou.

You have seen Jacob Lawrence's work.

You know more than a partial view of slavery told largely from a White perspective both without context and without any connection to the present, filled with well-meaning White people who fought to free enslaved Africans.

You know more than ancient Egypt, or bits and pieces of colonialism that you were taught over and over and still don't have a firm grasp of.

*Or you don't. Or you didn't.*

We imagine that for many readers, you did not have an opportunity to learn the above. The standards did not "allow for it" or the curriculum did not "cover it." If these omissions are more in line with your experience, you would be a typical student in the United States.

For many years, we have asked our college students what they remember learning about Black and African-descent people in schools. The responses are always the same: about slavery, the Civil War, perhaps the civil rights period, and they are done. Literature is just as sparse. It is a story of *omission* (not being included; being invisible) and *whitewashing* (the telling of half-truths about history in order to be less culpable). Both omission and whitewashing have similar consequences. They enable incomplete stories to dominate our understanding, skewing our collective memory. They suppress the contributions of Black people while exalting the contributions of White people. They allow students to remain ignorant of the astounding precolonial African civilizations that were pioneering in so many ways. They sanitize history in a way that makes it more about nostalgia and patriotism and less about what actually happened in the past. In all these effects, omission and whitewashing help support the structures of White supremacy.

We can easily find examples of omissions and whitewashing in effect right now. A research study showed that despite "85% of New York city public school students being Black, Latinx or Asian, 84% of the books in ten commonly used K–5th-grade curricula are written by white authors" (NYC Coalition for Educational Justice, 2020, p. 2). According to the nonprofit organization

We Need Diverse Books, "The top 10 most challenged books for 2020 include themes of racial justice, stories centered around BIPOC, and LGBTQIA+ content. Of the top 10 most challenged books,[1] 70% were by authors from marginalized groups" (Yao, 2021). This includes *Stamped* (Reynolds & Kendi, 2020), *The Bluest Eye* (Morrison, 1970), *The Hate U Give* (Thomas, 2017), and *All American Boys* (Reynolds & Kiely, 2015). When you think about your own schooling experience, do you remember reading books

- about Black people? In elementary school? In high school?
- written by Black people? In elementary school? In high school?
- about people currently living in Africa? By African authors?

It is an interesting self-check. In my (Kerri's) experience, I can recall reading a handful of books: *Black Ice* by Lorene Cary, *The Bluest Eye* by Toni Morrison, *Meridian* and *The Color Purple* by Alice Walker. Maybe one per year in high school? And I imagine this is many more than other students. As for Black history, I remember very little. Slavery, nothing about Africa; I do not remember "getting to" civil rights. What happens when you do not learn about an entire continent of people? This is a question I ask my undergraduates every semester. They often suggest that lack of attention conveys lack of necessity: What is there worth studying about Africa? Did important things happen there? Are there other stories beyond slavery in Black history? The omissions speak volumes and teach something in and of themselves; they reflect what is deemed important.

A recent example of misinformation comes from a widely used social studies resource. *Studies Weekly* is a social studies curriculum that is used by 4.3 million students. The format is a weekly newspaper that provides lessons on social studies topics for students in K–8 classrooms. A recently conducted internal audit found "400 examples of racial or ethnic bias, historical inaccuracies, age-inappropriate content, and other errors in the materials" (Schwartz, S., 2019, para. 5). These include the way American Indians are represented and how slavery is presented. For example, a publication stated that White colonists didn't enslave American Indians (untrue), and a 4th-grade article mischaracterized life for Africans who worked in tobacco fields. Part of the materials describe Africans who were brought to Jamestown to work on tobacco fields without pay: "It wasn't wonderful, but it was better than being a slave" (Schwartz, 2019, text box "Problematic Lessons"). We are unclear of the difference between "unpaid worker" and "enslaved."

Work by Brown and Brown (2015) can help illuminate patterns in the way we teach history. Brown and Brown argue that curriculum in the United States is about memory-making. We can see this in the above case. The lessons that are taught to youth are more about how we wish to memorialize the past, and less about the past itself.

Looking at textbooks and children's literature and how they depict race and racism, Brown and Brown's research identifies the substantial gap in how schools approach these subjects. Over time, despite there being more Black representation in both textbooks and literature, the omissions remain glaring:

> The characterization of African American images, culture, and histories consistently dehumanized African Americans through textbooks and children's literature. However, as the formation of race changed to a more inclusive, integrated society and postracial society, so did the presentation of African Americans in textbooks and children's literature. Within this period, the creation of a new kind of racial marking . . . emerged, in which children's literature and textbooks were able to implicitly present curricular texts as inclusive, while holding steadfastly to dominant, canonized knowledge, drawing at times from long-standing racialized tropes about Black people and deemphasizing the long-term and systemic effects of racism. (Brown & Brown, 2015, p. 124)

Racism continues to be a facet of life in the United States that goes unnamed. In a powerful condemnation, Brown and Brown state, "School curriculum, in the context of enduring racisms, has been one of the most effective mechanisms to (not) tell the story of race in the United States" (2015, p. 125). Loewen (2018) argues a similar point in *Lies My Teacher Told Me*. He explains that textbooks are starting to include some of the horrors of slavery. But, he cautions, "slavery's twin legacies to the present are the social and economic inferiority it conferred upon blacks and the cultural racism it instilled in whites" (p. 143). Both of these realities are largely missing. Racism is not taught about in most schools. Ighodaro and Wiggans call this "deliberate manipulation of academic programming" curriculum violence, in that it "compromises the intellectual or psychological well being of learners" (2010, as cited in Jones, 2020, para 16). The consistent omission of racism as a factor in U.S. society injures Black students by not giving voice or provenance to their lived experience. It is as if several hundred years of slavery evaporated into the mists, without leaving a hint of residue or any consequences that impact contemporary life. It is impossible to understand the development of the United States without understanding race, racism, culture, and ethnicity. But few students ever learn about these topics.

## On Teaching About Slavery

While slavery tends to be the one area that students do study about the experiences of African-ancestry people, they learn it incorrectly. Research by the Southern Poverty Law Center (Shuster, 2018) found that "only eight percent of high school seniors surveyed can identify slavery as the central cause of the Civil War" (p. 9). Current approaches to teaching slavery often "soften" the story. We can see this happen in several ways. There are examples in many textbooks where myths take center stage; slave owners are portrayed as benevolent and enslaved Africans "better off" in their care (Mineo, 2020).

We see this operationalized on a field trip to Beauvoir, Jefferson Davis's plantation in Mississippi. In a special report published by the Smithsonian, researchers followed schoolchildren on their tour to better learn what children are taught about enslaved Africans (Palmer & Wessler, 2018). The researchers questioned the tour guide about what she could tell them about slavery. She explained, "I want to tell them the honest truth, that slavery was good and bad. . . . It was good for people that didn't know how to take care of themselves, and they needed a job and you had good slave owners like Jefferson Davis who took care of his slaves and treated them like family" (Palmer & Wessler, 2018, p. 56). In an interview with the executive director of the same site, Thomas Payne, he reiterates this same point: "There's actually evidence where the individual who was enslaved was better off physically, and mentally and otherwise" (p. 59).

Palmer and Wessler followed 650 children around (many of them Black), as they were taught these messages. These stories, like so many others, have taken on a life of their own. The narrative of the contented enslaved African, who is bettered by the opportunity to do "honest work" and experience Christianity, is a persistent feature in the mistelling of slavery. But let's unravel the story a bit. Let's follow through with the logic presented to children on this field trip.

1. *It was good for people who didn't know how to take care of themselves.* Where is there a people group anywhere on the planet who cannot take care of themselves? The entire people group? Of course, individual people struggle and do without, but there are no people groups who in their entirety cannot take care of themselves. The people group we are referring to here of course is Africans. Millions and millions of Africans. No mind is paid to the fact that they were kidnapped, beaten, sexually abused, branded, removed from their culture, and stripped of their language, name, identity and family, as if these realities had no traumatizing effects. To suggest that the entire population of enslaved Africans could not take care of themselves renders them infantile and diminished. But it had to be this way, yes? An important tool in the maintenance of slavery was to make Africans appear very, very different from Europeans. This is one of the key elements of the story. Africans have to be distinctively different, childish, lacking sophistication or reason. They need to appear helpless. They need to be framed as reliant upon White people. Otherwise, justifying slavery is a harder argument to make.

2. *They needed a job.* They needed a job because they were stolen from the work they previously did. Or their grandparents previously did. There is a cause-and-effect relationship here that also goes unacknowledged in this line

of thinking. The slave owner is the original reason they did not have a job. They were kidnapped from it.

3. *There were good slave owners who loved their slaves.* James O. Lewis, back in the 1960s, pointed to this phenomenon: "Slave life is pictured as a not too unpleasant condition; in fact it was often described as having been rather nice" (Lewis, as cited in Greenlee, 2019, p. 5). The narrative of the kindhearted slave owner who loved his enslaved Africans as if they were family plays a really important psychological purpose. It allows an unjustifiable condition to be softened. It blunts the edges of owning people. It is quite odd that the default phrase employed here is treated "like family." We know of no families that enslave their members. It is simply an absurd comment. Yet it is one that is repeated consistently. The curators at Monticello, Thomas Jefferson's plantation, are more plain about the validity of the good slave owner trope: "Jefferson wrote that he wished to ameliorate the conditions of slavery and treat people less harshly than other violent slaveholders, but he still forced people to labor for the wealth and luxury of his white family. This force was upheld through violence, the threat of violence, family separation, and emotional, psychological, and sexual abuse" (Thomas Jefferson's Monticello, n.d. para. 2). They conclude, "There is no such thing as a good slave holder."

This softening perhaps explains how a teacher can casually throw in examples of slavery to teach mathematics, like in an elementary school in Atlanta (West Savali, 2012):

Each tree had 56 oranges. If eight slaves pick them equally, then how much would each slave pick?

If Frederick got two beatings per day, how many beatings did he get in one week? Two weeks?

How is this a valid educational endeavor? In what other context would physical violence be used to illuminate multiplication? Can you imagine a parallel example?

If Liza was stabbed twice a day, how many wounds were on her body by the end of the week? Two weeks?

No, right? This is outside the bounds of what is acceptable practice. However, this is far from rare, this casual reference to slavery in ways that minimizes its horror. The softening shows up in other school places. For years—literally years—I (Kerri) have heard stories of the Underground Railroad field trip, told to me by my college students. Several regional school districts took middle school students on an overnight field trip where part of it was to learn about the Underground Railroad. On its face, this would seem like a beneficial endeavor. We can imagine many ways in which this event could be viewed as progressive, and even "multicultural." But simply including people of color in a lesson or activity does not make it meaningful. We will use this example as a case study, to help discern what is helpful, and what is harmful, when it comes to teaching about race and racism.

On this trip, students were taken out at night and had to escape on the "Underground Railroad" through the woods. Counselors chased after them as if they were bounty hunters looking for escaped enslaved Africans. According to a local journalist who covered this field trip after a parent complaint (De La Torre, 2013), the experience "included threatening language and use of a racial epithet; packing together students in a dark room, as if they were on a slave ship; and hiding in the woods from 'white masters'" (para. 7). Students recalled that "They were told they would be whipped or worse if they ran, and some were asked to dance for their masters. 'I had to hold my head down and could not make contact with the white masters,' the 12-year-old student, who is black, said in a statement read to the Hartford school board this week. 'I heard the instructor ask kids behind me to open their mouths so their teeth could be checked'" (Associated Press, 2013, para. 2).

Year after year my own students recount being scared to death, crying, joking, and simply not getting the point of the activity. What is interesting is that I have never brought this up specifically in class: it was always an organic outgrowth of students noticing how they were taught about slavery, and then having a light bulb go off when they considered it with fresh eyes. I would hear something like, "Dr. Ullucci, have you ever heard of the Underground Railroad trip? I'm not sure about that trip now that I think about it." Every. Single. Year.

Now, we have no issue with students feeling uncomfortable discussing slavery; that is not our critique. Hard things are hard, and we owe it to our students to help them navigate these topics. Our critique, however, is twofold: (1) the way this affects Black youth fails to be taken into consideration and (2) there are certain events that simply cannot be simulated. Period. Schools should not try to make students feel like they are slaves. This is in part because there is no way for the school to actually do this authentically (your 2-hour run through the woods cannot mirror an enslaved African's lived experience; there is no way to approximate this). Instead, this simulation potentially trivializes it. I am reminded of a local school that did a battle reenactment each year. The elementary students used model weapons and "attacked" one another. If you are 10 years old, what does this teach you about the Revolutionary War? Can you actually replicate the fear, anxiety, horror? Or is it a fun game where you use cool guns and beat the other side doing something that is not remotely similar to the reality of war?

One goal of simulation as a pedagogical tool is to get students to imagine how others felt. We truly appreciate this. Building empathy and the ability to see through many vantage points is such an important skill. However, from our students' interpretations, youth leave the simulation feeling as if slavery was not that bad because they essentially played capture the flag at night. The educational purpose falls apart. We imagine that instead of building empathy for and knowledge of enslaved Africans, White students in particular might misread the experience as being more trivial. On the other hand, Black students have to live through being hunted, purchased, and commodified. Is that a lesson they need to learn?

To return to the larger point, this slavery simulation illustrates both the power of the softening of the story ("Slavery was not that bad. You can have students reenact it on a field trip!") and a caution to be critical about how we teach about slavery and Black history in general. We do not want to fall into the trap of essentializing slavery as the totality of Black history (Jones, 2020). While simulations and role-plays can help build understanding, much is lost and is not possible to learn through this method. In discussing the use of simulations to teach about the Holocaust, Totten (2000) argues that they should be wholly eliminated. He lists his cautions:

> These include, but are not limited to, the following: they are invariably simplistic; they frequently convey both skewed and incorrect information vis-a-vis the Holocaust; and more often than not, they are ahistorical. The simple fact is, no matter what a teacher and his/her students do in a simulation, *they will never, ever, even begin to approximate or simulate the horror that the victims suffered at the hands of the Nazis* [emphasis in original]. What is of critical importance here is that the use of such simulations often results in students believing that—at least to some extent—they do. (para. 24)

Both *Teaching History and Ourselves* (a social studies-focused website and professional development provider) and the Anti-Defamation League also caution against simulations for similar reasons, warning about potential trauma for students who are in the target group and potential reinforcing of stereotypes against victims (Drake, 2008). Jones (2020), writing for Teaching Tolerance (a website of the Southern Poverty Law Center), simply says, "Reenactments and simulations do not help students to understand slavery" (para. 15). It would be more beneficial, powerful, and authentic to allow people who went through these experiences to speak for themselves through autobiographies, primary sources, and oral histories.

Additionally, we need to consider the way in which Black children (not to mention Black teachers) in particular might experience this trip. In the districts many of Kerri's students come from, Black youth are in the minority. To be taken to a strange place and be attacked verbally by White people you do not know, while being made examples of in front of your peers, lacks empathy and humanity. When I (Joi) take my graduate students to study the Underground Railroad in Maryland, I am cognizant of the trauma my students experience when they visit an actual safe house. The safe house sits on the site of the Underground Railroad museum, and it served as part of the escape route for many enslaved individuals. As part of the tour, visitors can step into an underground crawl space, which was used to hide escaping slaves who were headed to free territory. During the visit, many of my students try out the space, stepping in and imagining what it must have been like. Others ask to have their pictures taken while in the crawl space, posting pictures on their social media platforms. Students are always respectful, and this time is generally one of quietness and reflection. What is important to note, though, is that without fail, none of my Black students ever venture into the crawl space. Instead, they typically congregate on the lawn outside during this portion of the tour (which, incidentally, is always where I find myself; I cannot face the crawl space either). This moment on the lawn becomes an unspoken time of solidarity and affirmation. We see one another and recognize our shared pain. The terror of slavery is close to us, living in our family histories and psyches.

Students come to us with different backstories and lived experiences. These experiences shape how students interact with schooling. The resonance of being in a space where actual enslaved Africans endured suffering hits our students in different ways. This only makes sense; this should be expected, right? However, our dominant discourse of colorblindness, where we interact with the world through the lens of we-are-all-the-same, interferes entirely with our ability to see this. It is OK for some students to need something that others do not. We are not calling out the non-Black students, at all, for wanting to see the crawl space. They are trying to wrap their minds around something that is not easy to grasp. However, for Black students, getting in the crawl space is potentially autobiographical. They may stand there imagining themselves, or their Grandma, in that space. It is not unfair, or unequal, to construct different learning experiences for different students. Instead, it is humane.

Moreover, we need to be savvy in general about how we include topics about race, racism, and culture. When we come across lessons that include these components, we need to think about what is being taught, whether the lesson is valuable, whether it reinforces or breaks stereotypes, and how it will affect *all* the students in the class. For example, I (Kerri) once watched a teacher read a book about a Muslim youth to her 5th-graders. I was happy to see this story being shared, as stories of Muslim people are a rarity. The teacher then went on to use the book to illustrate how strange the character was, and how their family did not value education. So instead of using the text to expand the students' understanding of people who were different from themselves, the teacher used the book to stereotype a group of people and make them seem like they were odd and not particularly smart. In this case, it was more damaging to her 5th-graders to read the book than it would have been to omit the book entirely, in that the teacher potentially introduced the children to new stereotypes. Some lessons are better left untaught.

4. *An individual who was enslaved was better off.* The question, of course, is: Better off than whom? We are not sure who enslaved Africans were better off than. If slavery caused a positive condition, shouldn't people who are currently struggling be enslaved? Following this logic? It's preposterous, right? Inconceivable. No matter how incapacitated, ill, developmentally delayed, or unable to care for oneself, this is never an option. Simply typing these sentences seems entirely surreal! There is no way to square slavery with love or family or goodness. We appreciate the words of Spivey, and will end this section with his words (2019):

> The truth is that the curve on which slave ownership is measured goes only from bad to worse. No slave, under the best of circumstances was exempt from the possibility of being sold away, separated from their families, at the whim of their master. They were subject to having their mates selected for them to breed the best slaves for sale or forced to submit to their master's desires. They could legally be beaten, or killed, and had to live each day of their life carrying that weight. (Final paragraph)

## The Legacy of Whitewashing and Omission, 2022 Version

As we write this chapter, examples of the dishonesty of whitewashing and omission abound. In a case of actual omission, a public school in Utah allowed students not to participate in a Black History Month curriculum. Parents were allowed to sign an opt-out form to remove their students from these lessons (Asmelash, 2021). The school ended up reversing the decision after public protest, but the message that Black history is marginal remains. In what other context would students be allowed to opt out of history lessons?

In a new twist, Black books are under particular fire, as they are increasingly finding themselves on banned book lists. In the context of the conservative social movement to ban critical race theory from schools, Black stories are believed to be inherently critical race theory stories (Bellamy Walker, 2022) and are getting swept up in that storm. The American Library Association cites rising challenges against books written by Black authors (Will, 2021). The Katy, Texas, school department removed two of Jerry Craft's (award-winning) books from their libraries, seemingly because they show Black boys experiencing racism. All Black stories, and stories mentioning the Black experiences, begin to look (to some people) like a criticism of White people and their histories, and opponents target Black books as promoting critical race theory despite the fact that the books never actually discuss critical race theory at all.

In a related mess, Texas State Representative Matt Krause (see Lopez, B., 2021) sent a letter in October 2021 to superintendents asking if their schools possessed books from a list of *850 titles* believed to make students feel "discomfort" or "guilt." Superintendents were asked to reply with (a) which books they had, (b) how many copies they had, (c) where they were located, and (d) how much they spent on them. Titles included: Amnesty International's *We Are All Born Free: The Universal Declaration of Human Rights in Pictures*, *The New Jim Crow: Mass Incarceration in the Age of Colorblindness* by Michelle Alexander, *All American Boys* by Jason Reynolds and Brendan Kiely, and *This is Your Time* by Ruby Bridges.

Just who are these books making uncomfortable or guilty? Who is being protected here and who has gone missing from the equation? Do Black boys who live in Texas not know that racism exists, and the Katy school department is trying to protect them by removing these titles? Or do they not want to let White children read about racism? Our professor used to tell us if you throw a rock into a pack of dogs, you know which one you hit because it is barking.

North Carolina has just passed rules that threaten discipline or dismissal of educators who "teach that American historical figures were not heroes, undermine the U.S. constitution in lessons or say that racism is a permanent part of American life" (Associated Press, 2021, para. 2). Rather, it states in this new policy that "*all* people who contributed to American society will be recognized and *presented as reformists, innovators and heroes* to our culture"(emphasis added) (para. 4).

Let's think this through. Teachers are being told that people who contributed to society must be painted in a positive light. So any contribution has to be seen as heroic? How do we teach Jefferson? Andrew Jackson? We will tell Black children (and all children) that Jefferson was a model Founding Father? Of course, he contributed to the country in indelible and important ways. But how do we overlook his participation with slavery? His plantation? His relationship with Sally Hemings and their enslaved children? When we omit these facts, the goal is not the truth, but a whitewashing of it.

Here we see yet another example of how storytelling has led us astray. Schools have been telling stories about the past, fictionalized stories about the greatness of White leaders who walk through history unblemished and pristine. But they—like the stories we tell about race—are inaccurate. They miss the full picture. They leave out key information. Students would have so much richer an experience if we told them the truth. If we told them that Washington was a pivotal leader *and* a plantation owner. That Jefferson penned much of the Declaration of Independence *and* held more than 600 slaves. That most people are not 100% good or 100% evil but instead a mind-numbing array of in-between and that people can do great things and horrific things and history, like life, is filled with this contradiction. We can teach them that the United States is a beautiful, messy, imperfect country that aspires to something we have not yet reached but we still keep trying. We can tell the truth.

## CENTERING ATHLETICISM OVER INTELLECT

In an interesting thought exercise, Cooper (2019a) asks readers to think of 10 Black athletes. Then he asks to think of 10 Black men who are not athletes or entertainers. It's a stunning self-check. Athletics takes up a lot of space in our understanding of Blackness.

There is a long and complex relationship between African Americans and sports (see for example, *Forty Million Dollar Slaves: The Rise, Fall, and Redemption of the Black Athlete* by William C. Rhoden, 2006). On the one hand, sports have increased the visibility of the Black community and even provided a platform for elevating their concerns and struggles for civil rights (see Colin Kaepernick and the WNBA in particular). On the other hand, the superior performance of Blacks in sports has been used to support arguments about their physical prowess, and to feed into stereotypes that they are closer to animals (and thus less intellectually developed). Cooper (2019b) lays out the many ways pseudoscience shaped how Black bodies were seen, and how tropes about genetics and breeding contributed to their dehumanization. When Jesse Owens, the renowned track and field athlete, broke records at the 1936 Olympics, his own coach chalked up his ability to his "primitive" ancestry in Africa: "It was not that long ago that his ability to spring and jump was a life-and-death matter to him in the jungle" (Maraniss, 2020, para. 5).

This complex relationship permeates school sports as well, most often negatively impacting African American children. The implicit socialization of Black students as athletes instead of scholars is problematic and often remains uninterrogated in school settings. Howard (2013)[2] uses the term Athlete Seasoning Complex (ASC) to describe the process by which "young Black boys as early as 4–5 years old are encouraged to play basketball, football, or baseball; follow the sport in an intense and persistent manner; compete at all costs; and practice to achieve perfection or a high degree of proficiency—often at the expense of their academic development" (p. 77). This framing of Black youth that focuses on their bodies instead of their minds is the primary concern of this section. We will argue that this focus on the physical over the intellectual is an act of dehumanization in itself. We seek to help principals, coaches, and teachers see how sports can reinforce anti-Blackness within and beyond their schools.

In this section, we chose to take a different approach in sharing our concerns. We begin with an actual letter that was sent by a Black family to the local high school (referred to pseudonymously here) their son was attending. We share it in its entirety as we sketch out the ways in which the overfocus on Black children and sports can limit Black youths' opportunities. We draw on this document because we believe in the importance of concrete experience (returning to Ladson-Billings's methodological approach in Chapter 1) and because this family illuminates anti-Blackness in clear detail. Several aspects

of ASC will become immediately apparent in the letter from the family. For
example, the family expresses a concern with the inordinate amount of time
that their child is expected to devote to basketball. We will then use the letter
as a case study to highlight our primary concerns regarding sports.

### Sports and Black Youth: A First-Person Account

Dear coaches and administration,
    We are writing to address an issue related to the boy's basketball
program at Thurgood Marshall High School. After a year at Marshall,
it is seemingly clear that Marshall is far more interested in African
American boys becoming athletes than scholars. Given that your school
is designed after one of our greatest leaders, Thurgood Marshall, the behaviors my family and I have seen in relation to the basketball program
are unconscionable. Our family is requesting a meeting with the
principal as well as the basketball coaching staff. Below I outline some
of our major concerns.
    *Off-season basketball games send harmful messages.* The coaching
staff has placed our children on a treadmill where the students are
playing and/or prepping for the same sport throughout the entire school
year. This includes summers, after school and off-season. This hyper
involvement can send a damaging message to youngsters that their
full life's energies and goals ought to be directed towards playing ball.
If our students are playing basketball all summer long, what space is
left for them to develop themselves academically or culturally, to take
additional courses, attend academic camps, travel, read, and envision
a life for themselves beyond what you have set up for them? While the
coaching staff and/or the school may see that a Black boy's only goal in
life should be to play basketball, we have a different vision for our son.
While we believe that sports can be a part of that vision, we reject the
notion that it is the **only** vision.
    *Games during finals week are unacceptable.* The coach informed
our son that if he did not play Junior Varsity games in June (which are
off-season and occur during spring semester finals) that he would not be
allowed to play on the Junior Varsity team at all. Our son was terrified
at the thought that despite all of his work throughout the school year
to help bring success to the freshman basketball team, that missing one
game during the off-season would ruin the rest of his chances to play
basketball at Marshall. This bullying message—delivered directly from
his coach—is an appalling example of a high school sports program.
That a coach would threaten a hard working student that if he did not
place his academics on the back burner on behalf of a so-called important game is **highly** upsetting. Sending students the message that they
are expendable at any given moment based upon the whim of a coach is

particularly disturbing. One could perhaps understand students having to play a game during finals when their sport is in season. However, requiring students to play during finals when their sport is off-season and threatening them that they will be dismissed from the team if they do not do so is completely unacceptable. This is a time when coaches ought to be reinforcing academic vigor and encouraging students to study. We are appalled that our son had to experience the antithesis of this.

*Concentration of African American boys in for-profit sports is harmful.* African American boys must wrestle with a legacy that tells them that their physical strength is the sum total of their worth. They, more than any other male students on your campus, are inundated with messages through the media and at large that they are academically and intellectually inferior, but physically superior. They are routinely told that their only hope for success is through some highly unlikely professional basketball or football contract. Instead of interrupting this messaging, and showing our students the full menu of opportunities available to them, Marshall justifies these messages through their behaviors. There is a clear concentration of African American boys on the campus engaged in for-profit sports such as basketball and football. Sports such as water polo, volleyball, cross-country, and golf (all of which are offered on your campus) are completely ignored when it comes to our children. These sports can provide young athletes with valuable skill sets, physical conditioning, and countless college and university opportunities. Why has our son never been encouraged to try these other sports? Were he to continue at Marshall, would he ever have such opportunities? Such behavior makes us question the coaching staffs' as well as the school leaders' true motives. It seems that you are more interested in the athletic prestige that African American boys can bring to your school than in their life-long development and opportunities. Again, we ask if our students are playing basketball 365 days out of the year, when will they engage in these other, valuable opportunities?

*Athletic efforts trump academic energies.* If Marshall would place as much effort into developing our boys academically as they place into preparing them for a life of ball bouncing, then they might actually succeed in closing the achievement gap. We urge you to place that same level of energy and commitment into preparing him to become a top scholar at your school and beyond. Encourage him to join the Science Olympiads, engage in Game Design competitions, take advanced mathematics courses, and join the National Honors Society (all of which are opportunities at your school that he has never been invited to participate in despite his strong academic achievement). Make it your business to see him succeed—truly succeed—in the 21st century.

Prepare him to become an active, educated, engaged citizen. Help him to truly beat the odds that far too many African American males succumb to. Get serious about his whole development and treat him in the manner that you would treat your very own child.

We look forward to the opportunity to speak with you all. We have always taught our son to respect school, his teachers, and his coaches and to respect the enterprise of education. In fact, we see schools as a partner in his development. This is why the coach's current stance is particularly egregious. Our son ought to be able to trust the judgment and decisions of his coach. Our goal is not merely to levy complaints. Rather, we want to engage in an active, forward-moving plan.

We look forward to hearing from you in the coming days.

The _____ family

To provide a bit more context, the above letter was sent from the family of a Black, male high school sophomore. What is not present in the letter, but important for readers to understand, is that while the parents and family had been educated in the inner city, they had sacrificed a great deal to raise the next generation of their family in the well-resourced, suburban schools 65 miles east of their hometown. At the time the letter was written, the Thurgood Marshall High School Black student population hovered around 8%, while their boys' basketball team was over 90% Black. While the letter represents years of frustration, the tipping point came when the school's basketball coach sent the boys a message requiring them to play in a tournament during finals week of their spring semester. As the letter denotes, the tournament fell outside the school's basketball season. This meant that even players who had successful seasons the previous winter would be cut from the team if they did not participate in the June tournament. So, at a time when students could finally place their full minds and energies into their academic pursuits, they were being required to play in a weeklong tournament. To the casual onlooker, the coach's requirement that students play in the tournament (a decision endorsed by the high school) might look benign. It is not. At its most basic, this policy unduly affects the academic progress of African American students and decreases their chances of doing well on their finals; it therefore interferes with future opportunities. It also reinforces rather than interrupts a racialized narrative about the significance that Black students should hold for sports over academics. Finally, this request commodifies Black youth. We will explore these ideas more fully in the next sections.

### Sports' Undue Impact on Black Students' Academic Progress

While there are numerous studies claiming a variety of benefits of participation in sports on student educational and academic outcomes (Braddock, 1981 [improved academic goals and aspirations]; Broh, 2002 [student development and social ties among students, parents, and schools]; Fejgin, 1994; Hanks & Eckland, 1976; Marsh, 1993 [grades, self-concept, locus of control and educational aspirations, course work selection, reduced absenteeism]; Melnick et al., 1992 [grades and achievement]), the outcomes for Black students are not clear-cut. Recent studies have disaggregated their findings to understand the differing impacts of sports on different social groups. Zeiser (2011) examined the Education Longitudinal Study of 2002 to investigate the effects of participation in varsity football and basketball on student GPAs and mathematics test scores. Her analysis showed that participation in varsity football had a negative effect on Black, but not White, students' GPAs. Likewise, participation in girls' varsity basketball led to higher GPAs for White, but not Black, students. Eitle and Eitle's 2002 study found that "sports participation may positively contribute to the achievement of some groups (whites and middle class males) but may not have any significant influence on the educational outcomes of other groups (e.g. lower socioeconomic strata youths and minorities)" (p. 126). In their analysis of the National Longitudinal Study of Adolescent Health, Rees and Sabia (2010) found "little evidence to support the claim that sports participation is positively related to academic performance in a causal sense" (p. 759).

Eitle and Eitle (2002) also found that there are racial differences in high school sports participation. Controlling for the factors of family structure (i.e., single parent, stepparent, or two-parent household) and cultural resources and capital, Black male high school students were 2.54 times as likely as White males to participate in football and 5.68 times as likely as White males to participate in basketball (p. 130).There is an overrepresentation of Black male students in profit-bearing sports, which requires a caution. This can easily lead to exploitation by coaches and commodification of Black youth, which we will explore in greater depth later.

Eitle and Eitle (2002) used data from the National Education Longitudinal Study (NELS)[3] to investigate the impact of sports participation on academic outcomes. Their study captures longitudinal versus cross-sectional data and thus allows us to understand causal relationships, and more clearly see the impacts of sports participation on African American youth. Note, for example, the argument that students who participate in sports have higher grades than those who do not. Given the minimum GPA requirements for students who participate in sports, are the higher grades a result of teachers loosening their grading standards for student athletes or perhaps student athletes taking less rigorous courses? Longitudinal studies like these help us to move beyond these conundrums by charting individual children over time

Eitle and Eitle were particularly interested in the impacts of sports on Black students from low-income/low-resourced communities and families. Citing Melnick et al. (1992), Eitle and Eitle provide two arguments that may unpack why Black youth do not get the same benefits out of sports participation as White youth:

1. The institutional matrix of high school sports helps those who are already advantaged more than it helps the disadvantaged (the reinforcement hypothesis) and/or
2. The advantages afforded by sports participation are more effectively taken advantage of by those who are already advantaged (the cumulative advantage hypothesis). (p. 125)

Examining Black and White students who participated in sports in 8th grade and 2 years later, a major finding of their study was that Black student athletes had less access to cultural capital and resources (music courses, educational resources in the home) than their White counterparts did. Following this reasoning, Black students, due to limited resources, may be less able to reap the benefits of participation in sports. Of great importance is the finding that differences in cultural capital (like participation in cultural courses such as dance or music) were strong predictors of participation in basketball and football. Stated differently, as the cultural capital of students decreased, participation in basketball and football increased. Eitle and Eitle (2002) further showed that sports might actually have a *detrimental* effect on the academic showing of Black students in basketball and football. Participation in these sports had a "negative relationship with standardized achievement scores" (p. 141) and showed no benefits to grades. Given that Black students in the study had less cultural capital overall, Eitle and Eitle argue that their finding may signal that "cultural disadvantage may contribute to an increased interest in and dependence on particular sports (namely basketball and football) and that this dependence on sports may have additional adverse consequences for its participants in terms of academic achievement" (p. 141). Stating this plainly, a lack of other forms of capital drives participation into basketball and football, which in turn predicts lower academic achievement. For Black students who see basketball and football as their ticket to greater wealth and resources, such participation may act against their envisioning other paths that would be more successful.

Eitle and Eitle's study also provides insight into the difficulty Black students who attend inner-city and otherwise predominantly minority high schools have with finding a space on their schools' sports teams. Startlingly,

Enrollment at a school that has a 50 percent to 100 percent minority enrollment vis-a-vis a school that has less than a 10 percent minority enrollment substantially decreases the odds of participating in football and basketball. Similarly, attending a school that has a 10 percent to 49 percent minority enrollment vis-a-vis a school that has less than a 10 percent minority enrollment decreases the odds of participating in basketball. This effect provides some support for the notion that participation in football and basketball is important in the black community—the more minorities in a school, the more competition for limited opportunities to play football and basketball. (p. 135)

I (Joi) have personally witnessed young Black male students moving from one high school to the next to find an open space on a football or basketball team. Likewise, we have all witnessed elite, predominantly White, well-resourced and even private schools opening their doors to Black student athletes. This is certainly common practice in Southern California, where such schools seem more willing to invest in the *athletic* promise of Black students than in their academic and intellectual gifts. The relationship between sports participation and academic success for Black students is at best spurious and at worst detrimental.

**Sports' Reinforcement of Racialized Narratives**

*Metanarratives* are "those grand stories used in a culture in order to legitimize mechanisms of social control" (Perry, 2005, p. 141). Racial metanarratives are ubiquitous. For example, the superiority of African Americans in sports is a grand story of our culture. This grand story is most often coupled with one that posits the intellectual inferiority of Blacks. There are consequences for metanarratives. Uncontested, these dominant stereotypical views have power, controlling how we see youth and the possibilities that we envision for their lives. Consider the fact that the young man for whom the letter above was written entered high school with a nearly perfect GPA. He excelled academically in elementary and middle school and even served as a peer mentor. Upon entering high school, the young man was never asked to join the school's robotics team, its academic decathlon, or its student government. He was, however, recruited heavily for the school's basketball team. On several occasions, during his freshman year, the basketball coach tracked him down during lunch and encouraged him to go out for the team. When the young man mentioned this to his counselor, she quickly rearranged his schedule to accommodate the team practices. He made the freshman basketball team, and they enjoyed a winning season. He played on the junior varsity team as a sophomore. It was during this year that for the first time in his academic career he struggled in one of his courses, second-year algebra. As his family recalls, they set up a conference and they, along with their son, met with the algebra teacher. She began the meeting educating the family on what Algebra II was and why her students found it so hard. She was shocked when the family shared that they knew what the course of study was and had questions about her teaching methods. The teacher then turned the conversation to the young man, saying that he ought to ask more questions in class and be more assertive. As she concluded her comments to the young man, she said, "Math is not like basketball. You have to work at it." As his parents recalled, the boy's head dropped. The conference ended. Through continued struggle, he passed the course, yet the experience had shaken his confidence.

Throughout his high school career, his parents urged and encouraged him to take AP courses, which he resisted again and again. Finally, in the second semester of 11th grade, he enrolled in the last half of an AP U.S. History course. Later that semester, he shared with his folks how much he appreciated the ideas he was learning about and the students that he was learning with in this course. "This is where I should have been all along," he commented.

The racial metanarrative of Blacks and athletics is not benign. In this case and countless others, it stifles the schooling enterprise, which is to grow and develop young people in all their capacities. It constricts teachers' views of Black students as well as Black students' views of themselves. It cuts off opportunities and vantage points, shutting down options that Black families have fought so hard to secure.

## Sports and the Commodification of Black Youth

Whom does the overemphasis on sports (particularly basketball and football) serve? Why are schools that are seemingly unwilling and unable to invest in the academic and social success of Black students so eager to put resources into the athletic development of Black youth? We argue that this overemphasis on Black youth's *athletic* development on one hand, and the underemphasis on and lack of investment in Black youth's *intellectual* development on the other hand, signals a *commodification* of African American youngsters. By commodification, we mean a valuing of them for the future profits, reputations, and overall financial gains that their physical prowess might accrue. We are all aware of the long and damning history of African bodies being used as wealth-generating property. In this historical arrangement, Blacks performed the arduous physical labor, yet White/European landowners reaped the profits. While the enslaved exerted the physical strength, owners maintained power through an elaborate system of laws, practices, and punishments.

Similar to slavery, the multibillion-dollar sports enterprise is built on the physical strength of professional athletes, many of whom are Black. While (those few) professional athletes are paid, their compensation does not compare to the immense wealth that they generate for team owners, corporations, television networks, and multimedia conglomerates. Rhoden (2006) calls out this imbalance of power and wealth in his treatise, *Forty Million Dollar Slaves: The Rise, Fall, and Redemption of the Black Athlete*. We dare say that many schools' overengagement of Black youth in profit-making sports such as basketball and football is painfully similar to these arrangements. The strict discipline and rules of conduct, the lengthy, military-like practices, and the insistence that young people commit all of themselves, their time (both during and after the season), their energy, and their interests to a given sport feels out of balance with the goals and purposes of schooling. While these young people are giving their all, to win a school title or perhaps land a remote yet coveted college scholarship or the even more unlikely professional team spot, who is watching out for their well-being?

Taylor (1999) writes that "although fewer than 2,000 African Americans are in the NBA and more than 30,000 African Americans are physicians, we would never know it from the images that surround our children" (p. 75). Despite this, Black youth are groomed to become the next LeBron James, but not the next Mae Jamison.

Moreover, there are a limited number of spaces to be the next LeBron. As of 2019, there were just 1,628 Black Big Ten athletes. Even at the Big Ten level (a feeder conference to professional sports teams) there is extremely limited space for their participation. There is intense competition for just a handful of spaces. However, the young man discussed in the school letter above was never asked to take an AP course or join one of the school's numerous academic clubs or teams. He was not set up to be one of those 30,000 physicians. Schools who want to enact justice on behalf of Black youth must account for their actions, responding to the questions: How well did we prepare Black students to face and surmount the challenges that they will face? What opportunities will they be able to take advantage of as a result of their time with us?

## Concluding Thoughts on Sports and Black Students

We do not dislike sports. We appreciate the many benefits team sports have for children's physical and mental health. Rather, we are opposed to the ways in which an unchecked devotion to them on school campuses impedes academic success, perpetuates harmful narratives, and commodifies Black youth. We believe that Black youth have an abundance of ideas, gifts, and skills to share with the world and that they have a right to attend schools where these talents are developed and actualized. Moving in this direction will require schools to be intentional. They must pay attention to patterns right in front of them. We question whether it is truly possible not to notice that a school with an 8% total Black student population has a basketball roster made up of over 90% such students. School communities must be intentional in interrupting stereotypical and harmful narratives. The lack of questioning disproportionalities (such as the 8%/90% disproportionality at Thurgood Marshall High) is evidence of the invisible manner in which racism remains in play in schools. Critical race theory (CRT) shows us that racism is a normalized component of our society (Ladson-Billings, 2021). Racialized patterns that are grossly disproportionate are neither noticed nor interrupted. Such arrangements are seen as normal.

We note also that sports teams can be spaces where *representation* exists, but *justice* is absent. Justice and diversity/representation are not the same. Diversity and inequity can exist simultaneously. For example, Black youth are represented on the basketball team. However, very few Black youth are succeeding academically, which is the goal of schools. In this regard, equity is not being achieved. Justice, for us, always trumps diversity. Justice changes the game.

We end this section with words from Kevin Merida, a *Los Angeles Times* sportswriter committed to telling the fuller stories of Black athletes. In his interviews with countless Black athletes, he has documented their intellectual gifts and pursuits, scholastic achievements, political activism, and business acumen. He reflects:

> Sometimes size or height, athleticism, poverty or just the limitations of your dreams propel you into a life of sports. The thrill of competition enlivens you, the cred you generate in your community empowers you. Athletic success opens doors that never seem to close—and you become defined by your physical skills. The world engages you through highlights and sound bites, and your Twitter feed. The rest of your genius—your tastes, passions, eclectic interests—the world sometimes misses. Or, sadly, just ignores. (Merida, 2018, paragraph 10)

It is our desire that Black student-athletes be seen in their fullness, given the opportunity to actualize, and allowed to develop "the rest of their genius."

## ADULTIFICATION

A Black girl, confused, asks her teacher a question, but it is misread as intentionally challenging the teacher's authority.

A Black girl is 14, but is believed to be 18 when picked up by police. They refuse to believe her age.

A Black boy with a toy gun is mistaken for a young adult with a real gun.

A Black child injures himself during sports but is not given comfort. He is seen as tough and not needing extra care.

We are moved by McKinney de Royston et al.'s (2021) claim that racism attacks Black childhood. Childhood is supposed to be a time of growth, where young people learn how to do and act and be. Childhood is where lots of mistakes are made, and boundaries tested, and space given to figure out how to rebound and make amends if needed. But Black children do not walk through childhood in the same way as White children. New research is exploring the ways in which Black children's childhoods are erased, constrained, and denied. A series of reports put out by the Center on Poverty and Inequality at Georgetown Law explores this phenomenon: *Girlhood Interrupted: The Erasure of Black Girls' Childhood* (Epstein et al., 2017) and *Listen to Black Women and Girls: Lived Experiences of Adultification Bias* (Blake & Epstein, 2019). This practice of not seeing Black children as children is called *adultification*. The authors define adultification as "a form of dehumanization, robbing Black children of the very essence of what makes childhood distinct from all other developmental periods: innocence. Adultification contributes to a false narrative that Black youths' transgressions are intentional and malicious, instead of the result of immature decision-making—a key characteristic of childhood" (Epstein et al., 2017, p. 6).

Adultification functions in different ways according to gender. Black boys are perceived as "older, more likely to be guilty than their white peers, and police violence used against them more justified" (Epstein et al., 2017, p. 4). In research with kindergarten data, Zimmermann (2018) noted, "Teachers are more likely to perceive and interact with black boys in early childhood in ways that mirror and reinforce the racialized depiction of them as problems. That is, given similar behavior as non-black boys, teachers view black boys' behavior more negatively and treat them more harshly than non-black boys" (p. 106). Here we see that what is typical childish behavior in White boys is seen as punishable with Black boys.

Making connections with a popular media example for a moment, Kerri was recently reading *Notes from a Young Black Chef* (2019), and was struck by Kwame Onwuachi's recollections on being a student in Nigeria, versus being a Black student in the United States:

> What I remember most of all was how differently our Nigerian teachers treated us. We were just boys, students, some of us better than others. What we weren't were problems. At the time I couldn't put into words or thoughts exactly why I felt the way I did—lighter, more joyful than I was in the Bronx—but now I know that this was it. I was fundamentally not seen as a problem first and a person second. (p. 72)

With Black girls, adultification blurs the line between Black girlhood and Black womanhood through age compression, making Black girlhood and Black womanhood one and the same (Morris, 2016). The problem with this compression, argues Morris, is that "latent ideas about Black females as hypersexual, conniving, loud, and sassy predominate, even if they make it to college and beyond. Public presentations of these caricatures . . . prescribe these traits to Black women. However, age compression renders Black girls as vulnerable to these aspersive representations" (Morris, 2016, p. 34).

In survey research conducted by Epstein et al. (2017), they found that across all age ranges, Black girls were seen as needing less protection and nurturing, and as being older than they were and more knowledgeable about adult topics. In subsequent focus-group research, Blake and Epstein (2019) found that many of the adultification beliefs about Black girls are related to negative stereotypes of Black women, mirroring Morris's claims above. For example, two themes that emerged from their data were the beliefs that Black girls had bad attitudes and that Black girls were hypersexual. In the case of "bad attitudes," this belief is tied to stereotypes of Black *women* being loud, difficult, and brash. Black *girls* are painted by this same brush. A respondent in Blake and Epstein's work expressed the idea that the word "attitude" was not used with White girls; it is a critique of Black girls alone (Blake & Epstein, 2019). Morris relays the story of a 6-year-old Florida girl who was *handcuffed and arrested* following a classroom temper tantrum (Morris, 2016). A 6-year-old. Handcuffed. And arrested. Temper tantrums in 6-year-olds fall firmly in the childhood behaviors category. Anyone who has taught 1st-graders has seen a child melt down. It is frustrating, and overwhelming and messy, but it is not criminal. This overreaction to Black girls' "attitude" is no small thing. Seeing them as particularly more violent, or dangerous, or resistant sets up problematic patterns. Research by the Office for Civil Rights at the U.S. Department of Education found "Black girls received in-school suspensions (11.2%) and out-of-school suspensions (13.3%) at rates almost two times their share of total student enrollment (7.4%)" (2021, p. 17). Moreover, their research showed that Black girls were the only group of girls that experienced this overrepresentation. So while Latina girls make up 13.3% of school enrollment, they are underrepresented in suspensions (at 7.4%). Again, Black girls make up 7.4% of the enrollment, but are 11.2% of the suspensions. They are the only group for which we see this overrepresentation.

A second theme of Blake and Epstein's research is the hypersexualization of girls. Black girls are seen as less innocent and more promiscuous. Morris argues that this is a holdover of slavery. "The sexual terrorism to which Black women were subjected as enslaved women was justified by casting them as immoral and sexually insatiable," writes Morris (2016, p. 115). This follows on from an earlier theme of needing Black people to be really, really different to justify slavery. One way of doing this was to make Black women really, really different from "proper," "delicate," "modest" White women. It also protects the "innocence" of White men, allowing them to deflect their sexual violence against Black women. Spinning stories of insatiability and "being loose" makes Black women different from other women. This othering is yet another way to justify slavery.

In truly stunning work done by Goff, Jackson, DiLeone, Culotta, and DiTomasso (2014), the researchers argue that Black childhood is diminished as Black children are dehumanized. They conducted four experiments including hundreds of people. Their findings paint a clear picture of how Black youth are adultified. Participants believe Black children are less innocent than White children are. The ages of Black targets (referring to characters in the research scenarios) were overestimated (by 4.5 years!), and these Black targets were seen as more culpable. Stunningly, in an implicit bias test, they found that the more participants "implicitly associated Blacks and apes, the greater the age overestimation and perceived culpability of Black children" (p. 532). The greater the degree of dehumanization, the greater the chance that children are seen as guilty adults. This research matters because it has tangible consequences. Black youth overall are 18 times more likely than

White youth to be sentenced as adults (Goff et al., 2014). Adultified this way, Black children and Black youth do not receive the affordances of childhood, and are set up for a host of real, life-altering obstacles. In their final conclusions to their study, Goff et al. argue:

> Sociologist Michael Kimmel (2008) has suggested that, for middle-class White males, the period of time when boys are not held fully responsible for their actions can extend well into their late 20s. In contrast, the present research suggests that Black children may be viewed as adults as soon as 13, with average age overestimations of Black children exceeding four and a half years in some cases. . . . In other words, our findings suggest that, although most children are allowed to be innocent until adulthood, Black children may be perceived as innocent only until deemed suspicious. (p. 541)

## Disciplining of Black Youth

The Office for Civil Rights at the U.S. Department of Education compiles data regarding discipline and racial disparities across the country (Office for Civil Rights, 2021). They found that beginning with the youngest children, Black children are subject to exclusionary discipline at higher rates than other youth. Some findings:

- Black preschool students accounted for 18.2% of total preschool enrollment but received 43.3% of one or more out-of-school suspensions (p. 7).
- Black preschool students were expelled at rates that were more than twice their share (38.2%) of total preschool enrollment (18.2%) (p. 8).
- Black students, who accounted for 15.1% of total student enrollment, were expelled at rates that were more than twice their share of total student enrollment (p. 12).
- In 2017–2018, Black students accounted for 28.7% of all students referred to law enforcement and 31.6% of all students arrested at school or during a school-related activity—twice their share of total student enrollment of 15.1% (p. 21).

Black students are overrepresented at every level of the disciplinary system (Dumas and ross, 2016). Black girls in particular are more likely to be suspended for subjective reasons, like disobedience, disruptions, and minor issues like cell phone use or dress code violations (Epstein et al., 2017). Black children with special needs are also disproportionately impacted by discipline policies. They are three times more likely to be suspended out of school than their White peers. In their research, Hines, King, and Ford (2018) suggest that the hypersurveillance of Black youth along with implied criminalization contribute to this disproportionality. This tells us that where teachers are looking matters. In one of Kerri's college courses, we listen to an NPR audio clip about bias in preschool (Turner, 2016), which is based on the findings of a Yale Child Study Center research report (Gilliam et al., 2016). Their findings show that teachers in preschool already spend more time watching Black children and surveilling them for perceived bad behavior. Using eye-tracking software and video clips, the researchers were able to assess where teachers were looking and whom they paid the most attention to when asked about challenging classroom behaviors. Black boys received the most attention in their experiment. This tells us something critical about how disproportionality and implicit bias function. For these teachers, this was not something spoken or explicitly acknowledged. Black boys are watched more, closer, and with more suspicion. So it isn't particularly surprising that Black youth are disciplined more, is it? You can only see what you are looking for. Gilliam et al. explain that a lot of this reaction is implicit and based on bias, biases that have significant consequences for Black children. Children who are denied educational opportunities in preschool are set up for long-term ramifications. Thus, schools can enact these early patterns of attributed criminality that impact youth for a lifetime. Hines et al. (2018) poignantly conclude that we must "examine schools as contexts of *and* for producing systematic oppression" (p. 8).

## Policing of Black Bodies

The policing of Black bodies shows up in a variety of ways at school, including rules about hairstyles, nails, dress, and other forms of self-expression. This is a form of Eurocentrism in which White standards of grooming, dressing, and expression are given priority and importance. Deviations from these standards are viewed as unkempt, dirty, thug-like, provocative, and a host of other negative terms. This kind of policing not only constrains Black expression and cultural practices in the moment, but has truly significant consequences.

- Faith Fennity, 11, was dismissed from her school in Louisiana for wearing box braids.[4] The use of "unnatural" hair was against school rules (Jacobo, 2018).
- Two black students in Texas were suspended for wearing dreadlocks, which broke the school rule on hair length for boys. D'Andre Arnold, a senior, was barred from attending the prom and his graduation (Schwartz, 2020).
- Two Black twins, Maya and Deanna Cook, were barred from extracurricular activities and the prom, and threatened with suspension, when they came to school in braids (Lattimore, 2017). The school handbook considers hair extensions "distracting."
- Tiana Parker, age 7 (!), was told by her Tulsa school that her dreadlocks needed to be removed. According to her father, she was

told she did not look "presentable." Her father is a barber. The child changed schools (Klein, 2013).

Black girls are particularly impacted by school dress codes and rules about grooming. In fascinating research by the National Women's Law Center (2018), young women in Washington, D.C., high schools reported the myriad ways in which Blackness is policed via rules about appearance. Many girls run afoul of rules when it comes to natural hairstyles (which are seen as "unprofessional") and hair wraps or head coverings (which are outright banned in many schools). According to their report, 68% of D.C. high schools that publish their dress codes online specifically ban head wraps and head scarves. The girls in the study also reported that while there were rules for girls about the length of shorts and being covered, there were no similar rules for boys. The girls went on to catalog rules banning clothes that were too big, clothes that were too small, makeup, long nails, and hair dye. In an insightful comment, one student relayed that:

> they really enforce their dress code especially towards the girls. You never hear a boy [say], "Oh, y'all got dress coded today, bro." And then the girls with curves, like really curvy, they just [say], "Oh, you're showing too much, you're revealing so much." I have this friend, she has no breasts, no butt. She wears crop tops, miniskirts. It doesn't matter. They don't care. (National Women's Law Center, 2018, p. 16)

Several students echoed this exact concern. They relate that curvy girls are much more apt to be called out for dress code violations and looking "inappropriate." They are very clear that skinny, less-developed girls with smaller breasts are not put through the same level of scrutiny. What explains this?

Let's add to this that the young women are quite clear that their sexuality is being policed as well. The report relates that many of the rules exist to ensure girls that will not tempt or distract boys. Admonitions to cover up or be less revealing are commonplace. Returning to our earlier explanation of adultification, you can see this in effect here. Girls who look more "developed," with breasts and curves and bottoms, are being policed in different ways than girls who appear more childlike. Young Black women are seen as older and more sexualized earlier. The more girls fit into White stereotypical imaginations of adolescent Black girls, the more they are constrained and controlled. So in shorthand:

Bitty girls = not seen as sexual (yet) = nothing to control.
Developed girls = young Black women, thus promiscuous = needing to be controlled.

Beyond the issues of fairness, dignity, and self-determination this kind of policing brings up, there are clear consequences for schooling. Children lose time in school. They lose time going home to change or when they are suspended for their braids or when they cannot participate in sports because their hair is not "right." For example, "74 percent of D.C. public high school dress codes authorize disciplinary action that can lead to missed class or school" (National Women's Law center, 2018, p. 26). Black girls in D.C. are 20 times more likely than White girls to be suspended (National Women's Law Center, 2018). This is beyond unfairness. When we chose the dress code as a focus, schools chose to prioritize how a child looks over their education. The issue of hair in particular is of such a concern that the NAACP Legal Defense Fund is currently working on legislation to end this kind of discrimination. Yes, that is hair-based discrimination. Because it is so widespread and consequential (people losing their jobs and children losing time in schools), they have proposed the CROWN Act,[5] which would decriminalize Black hair (NAACP Legal Defense Fund, n.d.). Stunning, yes? That in 2022 Black organizations are fighting for Black hair to be accepted? This is a long and complex fight, in that hair is being used as a proxy for conforming to White standards. We encourage readers to look at the original documents at the Legal Defense Fund site on natural hair discrimination (at https://www.naacpldf.org/natural-hair-discrimination). The site walks you through legal cases regarding Black hair since 1947.

## IN CONCLUSION

This chapter is wide and diverse. We have charted the myriad ways that anti-Blackness shows up in classrooms and on playing fields. In wrapping up, we have a few take-home thoughts that will link the reader back to larger themes we wish to prioritize. Again, we repeat these themes not to be redundant, but because patterns matter in analyzing racism. Patterns are the opposite of idiosyncratic individuals making personal choices. Patterns help us see the systemic webs.

Returning to Marshall High School for a moment, given the fact that merely 8% of students on Marshall's campus were Black while 90% of the boys' basketball team was, basketball games and practices are likely the largest regular gatherings of African American boys at the school. As students, families, and educators gather at games to celebrate and cheer on the team, consider the message that is sent. As the team of coaches assembles to provide instruction and discipline to the boys, often offering additional after-school practices, weight lifting sessions, and weekend clinics, consider the messages that are being delivered (to the boys, their families and the rest of the community) about what the boys are valued for and what the school is willing to invest on behalf of their success in the area of basketball. When schools do not interrupt narratives about Black youth, they are simply perpetuating them while at the same time teaching other kids at the school how to treat and value Black children. Like with the little boy being pulled in the boat at his baseball celebration in the Introduction, racism teaches White children the role of Black children. This is a theme. Black children being represented in a sport, but that representation actually signaling a problem, is a second theme. Representation cannot do the work of justice.

Recall from the Introduction that being intentional about goals is key to working against anti-Blackness in schools. Being intentional begins with facing the truth. However, research shows us that many White teachers resist discussions of racial issues and instead choose a "colorblind" approach. They choose "not to notice" the racial makeup of their students or different classes. We see this in action with sports. Instead of confronting obvious harms and patterns, they assume that schools' policies and practices are neutral (García & Guerra, 2004). We have already laid out the perils of colorblindness, but here we see a third theme at work. Colorblindness does not serve Black children. Can these students be educated well if they are not empowered to face the very real forces allied to defeat them (low academic achievement, racialized narratives/deficit thinking, low expectations, racism)? Teachers and coaches espousing a colorblind approach, where they bury the role of race, does nothing to help. It renders people incapable of seeing the harm right in front of our eyes.

### REFLECTION QUESTIONS FOR CHAPTER 3

- Do I see evidence of the overpolicing of Black youth in my school?
- Do Black children see themselves in your curriculum?
- Do teachers handle slavery and other hard topics with empathy and care?
- What examples of colorblindness do you see at your school? Your children's school?
- How can schools and coaches be intentional about undoing narratives that their Black students are athletically gifted, but not academically gifted?

# Part II

# BLACK-AFFIRMING POSSIBILITIES AND DOING THE WORK

## CHAPTER 4

# Imagining Black-Affirming Spaces

When I (Joi) was a kid, my dad had a sticker on the glove box of his van. It said, "Fight Black on Black crime with Black on Black love!" We did Black love in my family and in my community. We acknowledged folks when we saw one another, got called out when we did wrong, and uplifted each other with our words ("Little Man is really doing his thing!" or "Sister-girl is alright with me!") and actions. We shopped and ate at Black establishments and read Black books and magazines (there was always an *Ebony* or *Jet* magazine on our coffee table). We watched White television shows when they had Black people in them (like Mr. T on *The A-Team*, Alfonso Ribeiro on *Silver Spoons*, or Kim Fields on *The Facts of Life*) and without question faithfully viewed Black television shows and movies (like *Sanford and Son, Good Times, The Cosby Show, The Wiz,* and *Coming to America*). We did not read these books, watch these shows, or eat at those restaurants in response to some formalized campaign to build Black businesses or to "buy Black." While our desire to support Black enterprise was certainly a factor in our decisions, ultimately, we shopped, ate, read, and watched as we did because it was edifying to us. Our stories, our lives, our tastes, and our styles were reflected. We saw ourselves, and what we saw was good. There was no shame. In that beautiful place and at that moment in time, there was no schism between Black and beautiful or Black and accepted. It simply was a matter of fact. To be able to see yourself, your people, and your community and love what you see is the simplest, most foundational human dignity. To be at home in your body and mind and to know that there is nothing that needs to change for you to be accepted is the most basic human right. I was blessed to be raised in this environment.

As outlined in this book, we police Black children's bodies, their dress, and their hair. We over punish their infractions and under acknowledge their successes. We position them as intellectually inferior and suggest that their ancestors contributed little to the historical record. The slights go beyond what we chronicle in this book. Educators routinely shame and condemn Black children's language (Baker-Bell, 2020; Champion et al., 2012; O'Quin, 2021) and even styles of movement (Neal et al., 2003). There is so much that educators require Black children to change.

bell hooks in *All About Love* defines love as "a combination of care, knowledge, responsibility, respect, trust, and commitment" (hooks, 2001, p. xviii). Building Black-affirming spaces begins with love. There is simply no way around it. But love and care require effort and attention. Love is layered. Care requires consistent attentiveness to others. How can we bring love and care to our schools? We build by analogy here; a story helps us connect the practice of love and care to our classrooms.

I (Joi) watch a lot of nature programming (I am a science lover, too). Much of it is focused on the rescue and rehabilitation of injured animals. I am always struck by the level of care provided to a wounded sea turtle, elephant, or salamander. In one episode, a young koala had been injured by wildfires in Australia. Among the measures to save its life, they placed the animal into a home to be fostered by a woman who watched over it day and night. She hand-fed the baby, held it using a special blanket, and kept it warm with a carefully monitored heat lamp. She weighed it each day to make sure it was gaining the minimum number of ounces for it to thrive. At one point, the little koala lost some weight. She informed the veterinarian, who then traveled from one koala sanctuary to the next to collect a needed treatment. I provide the example to highlight the levels and nuances of *care* and how care unfolds. Care requires individualized attentiveness. Care requires doing. The caretakers invested time and resources to put the koala on the road to recovery. They had to learn how to feed it and at which intervals, and they gained *knowledge* of the particular nutrients it needed and the necessary formulation, as well as its ideal temperature and expected rate of growth. Care requires a *responsibility* to the animals and environments that the naturalists protect. In other words, they do not sit around and wait for someone else to come along and protect these species. When something goes wrong (like the massive fires in Australia), they step up and put in the work to make things right. They exhibit a deep *respect* for animals, plants, and the entire natural environment. Every effort is made to keep animals in the wild. Out of respect for species, infants are never allowed to imprint onto humans or to eat human food. Delicate plant species are handled with gloved hands. With tenderness and time, *trust* is built between the wildlife and their human caretakers. Finally, the naturalists exhibit *commitment* to the species that they care for. No matter how daunting the tasks (rebuilding the tiger population or reforesting the Amazon) or how ominous the outlook (widespread bleaching in the Great Barrier Reef, the diminishing polar ice caps or climate change), they remain committed to the goal of healing the natural world. The caretakers are not deterred. In fact, they are perhaps operating with increased fervor given the urgency of the situation. They show love, as bell hooks lays out, through the operationalizing of "care, knowledge, responsibility, respect, trust and commitment" (hooks, 2001, p. xviii). These are not abstract feelings but actualized actions. Love is made tangible. Although a far-afield example, to us, this illuminates the way in which we can do love. There is an intentionality in each step the caretakers make that allows the small ones to thrive. Care. Knowledge. Responsibility. Respect. Trust. Commitment. We add: intention. These are the building blocks we need in schools.

What would it mean to build schooling experiences where Black children are loved, cared for, known, and respected? What would educational spaces committed to Black youths' success feel like? What steps can be taken to build trust despite challenges? In this chapter, we paint a picture of Black-affirming educational spaces, where Black children can be whole, central and celebrated.

## CREATING HOMEPLACES

As with the previous chapters, we are seeking to build a new trajectory for educating Black children that is not resting on the status quo. We take up Ashley Woodson's (2021) challenge that toleration is not the goal. She argues, "Turning desegregation out means rejecting the assumption that merely being tolerated through desegregation makes us [Black people] more enough. It is aggressively celebrating with and for Black children until this assumption is vacated and condemned" (p. 21). We also agree with k. m. ross, who warns that the goals of integration remain unmet through her concept of the *afterlife of school segregation* (ross, 2021). She cautions, "Black students remain systematically dehumanized and positioned as uneducable" (ross, 2021, p. 48). Thus, Black education must happen in spaces that "create liberatory schooling experiences for Black students in an anti-Black world" (p. 51).

ross (2021) offers some ideas about what fugitive (as she terms them) Black educational spaces might look like. She focuses on the idea (adapted from hooks) of "homeplaces," spaces that provide safety and nurturance to Black people. These are places of "radical possibility," often on the margins (ross, 2021), where new worlds can be seen and resistance can be gathered. This is a place where "Black children dream weightless, unracialized and human" (Dumas & ross, 2016, p. 436).

Ladson-Billings reminds us that "students of color may become alienated from the schooling process because schooling often asks children to be something or someone other than who they really are. . . . It asks them to dismiss their community and cultural knowledge. It erases things that the students hold dear" (2001, p. xiv). Black-affirming spaces do not ask Black students to choose between being educated or being Black.

The goal of this chapter is to help readers imagine what they often do not see: a *Black-affirming* educational space. To do this, we use a case study of a summer STEM/Engineering camp. Through this case study, we provide a specific roadmap of how to develop Black-affirming spaces that move beyond the superficial. We seek to answer how Black-affirming spaces are created, what ideological commitments must be in place, and what challenges must be navigated. We provide a vision of these homeplaces.

## STEM ACADEMIES: AN OVERVIEW

We (Joi and her team) run our STEM Academies each summer. The academies serve students in grades 6–12. In addition, we train a cadre of diverse (Black, Indigenous, refugee, first-generation, DACA, White, Southeast Asian, immigrant, working class, struggling, middle class, etc.) college students, graduate students, and young educational professionals to serve as counselors and instructors.

The STEM Summer Academies are 1- to 2-week programs for middle and high school students focused on holistic academic enrichment. Through hands-on learning in engineering, arts, and mathematics, students engage their creativity, enhance problem-solving skills, and develop mathematical questioning, communication, and critical thinking skills. The goal is to provide a fun and enriching experience that increases students' STEM literacy, and to spur their enthusiasm about further education opportunities and careers in STEM fields. We conclude the academies with a Community Conference where students present the work that they have accomplished during the Academies to their larger community. Each Academy serves 40–50 students. The culminating Community Conference is open to all members of our region, but we particularly market it to families, educators, youth, and STEM-focused nonprofit organizations. The Conference generally has well over 400 participants in attendance.

We begin with a snapshot from one afternoon in our STEM Academy, to provide a glimpse into what we built. Then we will work backwards to unravel how we created this homeplace.

## A DAY IN THE LIFE OF THE ACADEMY

The Southern California sun shined brightly on our outdoor lunch gathering. Sitting at round umbrellaed tables attempting to shade the noontime sun, middle and high school students from all over our city laughed, relaxed, and enjoyed today's lunch: pupusas! Then, as if on some invisible cue, a group of four African American girls stood up and performed the full dance routine to New Edition's "If It Isn't Love." The other students looked on with smiles, some attempting to perform the moves. When the girls finished, there were claps and more smiles. Such a scene may not seem notable. After all, kids hang out together all the time, and laughter and dancing are sometimes part of the merriment. But this was different. This group was a gathering of young people in our summer STEM Academy, a camp where students spend hours each day solving challenging mathematics problems and sharing their solutions. This gathering was taking place on a predominantly White, private university campus on the patio of their elite

School of Engineering. This gathering was taking place in a county where at one of our local high schools, slightly over 2.5% of African American high school students are scoring proficient on standardized exams in mathematics (California Assessment of Student Progress and Performance, 2019). Just 2% of the undergraduate attendees at the local (public) University of California campus were Black/African American (University of California San Diego, 2018), and mathematically talented and gifted was routinely equated with Asian or White students and more often than not, males. Given this context, and the general invisibility of African Americanness in our region, how did this moment emerge, and in what ways did the STEM Academy engender this important and rare outcome?

Here, we unpack the features (both visible and invisible) of our STEM Academies and their specific focus on creating mathematics spaces where Black children can thrive. In particular, the camp begins by drawing on the funds of knowledge and cultural resources (González & Moll, 2002) of Black families who engage in the engineering design process alongside their children. Throughout the camp, families are asked to share stories with their children of when they have used engineering (problem solving, mathematics, science, etc.) in their lives. Here, Black families in all of their configurations are included and uplifted. Black music, culture and practices are centered in the curriculum and programming of the camp (e.g., studying the mathematics of hair braiding and barbering and tessellations in Black and African design). Likewise, instead of positioning STEM as a tool of American productivity and imperialism (Martin, 2019), students are invited to build a critical stance toward STEM and then to utilize it to investigate questions and challenges that are imperative to them and to their communities. In short, the Academies are a learning space where Black youth are not an afterthought, but central to the mission, processes, mindsets, and content matter of the STEM Academy.


## INTENTION AS OUR PHILOSOPHY

Few things in our STEM academies are done without intention. By this, we mean that our choices are guided by consideration for the children we serve. Every decision we make centers the lives and experiences of Black children. We are intentional in our recruiting, marketing, curriculum, guest speakers, field trips, and schedules. We are even intentional about snacks! We are unabashedly intentional about our beliefs about Black youth. Our beliefs about youth are premised on Martin's (2009) *Axioms for Researching Black Children in Mathematics*. We specifically embrace the ideas that:

    Axiom I: Black children are brilliant; researchers should not overly concern themselves with documenting how Black children differ from White children and reifying racial achievement gaps but with how Black children can best attain and maintain excellence in mathematics; and

Axiom II: Black children possess the intellectual capacity to learn mathematics as well as any other child; they do, however, often lack sufficient opportunities to engage in meaningful mathematical experiences. (p. 36)

Our beliefs about Black youth in our programs are based on their assumed competence, intelligence, and potential, while being mindful that obstacles stand in their way. We are intentional about seeing and attending to race and racism in the context of STEM. Intentionality allows us foresight into obstacles that our youth may experience. We are able to anticipate roadblocks. For example, we anticipate that the students who come to us may have had negative experiences in mathematics classrooms. We anticipate that students will have received a fairly anemic version of mathematics. We anticipate that more often than not they have been fed messages that they as well as other Black students are not good in mathematics and that other students of different racial backgrounds are superior to them. We anticipate that they are experiencing academic tracking and are likely on the lower rung of the mathematics tracks in their middle or high school. These anticipations are not the result of deficit views on our end (we are people of color ourselves and witness the genius of Black people in mathematics and STEM on a regular basis). Rather, what we anticipate reflects what we know about the status of Black children in mathematics through the research on school tracking (Oakes et al., 2004; Orfield & Lee, 2007), STEM educational outcomes across our state and the nation, deficit views that teachers hold for Black youth (Allen, 2015; Delpit, 1988, 2012; Solórzano, 1997) and the voices of Black STEM learners themselves (see for example McGee, 2016; McGee & Martin, 2011; Spencer, 2009). We understand that Black students have to contend with a metanarrative that suggests that they are athletically talented, but intellectually inferior. We intentionally work to undo the damage done by these metanarratives and to create new ones in our academies. We hire counselors who defy these stereotypes. Some are athletes, some love hip-hop, some are artists or musicians, others are all of the above. They are each living and breathing counternarratives. We do not operate from a colorblind platform because to do so would silence our students, deny them their lived experiences, and operate from a place of fiction, not reality. Instead, we notice race and purposely program in response to it. Intentionality is the bedrock of our programming.

It takes a great deal of organizational and administrative wizardry to run our highly interactive full-day summer programs for 45+ middle and high school students. Using the anchor of intentionality, we lay out the thinking and focus of our staffing, curriculum, family relations and other affective features of the STEM Academy.

## Intentionality in Student Recruitment and Outreach

The Academy is open to incoming 6th- to 12th-graders. While students who already have an interest in exploring engineering and mathematics often find their way to our academies, we focus a great deal of our energies on attracting nontypical mathematics/science/STEM students. This particular move (bringing so-called non-STEM students into the STEM space) is undoubtedly the most important step in our work. Recall our earlier discussion of metanarratives (Chapter 3). One of the most salient metanarratives in schools and in our society is the inferiority of Black students in mathematics and other STEM-based fields. This is, of course, connected to the more global narrative that questions the overall intelligence of Black people. There is clear evidence that this narrative materializes in the schooling experiences of African American students, shaping their access to high-quality instruction, university preparatory courses, and qualified and woke teachers (i.e., teachers who have belief systems and dispositions that acknowledge the intelligence of, understand, support, and edify Black people). Furthermore, these narratives shape the mathematics identity of Black students, molding how their teachers and classmates see them and ultimately how they see themselves in relation to mathematics.[1] We understand that Black students in mathematics classrooms must manage the narratives that teachers hold of them. As Nasir and Shah's (2011) study found,

> African American students do not typically have a choice to simply ignore these issues, as their awareness of the narratives means that the narratives are salient artifacts within the classroom space that may be deployed against them in some way, usually to position them in ways detrimental to learning. . . . The young men and boys that we interviewed were, thus, not simply aware of racialized narratives about school and math performance; they found themselves regularly needing to respond to these narratives. . . . As educators, and as a society, we cannot underestimate the burden such negotiation places on students. (pp. 41–42)

Our work recognizes that when it comes to Black students, tacit markers of achievement such as grades and standardized achievement scores are highly questionable artifacts of their actual capacity in STEM. Since success on these measures is often not reliable or valid, we see no need to recruit students based on them. Our understanding of the realities of Black students' schooling experiences allow us to have completely different conversations with potential students and their families. We see the STEM Academies as an opportunity for students to consider their identities anew, free from the noisy messaging that only certain people belong in STEM.

There is so much potential among students who have otherwise been written off in STEM. We have as much if not more interest in the 11th-grade student who is just completing their first year of algebra (generally a course taken in middle school) as we do in the 8th-grade student completing geometry (often taken in one's freshman or sophomore year of high school). We understand that writing off these students is an incredible loss to us and to the potential fields that they might work in. The STEM Academies, then, become an opportunity not to convince students that they need STEM, but rather that STEM, as a field, needs them: their ideas, perspectives, questions, and experiences. When it comes to climate change, superviruses, cancer, environmental degradation, and more, there is no "them and us." Rather, science's ability to do its work is contingent upon its willingness to open its fields to more folks.

In a city where success in STEM shapes so many future life chances for youth (high school graduation, college eligibility, job placement for enlistees in the military, etc.) and where very few Black students are succeeding in STEM or mathematics, we believe that serving these students is an imperative. As such, we recruit our students through every means possible. We understand that there are powerful, informal networks within Black and brown communities, networks that are overlooked and missed because they do not operate in the same way as those in the dominant culture. Black communities, specifically, have always had to organize in covert ways, as so many of their efforts to move forward have been brutally threatened and undermined (Faraj, 2007; Harding, 1981; Martin, T., 1986). She might not have official 501(c)3 status, but Mrs. Mohammed (the elder who was once a teacher's aide at the local middle school) may have supported and helped to educate an entire generation of young people in her community. You might not be able to locate their scholarship fund on Google, but the small Black church on the corner may have helped hundreds of youngsters pay their college tuition. Whether through churches, mosques, grocery stores, sporting events, restaurants, or theaters, when we see Black families with children who look to be in middle or high school, we speak to them and share about the Academy. We look for individuals who champion Black youth, whether those are teachers, mothers, organizers, or neighbors.

We also know the Black people on our campus. This includes executive assistants, police officers, deans, shuttle drivers, faculty, and students. Over the years, with care and consistency, we have built relationships and real trust. Time and again, we hear negative stories about Black communities, that the kids do not care about academics or that their neighborhoods are violent and dysfunctional. We do not want to romanticize the Black community (or any community, for that matter). There are certainly profound challenges that African American communities face, and we are well aware of these complexities. However, our experiences with Black youth and their families routinely tell a different story: that they care deeply about their education, have deep interest in STEM, and are invested in the success of their children.

### Intentionality about Staffing

*Who we hire.* We hire a cadre of diverse and talented counselors. These individuals will work closest with our middle and high school students. We recruit undergraduate and graduate STEM and education majors as well as early professionals in teaching (those in their first 5 years of classroom practice) to serve as counselors. Anyone who falls into these categories is eligible to apply. Still, we *seek out* Black, Latinx, Southeast Asian, immigrant, and refugee-status individuals to serve as counselors. In our quest, we also search for individuals with diverse interests, styles, and personalities. My research team and I (Joi) are struck by how often we are told that such individuals do not exist—that there are no qualified POC who can serve in these roles. We then defy them each year as we staff our Academies with a host of intelligent, skilled, and passionate STEM majors and educational professionals. Our camp is a veritable Wakanda, where for weeks, our predominantly White campus overflows with BIPOC counselors and students engaged in rich mathematical and STEM work.

We vet our counselors via an application process followed by an interview. During this process, we are reading and listening for more than high GPAs and extracurricular activities, and we are looking for something beyond diversity in its traditional sense (i.e., a mix of racial, cultural, and gender identities). While these matter, our focus is on the *dispositions* towards youth exhibited by the applicants. How do they talk about themselves in relation to the kids they will work with? Is there a distance ("I want to help underprivileged kids"), or is there affinity ("When I was in school, I was part of a community program that really helped me to grow and develop")? Do their responses reflect a deficit perspective towards youth of color?

*How we prepare them.* Once they are hired, counselors are required to attend a weeklong professional development in-service. Most STEM programs that we are aware of provide content-specific training to their new hires. For example, the science institute in Joi's community hires college students to run its afterschool STEM courses for local elementary school kids. To prepare their new hires, the institute provides the college students with training specific to the topics that they will teach. For instance, trainings include "How to dissect a lemon" or "Teaching Engineering 101." Our training reaches beyond a focus on the STEM topic. It is instead centered on the specific needs of BIPOC learners in STEM and in education. We educate counselors on best practices of STEM pedagogy as it specifically pertains to African American, Latinx, and multilingual learners. Many of the articles that have been cited in this book are part of the professional development and training that our counselors receive. In addition, they learn skills for mentoring adolescents and culturally responsive classroom management, and review research on how best to support the STEM identity of BIPOC students, the status and experiences of BIPOC youth in STEM, and culturally relevant pedagogy in STEM. We of course provide them with training in the lessons that they will deliver to their students, but, more importantly, we provide them with a wide, critical, research-based lens through which they can see and understand the youth that they will work with. Professional development sessions include time for discussion and reflection. We find that many of the readings help the counselors to better understand their own educational journeys and to place in perspective the challenges they have encountered.

## Intentionality in Curriculum

The curriculum of our STEM Academies reflects our beliefs as educators that youth are innately curious and that learning is the natural outgrowth of that curiosity. We believe that the questions of mathematics are engaging and that puzzling over them is fulfilling and enlightening. Furthermore, we believe that science, technology, engineering, and mathematics belong to all cultures. All people across time and location have asked mathematical questions, used quantitative thinking, and engineered solutions. Systems of science (while different across cultures) emerge in response to the ideas, ways of being, questions, and challenges of different societies (for a fuller discussion explore Greer et al., 2009). No one group owns STEM. Our curriculum demonstrates these principles by exposing students to mathematical ideas and practices that members of their (and other) communities engage in. For example, in one lesson students examine the mathematical patterns embedded in cornrows. On a field trip, students explore the murals of Chicano Park. While there, they then spend time with one of the muralists, who shares the process by which his notebook-sized sketches are transformed into massive works of art. The goal is to aid students in seeing themselves and their communities as a part of the enterprise, history, and evolution of STEM, something that they rarely experience in the mathematics and STEM courses in their schools.

The questions of STEM are the questions of society itself. We want our students to see STEM as a tool for unpacking the challenges that they and the larger society face. That the aim of STEM ought to be the social good—to help understand and solve society's most profound challenges—is a shift from the messaging that many youth receive about its purpose (i.e., to obtain a high-paying job or to gain privilege in the world). We use the 17 United Nations Sustainable Development Goals (SDGs) to introduce students to the grand global challenges that the UN has identified. For the full list of the 17 goals, see the United Nations Department of Economic and Social Affairs webpage at https://sdgs.un.org/goals. These goals are introduced in a video that features tennis champion Serena Williams.[2] Students begin their examination of the goals by asking as many questions as they can about each of them. This inquiry-based activity allows students to see that STEM is as much about the insightfulness of their questions as it is about solutions and answers. We are continuously struck by how effortlessly our students interrogate and unpack these 17 challenges. Their proclivity is evidence that they too have experienced poverty (Goal 1), unequal schooling (Goal 4), and inequality (Goal 10). Their families often live in communities with poor infrastructure (Goal 9) and know the realities of struggle due to poor jobs and economic opportunity (Goal 8).

Seeing that the challenges they grapple with are the very same challenges that others around the world face repositions our students to the very center of STEM's work. As Christensen (2009), author of *Teaching for Joy and Justice*, writes, "Teaching for joy and justice means creating a curriculum that matters, a curriculum that helps students make sense of the world, that makes them feel smart—educated even. . . . How do we live our lives as moral citizens of the world, how do we make the world a better place?" (p. 7).

Students' culminating tasks are to use the STEM knowledge and dispositions gained from their time in the Academy to craft a solution to address one of the SDGs. We witness our students produce novel, insightful solutions with skill, ingenuity, and passion. From ways to deliver vaccines to remote locations to methods of cleaning the ocean of plastics to the design of neighborhoods that produce their own food, students demonstrate that they are capable doers of mathematics and STEM.

The life stories and STEM journeys of our counselors are another part of the curriculum of our STEM Academies. Each counselor is required to give a presentation to the entire Academy where they detail their STEM journey. In their presentation, they must share a struggle that they have overcome along their academic and life path. These stories of persistence and resilience are a rare glimpse into the lives of young BIPOC STEM majors and educators. Their stories, like their very presence on our campus each summer, upend the myths that they are intellectually inferior or do not belong. While our original intention was to create an opportunity for our campers (middle and high school students) to see new possibilities for themselves as they listened to the stories of their counselors, the end product has yielded so much more. These moments of storytelling bring our noisy, busy Academy to a standstill. The entire camp (counselors, youth, leaders, visitors, families) stops what it is doing to listen and learn. There are tears, head nods, and cheering. There is recognition of our struggle together as people of color. These moments of *ubuntu* (we are in this together; you struggled to make things better for me, so I will struggle to make things better for others) are routinely noted as one of the most impactful aspects of the Academy.

A major impetus for starting the academies was to give BIPOC youth access to the beauty and resources on our university campus. Every summer prior to implementing the Academy, we saw hundreds of youth attending camps and participating in activities on our campus. They were playing tennis, learning how to code, eating in the cafeterias and preparing for college. Rarely did we see Black youth among these young people. When attempting to enroll my (Joi's) own kids into these camps, I quickly found out that they were cost-prohibitive. (If I, as a professor, could barely afford to enroll my kids, what was the likelihood that other BIPOC families would be able to?) Through fundraising efforts and in-kind donations of individuals on campus, we were able to bring STEM Academy to life.

Being on an actual university campus gives Black and other BIPOC youth firsthand experience with higher education. Professors from across our campus give workshops and share their expertise during the Academy. It is important for these professors to see and interact with our youth, and it is essential for our youth and their families to see that they belong on a university campus.

The last aspect of our curriculum relates to joy and play. Our academies are places where youth want to come. Each morning, before sessions officially begin, students work on a variety of puzzles, play games, and participate in paper folding. And each day our youth have a full hour of outdoor play. Yes, from the youngest 6th-grader to the eldest high school senior, there is running, jumping, chasing, and twirling. Through a combination of professional outdoor educators and volunteer staff, our students experience the joy of childhood, something so many Black and BIPOC youth miss. This is a permanent fixture of our curriculum, as we believe that joy is a central feature of learning well.

## Intentionality in Family and Cultural Practices

Families are central to the success of BIPOC youth, yet so many times Black families are disregarded. We see families as our partners and seek to provide an experience that includes, informs, and enriches them. Let's begin with our nomenclature. We intentionally use the term *family*, not *parent(s)*. Undoubtedly, the identities and backgrounds of Joi and her two Academy cofounders (which include Black, immigrant, English language learner, low-income) shape this decision. Many families of color are multigenerational. They routinely include cousins, grandparents, aunts, uncles, and fictive kin. These are not aberrant versions of "traditional nuclear" families. They are the way that Black families organize and operate. With this knowledge, we organize our academies to be inclusive of families. Because Black youth have a number of individuals engaged in their lives, our academies are an opportunity to have a wide impact. Our orientation is one such example. It is open to all family members of Academy students. We spend time explaining the purpose of the Academy, introducing ourselves and the counselors, and providing our families with a taste of what their kids will experience during the Academy. Families (grandparents, uncles, aunts, moms, cousins, dads, etc.) are introduced to the SDGs and watch an introductory video featuring Serena Williams (in English and Spanish). Families are then asked to share their initial thoughts about the SDGs. These discussions are always meaningful.

Next, orientation attendees are presented with an engineering challenge. Breaking up into their individual family units, they compete with other families. This activity is always lively and competitive. The creativity and skill of families are in full effect. Whether they are housekeepers, gardeners, receptionists, physicians, or mechanics, families rise to the thorny engineering challenge. There is a lot that we hope is learned from this activity. First, we want to give adults an opportunity to see their kids in action. We want them to see how they problem-solve, their insights and their challenges. At the same time, we want the children to see the adults in their family as the mathematicians, engineers, and scientists that they truly are. Whether the adults in their family have attended college or not, and regardless of their occupation, they have deep funds of knowledge to draw upon (Gutstein, 2006). Their family, and all of the families gathered, possess valid and effective mathematical and engineering knowledge, and this knowledge is capable of solving engineering problems assigned by university professors.

In addition to drawing on the knowledge of families and youth, we intentionally invite and include home languages in our academies. This includes Spanish and Black language/African American Vernacular English. We hire counselors from a variety of language backgrounds, and we pay attention to the language needs of our students. Many of our counselors use Black dialects (yes, our college students majoring in engineering and mathematics speak Black English!). We embrace this as one more way for our youth to see themselves in STEM. We appreciate the freedom that emerges when young people realize that their language is validated. Likewise, we recognize that wider language registers provide us and our students access to more ideas and perspectives.

Our own families (the families of Joi and her Academy codirectors) are an important part of the STEM Academy, and they are regular participants in it. The participation of our spouses, children, nieces, nephews, siblings, and parents provides one more mirror for our students (an opportunity for them to see themselves in STEM). Family structures reflect *relationships* within families. Who are you responsible for? Who is responsible for you? In working-class families, it is routine for youth to stay in the home after high school to work and help support the family. Older siblings may take care of younger ones. In many Black families, grandparents may have primary caregiving roles, and cousins may be as close as siblings. Family has a significant impact on how people live their lives, the responsibilities they have, and the choices they do and do not make (Brooks, 2015; Park et al., 2019). My family structure and the family structures of my colleagues in running the STEM Academies are similar to the families of the students we serve. Even though we are each professors with PhDs, we maintain close connection with our families and remain responsible to them. While there is generally a strong separation between work and family life in academia, we maintain our cultural practices.

Our family members serve as counselors, deliver lunch, participate in workshops, and help set up activities within the STEM Academy. Their participation is one more signal to Academy students that they can engage in the work of STEM while maintaining who they are (their culture, values, and ways of being).

## HALLMARKS OF BLACK-AFFIRMING SPACES

How might you bring these ideas back to your school? We appreciate that these academies are unique environments, where we have a great deal of autonomy and latitude. We are mindful that many schools do not have the same flexibility. Still, there are ways in which the intentionality of the Academies can be replicated in other spaces and places. We will walk you through some possibilities.

- Hiring African American professionals such as:
  » teachers, specifically those with a pro-Black stance.
  » Black paraprofessionals, who are often closely linked to Black communities.
- Committing to learning and understanding African American stories through ongoing staff development (we provide an extensive list of resources in Chapters 6 and 7).
- Joining/partnering with African American organizations and consulting with a variety of elders in the Black community.
- Committing to antiracism efforts that move beyond diversity or multiculturalism.
- Honoring linguistic diversity among children and adults. Providing space for children to use their many languages for meaning-making and for connection.
- Minimizing heavy-handed discipline and classroom management that is punitive in nature. Being mindful of the particular ways in which Black girls and boys are overdisciplined.
- Centering curriculum on real-world problems that engage and excite students, to show them the true potential of STEM and other academic areas.
- Linking youth to the larger world, to show how they, as individuals, can better it. STEM is a way to solve problems. It is a toolkit. Allow students to see that they own this toolkit and can use it to save orangutans in Borneo or support children without access to fresh water in Ethiopia (or Flint, Michigan).
- Building storytelling into your programs and classes. As we mentioned, counselors share their STEM journeys. Hearing from others who have gone before them and have succeeded matters.
- Connecting with families in ways that uplift their knowledge. Everyone uses math and science in their daily lives. Everyone. Allow students to see the wisdom embedded already in their families.
- Identifying local museums, STEM-focused nonprofits, and other community organizations that might have resources and events particular to Black youth.
- Locating and then learning from schools where African American students are thriving.

- Inviting BIPOC professionals in the STEM fields (or any field, really) to do classroom visits, mentor students, or host a visit-a-scientist's-lab day.
- Allowing youth to play. Play with math, play with one another, play with adults. The last few years have been awash in COVID trauma. We are mindful of this. We are mindful that Black children often have constrained childhoods. Build in moments to be light and goofy with your youth.
- Provide good snacks. Snacks always matter!

## IN CONCLUSION

As Delpit (2012) writes, "What we need to know at a very deep level is that African American children do not come into this world at a deficit" (p. 5). Our academies seek to provide meaningful mathematical experiences in contexts that embrace and support Black children. From the music we play while students are working, to the lunches and snacks that we serve and the problems that we work on, our goal is to produce a place where Black middle and high school students feel at home, experience alignment between themselves and the subject they were studying (mathematics), and ultimately find fulfillment and joy. In short, our academies seek to be homespaces where Black students did not have to become someone other than themselves in order to succeed. We believe that because they are free to be themselves, and free from managing the pressure and expectation to be something and someone else, they are able to invest much, much more of their energies into doing and learning mathematics. Our hope is the creation of unapologetically Black spaces in mathematics that are like the neighborhood and community I (Joi) grew up in.

### REFLECTION QUESTIONS FOR CHAPTER 4

1. Intentionality is our anchor in this work. How is your school intentional in its inclusion of Black youth? In what ways does it consider Black culture, history, voices, and experiences?
2. Love and care are often not discussed in schools or in teacher education. Should they be? What could they add to our work?
3. Are there obstacles to youth pursuing math and science in your schools? How can you cast a wider net in building STEM identities?
4. Much of what we talk about in this chapter is about taking a chance on something new. Which chance should your school be taking?

## CHAPTER 5

# Tools for Building
# Black-Affirming Schools

In this chapter, we focus on practical methods that educators can use to investigate anti-Blackness and its effects in their school spaces. We offer three tools to help educators analyze their school's culture and its programs and see how it is reflecting, and affecting, its Black students. For schoolwide endeavors, the Supporting Black/African American Youth inventory provides schools with criteria that address climate, policies, beliefs and practices. The second tool, a teacher-focused journal activity, can help to spur reflection on how and where race and racism show up in classrooms. Finally, we provide questions for interviewing Black youth and families. With this technique, we hope to encourage schools to seek feedback from those who are most impacted by anti-Black policies and procedures.

These tools can be used in a variety of ways. Of course, they can be used as actual inventories for research and information collecting purposes. A gentle note: we are former teachers. We have designed all these tools to be organic, flexible methods to learn more about what we do as educators and to be replicable by practitioners in the field. Many scholars in education specialize in instrument creation and calibration to measure all manner of variables in schools and to quantify outcomes and patterns. While we were both trained in how to create such measures, this is not our goal with these inventories. As with everything in this book, we strive to be transparent and forthright. These tools are based on strong research-based evidence. But they are not designed to support statistical analysis.

Beyond using the tools for data collection, they can be put to work as jumping-off points for faculty development and as frameworks for supporting Black youth. By this, we mean that tucked within the surveys and interview questions is plenty to talk about, whether you give the survey or not. Overall, our goal with this chapter is to provide schools and teachers with methods of engaging in data collection and self-reflection as to whether and how they support Black youth. These data can then inform subsequent professional development opportunities (which we will turn to in Chapter 6).

## A SCHOOLWIDE INVENTORY

We begin with a straightforward survey tool to examine the supports available for African American students across a school. This inventory is designed to be used by school and district teams to get a sense of the climate in your building. You will find the full survey in the Appendix. There are many ways this tool can be utilized:

- We imagine that members of leadership teams could complete these individually, and then share and compare their findings with one another.
- A trusted colleague from a partner school could help, as a critical friend, to facilitate meetings where findings are shared, providing space for the team to do this work. This would allow administrators to engage as participants and not facilitators.
- The modified tool could be given to students to complete; we can see doing this with youth ages 12 and older.
- Families could also complete the survey, as a way of gathering feedback on how the school is connecting with the larger community.
- All teachers and staff could complete the inventory together in small groups during a faulty meeting, using the questions more as discussion prompts or food-for-thought points.
- The tool could also be used as an exit survey, taken by graduating students and their families.
- Finally, the inventory could be administered online and distributed anonymously to all members of the school community.

Of course, once it is complete, tallying and sharing the findings are the heart of the work. Taking the time to look for trends, patterns, clear gaps, places of progress, and areas of pride is the most important step in the process.

We designed these indicators to be reflective of the themes we have laid out in the previous chapters. The indicators were chosen to locate potential areas of growth around how schools and teachers see Black intelligence, position students regarding sports, and discipline Black children, among other areas. We are purposefully wide in our indicators because we do not want to fall into the trap of essentializing Black inclusion to be simply about representation. We do not want to simply count resources (such as the number of books by Black authors), nor count Black bodies in spaces (for example, "there are four Black girls in AP Chemistry"). While both of these inclusions are important, they are *part of* building schools that affirm Black students and are not sufficient *on their own*. We are treading quite carefully here. In previous chapters we have specified that representation in books and courses matters. It does, unquestionably. There is no contradiction. As we discussed in Chapter 1, our goal is creating just educational spaces for Black youth. The work is deep, extensive, and continuous. What we worry about is anything that seems remotely like a "silver bullet." There is no silver bullet in this work. There isn't a single remedy that will fix racism in schools. The damage, quite frankly, is too diffuse. This is also why the single-shot professional development training does not work (but we digress). When people are working on how to address inequities in schools, a first line of response is often representative in nature (see Gorski, 2009, 2017, for a discussion of levels and stages). Schools will add posters or books to the school environment to increase "diversity." This is good! But as we said previously, this is an *initial* step. The survey is designed to capture representation and then keep going, to get to other equity and justice concerns.

As the reader will notice, the survey is an outgrowth of each of the preceding chapters and their research bases. Readers will be able to follow the research footprints through the prompts. We do this because any tool to examine anti-Blackness must be solidly grounded in the research and what we know about how anti-Blackness shows up in schools. Thus, each of the indicators traces back to some form of anti-Blackness we are trying to rupture in our work. As we said, the full survey is in the Appendix; a small sampling of the indicators/survey prompts is shown here.

1. Our school understands that the Black experience is not monolithic: that there is great variety within the Black community as to language, religion, family structure, immigrant status, gender, and sexual orientation.
2. Our school/district has a position dedicated to supporting African American students and families. Our school/district employs therapists and counselors with expertise in supporting African American students.
3. Our school celebrates and/or commemorates the African American experience in the United States through holidays, activities, and/or events.
4. Members of our school/district community understand the difference between individual and systemic racism. Members of our school/district recognize that both are real.

## A TEACHER REFLECTION TOOL

In 2018, the Black philosopher George Yancy came to Kerri's university to speak (Yancy, 2018a). In 2015, he had written a piece in the *New York Times* asking White people to acknowledge racism and their role in it (Yancy, 2015). The racist backlash he received after its publication was intense. From death threats, to being called the N-word, "ape," and "hoodrat," Yancy was so inundated with vitriol from White people who refused to acknowledge racism that he went on to write an entire book about the experience: *Backlash: What Happens When We Talk Honestly About Racism in America* (Yancy, 2018b).

In his talk, Yancy mentioned that his students are also inclined not to notice race. To help them to see, he asks his students to complete a journal in which they are tasked with documenting racism in their daily lives. He was concerned that many students felt they were untouched by racism, and that Whiteness had no impact on them (Yancy, 2018a). Their results were alarming. There was a wide array of racism demonstrated in their dorms, families, and jobs. When you go looking, racism is indeed all around.

Picca and Feagin (2007) capture a similar reality in their book *Two-Faced Racism: Whites in the Backstage and Frontstage*. Here, students are also asked to journal about race in their lives, and the book is a compilation of those findings. Picca and Feagin find that there is a lot of "backstage racism" in effect: racist sentiments expressed between White people in private, personal interactions that belie the public "nonracist" face they often present. This allows White people to be racist in White settings, while appearing non-racist when with POC.

This teacher reflection activity is based on both of these works. It uses the model of journaling in everyday life to get at the realities of racism. In this way, our second activity is essentially a field research project, in which teachers keep a keen eye on how race and racism intersect with their lives.

*Goal:* This tool is designed to help teachers understand how race and racism function in classrooms, schools, and communities. Individual schools can decide how wide or narrow to make the lens. Teachers could keep notes that look at the totality of their lives (say a week long, noting everything race-related at home, school, church, the CVS, waiting at the movies, etc.) or just specific to school (so just 8 a.m. to 3 p.m. for 2 weeks in classrooms, recess spaces, hallways, etc.). Facilitators can help teachers pick an appropriate length of time, and a field (what they are looking at).

A gentle caution: All these options require trust. This is not a good task to do with people who are new to one another or are particularly prickly, or if there are hierarchies at play. This is generally better for smaller groups or more established teams. Gentle caution #2: This task is designed to increase awareness that racism exists. Some folks do not need this lesson. If you are working with a mostly Black faculty or other faculty of color, this is a problematic task. You are asking them to keep track of painful daily indignities or traumas. This can be helpful in some contexts, for example, as a way of Black and brown folks being able to put on paper what they already know. But if you are facilitating this activity, tread lightly and check in with participants. Instead, we suggest you offer this alternative version of this task, where Black faculty note examples of Black resistance and Black micro-affirmations (Huber, 2018) as a way to document Black self-care and community support.

Instead of charting racism, ask participants to journal where they see examples of Black resistance and refusal in the news, online, on social media, and between people as well as incidents of micro-affirmation. Micro-affirmations refer to "everyday forms of affirmation and validation that people of color engage in, the nods, smiles, embraces, use of language, and other actions that express acknowledgment, respect, and self-worth" (Solórzano & Huber, 2021, para. 3). Rowe (2008) describes micro-affirmations as "tiny acts of opening doors to opportunity, gestures of inclusion and caring, and graceful acts of listening" (p. 46). Have teachers chart these small and large ways in which Black people support each other.

*Task:* To return to the original task, we want teachers to see if, how, and when their lives intersect with racism. We ask participants to pay attention to when race is relevant, both in positive and negative ways. Teachers can keep track of things they see, hear, read, watch, and so on. They can include all the ways in which race and racism are present. Think about examples of bias, discrimination, being included or disincluded, subtle remarks, positive experiences, places where people are ignoring difference, making assumptions, and so forth. A template follows that can help give structure to notes (see Table 5.1). Additionally, if a map of your school building is available, it can be helpful to print one out. Map any incidents that happen on the school campus. To do this, teachers can physically mark on the map where they heard or witnessed the event. Ask teachers to be aware of their surroundings and what they personally hear and see (watch the news, listen to the radio, flip through social media and the web). All examples should be anonymous, unless they are public comments made by people in the public eye (meaning you heard it in the news, saw it on Instagram, said by the mayor). Do NOT use the real name of any peer, family member, teacher, friend, and so on.

*Explaining the data:* Once data have been collected, your group will want to figure out how to share their information. Please be careful how you set this up. Think through in advance how you are going to deal with racist statements or actions coming from coworkers. To analyze at a macro level, some discussion prompts include:

- How prevalent are issues of race/racism in daily life?
- What form do racist events and comments take? Overt/covert? Individual/institutional/systematic?
- Based on the maps, where did you see or hear events? Does the location surprise you? What do you make of this?
- What do people do and how do they react when they hear or witness racist events? Do they react at all? What would you do?
- Is racism a problem in the United States? How do you know? What patterns do you see? If you did not see much racism, what can you infer?

**Table 5.1. Journal Note-Taking Template**

| Date | Event (comment heard or observation made) | Between whom or where? | Thoughts or questions? |
|---|---|---|---|
| 1/3 | A woman told a Black teen wearing a hijab to come sit next to her, when another rider gave her dirty looks on the bus. | Two people on the bus | I am happy to see this woman was trying to protect this girl. I like this standing up for one another. |
| 1/3 | Anthony told Andre he was "nappy" in class today. | Two students in my class. | This is between two Black boys, so I am not sure what to do. Is this okay? |
| 1/4 | "They need to go back home." | Facebook, about Haitian people | This is more and more common. We live in a dangerous moment right now. |

## INTERVIEW PROMPTS FOR BLACK YOUTH AND FAMILIES

We need to hear directly from Black youth and families about how they experience school. Our final tool is designed to provide practitioners with interview and focus-group questions. Like with the previous tools, these can be used in a variety of ways. Facilitators can interview students who self-select to participate. Black students can interview their families. Administrative teams and working groups can conduct focus groups of Black families or Black students. New teacher mentoring circles could invite Black families in for an after-school professional development opportunity and interview them as a group.

Our interview framework is a hybrid of several resources. Based on earlier research, Kerri created teacher quality indicators for children of color (Ullucci, 2005). This is supplemented by research used in the chapters, as well as by research in Boston public schools about school success for Black and brown boys, conducted by the Annenberg Institute and Center for Collaborative Education (Tung et al., 2015a). Two Annenberg/Center for Collaborative Education publications provide helpful models for schools of how districts can look at their own populations and outcomes: *Opportunity and Equity: Enrollment and Outcomes of Black and Latino Males in Boston Public Schools* (Miranda et al., 2014) and *Promising Practices and Unfinished Business: Fostering Equity and Excellence for Black and Latino Males* (Tung et al., 2015a).

*Promising Practices and Unfinished Business* collated indicators based on what works for Black and Brown boys in schools, building on evidence-based practices (Tung et al., 2015a). These indicators helped to give shape to our interview questions. Tung et al. organized indicators around six main clusters:

1. Mission and vision
2. School leadership and organizational policies
3. Curriculum and instruction
4. School culture and climate
5. Family engagement
6. Community partnerships

Below, we give a brief snapshot of their indicators verbatim to show some of the variety at work here (see Table 5.2). We share these samples to let readers know that there are many, many efforts that do support Black boys in schools, and a robust research base. Additional indicators can be found in the long-form report and would be useful for teams who want to modify the interview protocol

**Table 5.2. Indicator Framework for Black and Latino Male Equity and Excellence (from Tung et al., 2015a)**

| Indicator | References |
|---|---|
| The school has a mission of high expectations for student learning outcomes for all students (using measurable and monitored objectives), with explicit attention to Black and Latino males. | COSEBOC, 2014; Fergus & Noguera, 2010; Fergus et al., 2014; J. M. Lee & Ransom, 2011; Nieto & Bode, 2012; Tatum, 2007; Tung et al., 2011 |
| Curriculum and instruction is culturally responsive to Black and Latino males; curriculum is multicultural and stresses diversity; critical multicultural education challenges structural racism and other -isms. | Banks, 1993, 1999; COSEBOC, 2014; Duncan-Andrade, 2008; Fergus & Noguera, 2010; Fergus et al., 2014; Gay & Hanley, 1999; Ladson-Billings, 1998; J. M. Lee & Ransom, 2011; Lewis et al., 2010; May, 1999; Milner, 2012; Nieto & Bode, 2012; Sleeter & Grant, 1987, 2006; Tatum, 2007; Valenzuela, 1999; Yosso, 2005 |
| Teachers and students have strong, caring, accountable, and reciprocal relationships with each other; relationships originate with revealing the self rather than with academic knowledge and skills; teachers initiate connection with youth. | Alva & Padilla, 1995; Bryk & Schneider, 2002; Castellanos & Gloria, 2007; Chenoweth, 2009; Coleman, 1990; Collins, 2011; Comer, 2001; De los Reyes et al., 2008; Halx & Ortiz, 2011; Harper & Williams, 2014; Noguera, 2003; Pang, 2005; Valenzuela, 1999 |
| Discipline policies and practices emphasize justice/fairness. | Lewis et al., 2010 |

**Table 5.3. Black Youth and Families Interview Questions**

| Questions for interviews/focus groups | Based on what we know works with Black youth |
|---|---|
| • How is your culture represented in school?<br>• If I was in your classroom, who would I see speaking?<br>• Does your teacher have high expectations of students? How can you tell?<br>• Describe a usual math lesson in class.<br>• What happens if you struggle with an assignment?<br>• What are your hopes post-graduation? How do your teachers help you reach these goals?<br>• Do you learn about Black history, literature, art? | Teachers expect high levels of academic achievement from their students and include elements of the students' culture in curriculum and pedagogy (Ladson-Billings, 2009; Gay, 2018). |
| • Do kids get in trouble often at school?<br>• Are discipline policies fair?<br>• What are your thoughts about the dress code?<br>• If students are struggling with mental health/behavior, are supports available to help? | Youth are treated like youth and disciplinary practices reflect age-appropriate, restitution-focused processes (Morris, 2016; Tung, 2015a). |
| • Is there space to talk about issues like sexism or racism in school?<br>• Have you experienced racism at school?<br>• If something racist happened at school, would there be space to talk about it?<br>• Is there someone that you would feel comfortable speaking with if something racist happened at school? | Teachers are race-conscious. They understand inequalities exist and can be replicated by schools. They do not enforce colorblindness (Brown & Brown, 2015; Ladson-Billings, 2009; Ullucci & Battey, 2011). |
| • Good schools often feel like families. Does your school feel like this?<br>• How would you describe your relationships with teachers?<br>• Do you have opportunities to work with classmates, support one another, and help each other do better?<br>• Are the staff and faculty diverse? | Relationships and community are central to life in school. Students feel part of a larger family and look out for one another (Emdin, 2017; Tung et al., 2015b). |
| • Are Black families' concerns taken seriously?<br>• Do families have opportunities to participate in your child's education?<br>• Is there support for bilingual youth or other home languages?<br>• Are there many ways for families to be involved in school? | Parents are welcome and included. The school respects home cultures and languages and attempts to connect youths' home life with their school life. Communication is ample (Nieto & Bode, 2017; Tung et al., 2015a). |
| • Would you recommend this school to a Black friend?<br>• Is there something we have not asked about that you would like to share? | |

to fit their schools' needs (see Tung et al., 2015a). Following the selection from Tung et al., we share a selection of our interview prompts in Table 5.3.

As with the schoolwide survey, we connect the research to the interview questions to show the scholarly work that does exist in this field. We take this route because we feel it will yield richer results; the questions are linked with what matters in the education of Black youth (see Table 5.3). It is so rare that researchers seek feedback on schools from youth, never mind Black youth. We want to help ensure that the time engaged in this work is well spent.

## IN CONCLUSION

A gentle note (#435!): This is not easy work. There are tons of places where facilitators can experience backlash, hostility, reticence, the feigning of ignorance, and stalling. This is particularly the case when uncovering racism. We do not say this to be negative, but simply because we have been doing this a long time. For example, with the above journaling activity, we can imagine participants saying they did not see any racism. In their weeklong effort, there simply was none. This is where it is often helpful to have the rest of the group "right the ship." We will turn to other participants and have them weigh in with what they are seeing. This can help reluctant participants "see" in new ways, especially when other participants have long lists of examples. The facilitator can also come in with their own journal, chronicling what they saw over the week as a model. It is best to focus on public, well-known events that anyone paying attention would have heard or seen. It also can be helpful to have some go-to sites where you can direct people to see racism on the day-to-day (for example, see Driving While White at: https://www .facebook.com/DrivingWhileWhite/) as well as historically (a resource from the Smithsonian, *158 Resources to Understand Racism in America* [https:// www.smithsonianmag.com/history/158-resources-understanding-systemic -racism-america-180975029/; Solly, 2020], is a useful gathering of examples from the institution's collections; the photographs of the grieving Till family will take you apart). These can be a good counterbalance against folks who claim they saw nothing.

We caution facilitators not to lose faith. People can change. Really. Those of us who are teachers know this (or we would not be in this work). Reaching back to Baldwin again, he tells us, "I can't be a pessimist because I'm alive. To be a pessimist means that you have agreed that human life is an academic matter. . . . It is the work of human beings to make the world more human" (Baldwin, in Abdelfatah & Arablouei, 2020, audio recording). In the 20+ years we have been doing this work, we have been well served by humility and hope. Glaude, in an interview about James Baldwin, ends the conversation quoting Baldwin: "Hope is invented every day" (Abdelfatah & Arablouei, 2020). Indeed.

## CHAPTER 6

# New Paths in Professional Development

At this point, a look back for a moment seems warranted. As we near the end of the book, we have walked through understanding the complexities of race and racism and charted how anti-Blackness shows up in schools. Using research techniques, readers looked at how their own schools and classrooms support Black youth. In this chapter, we turn to resources that extend learning about how to make schools more affirming for Black youth. We have placed this chapter between tools and inventories (Chapter 5) and resources (Chapter 7) as a bridge; we regard these three chapters as mutually reinforcing. The findings that come out of research projects help to determine professional development opportunities; resources might spur curiosity about some aspect of your school, which can lead to a research project. So you will notice some overlap among these chapters.

In Chapter 6 you will find concrete readings, activities, and discussion topics for professional development that schools can use to become more race-conscious. For example, one module deconstructs "immigration lessons" for Black children. We look at a typical lesson plan, one that asks students to talk about their immigration and family history stories. The module helps teachers to see the complexity of immigration stories for Black youth, many of whom do not know critical pieces of their past. We help teachers to clarify their academic and social justice goals, understand the realities of Black youths' lived experiences, and imagine other methods of telling origin stories that are inclusive and whole.

We have built a selection of professional development modules that schools can use to engage practitioners across a wide variety of purposes: for in-service days, as part of department or faculty meetings, for teacher book groups, in new teacher mentoring programs, and with working groups that are exploring critical needs at your school. The modules vary in length and are modifiable to fit your school's needs. While each module can be utilized as a stand-alone experience, we hope readers will also look across the offerings and select individual components that best support their professional development goals. Of course, there are other scenarios and outcomes that we did not capture; the possibilities are endless. Our goal is to provide an assortment of goals, audiences, and activities that can set you on a productive path.

## MODULE ONE: WHITE MIDDLE SCHOOL TEACHERS

*Audience:* A self-selected group of middle school teachers, across content areas, who have joined a teacher book club.
*Goal:* To support White teachers in a majority-White school who are interested in learning more about racism and Whiteness.
*Plan of Action:*

1. Have teachers engage in the online survey created by the *New York Times* in 2020, "How much racism do you face every day?" (https://www.nytimes.com/interactive/2020/us/racism-african-americans-quiz.html). This interactive survey allows participants to self-assess how much their identity "shows up" in their everyday activities. It then allows them to compare their experience against the experiences of Black youth. This is often an eye-opening step in rendering the invisible visible.

2. Have your teachers discuss how they experience race/racism and how that compares with African American youth. This can be done through an email or chat string, on an online meeting platform like Zoom, or in person, based on the norms of the group.

3. *Teaching While White* (https://www.teachingwhilewhite.org) has a super blog that is filled with timely, relevant entries to understand better how Whiteness functions in schools. Read four posts of the group's choice.

4. In a follow-up posting or Zoom meeting, discuss the following questions:
   a. Which blog post stood out the most to you and why?
   b. Are you surprised by how often Black students face racism? Why or why not?
   c. How has your race shaped how you experience your life?
   d. Is our goal as teachers to be race-conscious or colorblind?

## MODULE TWO: CURRICULUM PLANNING TEAMS

*Audience:* Curriculum planning teams in high school.
*Goal:* To analyze and improve your school's diversity in literacy offerings. You will inventory students' access to literature by Black/African American authors.

***Plan of Action:***

1. Baseline data collection. Ask each teacher of English in your building which core books they teach. Ask librarians about the diversity of their collections regarding Black and African authors. Do a general analysis as to the degree of diversity represented in the books available to youth. Do the books provide both mirrors (opportunities for students to see themselves) and windows (opportunities to see others' experiences) when you look across the collection? (Sims Bishop, 1990).
2. Identify gaps: Whose perspective is missing from your collections? Think about the diversity of Black youth widely here (immigrant children and U.S.-born; English speakers and speakers of additional languages; Muslim youth; youth in foster care; youth in various family configurations, etc.).
3. Refer to We Need Diverse Books as a jumping-off point for remedying gaps (https://diversebooks.org). Also, see Coretta Scott King Book Award winners for additional resources to create updated book lists. The American Library Association's Coretta Scott King award is given to exceptional books by African American authors. A list of all winners since 1970 is available on the ALA website (https://www.ala.org/rt/emiert/cskbookawards/coretta-scott-king-book-awards-all-recipients-1970-present), as are discussion guides with age-appropriate questions (https://www.ala.org/rt/emiert/coretta-scott-king-book-awards-educational-resources).

## MODULE THREE: NEW TEACHERS

***Audience:*** New teachers to your district or building.
***Goal:*** To see how content that is frequently seen as "difficult" or "sensitive" can be incorporated into teaching. In doing so, we make space for students whose experiences and histories are often left out or marginalized.
***Plan of Action:***

1. Via Flipgrid,[1] have each teacher upload a 1-minute video discussing a content area, topic, or subject that they find difficult to talk about with students. Ask them to focus on social issues, history, or ideas that are challenging to raise.
2. Read Learning for Justice's guide, *Let's Talk: Facilitating Critical Conversations with Students* (https://www.learningforjustice.org/magazine/publications/lets-talk).

3. Review *Teaching Hard History: American Slavery* (https://www
.learningforjustice.org/frameworks/teaching-hard-history/american
-slavery). These are Teaching for Justice's collections on slavery,
niched to students throughout the K–12 grade span. There is a huge
array of materials here: professional development videos, articles,
podcasts, webinars, and classroom activities. This site is a rich
resource of ways to engage complex topics. Have each teacher read
or view 4–6 sources.

4. Returning to Flipgrid, have teachers do 2–3-minute videos, returning
to the topic they originally struggled with and offering suggestions
as to how they might teach the topic differently in the future. Use
both the *Let's Talk* guide and the *Teaching Hard History* resources as
models and inspiration.

5. Ask teachers to review one another's second Flipgrid videos as a form
of collaborative learning.

## MODULE FOUR: MATHEMATICS EDUCATORS

*Audience:* Mathematics teachers, K–12, differentiated below.
*Goal:* To investigate the context of mathematics education for Black students
in order to improve their math outcomes.
*Plan of Action:* (Note: This is designed to be a long-term project and has
many steps.)

1. Host a small-group discussion between teachers to orient them to the
relationship between race and math. Some potential questions:
   a. What is the role of racism in the teaching and learning of mathematics?
   b. How does racism affect the teaching and learning of mathematics?
   c. What is the role of culture in mathematics classrooms and/or at
your school?
   d. Does bias impact how Black students experience mathematics?
How might you find out?
   e. Do we expect excellence in mathematics from our Black students?
How might you find out?

2. Plan a longer reading on math for Black youth. For middle and high
school teachers, read "The Racialization of Mathematics Education"
(Spencer & Hand, 2015; available online through STEM Teacher
Leadership Network at https://stemtlnet.org/resources/racialization
-mathematics-education) in grade-level teams. For elementary school
teachers, read *The Brilliance of Black Children* (Leonard & Martin,
2013) in grade-level teams. We particularly suggest Chapters 2, 3,
5, and 14 to get a firmer foundation on Black children's experiences

in learning mathematics. Discuss the major themes of the readings, asking these questions:

  a. It is often argued that mathematics is colorblind. In what ways do race and racism show up in the readings?

  b. It is often argued that mathematics is culture-free. In what ways does culture show up in the readings?

  c. In what ways have policies undermined the success of Black students in mathematics?

  d. In *The Brilliance of Black Children*, what examples do you encounter where Black children have a positive mathematics identity? How is this identity promoted and achieved?

3. Along with your leadership team, think about and document the following:

  a. How (the criteria) and when (in which grade) are decisions made about student placements in mathematics courses? For example, how do you determine which students will and will not take more advanced mathematics courses?

  b. Who makes the final decisions regarding which mathematics courses students are placed in? What alternative ways (beyond test scores) are used and can be used to determine what students know in mathematics?

  c. What additional and/or non–school-based experiences do students in your school have with mathematics (games, sports, elective courses)?

  d. What opportunities do students have to be creative and have fun with mathematics?

  e. What opportunities do students have to interact with people of color in STEM fields?

  f. How do you actively interrupt the long-held stereotype that Black students are not good at mathematics?

## MODULE FIVE: WHOLE HIGH SCHOOL FACULTY

*Audience:* This could be a collaborative activity across your faculty.

*Goals:* To read positive stories about boys of color in schools and gain insights from these counternarratives. To break stereotypes about Black boys, often seen as academically low-performing and not particularly motivated by school.

*Plan of Action:*

1. Have your team read "Radical Care to Let Black Boys Thrive" (Howard & Howard, 2021) and *The Counter Narrative: Reframing Success for High Achieving Black and Latino Males in Los Angeles County* (Howard et al., 2016).

**Table 6.1. Black Boys' Support Tally**

| Building Blocks | Does our school provide this? |
| --- | --- |
| Diverse faculty and staff | Not yet |
| Extended school hours/safe haven/ activities to keep youth safe and busy | Currently 'til 3:30. Can we push this out? |
| Rigorous, relevant, responsive teaching | Teacher-dependent; not comprehensive at this point |

2. Looking across these texts, what are some of the building blocks that support Black males' success in schools? Come up with lists in small groups.
3. Using the small-group feedback, create a whole-group cumulative list of the building blocks identified in the small groups. This will provide the group with their cross-group main list.
4. Next, compare the main list with what your school provides (see Table 6.1 as an example). Keep track of where your school is doing well and where there are gaps. Come up with a concrete, productive plan for prioritizing and then tackling these goals.

## MODULE SIX: SOCIAL STUDIES TEACHERS, K-8

*Audience:* Elementary and middle school teachers.
*Goal:* To conduct a microanalysis of a commonly used lesson about immigration and see where it might pose difficulties for Black children.
*Plan of Action:*

1. Share the lesson plan below with your teachers (see Figure 6.1). This is from the Utah Education Network and was chosen simply because we were looking for a family history lesson. We have modified and condensed it here; the original lesson can be found online (https://www.uen.org/lessonplan/view/1092). Gentle note: We love lessons that capitalize on students' backgrounds, family histories, immigration stories, and home knowledge. These are all important dimensions of knowing your students. We wish we saw more of these. We highlight difficulties with this lesson to point out complexities to keep in mind when doing this work.
2. Have teachers discuss potential obstacles to children doing these activities. Begin with a discussion of what the academic/learning goals of this assignment are. What do we want students to learn? What new skills and understandings will students gain? These will be the anchors for making decisions about this lesson.

## Figure 6.1. Family Heritage Lesson Plan Example

Intended Learning Outcomes:

The students will learn how to keep a journal, write an autobiography, and develop their own family tree.

You will be required to write in journals for 2 weeks. You will also be writing autobiographies, reading journal entries of some of the pioneers, and designing a family or personal shield. In addition, we will be researching our roots and filling out a family tree chart.

After the journal entries are completed, give the following handouts to the students and have them take the handouts home to be worked on with parents.

- A family tree chart with spaces for at least 4 generations.
- The following outline to follow to complete a mini-autobiography.
  » Autobiography Instructions: Your autobiography should include the following.
    - A family tree (4 generations)
    - A personal or family crest (coat of arms)
    - 1 page about early years (birth–4 years)
    - School years
    - Family memories, traditions, trips, funny stories, grandparents
    - Personal goals, friends, hobbies, talents, pictures, etc.
    - Any other information you wish to include.

Have them take these things home to be worked on with parents or grandparents.

---

Some considerations: Lessons on family trees, family history, and immigration stories are all really common in elementary and middle schools. However, different children have different hurdles to clear with these assignments. Family trees can be difficult with blended families, divorced families, families with a parent who has died, children in foster care or adopted children, children with same-sex parents (if trees are labeled mom and dad), or any family structure that doesn't fit into the typical tree template (for example, raised by Mom only). There are ways for students to acknowledge and chronicle those who have come before them without potentially injuring or shaming a child. A twist of the family tree is the family roots assignment. Draw a central tree and label it with the child's name. Then draw roots from the tree into the earth; how many is up to the child. The roots are all the people in their ancestry. The roots are just drawn in and labeled—there isn't a set template or boxes—so the child can capture who is most important to them more organically.

Family histories and immigration stories can be particularly tough for African American families who have been in the

United States for a long time, but do not always have sufficient documentation of their ancestors. Asking a child "Where are you from?" is not always straightforward for children whose ancestors were enslaved. Of course, not all Black families will have this issue. For some folks, their immigration stories are quite new and well known to them and their families. However, we have worked (for example) with Black children who have family ties to plantations in Texas, and they did not want that plantation to be their origin story. Again, we are not suggesting you throw away lessons on family history. Teaching children they are part of a long continuum of history is an important lesson, but thinking through nuances and obstacles is warranted.

3. Generate alternative assignments that could get at similar learning outcomes as the original intent. In the family history theme, perhaps allow the child to focus on the story of a particularly impactful ancestor and do a biography of them. Or try a "Where I am from" poem (search "Where I'm from" and George Ella Lyon for examples) as a way of capturing family history. The Association for the Study of African American Life and History offers a program on Black family storytelling and culturally relevant methods of exploring Black history, complete with videos and a guidebook. Look up the Family History Toolkit (https://asalh.org/family-history-toolkit/) at the asalh .org website.

We encourage readers to consider a twist on the coat-of-arms activity that would be less European in its orientation. Adinkra symbols are visual images from Ghana. They represent different important concepts and collective wisdom of West Africa. For those readers with sharp eyes, these symbols were used frequently in the movie *Black Panther*. Google "Adinkra Ghana stamps" to see an explanation of these symbols and the symbols themselves. The central idea in a coat-of-arms assignment is to visually represent a family through images. This can easily be done using Adinkra symbols as the visual pool that students can select from as they design their crests (see adinkra.org). There are so many positive upsides to making this small flip to a traditional lesson. It shows students an intellectual history of Africa. It reminds them older African civilizations existed. It lets students in on another language; many Black-led businesses and organizations include these symbols or their titles in their work (the Sankofa—a bird with its head turned backwards—for example). It shows how cultures represent themselves without words, an important social studies analysis skill. The symbols are lovely in and of themselves and worth studying as forms of art. Many readers will be familiar with the symbol *Sankofa*, which represents "return and get it." This is an admonition to learn from the past. There are many Adinkra symbols related to education and learning, which reinforces a pan-African, well-established commitment to knowledge.

4. By being clear about the academic goals of this activity from the outset, teachers can omit any options that would be meaningless or shift from the learning goal. As you can see, however, there are very easy ways to keep fidelity to the academic anchors (helping students see their family's ancestry) while being culturally respectful and inclusive. These components are not mutually exclusive.

## MODULE SEVEN: SECONDARY ENGLISH/ SOCIAL STUDIES TEACHERS

*Audience:* This would best fit a group of history/English high school teachers who have been doing DEI work and want to expand their repertoire.
*Goal:* To explore Bettina Love's Hip Hop Civics as a way to incorporate resistance as a unit focus. We have seen social studies units on resistance as a theme, often for World War II. This could be done as a comparative unit.
*Plan of Action:*

1. Listen to this initial podcast with Dr. Bettina Love (professor at the University of Georgia) and what can be learned via hip-hop. You can find it at https://www.hiphopadvocacy.org.
2. Review Love's "GetFree" hip-hop civics curriculum at http:// getfreehiphopcivics.com. There are tons of resources that would be appealing to high school youth. A particular area to look into is resilience and acts of self-preservation. This could be an interesting project to watch, read, and listen to Black resistance in action. This could easily be utilized in social studies units comparing modes of resistance over time, or looking at patterns in the ways Black people have shown resilience in the face of racism.

## MODULE EIGHT: ANY GRADE, TEACHING FACULTY

*Audience:* This professional development option can serve a wide variety of teachers K–12 who have an interest in including Africa in their curriculum.
*Goal:* To expand access to curriculum that includes Africa and African people groups in rich and meaningful ways.
*Plan of Action:*

1. University research centers can be good places to find materials, resources, and ongoing professional development. One such spot

is the K–16 Education Outreach Program, in the African Studies Center at Boston University. Let's start with an article written by their Outreach Manager, Dr. Elsa Wiehe, about why we should be teaching about Africa, titled *Teaching African History and Cultures Across the Curriculum* (2020) This article points to diverse ways in which African history and culture can be incorporated across the curriculum.

2. You can move on to the Outreach Program's Teacher Resources, which are broken down by grade level and content areas at https://www.bu.edu/africa/outreach/. Teachers could jigsaw different resources to look at and listen to and report back on. For example, in a team of three:

   a. Teacher One could listen to a What Teachers Need to Know About Africa podcast (maybe choose the music as resistance option, "Soundscapes of Protest: Music in Social Movements Across Africa"). This series of podcasts was made in conjunction with Primary Source to provide nuanced resources on teaching about Africa. See their offerings at https://primarysource.org/for-teachers/podcasts.

   b. Teacher Two could explore the How Big Is Africa lesson. Using maps and geography, teachers (and students!) can uncover some false assumptions that are made about Africa and its size, importance and diversity (https://www.bu.edu/africa/outreach/teachingresources/geography/curriculum-guide/).

   c. Howard University's website on the Gold Road, looking at medieval African societies, is fascinating. Teachers can investigate this overlooked history: https://cfas.howard.edu/outreach/gold-road.

## MODULE NINE: WHOLE MIDDLE SCHOOL FACULTY

*Audience:* The whole faculty or social studies teachers, depending on whether you imagine this as a field trip or a classroom project.

*Goals:* (1) to look for evidence of Black history in your own backyards by visiting local sites of interest; (2) to bring awareness that Black history is everywhere, but often hidden or overlooked.

*Plan of Action:* This professional development activity requires a bit of backstory. Last year, I (Kerri) read an intriguing article in *The Atlantic* called "A Forgotten Black Founding Father" (Allen, 2021). It is the story of Prince Hall, a Black contemporary of John Adams, who lived in Massachusetts, not far from where Kerri now lives. Prince founded the first Black Masonic lodge, around 1775. Allen explains that membership in the Freemasons was a kind of proof-of-status for free Black men; she tells a story of free Black man being kidnapped into slavery, and when he was sold in the Caribbean to a man who was also a Mason, their shared membership nullified the sale (Allen, 2021). Prince Hall's Masonic lodge exists to this day; the original chapter is the oldest continuously active African American association in the United States. Like with this activity, the article stresses that Black history is all around, hidden in plain sight. We just need to uncover it.

So it was with a bit of shock and embarrassment, and a lot of head-nodding, yes-indeed-hidden-in-plain-sight realization, that I drove by Prince Hall Masonic temple *the next day*. You see, I had been driving by Prince Hall Masonic temple every day for years. Upon doing some research, I learned that Prince Hall Freemasons have been in the area contributing to the community since 1797. I am shaking my head myself, for what it's worth.

Black history is everywhere. We can help students locate and explore these local treasures. We will use Rhode Island as a model. A quick look online can yield all kinds of field trip sites (in person or otherwise). For example:

- The Providence tourism office offers a digital Black history tour of Rhode Island. See https://www.goprovidence.com/things-to-do /providence-walking-tours/early-black-history-historic-walking-tour/.
- Historic, educational and preservation sites, like preserveri.org and the Center for Reconciliation Rhode Island (cfrri.org) also have Black history maps and tours.

Rhode Island is fabulous and we invite you to visit the Black history sites in Kerri's fine state. However, we (sadly) imagine you are not heading out here, so please use the above as a way of finding resources in your region. Google your state + :

- local tourism offices
- preservation and historical societies
- Historically Black Colleges and Universities (HBCUs)
- Black churches
- Black cultural groups
- "black history tour"
- "black history site"
- "civil rights map"

These can help you locate sites to plot out your tour. If you cannot actually take a field trip, you can still "bring" students to different sites virtually. Even better, you could have students look up sites themselves and make their own maps (using a platform like MapMaker from National Geographic [https://mapmaker.nationalgeographic.org/]) that allows them to pin and annotate maps.

## MODULE TEN: ADMINISTRATIVE OR MENTAL HEALTH TEAMS

*Audience:* Administrators and mental health workers in 6–12 schools. Anyone involved in discipline and classroom management of youth could benefit.

*Goal:* To explore the idea of adultification of Black girls and how it plays out in school settings, and to look at how communities and schools are working to connect Black girls to school more holistically.

*Plan of action:*

1. Introduce the idea of adultification using this brief animated clip from Georgetown Law Center on Poverty and Inequality called *End Adultification Bias:* https://www.youtube.com/watch?v =L3Xc08anZAE.

2. Depending on the length of the PD, you could read Monique Morris's book *Pushout* (2016) or watch her TED talk: https://www .ted.com/talks/monique_w_morris_why_black_girls_are_targeted_for _punishment_at_school_and_how_to_change_that.

3. Review how other communities and schools have helped address in-equality for Black girls by reading *Increasing School Connectedness for Girls: Restorative Justice as a Health Equity Resource* (González, T., & Epstein, 2020) or *The Innocence Initiative: Translating National Research Into Local Action in Central Texas* (Georgetown Center on Poverty and Inequality, 2020). Both can be downloaded at https://genderjusticeandopportunity.georgetown.edu.

4. Review your school's student handbook for discipline policies that might have disparate impacts on Black girls. Consider revising or removing policies that overpolice them. Even better yet would be to do all of the above, *with* Black girls from your school.


### FINAL THOUGHTS

This chapter proposes 10 modules that allow educators and their schools to build new knowledge and grow their capacity to support Black youth and challenge anti-Black racism. Intentionality matters here. As with all professional development, work can be done to "look busy," or it can be done to undo harm. Since you are reading this book and have made it this far, we imagine that you are on Team Undo Harm. Help your colleagues to see this. Approach the activities with the intention to do better by Black youth. Encourage one another to stop at regular intervals, track your progress, and continue forward despite obstacles. If a school commits to even a fraction of the above activities—working with intention—it will make itself immeasurably more just for its Black students.

Do not allow yourselves to be blown off-course with critiques that this work is beyond what schools should do, beyond the curriculum, or beyond our expertise. Because schools are sites of the social reproduction of racism, there is no better place to do the work. The curriculum is wide. We can reach academic standards (say, chronological thinking/ how to interpret a timeline, a social studies standard) with content that reflects our youth. For example, teach this standard through the ancient civilizations of Mali. Chronologies happened in Africa too! If we need to teach about poetry structure (a Common Core English standard), use poets of the Harlem Renaissance. Teaching the relationships between people and their environment (a Next Generation Science standard)? Compare and contrast how Gullah Geechee farmers of the South Carolina seacoast raise crops and how West African planters grow rice. What are the similarities? How are resources used and protected?

See? It's possible. Just need to expand our vision.

What to do with the critique of "beyond our expertise"? That is a legitimate place to pause. But again, this is just wind; stay the course. There are so many fine resources at your disposal. Chapter 7 is filled with them. We have enough stories, documentaries, podcasts, articles, and research reports to do professional development on these issues every day for the next 20 school years. We just need to choose to do it.

## CHAPTER 7

# Resources

The previous chapters have navigated through the realities of anti-Blackness, the possibilities of Black-affirming spaces, and the ways in which we can learn and grow as educators and people. In this final section, we provide educators with additional resources to continue working against anti-Blackness in schools. The resources include online, print, webinar, and podcast options. We have organized them in sets that allow readers to select areas that are tailored to their needs. We begin with book recommendations. These are selected for particular entry points (be that age, profession, interest) and level (how much familiarity you have with the topics). The resources are also briefly annotated.

We then move into what we are calling "learning circle" materials. Here, we take our inspiration again from Gholdy Muhammad (Muhammad, 2020). When we looked at Black literary societies in Chapter 1, it was to highlight the long lineage of Black scholarship and learning. In this chapter, we take our inspiration from the literary society's goal of communal learning in the service of Black uplift. Muhammad stresses that these literary societies were interdisciplinary, ideological, focused on skill and identity building, and a way to organize (Freitag & Knight-Justice, 2020). At their heart, the members had "abolitionist, strategic, and humanizing plans to improve the social conditions of black people and all people" (Freitag & Knight-Justice, 2020, question 2). We imagined groups of people coming together to better the school experiences of Black youth, and matched these imagined teams to resources. The materials for these circles both expand and contract our lens: we expand the type of resources (online, podcast, video, etc.) and narrow the entry points (sorting resources by teaching or school role, age level and discipline), as this is generally how school people sort themselves.

A gentle note on the lists: These could be endlessly reorganized, sorted, and reconstituted. There is so much scholarship to select from, and we sifted through an abundance of riches when we made choices for these lists. We will be plain that these are not necessarily the best or only sources, but ones we know of and respect, as well as resources that represent diversity across authors. We tried to balance older works with younger authors; to balance fiction and nonfiction in the book offerings; to include multiple ethnicities, genders, and people groups among the writers; and to highlight academic texts as well as more popular reads. Any omission does not convey a slight or disrespect, but simply the limits of two authors overwhelmed by the good work around us.

## RECOMMENDED BOOKS

**The Basics**

Books will be our anchor for these next few resource lists. We have organized the lists by whom we think would most benefit from the titles. For readers who feel familiar with these topics, you may wish to skip to the intermediate or advanced levels to find the right fit.

| Calling all readers! This is the entry point set. To us, these are the basics, and no matter what you do or teach, these books can benefit you. Share with your mom, auntie, best friend, or partner. | |
| --- | --- |
| *Caste: The Origins of Our Discontents* by Isabel Wilkerson | A masterpiece of writing about how caste (be it race, class, religion, etc.) divides people in the United States and abroad. A Pulitzer Prize winner. |
| *Lies My Teacher Told Me* by James Loewen | An insightful look at how history teaching misses important (Black) stories. |
| *Why We Can't Wait* by Martin Luther King, Jr. | MLK's work on the pivotal year 1963; we suggest you read "Letter from Birmingham Jail" in particular. |
| *Invisible Man* by Ralph Ellison | A classic, must-read about being a Black man in the United States in 1952. |
| *Beloved* by Toni Morrison | A Pulitzer Prize–winning masterwork, a study in storytelling, about the consequences of slavery. This is a book that will change you. |
| *So You Want to Talk About Race* by Ijeoma Oluo | A good beginning spot for thinking through how race functions in the United States; the structure of the book makes it an easy read. |
| *The Color Purple* by Alice Walker | Our third classic Black literature selection; captures early-20th-century life in a Southern Black community through the eyes of Celie, an unforgettable character. A Pulitzer winner. |

Are you looking for books for teens in your life or for a high school student who is interested in these topics? These are selected for curious adolescents who are starting to expand their understandings of race and racism.

| | |
|---|---|
| *The March Series* by John Lewis et al. | A fabulous graphic novel set, a good entry point if you have a hesitant reader. |
| *It's Trevor Noah: Born a Crime: Stories from a South African Childhood* (Adapted for Young Readers) by Trevor Noah | Super autobiography about growing up in South Africa under apartheid. |
| *100 Amazing Facts About the Negro* by Henry Louis Gates Jr. | A primer on Black history, this is an easy-to-read journey through important people and events. |
| *We Should All Be Feminists* by Chimamanda Ngozi Adichie | For all young people in your life, a short, elegant argument for intersectional feminism. |
| *Malcolm X Talks to Young People: Speeches in the United States, Britain, and Africa* by Malcolm X and Steven Clark | A collection of talks to young people around the world. An entryway for teens on Malcolm. |
| *The Hate U Give* by Angie Thomas | A searing story of police brutality by a gifted writer. |
| *Call Us What We Carry: Poems* by Amanda Gorman | A poetry collection from the Youth Poet Laureate (and the young poet who spoke at the Biden/Harris inauguration!) |
| *Long Way Down* by Jason Reynolds | Jason Reynolds is a stunning writer of contemporary fiction. His works are well-loved by students. |
| *Becoming* by Michelle Obama | Because everyone needs more time with Michelle. |
| *All Boys Aren't Blue* by George Johnson | A look into queer, Black boy life. Buy it for the cover, keep it for the story. |
| *Children of Blood and Bone* by Tomi Adeyemi | West African magical fantasy in a genre that is overwhelmingly White |
| *Stamped: Racism, Antiracism, and You* by Jason Reynolds and Ibram Kendi | Youth adaptation of the wildly popular *Stamped from the Beginning*. (Note: there are three different editions of *Stamped*, each written for a different audience: adults, teens, and kids. Just a kind caution if you are looking to find the correct version.) |

| Are you trying to raise race-conscious children ages 11–16? Do you teach grades 5–11? | |
|---|---|
| *The Beautiful Struggle* Adapted for Young Readers by Ta-Nehisi Coates | An adapted youth version of Coates's memoir about father/son relationships. |
| *Brown Girl Dreaming* by Jacqueline Woodson | National Book Award–winning memoir by Woodson about growing up in the 1960s and 1970s. |
| *Stamped: Racism, Antiracism, and You* by Jason Reynolds and Ibram X. Kendi | Kendi's important book on charting the history of racist ideas, adapted for youth. |
| *Uncomfortable Conversations With a Black Boy* by Emmanuel Acho | Another adapted book (we are so glad these conversations about injustice are being modified for younger readers) by a former NFL player. |
| *The Watsons Go to Birmingham* by Christopher Paul Curtis | Insightful story of a family road trip during the Civil Rights movement. |
| *The Track Series* by Jason Reynolds | A series about a track team by the wildly talented Jason Reynolds. |
| *The Skin I'm In* by Sharon Flake | Relatable story about a Black girl's struggle to find her place. |
| *Chains* by Laurie Halse Anderson | A story of slavery in the North, bringing insights into an overlooked history. |
| *A Long Walk to Water* by Linda Sue Park | True story of two Sudanese children whose lives overlap in unexpected ways. |
| *Roll of Thunder, Hear My Cry* by Mildred Taylor | The Newberry Award–winning classic story of a Black family surviving the Depression in Mississippi. |

| Do you have little ones, ages 5–11, whom you would like to read Black-affirming titles? Do you teach grades K–5? | |
|---|---|
| *Black Boy Joy* edited by Kwame Mbalia | A celebration of Black boyhood by many different authors. Delightful. |
| *Life Doesn't Frighten Me* by Maya Angelou, with art by Jean-Michel Basquiat | A unique collaboration between two fine artists. Perfect to use in class. |
| *Happy to Be Nappy* by bell hooks | Sweet affirmations about Black hair with lovely illustrations. |

(*continued*)

| | |
|---|---|
| *Stamped (For Kids): Racism, Antiracism, and You* by Jason Reynolds & Ibram X. Kendi | This is the version for the youngest readers of *Stamped*. |
| *Martin's Big Words: The Life of Dr. Martin Luther King, Jr.* by Doreen Rappaport and Bryan Collier | A beautifully illustrated book about MLK for younger readers |
| *Born on the Water* by Nikole Hannah-Jones & Renée Watson | A companion piece to the 1619 Project for young readers; a story of resistance. |
| *We Are the Ship* by Kadir Nelson | An absolutely beautiful book about the Negro leagues. Kadir Nelson is an exceptional artist. We recommend any of his works. |

| Are you a new teacher or student teacher? Are you going to school to be a teacher? These titles are good foundational books for new teachers. | |
|---|---|
| *Dreamkeepers* by Gloria Ladson-Billings | One of the books that started Kerri on this path. Gloria Ladson-Billings is the queen for a reason; her warm prose and insightful observations keep us coming back. |
| *Black Male(d): Peril and Promise in the Education of African American Males* by Tyrone Howard | A multifaceted look at the way Black boys are framed at school. |
| *Why Are All the Black Kids Sitting Together in the Cafeteria?* by Beverly Tatum | Another classic. A look into the psychology of racism and racial identity. |
| *Teaching for Black Lives* by Dyan Watson, Jesse Hagopian, & Wayne Au | Rethinking Schools puts out useful, teacher-centered books. This one addresses how to support Black kids in school. |
| *An Introduction to Multicultural Education* by James Banks | The classic introduction to multicultural education from a giant in our field. |
| The *Shame of the Nation* by Jonathan Kozol | Moving look at inequality in U.S. schools. |
| *Other People's Children* by Lisa Delpit | An influential book about how culture plays out in the classroom. |
| *Why Race and Culture Matter in School: Closing the Achievement Gap in America's Classrooms* by Tyrone Howard | Howard is a heavyweight in this field; any of his books is worth a read. Here we get a primer on how race and culture play out in classrooms. |
| *Cultivating Genius* by Gholdy Muhammad | Lovely, uplifting, teacher-centric book on equity and literacy. |

| Do you want an introduction to Black history and literature written by African authors? These are not specifically focused on education, but are selected to highlight authors from Africa. | |
|---|---|
| *Things Fall Apart* by Chinua Achebe | A masterpiece by a singular author on the colonial African experience in Achebe's home country of Nigeria. |
| *Sulwe* by Lupita Nyong'o and Vashti Harrison | For young children, an age-appropriate story of colorism and of beautiful Black skin. |
| *The Long Walk to Freedom* by Nelson Mandela | Another pivotal read. Nelson Mandela's autobiography, in keen detail. |
| *The Boy Who Harnessed the Wind* by William Kamkwamba & Bryan Mealer | For children, a story of an ingenious young boy in Malawi and how he helps his community. |
| *Americanah* by Chimamanda Ngozi Adichie | Adichie, a super storyteller, follows the lives of two Nigerians as they navigate life and race. |
| *We Should All Be Feminists* by Chimamanda Ngozi Adichie | Based on a TED talk. Adichie has a compelling voice, and her points are elegantly argued. This is also quite short, so a good shared read for you and your workmates, cousins, co-teachers, etc. |
| *Born a Crime* by Trevor Noah | We may know him as a comedian and talk show host, but in this fine book, we learn of his growing up under apartheid. This is the adult version. |

| For White people in particular who would like to explore Whiteness, White supremacy, and how to be anti-racist. | |
|---|---|
| *White Fragility* by Robin DiAngelo | Popular book about how White people deflect racism. |
| *For White Folks Who Teach in the Hood* by Chris Emdin | A fresh voice on actual classroom practices to connect with youth. |
| *The History of White People* By Nell Irwin Painter | A look at how Whiteness has functioned over time, by a Princeton historian. |
| *Good White People* by Shannon Sullivan | A really important book on the role of "good White people" in maintaining racism. |

### For Folks Ready to Move On/Intermediate Selections

We are categorizing the next round of books as intermediate for a couple of reasons. Depending on the text, they might be better off reading after more foundational texts are finished, they are more specific in their focus (rather than more general in their treatment of race or racism), or the writing is more academic in its style. All are valuable.

| Are you a teacher who is ready to take the next steps or a reader with some background in these topics? | |
|---|---|
| *Culturally Responsive Teaching* by Geneva Gay | An introduction to culturally relevant teaching from one of the greats in the field. |
| *Racism Without Racists: Color-Blind Racism and the Persistence of Racial Inequality in the United States* by Eduardo Bonilla-Silva | Truly fascinating look at how racism perseveres despite so many people denying they are racist. And Bonilla-Silva is funny, too. This was a game-changer for Joi.[1] |
| *The Fire Next Time* by James Baldwin | A must read. Baldwin is a giant and all teachers should read his work. These essays will add depth and nuance to your understanding of American racism. |
| *Pushout: The Criminalization of Black Girls in Schools* by Monique Morris | Exceptionally readable and accessible book about how Black girls are overpoliced. |
| *Multiplication Is for White People* by Lisa Delpit | Delpit's second book pushes back on the idea of the achievement gap. |
| *These Kids Are Out of Control: Why We Must Reimagine "Classroom Management" for Equity* by H. Richard Milner, Heather B. Cunningham, Lori Delale-O'Connor, & Erika Gold Kestenberg | Proposes and supports equity-based classroom management. |
| *Why Are There So Many Minority Students in Special Education?* by Beth Harry and Janette Klinger | An important book about students of color and special education. |
| *Everyday Antiracism* edited by Mica Pollock | Great edited volume that explores antiracism in schools from many vantage points. |
| *Young, Gifted and Black* by Theresa Perry, Claude Steele and Asa Hilliard | Essays on Black achievement by influential thinkers in our field. Crisply counters deficit narratives of Black youth. |
| *Radical Equations: Civil Rights from Mississippi to the Algebra Project* by Robert Moses | Looks at math as a civil rights issue. Compelling, whether you teach math or not. |

| Do you want to go deeper on issues of race and racism? We consider this set intermediate for general audiences. | |
|---|---|
| *Between the World and Me* by Ta-Nehisi Coates | Moving letters from a father to his son, by an extraordinary writer. National Book Award winner. |
| *How to Be an Antiracist* by Ibram X. Kendi | A pivotal guide to antiracism work. |
| *The 1619 Project* by Nikole Hannah-Jones | The book that sparked backlash and outrage about the telling of American history; read it for yourself for its depth and truth telling. |
| *Begin Again: James Baldwin's America and Its Urgent Lessons for Our Own* by Eddie Glaude | One of Joi and Kerri's favorites, the book draws the work of Baldwin into the present day. Elegant and impactful. |
| *Kindred* by Octavia Butler | Black science fiction at its best. |
| *The New Jim Crow* by Michelle Alexander | A deeply important book about how incarceration has taken the place of slavery in controlling Black men. |
| *We Were Eight Years in Power* by Ta-Nehisi Coates | A series of essays that follow the 8 years of the Obama presidency. Profound and troubling. |

## Advanced Selections

Our final set of books is for teachers who wish to go deeper and look at some more academic titles. These are the kind of books that would be read in graduate school. We think they are worth reading even if you are not in grad school, though. They are more academic in their style and focus more tightly on a subject, like Black language styles or critical race theory.

| Are you a grad student? Teacher dedicated to these issues? | |
|---|---|
| *Fugitive Pedagogy: Carter G. Woodson and the Art of Black Teaching* by Jarvis Givens | A powerful look at the life of Carter G. Woodson. |
| *We Want to Do More Than Survive: Abolitionist Teaching and the Pursuit of Educational Freedom* by Bettina Love | We love Bettina's voice and candor. Read her. You will be lifted. |

(*continued*)

| *The Education of Blacks in the South, 1860–1935* by James Anderson | A favorite of Joi's. Documents the historical and legal quest of the African American community for equality and equal schooling. |
| *Choosing to See: A Framework for Equity in the Math Classroom* by Pamela Seda & Kyndall Brown | This book offers interventions to increase equity in the mathematics classroom written by longtime classroom practitioners. |
| *Articulate While Black: Barack Obama, Language, and Race in the U.S.* by H. Samy Alim & Geneva Smitherman | Using Obama's speech as a starting point, this book looks at the politics of Black language. The analysis of Obama saying "Nah, we straight" is alone worth reading the book. |
| *Critical Race Theory in Education: A Scholar's Journey* by Gloria Ladson-Billings | Latest book by one of our favorites, tackling one of the most controversial issues of our day. |

## LEARNING CIRCLES

We now turn more squarely to school-based folks (teachers, administrators, social workers) as we lay out additional resources for ongoing professional development. Here, we clustered resources around particular groups of people (like secondary history teachers, or school librarians) and then listed books, websites, and other materials that would be of use to this team. It is a bit fraught listing website materials in a book for obvious reasons. They change and go missing with such frequency. We have worked around this by sending you to well-established websites where you can find a host of information, rather than to discrete web pages that are more apt to disappear into a dark hole. When you get to the website, search it for the individual text you are looking for, or just browse. Serendipity is a powerful thing, so you never know what you might find.

| An Elementary/Middle Grades Circle | |
| --- | --- |
| **Participants:** K–8 teachers | **Goals:** Learn about antiracist standards, locate age-appropriate resources for curriculum |
| **Anchor Resources:** <br> 1. *Teaching Tolerance/Learning for Justice*. This group recently changed their name to Learning for Justice and can be found at https://www.learningforjustice .org/. This is one of the most well-established websites linking teachers and issues of diversity and inclusion. They are an arm of the Southern Poverty Law Center. They publish Social Justice Standards that provide teachers with concrete ways to think about diversity, equity, and inclusion (DEI) work in the classroom. They have a lot of resources and lesson plans. One of Kerri's go-to sites. | |

2. *Rethinking Schools*. A print magazine that you can find at https:// rethinkingschools.org/. The magazine is well worth subscribing to, as they provide timely articles and resources with a clear antiracist focus.

3. *Hechinger Report*. An online news site that covers inequality and innovation in education in particular. This site is appropriate for all teachers who are trying to stay up to date on DEI issues. https://hechingerreport.org/

4. *We Need Diverse Books*. A website on sourcing books that match your students; it can be found at https://diversebooks.org/. The Resources for Parents, Educators and Librarians menu provides links to find books that represent all kinds of youth.

5. *A Pathway to Equitable Math Instruction*. This guidebook/activity set/ workbook helps grade 6–8 math teachers dismantle racism in math. Find the download at https://equitablemath.org/.

| A Secondary STEM circle | |
| --- | --- |
| **Participants:** High school math and science teachers | **Goals:** Increase representation in STEM fields; reimagine Black children's success in science and mathematics |

**Anchor Resources:**

1. *The Brilliance of Black Children in Mathematics* by Jacqueline Leonard and Danny Martin (book).

2. *Rethinking Mathematics* by Rethinking Schools (Gutstein & Peterson, 2013) (book).

3. *Benjamin Banneker Association at bbamath.org*. Organization devoted to math advocacy and issues particular to Black youth and their experiences with math.

4. *Blood on the Tracks: Why Are There So Few Black Students in Our Science Class?* (Lindahl, 2015). Practical article from Rethinking Schools about racial inequities in science. https://rethinkingschools.org/

5. *STEM Stories: The Power of the Influencer*. A digital storybook featuring contemporary people of color in STEM fields. Designed and written entirely by high school students. http://dmdstem.weebly.com/

6. *Girls Who Code*. Provides access to coding for girls of color. The organization addresses the gender gap in technology with the goal of changing the image of who can code. https://girlswhocode.com/

7. *RadicalMath* (radicalmath.org). Looks at social justice and race in mathematics classrooms. Uses math as a tool for looking at issues of justice. Curriculum materials are also available.

| A Secondary History Circle | |
| --- | --- |
| **Participants:** Secondary social studies teachers | **Goals:** The telling of lesser-told stories, Black-focused history lessons |

**Anchor Resources:**

1. *The Education of Blacks in the South* by James Anderson (book). Anchors teachers in the long history of Black educational efforts.

2. *Zinn Education Project.* A race-forward site on teaching social studies and history with an eye on equity. Check their Facebook page for timely links to useful materials. https://www.zinnedproject.org/

3. *The Black History Bulletin.* Published by the Association for the Study of African American Life and History (ASALH), this journal provides high-quality, easily accessible lessons and resources on the teaching of African American history in schools. Carter G. Woodson established ASALH in 1915. They have quite a record of accomplishment. https://asalh.org/

4. *Facing History and Ourselves.* This organization for educators' professional development has many resources on teaching about race, ethnicity, and oppression in history. We find their work quite creative. They wrote a guide for teachers on discussing George Floyd (which can be used as a model for broaching hard conversations about police violence). https://www.facing history.org

5. *Reconstruction: America After the Civil War.* Four-part documentary series produced by PBS, narrated by Dr. Henry Louis Gates, exploring the pivotal years of American Reconstruction and the lasting impact of its failures on the lives of African Americans today. This is often an underexplored component of American history. https://www.pbs.org/

6. *Freedom's Unfinished Revolution* by the American Social History Project (1996). Highly accessible, inquiry-based high school textbook and teaching guide centered on the experiences of African Americans during the Civil Rights Era. Rich with primary sources.

7. *National Museum of African American History & Culture.* The NMAAHC website provides videos, images, and lessons that educators can use when teaching students about African American history and culture. At https://nmaahc .si.edu. We particularly like their "Reading Resources" (under Educators), which link their museum galleries to reading materials, and their "Learning Lab collections," which give teachers access to artifacts and other visuals.

8. *Teaching Africa: The K–16 Education Outreach Program.* Housed at Boston University, this program offers a resource library, training opportunities, and special events to expand teachers' abilities to teach about Africa with depth and knowledge. https://www.bu.edu/africa/outreach/

| A School Social Workers and Mental Health Care Circle | |
| --- | --- |
| **Participants:** Anyone assisting youth with mental health needs, supporting youth in the juvenile justice system | **Goals:** Find trauma- and self-care–related resources that are culturally responsive and relevant |

**Anchor Resources:**

1. *A Black Psychologist's Guide to Talking With Your Children About Race and Police Violence*. A video developed by psychologist Faith Sproul for families of color about discussing racial violence with their child. https://www.youtube.com /watch?v=KSeKOCDQF6Q

2. Antiracist Resources from *Greater Good*. This is UC Berkeley's excellent site on the science of well-being; it has many resources on the psychology of racism as well as self-care resources. https://greatergood.berkeley.edu/

3. *Girlhood Interrupted: The Erasure of Black Girls' Childhood* (Epstein, Blake, & González). From Georgetown University Law School's Center on Poverty and Inequality. Explores the idea of "adultification" and the ways in which black girlhood is constructed. https://genderjusticeandopportunity.georgetown.edu/

| A Teacher and School Staff Circle | |
| --- | --- |
| **Participants:** Anyone assisting youth with mental health needs after an incident of police-involved violence | **Goals:** Build resources for discussing police violence with youth |

**Anchor Resources:**

1. *Listening Circle on George Floyd*. This is part of the Morningside Center's work; you can see a script for teachers about talking through racial violence that can be used as a model. They have other great social–emotional learning materials. Located at: https://www.morningsidecenter.org/

2. *Teaching About Race, Racism and Police Violence*. This is Learning for Justice's curated set for talking about police violence. Learning for Justice is a leader in this work and has a wealth of reliable, meaningful materials. https:// www.learningforjustice.org/moment/racism-and-police-violence

3. *Black Girls Matter: Pushed Out, Overpoliced and Underprotected* is a report from the African American Policy Forum at https://www.aapf.org/. This is an important look at school discipline and the ways in which Black girls are particularly targeted.

4. *The Center for Racial Justice in Education* has an expansive list on its website (centerracialjustice.org) called "Resources for Talking about Race, Racism and Racialized Violence with Kids." Includes interview suggestions, articles, and video clips.

| A Secondary English Circle | |
|---|---|
| **Participants:** Secondary English teachers | **Goals:** Widening access to diverse books; teaching about media literacy through Ferguson, Missouri |

**Anchor Resources:**

1. *Social Justice Books: A Teaching for Change Project.* This site provides updated lists of the best children's, young adult, and educators' books on social justice. https://socialjusticebooks.org/

2. *We Need Diverse Books.* Excellent resource for finding books that represent all children. Useful for diversifying text choices/library offerings. https://diverse books.org

3. *Facing Ferguson: News Literacy in a Digital Age*, from Facing History and Ourselves (https://www.facinghistory.org/resource-library/facing-ferguson -news-literacy-digital-age). 11 lessons to use to teach about what happened in Ferguson, Missouri, through the lens of digital literacy. Could be used as a model for teaching current events and the role of media in society.

4. *The King Legacy* is a partnership between Beacon Press and the King estate. Here, teachers can find teacher guides for some of King's most famous books. http://thekinglegacy.org/


| A Black Affinity Group Circle | |
|---|---|
| **Participants:** Advisors and facilitators of Black affinity groups | **Goals:** Connecting with Black Lives Matters, helping to plan for special events and meetings |

**Anchor Resources:**

1. *BLM: Continuing the Civil Rights Movement.* Unit from the Choices Program at Brown University; focuses on Black activism. Lessons and materials are available. Additionally, at the main Choices website, there are 1,700 short video clips on a variety of topics (civil rights, colonization in Africa, slavery). https://www .choices.edu/

2. *DC Teachers/Black Lives Matter Week.* Curriculum from Black Lives Matters Week of Action, run by DC Area Educators for Social Justice. Very well developed resources that are very teacher-friendly. They also have great local DC area history links, if you live in that neck of the woods. https://www.dcarea educators4socialjustice.org/

3. *Racial Equity Tools.* Extensive tools to understand and address racism and issues around power, for groups in all phases of development. They offer a broad selection of sources, including interesting data sets and curricula. https://www.raciale quitytools.org/

4. *The Lemonade Syllabus*: A huge collection of feminist and Black women empowerment resources written by Black ministers, academics, and graduate students; inspired by Beyonce's album. https://issuu.com/candicebenbow/docs/lemonade_syllabus_2016

| Circle for Teachers Who Teach About Slavery | |
| --- | --- |
| **Participants:** Anyone teaching about slavery | **Goals:** To tell the truth about slavery in age-appropriate ways |

**Anchor Resources:**

1. *Teaching Hard History: American Slavery*. A very useful set of materials for teachers at all teaching levels to teach about slavery. There are podcasts, videos, and lessons. A really rich resource by Learning for Justice. https://www.learningforjustice.org/frameworks/teaching-hard-history/american-slavery

2. *The Whitney Plantation Museum (https://www.whitneyplantation.org/)*. The first U.S. plantation historical site interpreted entirely through the experiences of the enslaved. Abundant with resources on American slavery.

3. *Center for the Study of Slavery and Justice at Brown University*. A research center that looks at the contemporary legacy of slavery. https://cssj.brown.edu

4. *Slave Voyages website at https://www.slavevoyages.org/*. A digital repository of primary documents relating to the slave trade. Hosted by Rice University.

5. *National Park Service*. An often-overlooked option for helping to understand slavery. The Harriet Tubman National Historic Park in New York and the Harriet Tubman Underground Railroad National Historical Park in Maryland are both sites where you can take students. If you are not able to tour these sites, the website provides readings, lesson plans, and videos about Harriet Tubman and the Underground Railroad. Materials can be found at https://www.nps.gov/hart/index.htm and https://www.nps.gov/hatu/index.htm.

| A Librarians and Literacy Coaches Circle | |
| --- | --- |
| **Participants:** Anyone who is making book selections for students | **Goals:** Diversifying book offering for youth through vetted, reliable sites |

**Anchor Resources:**

1. One reliable way to find quality books written by African American authors is to look up Coretta Scott King Book Award winners. This award is given yearly in remembrance of Coretta Scott King, for books that focus on African American culture. Winners can be found at https://www.ala.org/

(*continued*)

2. Books that represent Black youth in the LGBTQ community can be found at Lambda Literary's LGBTQ Books for Children, Teens, and Young Adults at http://lambdaliterary.org

3. Recommended books that are LGBTQ-family friendly can be found at https://www.familyequality.org/

4. Dr. Nicole Cooke, faculty at the University of South Carolina and a librarian, put together the following padlet after the deaths of George Floyd and Breonna Taylor. It is awash with interesting sources, compellingly laid out: https://padlet.com/nicolethelibrarian/nbasekqoazt336co

## IN CONCLUSION

As you can see, there is a wide ocean of resources available to you. And we happily report that these lists are by no means complete. If you are new to this work, what you see here is literally just a sprinkling of what exists. We do not say this to undercut our efforts, but instead to highlight the many scholars, practitioners, and teachers doing anti-Blackness work. We encourage you to look for teacher activist groups in your communities as well as local anti-racism organizations/BLM organizations to supplement your efforts. Having like-minded folks to work with can make all the difference.

# Postscript

We will end very much as we began, with us each speaking for ourselves, and with our attention on the ancestors who preceded us. But first, a story.

Let's take a short tangent as we finalize our work. Inkwell Beach? Have you heard of it? Located on the tiny island of Martha's Vineyard (in Massachusetts), Inkwell Beach has been a site of quiet Black resistance for over a century (Osterheldt, 2020). Beginning in the 1800s, freed slaves purchased property on the island, and eventually an inn for Black travelers was opened. For generations, Black folks would visit the island and swim at Inkwell Beach, one of the few Black beach destinations in the United States. Jenee Osterheldt, a *Boston Globe* columnist, writing about her visit there in 2020, focused on the feeling of safety Black people experience when they are at Inkwell. And kinship. She interviewed Ariel Weekes, a Black man, about his visits to the island when he was small. He explained, movingly, that at Martha's Vineyard he was just Ariel. Just a boy.

We end at Inkwell Beach because it provides a tangible representation of what we aspire to in this book: Black-affirming spaces. At Inkwell Beach, Ariel was just a boy. While it is not said, we imagine that is in contrast to being "just a Black boy," with all the stereotypes and baggage that come with it. In thinking through what makes for places that uplift and support Black children, we are humbled by this most basic requirement: to provide a space where Black youth can just be.

This idea of finding space to be has been on Kerri's mind.

Kerri: I keep thinking about a memory I have carried with me for 20 years. When I was teaching 4th grade, my student asked me one day, "I am not Black, am I?" The child was from the Dominican Republic, and to tell you the truth, it does not matter what the child *was*. What is haunting is what the child *was afraid he was*. At nine, he knew he did not want to be considered Black. This child had already been poisoned by anti-Black racism.

Glaude and Baldwin and Wilkerson underscore how racism is a moral failure, and for me, this is the heart of the work. White people have bought into stories that have corrupted our understanding of the world and its people. We have been carrying around these stories, based on the lies of anti-Blackness, which taint our minds in fundamentally dangerous ways. We reissue and recycle the stories over and over again, stories about Black abilities and cognition and culpability. The stories are so ubiquitous that we do not even notice them as stories. They are simply the way things are. This lack of consciousness, willful ignorance, or comfort with the status quo is literally killing Black people, bodily and otherwise. This is not hyperbole. These lies matter. They have consequences. They are not an issue of kindness or being nice. To know that our stories can damage the well-being of others, and yet we hold onto them nonetheless? That is the moral failure.

We who teach are in the youth uplift field. We cannot spread poison and lies. It is morally indefensible. It is a dereliction of our duties. Ladson-Billings talks about "defunding" racism (2021). Indeed. We need to defund anti-Blackness. We need to starve it. Expose it as the lie it is and make it useless (Ladson-Billings, 2021). Drain off the poison. Take responsibility for what we do and say and how these actions affect others. Then we can create spaces where a child can just be.

Joi: While we were in the process of writing this book, all people lost an incredible voice for love in the world, bell hooks. In her book *Salvation: Black People and Love*, she wrote, "Black folks and our allies in struggle who care about the fate of Black America recognize that the transformative power of love in daily life is the only force that can solve the myriad crises we now face" (p. xxiv). It is hard to argue with love. While we rarely hear it spoken about in the context of schools and education, we all recognize that deep care for and commitment to youth and their communities is the solution to what we face.

My mother spent her early years attending an all-Black elementary school in Florida. I have always cherished her reflections on her time in this school. "If one kid didn't understand something, the teacher would have a student who did sit and work with them," she has often said. Students' achievements were a reflection on the teacher, and there was a pride she took in their success. "Have you heard how well Tommy can read?" or "Jean is an excellent writer!" When they shined, she shined. When they struggled, she put her energies into helping them overcome. Above all, there was a deep understanding that educating her students well was for a greater goal: the liberation and uplift of all Black people. I recognize that for non-Black teachers, working for the liberation and uplift of Black people might seem odd or antithetical to the notion of care for "all people." By working for the liberation of Black students, I am not suggesting that you ignore the needs of your other students. It is not anti-White to be pro-Black. Rather, when we work for the liberation of those who have been oppressed, we are all freed. At the very least, we are freed from the illusions of our own success (after all, it is easy to succeed academically when the ones you are competing against have fewer resources, fewer opportunities, and a litany of negative dispositions and narratives to wade through). What would it look like if we were competing on more equal footing? Undoubtedly, the greatest thing we are freed from is the illusion that we can somehow succeed and survive without the success and survival of others. Overincarceration harms us all. The school-to-prison pipeline and overpolicing of Black youth threaten everyone. The academic underdevelopment of Black youth serves no one. I am diminished (morally, socially, economically) when my sister, brother, companion, fellow sojourner is diminished. Black liberation and love must be everyone's goal. "Love is our hope and our salvation" (hooks, 2001, p. xxiv)

We opened this book in awe of Mary McLeod Bethune, and we will close equally in awe. Because she left no stone unturned, before her death Bethune (1954) wrote an eloquent "Last Will and Testament" in which she spelled out what she wanted to leave her community and what she hoped others would take from her work. She tells us, "I leave you with racial dignity"; explaining that Black people are the heirs of great civilizations and they must uphold their dignity no matter what. She also leaves us "a responsibility to our young people" that they "not be discouraged from aspiring towards greatness." We are responsible for this work. Young people are watching. Seventy years later, her work is as relevant, poignant and needed as ever.

With dignity upheld for young people,
With truth-telling and humility as our guides,
With grace, justice, and morality as our anchors,
We wish you fruitful work.

—Joi and Kerri

# Supporting Black/African American Youth in School

| Indicator | A strength | We are in progress | A weakness | Comments |
|---|---|---|---|---|
| 1. Our school understands that the Black experience is not monolithic: that there is great variety within the Black community as to language, religion, family structure, immigrant status, gender, and sexual orientation.[1] | | | | |
| 2. Our school/district has a position dedicated to supporting African American students and families. Our school/district employs therapists and counselors with expertise in supporting African American students. | | | | |
| 3. Our school celebrates and/or commemorates the African American experience in the United States through holidays, activities, and/or events. | | | | |
| 4. Members of our school/district community understand the difference between individual and systemic racism. Members of our school/district recognize that both are real. | | | | |
| 5. The experiences, perspectives, voices, and ways of knowing of Blacks/African Americans are infused throughout the curriculum and across disciplines and are accessible to all students. | | | | |

| Indicator | A strength | We are in progress | A weakness | Comments |
|---|---|---|---|---|
| 6. Our teachers are particularly knowledgeable of and careful about how slavery is taught, ensuring that students have access to accurate information that is thoughtful in its presentation. Teachers are mindful of the way Black children psychologically experience lessons about slavery and the potential emotional toll it takes. | | | | |
| 7. The percentage of Black students in our school's gifted and honors program is at least as high as the percentage of Black students on any given sports team (specifically football and basketball). Black student athletes are recruited for and participate in a variety of extracurricular activities beyond sports. Our school/district has programming and personnel dedicated to supporting the academic achievement of Black student athletes. | | | | |
| 8. Our school supports many manifestations of Black maleness, which move beyond the athlete, and include the scholar, artist, mathematician, writer, and scientist. | | | | |
| 9. Our school actively works to counter stereotypes of Black femaleness by not overpolicing the language, dress, and hairstyles of Black girls. | | | | |
| 10. Our school/district provides a variety of culturally responsive extracurricular opportunities for students (cultural affinity groups, step teams, opportunities to learn heritage languages, gay/straight alliances for POC, service clubs, etc.). | | | | |

*(continued)*

| Indicator | A strength | We are in progress | A weakness | Comments |
|---|---|---|---|---|
| 11. Our school community actively and consistently teaches, learns, and celebrates the historical, literary, artistic, and political contributions of Black people, not just in February. | | | | |
| 12. Our school/district has a program that supports the recruitment and retention of African American teachers and administrators. | | | | |
| 13. The authors of our textbooks and instructional resources come from a variety of racial and ethnic backgrounds, including Black and African scholars. | | | | |
| 14. Our school provides space in the curriculum to discuss race and its intersections with culture, gender, identity, religion, immigration status, and other social identities. | | | | |
| 15. Our school thinks of familial and parental involvement beyond PTAs. It understands barriers to involvement (logistical, work-related, based on parents' own previous school experience) and works to mediate these. For example, we meet with families/parents/guardians in locations and times that are convenient for them (like during half-times at athletic events). | | | | |
| 16. While physical manifestations of inclusion (diverse library books, dolls of various skin tones, signs in multiple languages) are meaningful, we also have **policies** that promote inclusion and justice (critiquing who is in gifted and talented programs; spelling out consequences for racist behavior; allocating college-planning resources equitably; translating parent communication into several languages). | | | | |

| Indicator | A strength | We are in progress | A weakness | Comments |
|---|---|---|---|---|
| 17. Our school moves beyond a focus on the "achievement gap" and notices and responds to gaps in resources and learning opportunities (focusing rather on the "opportunity gap").[2] | | | | |
| 18. Our school enacts best practices for supporting children and youth in the foster care system. | | | | |
| 19. Discipline policies are based on age-appropriate, developmentally sound principles, which remember we are working with youth. | | | | |
| 20. Discipline policies are equally enforced, with the end goal being the child learning new skills and/or restitution rather than punishment. | | | | |
| 21. Our school does not expect Black/African American and other POC to do all the heavy lifting regarding issues of race, multiculturalism, fairness, and equity. | | | | |
| 22. Our school draws upon the larger Black/African American community (churches/mosques, museums, sororities and fraternities, businesses/business owners, universities, etc.) as well as our school-based paraprofessionals, custodians, cafeteria workers, teaching assistants, and other staff as resources in the educating and nurturing of our Black students. | | | | |
| 23. We actively pay attention to counter negative metanarratives[3] and deficit views of Black people. We invite experts to assist us when we are stuck. | | | | |

# Notes

## Introduction

1. For a fuller discussion on the concept of Black as nonhuman, we suggest reading Dr. Sylvia Wynter (famed Jamaican theorist, scholar, and Stanford University professor), *No Humans Involved: An Open Letter to My Colleagues* (1994), and Bauman's discussions of how Jews became nonhuman (in a parallel argument) in Bauman (1989), *Modernity and the Holocaust.*

2. See Trump Memo 20–34, "Memorandum for the heads of executive departments and agencies" (Vought, 2020), which seeks to end federal trainings "on 'critical race theory', 'white privilege', or any other training or propaganda effort that teaches or suggests either (1) that the United States is an inherently racist or evil country or (2) that any race or ethnicity is inherently racist or evil" (p. 1).

3. Located in Rusk County, Texas, the Monte Verdi Plantation Family Slaves Marker was unveiled on September 1, 2018 (Texas Historical Commission, 2018).

## Chapter 1

1. Anderson's research revealed several such Southern pre-Civil War schools, including: New Orleans' Pioneer School of Freedom, founded in 1860; a school at Fortress Monroe, Virginia, beginning in 1861; and a school in Savannah, Georgia, which "had existed unknown to the slave regime from 1833 to 1865" (Anderson, 1988, p. 7).

2. Woodson's organization, now the Association for the Study of African American Life and History (ASALH), is still in existence and is home to Black historians throughout the world.

3. The Association for the Study of African American Life and History continues to publish the *Black History Bulletin* as well as the *Journal of African American History.*

## Chapter 2

1. Dan Smith, age 88, in 2020. His father was born enslaved, in 1862 (see Trent, 2020).

2. Psychologists use the term "attributional ambiguity" to describe the psychological state of uncertainty that members of a stigmatized group face when interpreting outcomes such as feedback (Crocker et al., 1991). Mendes et al. write, "Interracial interactions are more attributionally ambiguous . . . including the attribution that one may have experienced discrimination" (2008, p. 3).

## Chapter 3

1. A book is challenged if it has a documented request to remove it from a school or library (per American Library Association).

2. Howard (2013) presents four tenets of ASC, including 1) early and persistent exposure to sports; 2) inordinate time commitment to deveoping high-level competency in sports; 3) holdback phenomenon (the intentional grade retention/holding back of Black males in earlier grades to allow them to increase their physical growth and strength and therefore improve their chances of athletic success); and 4) save the family syndrome (the idea that a lucrative sports contract will help pull up an impoverished African American family).

3. Conducted by NCES, this was a nationally representative study capturing student, parent, teacher and administrator data. The longitudinal study captured students when they were in the 8th grade and then 2 years later when they were high school sophomores.

4. Box braids are small individual plaits that are parted at the scalp in a way that forms small squares. They often involve extensions.

5. At the time of publication of this book, the CROWN Act has been signed into law in 18 states (Dall'Asen, 2022). The U. S. House of Representatives passed the CROWN Act on March 18, 2022 (Stracqualursi, 2022).

## Chapter 4

1. Much important research has been produced on the mathematics identity and stereotype/narrative management that Black students must engage in. For those interested in learning more, we suggest Nasir's (2011) and Nasir and Shah's (2011) studies as a good start.

2. Watch this video to see Serena Williams introduce the global Sustainable Development Goals: https://www.youtube.com/watch?v=s5bti_B6mLc.

## Chapter 6

1. Flipgrid is a free online platform that allows participants to video-record themselves and then post their video for classmates or team members to view and then respond to. https://info.flipgrid.com/

## Chapter 7

1. A full review of this book can be found at Ullucci, 2006.

## Appendix

1. As an example, the last year Kerri taught 4th grade, she had Black children in her school from Liberia, South Africa, Haiti, the Dominican Republic, and all over the United States (New York, Rhode Island, Florida). On the West Coast, Joi taught Black youth from Panama, Belize, Oakland, and New Orleans. Together, they spoke English (standard and African American vernacular English), Spanish, and Haitian Kreyòl.

2. We suggest this switch in focus from achievement gap to opportunity gap. We find that with the achievement gap, the blame for the "gap" is placed on youth. So, when Black boys do not graduate at the same level as White boys, attention is focused on what is "wrong" with Black boys. Instead, it is more fruitful, and more fair, to look at the opportunity gap and assess whether youth have access to similar inputs in their educations (see Carter & Welner, 2013a; Gutiérrez, 2008; Ladson-Billings, 2006; or the remarkably titled "It's the opportunity gap, stupid," also by Carter and Welner, 2013b).

3. See Perry (2005) and Howard et al. (2016).

# References

Abdelfatah, R., & Arablouei, R. (Hosts). (2020, September 17). James Baldwin's fire [Audio podcast episode]. *Throughline*. NPR. https://www.npr.org/transcripts/912769283

Achebe, C. (1958). *Things fall apart*. Heinemann.

Acho, E. (2021). *Uncomfortable conversations with a Black boy*. Roaring Brook Press.

Adeyemi, T. (2019). *Children of blood and bone*. Macmillian.

Adichie, C. N. (2014). *Americanah*. Anchor Books.

Adichie, C. N. (2015). *We should all be feminists*. Anchor Books.

Agada, E. (2015). Sidney Poitier, Mike Brown, and the myth of Black exceptionalism. *Celluloid in Black and White*. http://celluloidinblackandwhite.blogspot.com/2015/01/sidney-poitier-mike-brown-and-myth-of.html

Alexander, M. (2020). *The new Jim Crow*. The New Press.

Alim, H. S., & Smitherman, G. (2012). *Articulate while Black: Barack Obama, language, and race in the U.S.* Oxford University Press.

Allen, D. (2021, March). A forgotten Black founding father. *The Atlantic*. https://www.theatlantic.com/magazine/archive/2021/03/prince-hall-forgotten-founder/617791/

Allen, Q. (2015). Race, culture and agency: Examining the ideologies and practices of US teachers of Black male students. *Teaching and Teacher Education, 47*, 71–81.

American Social History Project. (1996). *Freedom's unfinished revolution: An inquiry into the civil war and reconstruction*. The New Press.

Anderson, J. (1988). *The education of Blacks in the South, 1860–1935*. University of North Carolina Press.

Anderson, L. H. (2010). *Chains*. Atheneum Books for Young Readers.

Angelou, M., & Basquiat, J. M. (1993). *Life doesn't frighten me*. Stewart, Tabori, & Chang.

Asmelash, L. (2021, February 9). *After allowing parents to opt-out of the Black History Month curriculum, a Utah school is switching the decision*. CNN. https://www.cnn.com/2021/02/09/us/maria-montessori-academy-black-history-trnd/index.html

Associated Press. (2013, September 21). Connecticut students re-enact slavery during school trip by picking cotton and being sold at auction. *New York Daily News*. https://www.nydailynews.com/news/national/connecticut-students-re-enact-slavery-school-trip-article-1.1463361

Associated Press. (2021, October 4). North Carolina school board passes strict rules for teaching race. *The Virginian-Pilot*. https://www.pilotonline.com/news/education

/vp-nw-teaching-race-north-carolina-20211002-qlunf7d2trhghgc6tywashd2j4
-story.html

Baker-Bell, A. (2020). *Linguistic justice: Black language, literacy, identity, and pedagogy.* NCTE-Routledge Research Series.

Baldwin, J. (1992). *The fire next time.* Vintage. (Original work published 1963).

Banks, J. (2019). *An introduction to multicultural education* (6th ed.). Pearson.

Baptist, E. E. (2016). *The half has never been told: Slavery and the making of American capitalism.* Hachette UK.

Bauman, Z. (1989). *Modernity and the holocaust.* Cornell University Press.

Bell, D. (1992). *Faces at the bottom of the well: The permanence of racism.* Basic Books.

Bell, D. (2004). *Silent covenants: Brown v. Board of Education and the unfulfilled hopes for racial reform.* Oxford University Press.

Bell, L. (2010). *Storytelling for social justice. Connecting narrative and the arts in antiracist teaching.* Routledge.

Bellamy Walker, T. (2022, January 6). *Book bans in schools are catching fire. Black authors say uproar isn't about students.* NBC News. https://www.nbcnews.com/news/nbcblk/book-bans-schools-are-catching-fire-black-authors-say-uproar-isnt-stud-rcna10228

Bennett, B. (2020). *The vanishing half.* Riverhead Books.

Bethune, M. (1954). *Dr. Bethune's Last Will & Testament.* Bethune-Cookman University. https://www.cookman.edu/history/last-will-testament.html

Bethune-Cookman University (n.d.). *Dr. Mary Mcleod Bethune.* https://www.cookman.edu/history/our-founder.html

Black, G. (2020, October 12). The whitewashing of Black genius. *Scientific American.* https://www.scientificamerican.com/article/the-whitewashing-of-black-genius/

Blake, J., & Epstein, R. (2019). *Listening to Black women and girls: Lived experiences of adultification bias.* The Georgetown Law Center on Poverty and Inequality.

Bonilla-Silva, E. (2017). *Racism without racists.* Rowman and Littlefield.

Boykin, A. W. (1994). Afrocultural expression and its implications for schooling. In E. R. Hollins, J. E. King, & W. C. Hayman (Eds.), *Teaching diverse populations: Formulating a knowledge base* (pp. 225–273). State University of New York Press.

Braddock, J. H. (1981). Race, athletics, and educational attainment: Dispelling the myths. *Youth and Society, 12*(2), 335–350. https://doi.org/10.1177/0044118X8101200304

Branigin, A. (2018a, February 12). NYC investigates principal who barred Black History Month lessons from being taught at her middle school: Report. *The Root.* https://www.theroot.com/department-of-education-investigating-principal-who-bar-1822921670

Branigin, A. (2018b, February 14). Lena Horne's family responds to NYC principal accused of blocking Black History Month lessons. *The Root.* https://www.theroot.com/bronx-middle-school-teacher-accused-of-blocking-black-h-1822990922

Broh, B. A. (2002, January). Linking extracurricular programming to academic achievement: Who benefits and why? *Sociology of Education, 75*(1), 69–95. https://doi.org/10.2307/3090254

Brooks, J. E. (2015). The impact of family structure, relationships, and support on African American students' collegiate experiences. *Journal of Black Studies, 46*(8), 817–836.

Brown, A., & Brown, K. (2015). The more things change, the more they stay the same: Excavating race and the enduring racisms in U.S. curriculum. *Teachers College Record, 117*(14), 103–130.

Butler, O. (2003). *Kindred*. Beacon Press.

California Assessment of Student Progress and Performance. (2019). https://www.cde.ca.gov/ta/tg/ca/

California Newsreel. (2003). *Interview with Beverly Daniel Tatum* [Transcript]. https://www.pbs.org/race/000_About/002_04-background-03-04.htm

Cary, L. (1992). *Black ice*. Vintage.

Carter, P. & Welner, G. (2013a). *Closing the opportunity gap: What America must do to give every child an even chance*. Oxford University Press.

Carter, P. L., & Welner, K. G. (2013b, May 13). It's the opportunity gap, stupid. *New York Daily News*. http://www.nydailynews.com/opinion/opportunity-gap-stupid-article-1.13409

Champion, T. B., Cobb-Roberts, D., & Bland-Stewart, L. (2012). Future educators' perceptions of African American Vernacular English (AAVE). *Online Journal of Education Research, 1*(5), 80–89.

Christensen, L. (2009). *Teaching for joy and justice: Reimagining the language arts classroom*. Rethinking Schools.

Ciurczak, P., Marinova, A., & Schuster, L. (2020). *Kids today: Boston's declining child population and its effect on school enrollment*. Boston Indicators. https://www.bostonindicators.org/-/media/indicators/boston-indicators-reports/report-files/kids-today.pdf

Coates, T. (2015). *Between the world and me*. One World.

Coates, T. (2018). *We were eight years in power: An American tragedy*. One World.

Coates, T. (2021) *The beautiful struggle* (young adult version). Delacorte Books.

Cooper, J. (2019a, August 21). Why are black males supported only when they're athletes? *The Boston Globe*. https://www.bostonglobe.com/magazine/2019/08/21/why-are-black-males-only-supported-when-they-athletes/QwspMiHYgujEvhWi3VSI7L/story.html

Cooper, J. (2019b). *From exploitation back to empowerment: Black male holistic (under)development through sport and (mis)education*. Peter Lang.

Crocker, J., Voelkl, K., Testa, M., & Major, B. (1991). Social stigma: The affective consequences of attributional ambiguity. *Journal of Personality and Social Psychology, 60*(2), 218–228. https://doi.org/10.1037/0022-3514.60.2.218

Curry, C. (1996). *Silver rights: The Story of the Carter family's brave decision to send their children to an all-white school and claim their civil rights*. Harvest Books.

Curtis, C. P. (1997). *The Watsons go to Birmingham*. Yearling.

Dall'Asen, N. (2022, July 27). The CROWN Act Is now law in 18 states. *Allure*. https://www.allure.com/story/the-crown-act-congress-senate-passage

Dawson, M. C., & Bobo, L. (2009). One year later and the myth of a post-racial society. *Du Bois Review: Social Science Research on Race, 6*(2), 247–249.

De La Torre, V. (2013, September 19). Parent files complaint against Hartford schools over slavery reenactment on field trip. *The Hartford Courant*. https://www.courant.com/community/hartford/hc-xpm-2013-09-19-hc-hartford-parent-complaint-0920-20130919-story.html

Delmont, M. (2016, December 27). *Rethinking "busing" in Boston*. National Museum of American History. https://www.si.edu/object/rethinking-busing-boston%3A posts_1f1ea8975488d418b47d30813d64186d

Delpit, L. (1988). The silenced dialogue: Power and pedagogy in educating other people's children. *Harvard Educational Review, 58*(3), 280-299.

Delpit, L. (2006). *Other people's children: Cultural conflict in the classroom*. The New Press.

Delpit, L. (2012). *Multiplication is for White people: Raising expectations for other people's children*. The New Press.

Demby, G. (2014, January 6). The ugly, fascinating history of the word "racism." *Code Switch*. https://www.npr.org/sections/codeswitch/2014/01/05/260006815 /the-ugly-fascinating-history-of-the-word-racism

DiAngelo, R. (2018). *White fragility: Why it's so hard for White people to talk about racism*. Beacon Press.

Doiron, S. (2021, June 2). *South Kingstown school committee claims woman has filed 200+ public records requests*. WPRI. https://www.wpri.com/news/local-news /south-county/south-kingstown-school-committee-claims-woman-has-filed-200 -public-records-requests/

Douglass, F. (1845). *Narrative of the life of Frederick Douglass, an American slave*. Anti-Slavery Office.

Drake, I. (Spring, 2008). Classroom simulations: Proceed with caution. *Teaching Tolerance, 33*.

Du Bois, W. E. B. (1903). *The souls of black folk; Essays and sketches*. McClurg and Co.

Dumas, M. J., & ross, k. (2016). "Be real Black for me": Imagining BlackCrit in education. *Urban Education, 51*(4), 415–442. https://doi.org/10.1177/0042085916628611

Eitle, T., & Eitle, J. (2002, April.) Race, cultural capital, and the educational effects of participation in sport. *Sociology of Education, 75*(2), 123–146.

Ellison, Ralph. (1995). *Invisible man*. Vintage International.

Emdin, C. (2017). *For White folks who teach in the hood . . . and the rest of y'all too: Reality pedagogy and urban education*. Beacon Press.

Epstein, R., Blake, J., & González, T. (2017, June 27). *Girlhood interrupted: The erasure of Black girls' childhood*. Georgetown Law Center on Poverty and Inequality. http://dx.doi.org/10.2139/ssrn.3000695

Equity Collaborative. (2019). *Systemic equity assessment: A picture of racial equity challenges and opportunities in Loudoun County Public School District*. Loudon County Public Schools. www.lcps.org. https://www.lcps.org/cms/lib/VA01000 195/Centricity/domain/60/equity_initiative_documents/LCPS_Equity_Report _FINALReport12_2_19.pdf

Faraj, G. (2007). *Unearthing the underground: A study of radical activism in the Black Panther Party and the Black Liberation Army*. [Doctoral dissertation, University of California, Berkeley].

Fejgin, N. (1994). Participation in high school competitive sports: A subversion of school mission or contribution to academic goals? *Sociology of Sport Journal, 11*(3), 211–230. doi: 10.1123/ssj.11.3.211

Feldscher, K. (2021, May 19). *The downside of "John Henryism."* Harvard T.H. Chan School of Public Health. https://www.hsph.harvard.edu/news/features/the -downside-of-john-henryism/

Ferlazzo, L. (2020, January 28). Author interview with Dr. Gholdy Muhammad: Cultivating genius. *Education Week.* https://www.edweek.org/teaching-learning /opinion-author-interview-with-dr-gholdy-muhammad-cultivating-genius/2020 /01

Flake, S. (2018). *The skin I'm in.* Little, Brown Books for Young Readers.

Flores, A. (2007, October/November). Examining disparities in mathematics education: Achievement gap or opportunity gap? *The High School Journal, 91*(1), 29–42.

Forman, T. (2021, October 6). Charter school under fire for teacher's comments. *Salisbury Post.* https://www.salisburypost.com/2021/10/06/charter-school-under-fire -for-teachers-comments/

Freitag, M.,& Knight-Justice, N.(2020, December 2). *Rethinking intervention: An interview with Gholdy Muhammad.* Instruction Partners. https://instructionpart ners.org/2020/12/02/dr-gholnecsar-gholdy-muhammad/

García, S. B., & Guerra, P. L. (2004). Deconstructing deficit thinking: Working with educators to create more equitable learning environments. *Education and Urban Society, 36*(2), 150–168. https://doi.org/10.1177/0013124503261322

Gates, H. L. (2017). *100 amazing facts about the Negro.* Knopf Doubleday Publishing Group.

Gay, G. (2018). *Culturally responsive teaching: Theory, research, and practice.* Teachers College Press.

Georgetown Law Center on Poverty and Inequality, Initiative on Gender Justice and Opportunity. (2020). *The innocence initiative: Translating national research into local action in central Texas.* https://genderjusticeandopportunity.georgetown .edu/wp-content/uploads/2021/06/The-Innocence-Initiative-Translating-National- Research-into-Local-Action-in-Central-Texas-FINAL.pdf

Getachew, S. (2021, July 1). The toxic trope of Black exceptionalism. *New York Times,* A23(L).

Gholson, M., Bullock, E., & Alexander, N. (2012). On the brilliance of black children: A response to a clarion call. *Journal of Urban Mathematics Education, 5*(1), 1–7.

Gilliam, W. S., Maupin, A. N., Reyes, C. R., Accavitti, M., & Shic, F. (2016). *Do early educators' implicit biases regarding sex and race relate to behavior expectations and recommendations of preschool expulsions and suspensions?* Yale University Child Study Center. http://ziglercenter.yale.edu/publications/Preschool%20Im- plicit%20Bias%20Policy%20Brief_final_9_26_276766_5379_v1.pdf

Givens, J. (2021). *Fugitive pedagogy: Carter G. Woodson and the art of Black teaching.* Harvard University Press.

Glaude, E. (2020). *Begin again: James Baldwin's America and its urgent lessons for our own.* Crown.

Goff, P., Jackson, M., Di Leone, B., Culotta, C., & DiTomasso, N. (2014). The essence of innocence: Consequences of dehumanizing Black children. *Journal of Personality and Social Psychology, 106*(4), 526–45.

González, N., & Moll, L. C. (2002). Cruzando el puente: Building bridges to funds of knowledge. *Educational Policy, 16*(4), 623–641.

González, T., & Epstein, R. (2020, February). *Increasing school connectedness for girls: Restorative justice as a health equity resource.* Georgetown Law Center on Poverty and Inequality. https://genderjusticeandopportunity.georgetown.edu/wp-content/ uploads/2020/06/Restorative-Justice-as-a-Health-Equity-Resource.pdf

Gorman, A. (2021). *Call us what we carry: Poems*. Viking.

Gorski, P. (2009). *Toward a critical approach to multicultural teacher education*. Equity Literacy Institute. http://www.edchange.org/handouts/MTE-Approaches.pdf

Gorski, P. (2017). *Toward a transformative approach to equity*. Equity Literacy Institute. http://www.edchange.org/handouts/approaches-to-equity.pdf

Gorski, P. (2019). *Taco night*. Equity Literacy Institute. http://www.edchange.org /publications/TacoNight.pdf

Gorski, P. (2020). *Basic principles of equity literacy*. Equity Literacy Institute. https:// www.equityliteracy.org/equity-principles

Greenberg, A. (2020, July 14). *How the stress of racism can harm your health—and what that has to do with COVID 19*. Nova/PBS. https://www.pbs.org/wgbh/nova /article/racism-stress-covid-allostatic-load/

Greenlee, C. (2019). How history textbooks reflect America's refusal to reckon with slavery. *Vox*. https://www.vox.com/identities/2019/8/26/20829771/slavery -textbooks-history

Greer, B., Mukhopadhyay, S., Powell, A. B., & Nelson-Barber, S. (Eds). (2009). *Culturally responsive mathematics education*. Routledge.

Groeger, L., Waldman, A., & Eads, D. (2018, October 16). Miseducation: Is there racial inequality at your school? *ProPublica*. https://projects.propublica.org/miseducation/

Guidi, J., Lucente, M., Sonino, N., & Fava, G. (2021). Allostatic load and its impact on health: A systematic review. *Psychotherapy and Psychosomatics, 90*, 11–27. doi: 10.1159/000510696

Gutiérrez, R. (2008). Research commentary: A gap-gazing fetish in mathematics education? Problematizing research on the achievement gap. *Journal for Research in Mathematics Education, 39*(4), 357–364.

Gutstein, E. (2006). *Reading and writing the world with mathematics: Toward a pedagogy for social justice*. Taylor & Francis.

Gutstein, E., & Peterson, B. (2013). *Rethinking mathematics: Teaching social justice by the numbers*. Rethinking Schools.

Hanks, M. P., & Eckland, B. K. (1976). Athletics and social participation in the educational attainment process. *Sociology of Education, 49*(4), 271–294.

Hannah-Jones, N. (2021). *The 1619 Project: A new origin story*. Random House/ One World.

Hannah-Jones, N., & Watson, R. (2021). *The 1619 Project: Born on the water*. Kokila.

Harding, V. (1981). *There is a river: The Black struggle for freedom in America*. Harcourt, Brace and Company.

Harry, B., & Klinger, J. (2014). *Why are there so many minority students in special education?* Teachers College Press.

Hays, G. (2021, November 24). *Students who launched pro-slavery petition at Missouri high school sue after suspensions, expulsion*. PBS NewsHour. https://www .pbs.org/newshour/education/students-who-launched-pro-slavery-petition-at -missouri-high-school-sue-after-suspensions-expulsion

Hines, D., King, R., & Ford, D. (2018). Black students in handcuffs: Addressing racial disproportionality in school discipline for students with dis/abilities. *Teachers College Record, 120*(13), 1–24.

hooks, b. (2001). *Salvation: Black people and love*. Perennial.

hooks, b. (2017). *Happy to be nappy*. Little, Brown Books for Young Readers

Howard, B. L. (2021, September 22). Beloved Black principal fired in ludicrous critical race theory spat. *The Daily Beast.* https://www.thedailybeast.com/grapevine-colleyville-texas-school-board-ousts-black-principal-james-whitfield-over-critical-race-theory

Howard, T. (2013). *Black male(d): Peril and promise in the education of African American males.* Teachers College Press.

Howard, T. (2020). *Why race and culture matter in schools: Closing the achievement gap in America's classrooms.* Teachers College Press.

Howard, T., & Howard, J. (2021, March). "Radical care" to let Black boys thrive. *Educational Leadership, 78*(6), 22–29.

Howard, T. C., Woodward, B., Navarro, O., Haro, B.N, Watson, K.T, Huerta, A.H, & Terry, C.L. (2016). *The counter narrative: Reframing success for high achieving Black and Latino males in Los Angeles county.* UCLA Black Male Institute. https://escholarship.org/uc/item/2sv226tf

Huber, L. (2018, June). *Racial microaffirmations as a response to microaggressions.* Center for Critical Race studies at UCLA Research Brief #15.

Huntley, K. (2021, September 24). *Winooski student-athletes allegedly targeted with racial slurs during soccer game.* WCAX News. https://www.wcax.com/2021/09/24/winooski-student-athletes-allegedly-targeted-with-racial-slurs-during-soccer-game/

Isensee, L. (2015). *Why calling slaves 'workers' is more than an editing error.* NPREd. https://www.npr.org/sections/ed/2015/10/23/450826208/why-calling-slaves-workers-is-more-than-an-editing-error

Jacobo, J. (2018, August 21). *6th grader asked to leave private school over rule banning hair extensions, family says.* ABC News. https://abcnews.go.com/US/6th-grader-asked-leave-private-school-rule-banning/story?id=57311484

James, S. (2021) *The 172nd Cutter Lecture in Preventative Medicine: To Race with the World: John Henryism and the Health of Black Americans.* Harvard T. H. Chan School of Public Health, Harvard University.

Johnson, B. (2021, September 22). *Park Hill South High School condemns petition students circulated calling to bring back slavery.* KMBC News. https://www.kmbc.com/article/high-school-condemns-petition-students-circulated-calling-to-bring-back-slavery/37699523

Johnson, G. M. (2020). *All boys aren't blue: A memoir-manifesto.* Farrar Straus & Giroux.

Jones, S. (2020, Spring). Ending curriculum violence. *Teaching Tolerance, 64.* https://www.learningforjustice.org/magazine/spring-2020/ending-curriculum-violence

Kamkwamba, W., & Mealer, B. (2016). *The boy who harnessed the wind.* Puffin Books.

Kaur, H. (2021, June 3). *A Florida teacher is suing her school district for allegedly retaliating against her after she spoke out about racism.* CNN. https://www.cnn.com/2021/06/03/us/florida-teacher-blm-flag-lawsuit-trnd/index.html

Kendi, I. (2017). *Stamped from the beginning: The definitive history of racist ideas in America.* Bold Type Books.

Kendi, I. (2019). *How to be an antiracist.* Random House Publishing Group.

King, M. L., Jr. (1964). *Why we can't wait.* New American Library.

Klein, R. (2013, September 5). Tiana Parker, 7, switches schools after being forbidden from wearing dreads. *Huffington Post.* https://www.huffpost.com/entry/tiana-parker-dreads_n_3873868

Kohli, R., Pizarro, M., & Nevárez, A. (2017). The new racism of K–12 schools: Centering critical research on racism. *Review of Research in Education, 41*(1), 182–202.

Kozol, J. (2006). *The shame of the nation: The restoration of apartheid schooling in America.* Crown.

Ladson-Billings, G. (1995). Toward a theory of culturally relevant pedagogy. *American Educational Research Journal, 32*(3), 465–491.

Ladson-Billings, G. (2001). *Crossing over to Canaan.* JosseyBass.

Ladson-Billings, G. (2004). Landing on the wrong note: The price we paid for Brown. *Educational Researcher, 33*(7), 3–13. http://www.jstor.org/stable/3700092

Ladson-Billings, G. (2006). 2006 Presidential address: From the achievement gap to the education debt: Understanding achievement in U.S. schools. *Educational Researcher, 35*(7), 3–12.

Ladson-Billings, G. (2007). Can we at least have Plessy - The struggle for quality education. *The North Carolina Law Review 85.* http://scholarship.law.unc.edu/nclr/vol85/iss5/2

Ladson-Billings, G. (2009). *The dreamkeepers: Successful teachers of African American children.* Jossey-Bass.

Ladson-Billings, G. (2021). *Critical race theory in education: A scholar's journey.* Teachers College Press.

Lattimore, K. (2017, July 17). *When Black hair violates the dress code.* NPREd. https://www.npr.org/sections/ed/2017/07/17/534448313/when-black-hair-violates-the-dress-code

Lee, E., Menkart, D., & Okazawa-Rey, M. (2011). *Beyond heroes and holidays: A practical guide to K–12 anti-racist, multicultural education and staff development.* Teaching for Change Publishers.

Leonard, J., & Martin, D. (2013). *The brilliance of Black children in mathematics.* Information Age Publishers.

Lewis, J., Aydin, A., & Powell, N. (2013). *March: Book One.* Top Shelf Productions.

Lewis, J., Aydin, A., Powell, N., & Ross, C. (2015). *March: Book Two.* Top Shelf Productions.

Lewis, J., Aydin, A., & Powell, N. (2016). *March: Book Three.* Top Shelf Productions.

Lindahl, A. (2015, Summer). Blood on the tracks: Why are there so few Black students in our science classes? *Rethinking Schools, 29*(4).

Loewen, J. (2018). *Lies my teacher told me: Everything your American history textbook got wrong.* The New Press.

Lopez, A. E., & Jean-Marie, G. (2021). Challenging anti-Black racism in everyday teaching, learning, and leading: From theory to practice. *Journal of School Leadership, 31*(1–2), 50–65. https://doi.org/10.1177/1052684621993115

Lopez, B. (2021, October 26). Texas House committee to investigate school districts' books on race and sexuality. *The Texas Tribune.* https://www.texastribune.org/2021/10/26/texas-school-books-race-sexuality/

Loudoun County Public Schools. (2020, September 25). *An apology to the Black community of Loudoun County.* https://www.lcps.org/cms/lib/VA01000195/Centricity/domain/60/equity_initiative_documents/An_Apology_to_the_Black_Community.pdf

Love, B. (2019). *We want to do more than survive: Abolitionist teaching and the pursuit of educational freedom.* Beacon Press.

Lubienski, S. T. (2002). A closer look at Black–White mathematics gaps: Intersections of race and SES in NAEP achievement and instructional practices data. *Journal of Negro Education, 71*(4), 269–287.

Magee, N. (2021, September 29). *UMass Amherst investigating 'blatantly racist' emails sent to Black students*. The Grio. https://thegrio.com/2021/09/29/umass-amherst-investigating-racist-emails/

Mandela, N. (1995). *The long walk to freedom: The autobiography of Nelson Mandela*. Back Bay Books.

Maraniss, A. (2020, February 10). *Jesse Owens vs. Hitler wasn't the only story at the 1936 Olympics*. Andscape. https://andscape.com/features/jesse-owens-vs-hitler-wasnt-the-only-story-at-the-1936-olympics/

Marsh, H. W. (1993). The effects of participation in sport during the last two years of high school. *Sociology of Sport Journal, 10*(1), 18–43. https://doi.org/10.1123/ssj.10.1.18

Martin, D. B. (2007). Beyond missionaries or cannibals: Who should teach mathematics to African American children? *The High School Journal, 91*(1), 6–28.

Martin, D. B. (2009). Little Black boys and little Black girls: How do mathematics education research and policy embrace them? In *Proceedings of the 31st annual meeting of the North American Chapter of the International Group for the Psychology of Mathematics Education* (pp. 22–41).

Martin, D. B. (2011). *Proofs and refutations: The making of Black children in mathematics education*. Lecture presented at the 2011 Benjamin Banneker Association Conference, Atlanta, GA.

Martin, D. B. (2019). Equity, inclusion, and antiblackness in mathematics education. *Race Ethnicity and Education, 22*(4), 459–478.

Martin, T. (1986). *Race first: The ideological and organizational struggles of Marcus Garvey and the universal Negro improvement association*. The Majority Press.

Massachusetts Department of Elementary and Secondary Education. (2020, March 13). *District review report Boston public schools, comprehensive review*. https://www.doe.mass.edu/accountability/district-review/nolevel/2020-0035.docx

Mbalia, K. (2021). *Black boy joy: 17 stories celebrating Black boyhood*. Delacorte Press.

McArdle, N. (2004, December 18). Should Lynn schools use Boston's model? *The Boston Globe*. http://archive.boston.com/news/education/higher/articles/2004/12/18/should_lynn_schools_use_bostons_model/

McCluskey, A.T., & Smith, E. M. (1999). *Mary McLeod Bethune: Building a better world: Essays and selected documents*. Indiana University Press.

McGee, E. O. (2016). Devalued Black and Latino racial identities: A by-product of STEM college culture? *American Educational Research Journal, 53*(6), 1626–1662.

McGee, E., & Martin, D. (2011). "You would not believe what I have to go through to prove my intellectual value!" Stereotype management among academically successful Black mathematics and engineering students. *American Educational Research Journal, 48*(6), 1347–1389.

McKinney de Royston, M., Madkins, T. C., Givens, J. R., & Nasir, N. S. (2021). "I'm a teacher, I'm gonna always protect you": Understanding Black educators' protection of Black children. *American Educational Research Journal, 58*(1), 68–106. https://doi.org/10.3102/0002831220921119

Melnick, M. J., Sabo, D. F., & Vanfossen, B. (1992). Educational effects of interscholastic athletic participation on African-American and Hispanic youth. *Adolescence, 27*(106), 295–308.

Memory, J. (2019). *A kids book about racism.* A kids book about, inc.

Mendes, W. B., Major, B., McCoy, S., & Blascovich, J. (2008). How attributional ambiguity shapes physiological and emotional responses to social rejection and acceptance. *Journal of personality and social psychology, 94*(2), 278–291. https://doi.org/10.1037/0022-3514.94.2.278

Merida, K. (2018, January 3). *The state of the Black athlete: What does it mean to be Black and play sports?* The Undefeated. https://andscape.com/features/state-of-the-black-athlete-what-does-it-mean-to-be-black-and-play-sports/

Miles, T. (2021). *All that she carried.* Random House.

Milner, H. R, Cunningham, H. B., Delale-O'Connor, L., & Kestenberg, E. G. (2018). *These kids are out of control: Why we must reimagine "classroom management" for equity.* Corwin.

Mineo, L. (2020). How textbooks taught white supremacy. *The Harvard Gazette.* https://news.harvard.edu/gazette/story/2020/09/harvard-historian-examines-how-textbooks-taught-white-supremacy/

Miranda, H. P., Mokhtar, C., Tung, R., Ward, R., French, D., McAlister, S., & Marshall, A. (2014). *Opportunity and equity: Enrollment and outcomes of Black and Latino males in Boston Public Schools.* Center for Collaborative Education and Annenberg Institute for School Reform at Brown University.

Moore, E., Michael, A., & Penick-Parks, M. (2017). *The guide for White women who teach Black boys.* Corwin.

Morris, M. (2016). *Pushout: The criminalization of Black girls in school.* The New Press.

Morris, M. (2019). *Sing a rhythm, dance a blues: Education for the liberation of Black and Brown girls.* The New Press.

Morrison, T. (1970). *The bluest eye.* Holt, Rinehart and Winston.

Morrison, T. (2007). *Beloved.* Vintage Classics.

Moses, R. (2002). *Radical equations: Civil rights from Mississippi to the Algebra Project.* Beacon Press.

Muhammad, G. (2020). *Cultivating genius: An equity framework for culturally and historically responsive literacy.* Scholastic.

NAACP Legal Defense Fund (n.d.). Natural hair discrimination. https://www.naacpldf.org/natural-hair-discrimination/

Nasir, N. S. (2011). *Racialized identities: Race and achievement among African American youth.* Stanford University Press.

Nasir, N. S., Givens, J. S., & Chatmon, C. P. (2018). *"We dare say love:" Supporting achievement in the educational life of Black boys.* Teachers College Press.

Nasir, N. S., & Shah, N. (2011). On defense: African American males making sense of racialized narratives in mathematics education. *Journal of African American Males in Education, 2*(1), 24–45.

National Museum of African American History and Culture. (2014). *Historical foundations of race.* https://nmaahc.si.edu/learn/talking-about-race/topics/historical-foundations-race

National Park Service. (2021). *Carter Woodson Home.* https://www.nps.gov/cawo/learn/carter-g-woodson-biography.htm

National Public Radio. (2014, March 21). Black preschoolers far more likely to be suspended. *Code Switch*. https://www.npr.org/sections/codeswitch/2014/03/21/29 2456211/black-preschoolers-far-more-likely-to-be-suspended

National Women's Law Center. (2018). *Dress coded: Black girls, bodies, and bias in D.C. schools*. https://nwlc.org/wp-content/uploads/2018/04/5.1web_Final_nwlc _DressCodeReport.pdf

Neal, L., McCray, A.D., Webb-Johnson, G., & Bridgest, S.T. (2003). The effects of African American movement styles on teachers' perceptions and reactions. *The Journal of Special Educations, 37*(1), 49–57.

Nelson, K. (2008). *We are the ship: The story of Negro League baseball*. Little, Brown Books for Young Readers.

New York City Coalition for Educational Justice. (2020). *Diverse city, White curriculum: The exclusion of people of color from English language arts in NYC schools*. NYC Collective For Educational Justice. http://www.nyccej.org/wp -content/uploads/2019/12/Diverse-City-White-Curriculum-3.pdf

Nieto, S., & Bode, P. (2017). *Affirming diversity: The sociopolitical context of multicultural education*. Pearson.

Noah, T. (2016). *Born a crime: Stories from a South African childhood*. Random House/One World.

Noah, T. (2019). *It's Trevor Noah: Born a crime: Stories from a South African childhood (adapted for young readers)*. Random House Children's Books.

Nxumalo, F. (2021). Disrupting Anti-Blackness in early childhood qualitative inquiry: Thinking with Black refusal and Black futurity. *Qualitative Inquiry, 27*(10), 1191–1199.

Nyong'o, L., & Harrison, V. (2019). *Sulwe*. Simon & Schuster Books for Young Readers.

Oakes, J., Joseph, R., & Muir, K. (2004). Access and achievement in mathematics and science: Inequalities that endure and change. In J. A. Banks & C. A. M. Banks (Eds.), *Handbook of research on multicultural education* (2nd ed., pp. 69–90). Jossey-Bass.

Obama, M. (2018). *Becoming*. Crown.

Office for Civil Rights, U.S. Department of Education. (2016). *A first look: Key data highlights on equity and opportunity gaps in our nation's public schools*. U.S. Department of Education. https://ocrdata.ed.gov/assets/downloads/2013-14-first -look.pdf

Office for Civil Rights, U.S. Department of Education. (2021, June). *An overview of exclusionary discipline practices in public schools for the 2017–18 school year*. U.S. Department of Education. https://ocrdata.ed.gov/assets/downloads/crdc -exclusionary-school-discipline.pdf

Ogbunu, C.B. (2021). *From 'fear of a Black planet' to 'fear of a Black universe.'* The Undefeated. https://andscape.com/features/stephon-alexander-fear-of-a-black -universe/

Oluo, I. (2018). *So you want to talk about race*. Seal Press.

Onwuachi, K. (2019). *Notes from a young black chef*. Knopf.

O'Quin, C. B. (2021). *Exploring African American vernacular English and disproportionality in special education*. [Doctoral dissertation, Illinois State University].

Orfield, G., & Lee, C. (2007). *Historic reversals, accelerating resegregation, and the need for new integration strategies*. The Civil Rights Project / Proyecto Derechos Civiles, UCLA. https://escholarship.org/uc/item/8h02n114

Osterheldt, J. (2020, November 11). Claiming land and water on Martha's Vineyard. *The Boston Globe.* https://www.bostonglobe.com/2020/11/11/metro/claiming -land-water-marthas-vineyard/

Painter, N. I. (2011). *The history of white people.* W. W. Norton & Company

Palmer, B., & Wessler, S. (2018, December). The costs of the Confederacy. *Smithsonian Magazine.* https://www.smithsonianmag.com/history/costs-confederacy -special-report-180970731/

Park, L. S. (2011). *A long walk to water.* HMH Books for Young Readers.

Park, S. S., Wiemers, E. E., & Seltzer, J. A. (2019). The family safety net of black and white multigenerational families. *Population and Development Review, 45*(2), 351–378.

Pattillo-McCoy, M. (2013). *Black picket fences: Privilege and peril among the black middle class.* University of Chicago Press.

Pearman, F. (2020, July 1). *Anti-Blackness and the way forward for K–12 schooling.* The Brown Center Chalkboard. https://www.brookings.edu/blog/brown-center -chalkboard/2020/07/01/anti-blackness-and-the-way-forward-for-k-12-schooling/

Perry, I. (2005). Of Desi, J. Lo and color matters: Law, critical race theory the architecture of race. *Cleveland State Law Review, 52*(1 & 2), 139–154.

Perry, T., Steele, C., & Hilliard, A. (2004). *Young, gifted and Black: Promoting high achievement among African-American students.* Beacon Press.

Picca, L., & Feagin, J. (2007). *Two-faced racism: Whites in the backstage and frontstage.* Routledge.

Pietsch, B. (2021, April 14). Texas high schoolers set prices for classmates in "slave trade" chat. *New York Times.* https://www.nytimes.com/2021/04/14/us/slave -trade-auction-snapchat-aledo-isd.html

Pollock, M. (Ed.). (2008). *Everyday antiracism: Getting real about race in school.* The New Press.

*Race, the Power of an Illusion.* (2003). [Video]. California Newsreel.

Rappaport, D. (2017). *Martin's big words: The life of Dr. Martin Luther King, Jr.* Little, Brown Books for Young Readers

Rees, D. I., & Sabia, J. J. (2010). Sports participation and academic performance: Evidence from the National Longitudinal Study of Adolescent Health. *Economics of Education Review, 29,* (751–759).

Reynolds, J. (2017). *Long way down.* Atheneum/Caitlyn Dlouhy Books.

Reynolds, J. (2018). *Track Series: Ghost; Patina; Sunny; Lu.* Atheneum/Caitlyn Dlouhy Books.

Reynolds, J., & Kendi, I. (2020). *Stamped: Racism, antiracism, and you.* Hachette Book Group.

Reynolds, J., & Kendi, I. (2021). *Stamped (for kids): Racism, antiracism, and you.* Little, Brown Books for Young Readers.

Reynolds, J., & Kiely, B. (2015). *All American boys.* Atheneum Books for Young Readers.

Rhoden, W. (2006). *Forty million dollar slaves: The rise, fall, and redemption of the Black athlete.* Crown.

Rodriguez, D. (2021, September 8). Defaced Black doll at California high school sparks calls for accountability on racist incidents. *USA Today.* https:// www.usatoday.com/story/news/nation/2021/08/26/salinas-students-stand -solidarity-against-alleged-racism-campus-black-baby-doll-high-school-suhsd /5599239001/

ross, k. m. (2019). *Revisiting BlackCrit in education: Anti-Black reality and liberatory fantasy.* Center for Critical Race Studies in Education at UCLA, *17*(1), 1–4.

ross, k. m. (2020, June 4). Call it what it is: Anti-Blackness. *New York Times.* https://www.nytimes.com/2020/06/04/opinion/george-floyd-anti-blackness.html

ross, k. m. (2021). Black space in education: Fugitive resistance in the afterlife of school segregation. In C. Grant, A. N. Woodson, & M. J. Dumas (Eds.), *The future is Black: Afropessimism, fugitivity, and radical hope in education* (pp. 47–54). Routledge.

Rowe, M. (2008). Micro-affirmations and micro-inequities. *Journal of the International Ombudsman Association, 1,* 45–48.

Schwartz, M. (2020, July 22). *Texas school board keeps grooming code that led to suspension of Black students.* National Public Radio. https://www.npr.org/2020/07/22/893970329/texas-school-board-keeps-grooming-code-that-led-to-suspension-of-black-students

Schwartz, S. (2019, June 14). A popular social studies curriculum got an internal review. The findings weren't pretty. *Education Week.* https://www.edweek.org/teaching-learning/a-popular-social-studies-curriculum-got-an-internal-review-the-findings-werent-pretty/2019/06

Schwebke, S. (2021, March 25). Teacher's profane, racist rant captured on video by mother of Black sixth-grader in Palmdale. *Los Angeles Daily News.* https://www.dailynews.com/2021/03/25/teachers-profane-racist-rant-captured-on-video-by-mother-of-black-sixth-grader-in-palmdale/

Seda, P., & Brown, K. (2021). *Choosing to see: A framework for equity in the math classroom.* David Burgess Consulting, Inc.

Shuster, K. (2018). *Teaching hard history: American slavery.* Southern Poverty Law Center. https://www.splcenter.org/sites/default/files/tt_hard_history_american_slavery.pdf

Silverstein, J. (2019, December 20). Why we published the 1619 Project. *New York Times Magazine.* https://www.nytimes.com/interactive/2019/12/20/magazine/1619-intro.html

Sims Bishop, R. (1990). Mirrors, windows, and sliding glass doors. *Perspectives: Choosing and Using Books for the Classroom, 6*(3).

Snider, J. M., (2018). *Claiming Sunday: The story of a Texas slave community.* Snider Family Publications.

Solly, M. (2020, June 4). 158 Resources to understand racism in America. *Smithsonian Magazine Special Report.* https://www.smithsonianmag.com/history/158-resources-understanding-systemic-racism-america-180975029/

Solórzano, D. (1997). Images and words that wound: Critical race theory, racial stereotyping, and teacher education. *Teacher Education Quarterly, 24*(3), 5–19.

Solórzano, D., & Huber, L.P. (2021, September 21). *The strategies of resistance.* UCLA Graduate School of Education & Information Studies. https://seis.ucla.edu/news/how-microaffirmation-empowers-communities-of-color

Spencer, J. A. (2009). Identity at the crossroads: Understanding the practices and forces that shape African American success and struggle in mathematics. In D. B. Martin (Ed.), *Mathematics teaching, learning and liberation in the lives of Black children* (pp. 200–230). Routledge.

Spencer, J., & Hand, V. (2015). The racialization of mathematics education. In L. Drak-
eford (Ed.), *The race controversy in American education* (pp. 237–258). Praeger.

Spivey, W. (2019, October 25). The fallacy of "good" slave owners. *Medium*. https://
medium.com/discourse/the-fallacy-of-good-slave-owners-7dd2ea2dad2f

Stracqualursi , V. (2022, March 18). *US House passes CROWN Act that would ban
race-based hair discrimination*. CNN. https://www.cnn.com/2022/03/18/politics/
house-vote-crown-act/index.html

Steele, C. M., & Aronson, J. (1995). Stereotype threat and the intellectual test performance of African Americans. *Journal of Personality and Social Psychology*,
69(5), 797–811. https://doi.org/10.1037/0022-3514.69.5.797

Strutchens, M. E., & Silver, E. A. (2000). NAEP findings regarding race/ethnicity:
Students' performance, school experiences, and attitudes and beliefs. In E. A.
Silver & P. A. Kenney (Eds.), *Results from the seventh mathematics assessment of
the National Assessment of Educational Progress* (pp. 45–72). National Council
of Teachers of Mathematics.

Sullivan, S. (2014). *Good white people: The problem with middle-class White antiracism*. State University of New York Press.

Tatum, B. (2003). *Why are all the Black kids sitting together in the cafeteria and other
conversations about race*. Basic Books.

Taylor, E. (1999). Bring in "da noise": Race, sports, and the role of schools. *Educational Leadership*, 56(7), 75–78.

Taylor, M. (2001). *Roll of thunder, hear my cry*. Pearson Education Limited.

Texas Historical Commission. (2018). *Monte Verdi family slaves historical marker
dedication*. https://www.thc.texas.gov/news-events/events/monte-verdi-family-slaves
-historical-marker-dedication

Texas House Bill 3979. (2021, June). https://legiscan.com/TX/text/HB3979/2021

Thomas, A. (2017). *The hate u give*. Balzer + Bray/HarperCollins Publishers.

Thomas Jefferson's Monticello. (n.d.). *Slavery at Monticello*. https://www.monticello
.org/slavery/slavery-faqs/property/

Totten, S. (2000). *Diminishing the complexity and horror of the Holocaust: Using
simulations in an attempt to convey historical experience*. National Council for
the Social Studies. https://www.socialstudies.org/sites/default/files/publications/se
/6403/640308.html

Trent, S. (2020, July 27). At 88, he is a historical rarity—the living son of a slave. *The
Washington Post*. https://www.washingtonpost.com/history/2020/07/27/slave
-son-racism-george-floyd/

Tung, R., Carlo, V. D., Colón, M., Del Razo, J. L., Diamond, J. B., Frazier Raynor,
A., Graves, D., Kuttner, P. J., Miranda, H., & St. Rose, A. (2015a). *Promising
practices and unfinished business: Fostering equity and excellence for Black and
Latino males. FINAL STUDY*. Annenberg Institute for School Reform at Brown
University and Center for Collaborative Education. https://www.cce.org/uploads
/files/PromisingPractices_UnfinishedBusiness_FullStudy_FINAL.pdf

Tung, R., Carlo, V. D., Colón, M., Del Razo, J. L., Diamond, J. B., Frazier Raynor,
A., Graves, D., Kuttner, P. J., Miranda, H., & St. Rose, A. (2015b). *Promising
practices and unfinished business: Fostering equity and excellence for Black and
Latino males* (Executive summary). Annenberg Institute for School Reform at
Brown University and Center for Collaborative Education.

Turner, C. (2016, September 28). *Bias isn't just a police problem, it's a preschool problem.* Morning Edition, NPR. https://www.npr.org/sections/ed/2016/09/28/495488716/bias-isnt-just-a-police-problem-its-a-preschool-problem

Ullucci, K. (2005). *Learning to see: The development of race consciousness in White teachers.* [Doctoral dissertation, University of California, Los Angeles]. ProQuest Dissertations Publishing.

Ullucci, K. (2006). Book review. Racism without racists: Color-blind racism and the persistence of racial inequality in the United States, by Eduardo Bonilla-Silva. *Urban Education, 41*(5), 533–540.

Ullucci, K., & Battey, D. (2011). Exposing colorblindness/Grounding color consciousness: Challenges for teacher education. *Urban Education, 46*(6), 1195–1225.

University of California San Diego. (2018). *UCSD Institutional research: Student profile 2018-2019.* https://ir.ucsd.edu/_files/stats-data/profile/profile-2018-2019.pdf.

Vought, R. (2020, September 4). *Training in the Federal government* [Memo 20–34]. Executive Office of the President. https://www.whitehouse.gov/wp-content/uploads/2020/09/M-20-34.pdf

Waldman, A., & Green, E. (2018, October 15). *Charlottesville's other Jim Crow legacy: Separate and unequal education.* ProPublica. https://www.propublica.org/article/charlottesville-other-jim-crow-legacy-separate-and-unequal-education

Walker, A. (1976). *Meridian.* Harcourt Brace Jovanovich.

Walker, A. (1982). *The color purple.* Harcourt Brace Jovanovich.

Walker, V. S. (1996). *Their highest potential: An African American school community in the segregated south.* The University of North Carolina Press

Washington, B. (1903). The fruits of industrial training. *The Atlantic.* https://www.theatlantic.com/magazine/archive/1903/10/the-fruits-of-industrial-training/531030/

Watson, D., Hagopian, J., & Au, W. (2018). *Teaching for black lives.* Rethinking Schools.

Wellman, D. (1993). *Portraits of white racism.* Cambridge University Press.

West Savali, K. (2012, January 10). Atlanta metro-area school district defends using slavery equations to teach math to third graders. *Huffington Post.* https://www.huffpost.com/entry/slavery-third-grade-math_b_1191813

Wiehe, E. (2020, July 23). *Teaching African history and cultures across the curriculum.* Edutopia. https://www.edutopia.org/article/teaching-african-history-and-cultures-across-curriculum

Wilkerson, I. (2020). *Caste: The origins of our discontents.* Random House.

Will, M. (2021, September 30). Calls to ban books by Black authors are increasing amid critical race theory debates. *Education Week.* https://www.edweek.org/teaching-learning/calls-to-ban-books-by-black-authors-are-increasing-amid-critical-race-theory-debates/2021/09

WKRC. (2021, October 14). *Texas teacher off the job after being caught on camera using racist language.* Local 12 News. https://local12.com/news/nation-world/texas-teacher-off-the-job-after-being-caught-on-camera-using-racist-language-klein-student-race-racial-white-black

Wollenberg, C. (1976). *All deliberate speed: Segregation and exclusion in California schools, 1855–1975.* University of California Press.

Woodson, A. N. (2021). Afropessimism for us in education: In fugitivity, through fuckery and with funk. In C. Grant, A. N. Woodson, & M. J. Dumas (Eds.),

*The future is Black: Afropessimism, fugitivity, and radical hope in education* (pp. 16–21). Routledge.

Woodson, C. (2009). *The mis-education of the Negro.* Associated Publishers. (Original work published 1933)

Woodson, J. (2016). *Brown girl dreaming.* Nancy Paulsen Books.

Woolhouse, M. (2021, September 30). *Boston Schools desegregation, then and now: Through the eyes of a Black Student who survived the 1970s turmoil.* Learning Curve [Podcast]. https://www.wgbh.org/news/education/2021/09/30/boston-schools-desegregation-then-and-now-through-the-eyes-of-a-black-student-who-survived-the-1970s-turmoil

Wynter, S. (1994). No humans involved: An open letter to my colleagues. *Forum N.H.I. Knowledge for the 21st Century, 1*(1), 42–73.

X, M., & Clark, S. (1965). *Malcolm X talks to young people.* Young Socialist.

Yancy, G. (2015, December 24). Dear White America. *New York Times.* https://opinionator.blogs.nytimes.com/2015/12/24/dear-white-america/

Yancy, G. (2018a, September 17). *Gift giving and the violence of White backlash* [Video]. Roger Williams University. https://www.youtube.com/watch?v=Zxf7S-iPayw

Yancy, G. (2018b). *Backlash: What happens when we talk honestly about racism in America.* Rowman & Littlefield Publishers.

Yao, J. (2021, October 2). *Resources for banned books week and beyond.* We Need Diverse Books. https://diversebooks.org/resources-for-banned-books-week-and-beyond/

Young, D. (2020). *What doesn't kill you makes you blacker: A memoir in essays.* Ecco.

Zeiser, K. L. 2011. Examining racial differences in the effect of popular sports participation on academic achievement. *Social Science Research, 40*(4), 1142–1169.

Zimmermann, C. (2018). *Before Black boys are criminalized?: Race, boyhood, and school discipline in early childhood* [Doctoral dissertation, University of Pennsylvania]. Publicly Accessible Penn Dissertations, 3076. https://repository.upenn.edu/edissertations/3076

# Index

The letter *t* following a page number represents a table.

# About the Authors

*Joi A. Spencer,* PhD, is professor of mathematics education and the incoming Dean of the School of Education at the University of California, Riverside. Her work focuses on improving the mathematics educational opportunities of African American as well as other minoritized youth and improving teachers' capacity to serve these students. Joi has served on the editorial board of the *Journal for Research in Mathematics Education* and as the president of the California Association of Mathematics Teacher Educators, and has published in a variety of venues including *Dissent, Urban Education,* and *Journal for Research in Mathematics Education.*

    Dr. Spencer received her PhD at UCLA, where she was a fellow of the National Science Foundation–funded Diversity in Mathematics Education (DiME) Center for Learning and Teaching. As a higher education leader, she has implemented numerous initiatives to improve the experiences and success of faculty of color and underrepresented graduate and undergraduate students. Joi grew up in Los Angeles and received her MA and BA degrees from Stanford University.

*Dr. Kerri Ullucci* is currently an associate professor of diversity and equity in schools at Roger Williams University in Rhode Island. Kerri was born and raised in Rhode Island. She is a first-generation college student. She received her PhD from UCLA in urban schooling and her MAT from the University of Pittsburgh in education. She is a former elementary teacher. Her research interests include race and poverty issues in schooling and the development of culturally relevant teaching practices. Dr. Ullucci has been published in many journals, including *Urban Education, Race Ethnicity and Education,* and *Teacher Education Quarterly.* She prepares K–12 teachers for urban schools. This is her first book.